30 YEARS
Under the Beam

Bethlehem Steel Exposed
As Told by Those Who Worked There

Frank A. Behum, Sr.

CSP
CONTINENTAL SHELF PUBLISHING, LLC
Savannah, GA

Photographs. Front Cover Top: Chris Richie; plant and worker, Bethlehem Steel, courtesy of author. Back Cover: Frank Behum, Sr. Author Photograph: Richard Goodbody.
Cover design adapted from Brian Bloch

Library of Congress Cataloging-in-Publication Data

Behum, Frank.
 30 years under the beam : Bethlehem Steel exposed : as told by those who worked there / Frank Behum.
   p. cm.
Summary: "A history of the last years of Bethlehem Steel, the world's second largest steel company, told by steelworkers in interviews with laborers and management. Public perception was that the union employees were responsible for its downfall, with inflated wages and benefits. Here they make their case to the contrary"--Provided by publisher.
 ISBN 978-0-9822583-7-8 (pbk. : alk. paper)
1. Bethlehem Steel Corporation--History. 2. Bethlehem Steel Corporation--Interviews. 3. Steel industry and trade--United States--History. 4. Iron and steel workers--Interviews. I. Title. II. Title: Thirty years under the beam.

 HD9519.B4B44 2010
 338.7'6691420973--dc22

                              2010044344

Also in eBook version: ISBN 978-0-9831483-3-3 (eBook)

Continental Shelf Publishing books are available at special quantity discounts for premiums, sales promotions, or use in educational, corporate and community training programs. For information, please contact: Editor@CSPBooks.com

For book signings, please contact Frank Behum: fabbfrank1@yahoo.com

Printed in America
Sixth Printing, 2015

IN MEMORIUM

Valent Ulincy – Blast Furnace
John Sabol – Blast Furnace
Joseph Behum – Central Tool
Frank E. Behum – Alloy & Tool
Thomas J. Petro Sr. – Alloy & Tool/ Safety
William Danner – Combustion
Pearl Danner – Electric Furnace
William Wiley – Central Tool
Margaret Wiley – Reddington Test Center
Michael Wiley – #2 Machine Shop
John Wiley – Saucon Mills
Stephen Wiley – Central Tool
George Wiley – Lehigh Plant
Donald Wiley – Beam Yard
George A. Pinkey – Pipe Shop
Calvin Reszek – Beam Yard
Thomas J. Cooper – Ore Handling
Dave Goldstein – Press Forge
Bill Molitorisz – 48" Roller
Elsie Pribula – Main Dispensary
Frank Zelina – Ingot Mould
Vince Zoppi – Saucon Roll Shop
Larry Shea – Hydraulics Engineer
Claude "Wang" Buskirk – Beam Yard
Ray Rosati – Shipping Yard Maintenance

IN APPRECIATION TO:
The United Steelworkers of America

For doing an outstanding job of representing the men and women of the bargaining units of the Bethlehem Plant of Bethlehem Steel. In solidarity the author salutes you for a job well done.

CONTENTS

ACKNOWLEDGMENTS

The author is grateful to many friends and relatives who assisted him in producing this book. *Thirty Years Under the Beam* is a labor of love, and the author finds it very difficult to express his feelings adequately. He will try to.

First of all, he thanks his family who shared his journey through uncharted territory. Just listening to my many cries for help must have driven them crazy.

Beyond a doubt, he cannot downplay the assistance of Ms. Jill Schennum who edited and organized *Thirty Years Under the Beam*. Final proof reading was done by Nick Politi, my English professor at Penn State. Nancy Reinbold was my first transcriptionist and the work was completed by Donna Turek. These people were a driving force who pushed me on to the finish line. They were assisted by my wife Nancy who helped with the typing and also with staying focused.

The real stars of this book are the people I interviewed. I know many of them found it difficult to recall their years working at the Bethlehem plant of Bethlehem Steel.

Special thanks go to my wife Nancy, my mother Evelyn Wiley, my uncle Bill Wiley, and a special friend, Richie Check.

This book is dedicated to those who made Bethlehem Steel what it was, part of their lives. And also to those who gave their lives over 99 years of operation. Special thanks to Charles "Chuck" Bednarik, HOF 67 of the Philadelphia Eagles who inspired me to write the following: Bethlehem Steel was built on the backs of the Slovaks and Hunkies of South Bethlehem.

ROBERT HOLLY
23 years of service

Billet Yard, Tool Steel Inspection, Observation, Basic Oxygen Furnace

One of the few people in the plant who was an assistant grievance committeeman in Local 2598, 2599, and 2600. An active member of the joint safety committee. Bob's only goal at Bethlehem Steel was to work as many day shifts as he could.

* * * * * * * * * *

Today is May the 14ᵗʰ, 2000, we're here with Robert A. Holly, nicknamed Buddy. Should we call you Buddy or should we call you Bob?
RH: Yeah, I haven't been Buddy in a long time, so…

So we'll call you Bob. How's that sound?
RH: Good.

All right, Bob, how did you become a Bethlehem Steel employee?
RH: Um, I worked for Mobil Oil Corporation as a trainer in a facility near the Bethlehem Allentown border, and they decided to do away with the job. I was offered jobs at other bulk plants, and I refused, and the Bethlehem Steel was always hiring periodically, so what can I say?

So I see you were hired in March of 1973.
RH: Two weeks after I filled out an application, I was working at the Bethlehem Steel.

How about that? So you became known, as what, Dick Adams, the head of labor relations, always referred to as the famous Class of '73.
RH: Famous class of '73; I've heard that before.

Yes, he always said that. He said the class of 73 was different from all the others. And we won't get into any details, because I expect to interview Dick Adams before this is all over, because I know he'll have a lot to talk about. So when you first came into the plant, where exactly did you first touch base?

9

RH: Uh, 620 department, which was the Billet Yard, right underneath the Fahy Bridge, and it included the tool steel mills all the way into the shipping end, which was the annex.

Now the tool steel was a high-powered basic bread and butter big money maker for Bethlehem Steel, wasn't it?
RH: In '73 it was 24 hours a day seven days a week, and six days a week was your average schedule.

I was a crane man there.

A crane man, that's pretty easy. I mean you operated, what, most of those were like ten ton cranes in there?
RH: 10 to15.

So you worked in the bays?
RH: I worked in the bay. I worked in the annex most of the time, over the pickling tanks, over the test saws. I had good jobs.

So when we talk about your working in the annex, the best way to describe that is where the Starters Riverport is right now.
RH: Absolutely.

That is right there. In fact, you know when you walk in that drive-in there at Starters, and just before you make the right-hand turn to go into the parking, that used to be the Beardsley Piper Grinder there.
RH: Correct. I used to work over the grinders, I used to work over the scarfers, which were the ones that took the imperfections out before they re-rolled the steel.

And those guys were, we used to call those guys the hungry hippos, when we were maintenance people, because we hardly ever got a call from 3 bay, because they were too busy making money.
RH: They had to.

And that included every shift they had. And I guess you know all about that. It must have driven you nuts when you worked like the bicycle grinders and that.
RH: When you worked in 3 bay, you were lucky to catch a break. Something bad had to happen, or they had a lot of bad steel that they were grinding, because normally there was always somebody with a hand up. They were very hungry people.

Yes, I remember the one guy, the crane man, said to me, he says, "Could you take my heater?" He says, "And instead of having it flushed along the wall, could you make a bracket and have it lay horizontal, so I can heat my sandwiches and my soup up on it?" And I said, "Okay, I'll do it." So one day we're up there with my boss, and he says, what on earth is this? I says, "The guy likes to heat his sandwich and his soup." Oh, you know what? He went and he started changing them around on guy's cranes, and we had several cranes up there by the time I left, you know, that were set up like that, and uh, the guys loved it. I mean, everything wasn't a bed of roses at the Bethlehem Steel like everyone thought. And you know yourself.

RH: I was a worker.

If you worked middle or night shift on one of those cranes up there, if you got to eat your lunch, you were having a good day.

RH: Even on day shift, if you got to eat your lunch, you were having a good day.

That's right, and it was always a nice thing when they had a longer safety talk than normal in the morning, how about it?

RH: Every shift.

Where did you end up from there Bob? Where did you move on? Oh, I see right here you did some inspection work too.

RH: Right. After eight months of being in the crane, and being crane man instructor at the end, which was a good job, steady days, which was always my goal to get as many day shifts and as many weekends off as possible. I was different from your average steelworker. I had a life. I had a young bride, and we decided that instead of making all the money, I would spend more time and do…

The very honorable thing.

RH: Enjoy life.

So now you became an inspector. What exactly did an inspector do?

RH: Um, prior to steel being re-rolled into a smaller shape or into, like some of it was even surgical steel which was forged, and very little of that was rolled. It was mostly heavy machining, but you had to make sure all the imperfections were out, it was the correct grade, and it was the correct application for the right customer. Um, we did cam shafts for Chrysler, we did a lot of stuff, fill collars.

I remember we used to do, at one time when I started up there at the 35 inch mill they had a run of nine by nines that went on for years, they were crank shaft steel for Ford Motor Company.

RH: Correct.

We made every crankshaft for every Ford passenger car for years and years and years on end.

RH: And the four and halves were Chrysler camshafts.

Yeah, how about that? That is, that's really something.

RH: But you had to make sure that they were, that the imperfections were minimal. You were allowed so many thousands, and you'd have to grind them to make sure that they were within tolerance. It was a very tedious job, but you know what, it was a great job. We had great bosses, very understanding people.

And actually the quality of the product hinged directly on what you guys did in the inspection department.

RH: And that's why we never got the incentive or any of the money that the other guys made, but again, it was steady days, weekends off, and then when we got busy it went to days and middles, weekends off, which I became a safety, I'm sorry I became a union rep by attrition. Maco, the gentleman that had the job before me, when he retired, I inherited it, because I had his job.

How about that?

RH: And it was an easy hat to wear in those days because we basically had a good boss and a good following, and we didn't have any problems.

If my memory serves me right, I believe John Maco put 44 years in. In fact it may even have been more than that. But I know it was at least 44.

RH: He was there before my father, and my father retired with 42 years in 1975. And he retired in '77, I think it was, that's when I became a union rep.

How about that? And, uh, when you first came into the plant. Let's say you're still a crane man, you're in your first year, I mean, what was your first idea when you walked in there? What were you thinking?

RH: I was going to run.

You were ready to turn around and go back out the door.

RH: On the tour, after you got your shoes, your helmet and the red stripes on your helmet

What were the red stripes for?

RH: Temporary employees or new employees of the department. So that was for crane men could see people that didn't have the experience in the shop.

And watch them closely.

RH: Absolutely.

And how about the scheduling? I guess it must have been atrocious until you got into the inspection end.

RH: I hated it, hated it.

How did that work?

RH: Well, one of the smartest things the boss ever said to us, and this is the schedule clerk now, and Johnny Feight was our general foreman, who was a very hard-nosed hard working, didn't want to get in his way. But he said if you want a weekend off, you're going to have to take it off. I think I missed 60 days my first eight months in the Bethlehem Steel.

Wow.

RH: Mostly weekends, believe it or not. I was reprimanded a few times for that.

And you know, I'll never forget John sitting at his desk and right to the right of it was the palm depressor that he used to blow all the sirens and whistles, because everything worked on a whistle or a siren in the alloy division. From the 35-inch mill all the way up to six bay.

RH: You stopped working on a whistle, and you started working on a whistle. Lunch breaks, everything was on a whistle.

And when you talk about a whistle shop, I mean, that's exactly what a whistle shop was.

RH: But not as bad as some of the whistle shops.

No, that's true. So now you're in tool steel inspection. You spent some time there, didn't you?

RH: I was in that until they were closing tool steel down, which I believe was in '83/'84, it started really slowing, oh there '81. I was going to say '82 or '83, but I guess '81 was when it really started to slow down. We were getting laid off. You know, periodically I would take jobs in other departments. I ended up in the beam yards and a few other departments, and machine shops always had good jobs, and they always cut my crane check, which was one of the things I was told never to give up. So every six months as long as I went for a physical, I got to keep my crane check. So it was one of the things that I held until the very end.

And it always served you well I would imagine.

RH: Oh, I used to get up and do things that I wasn't supposed to do, especially middle shift as an inspector, if I didn't have a crane man out, I go in and make the lift myself just to get the things done so we could get our jobs done and get out of there.

Well you know, George Bush always used the theory that, you know, everything's legal until you're caught, and it served him well, so.

RH: I never got caught.

Okay, there you go. Now, after the inspection job there, went away more or less, where did you end up?

RH: Uh, right before inspection, tool steel closed, I saw a posting for Observation Department, and I thought what a job, anybody that couldn't be an observer isn't worth his salt as a steelworker.

But then you got a big surprise didn't you?

RH: Well the test was, I barely squeaked by the test, because there was a lot of metallurgy and a lot of questions asked that I just had no clue. I was shooting from the hip. Luckily I had enough practical experience as an inspector. I knew how things worked. I knew about treatment. I knew, you know, how things happened, and basically I just did a reverse and answered most of the questions right, I was accepted.

Yeah, what did an observer do Bob?

RH: A lot more than what I expected. You had to be on the floor of the electric furnaces during the melts to make sure they were using the proper temperatures, the alloys going into these heats were, you know, very critical, as far as them getting the right composition to make the right grade, and that would be very important to the customer. You know, making sure that if he was getting 18/8 surgical stainless; it had to be 18 chrome to 8 parts of nickel.

So, in reality we can say in layman's terms you were like a process inspector. You made sure that everything was done the same way every time.

RH: Very critical also. And the right times, how long, the temperatures were also important because you could burn the steel. And if it wasn't hot enough, again you're not getting the proper mix.

And you did that for how long?

RH: I did that all the way up until 1992.

Now that was a shop where you did work all three shifts wasn't it?

RH: At times I did. When I would work in Saucon and the BOF that would be three shifts. You know, seven-seven-six cycle, um, and by that time my kids were young enough that they understood dad wasn't home because he was at work. Most of the time they were used to having me around, because like I said I always sought the day shifts. And then I ended up in the Press Forge for eight years as an observer, which was a steady day shift job.

Wow, eight years on a steady day shift. And you know what, I don't know of anybody else in the company that could tell me they worked eight years on day shift at Bethlehem Steel.

RH: Straight.

That is really saying something. Because let's face it, you were at the mercy of the schedule clerk.

RH: Yeah, but like the people that I would work with, even people in my own department were making $10,000-$15,000 a year more than I was. I shunned the overtime. I didn't work the weekends when I could have been working the weekends. I would give it to the younger guys that were hungry and they wanted it. I would rather be home. I also coached basketball. I coached baseball.

Now at the time when you were day shift like that, was your wife working?

RH: Yes, my wife.

Or was she just a full-time mom at the time?

RH: No my wife always worked, always worked. She was a dental assistant, then she was a chair-side assistant, and then an orthodontist bought the practice, and then she's still in the dental field today yet.

Yeah, well, that's a long time. '92 you say you went to the BOF.

RH: '92 when they closed. They started cutting back again, and one of the first departments to go were all the inspection and observation departments. They eliminated the quality control end of the Bethlehem Steel. So we got absorbed into the BOF. That was where most of the observers worked, and they created a position called the teaming person, which was you were either a steel pourer, you were a test taker, you were setting nozzles for the ladles before you poured them. Um, it was a conglomeration of about fourteen or thirteen jobs that they condensed into five.

But the company was smart enough to know they were better with you guys than anybody else.

RH: I don't. I think they expected it would fail, because the first crew was all observers. We didn't have any experienced personnel from the BOF. As I said, we were designed to fail. And they gave us a foreman from Lackawanna, and Mr. Brown, as we referred him to, was one of the nicest guys you could work for. He explained everything, showed you how to do it right the first time, and most of us learned the jobs from watching and being an observer in the past. You had to learn how to take a test, or you had to learn how to pour steel just so some guy could get a pee break or whatever else.

Yeah. So you, uh, you must have had a lot of things that happened. You spent a lot of time with a lot of different people. Some guys come to me and they say, we spent more time at Bethlehem Steel than we spent with our own families.
RH: True.

Okay, what are some of the best memories you've had working at Bethlehem Steel?
RH: The best memories, the people you work with. It was like a giant family. I mean you basically ate together, you worked together, you cried together, and you laughed together.

And when you went out sometimes, you even drank together.
RH: Oh, once in a while yes, not…

I mean, you did what you could. And then there was the clam bakes, all the, there's a lot of different shops had things going on. Did the BOF have anything like that where the guys got together once a year, or pension party?
RH: Actually we used to get together once a month after our middle shift.

I like that.
RH: Until they found out that the general foreman was actually with us. He used to pay for the beer and the pizza, and he was a real nice guy. He got a lot of work out of us. We were in 90 some percentile as far as efficiency rate. And they said we were designed to fail, and here we are the highest percentile of all the different crews; there were four different crews.

Yeah, so your general foreman more or less took care of you because he recognized, you know, that you guys were going the extra mile for him.
RH: Absolutely.

Absolutely. Good, you want to mention his name?
RH: I did, Brown.

Oh, okay, that was Brown, Dick Brown. Good for him. I'm not even going to pursue what's your worst memory, because I know down at the BOF you could have had a lot of bad memories, so if you don't want to talk about it, you don't have to; if you do, go ahead.
RH: Well, Mike Ryan got killed while I was a safety rep. Right near the end we were. Honestly we were less than a year, probably within six months of closing down the whole shop, and he made a mistake.

I believe he was the last person that was a fatality in the Bethlehem plant.
RH: I couldn't say that for sure, but it still, I still think about the guy.

I run into his ex-girlfriend every now and then. And, uh, when did you actually realize, come to the conclusion, you know, the plant was in big trouble?
RH: Probably in the early '80s.

In the early '80s?
RH: Yeah, when they were getting ready to close tool steel, it might have been late '70s even.

Yeah.
RH: Uh, they kept telling us that we're landlocked and the union and the company weren't exactly, uh, how would you say, trying to get along. The union was fighting their fight, and the company just kept telling us that we're wrong, and we're doomed, you know, because we were landlocked and we didn't have a seaport or anything else, like some of the other plants.

Well, you know, I think a lot of that was predicated by Charlie Schwab having the Bethlehem plant as the starship plant. I mean, let's face it, without the Bethlehem plant, none of the other operations at Bethlehem Steel would have ever existed. And a lot of people fail to understand that. They just think that, well, why did Bethlehem go under and the other ones were still going? Well, it was just the way it was, for some of the reasons that you spoke. I interviewed a guy the other day who said the alloy division never lost a penny the entire time it was in operation, but they closed it anyway.
RH: Well, they told us they were losing money. We had a tough time believing that.

Yeah, well, I was told otherwise. But the bottom line, the bottom line came down to, the company, it seems, the company's idea is if you made one million on the product this year, and the next year you made $850,000, you lost $150,000.
RH: That's the way they looked at it, exactly.

And we couldn't figure that out, because you know the figures were right there. But you know they have a saying about that, you know about liars and figures, and we won't go into that. But anyway, you were a shop steward most of the time you were at Bethlehem Steel weren't you?
RH: In three different locals.

No kidding, all three locals.
RH: All three locals.

Do you think you could have worked at Bethlehem Steel without the union?

RH: Never.

Why's that?

RH: Well, just for instance starting off in a whistle shop. I mean, they actually wanted you to drop your sandwich when that whistle blew and get back to work.

Yeah.

RH: And from what I understand from back in the '40s it was people getting killed left and right. There was no safety. There was no, there was a lot of things that the union brought into the workplace which was, number one, I think was safety. I was always involved in safety and ended up becoming joint safety rep at the end.

Did you ever hear in all the time at Bethlehem Steel that there were two problems with the safety department? One: they didn't like to spend money on anything.

RH: Correct.

And two: if 100 drop dead, go get 101. What do you say to that? I mean, what's your opinion on that?

RH: It was different by the time we came in '73. By the time we came in '73 we inherited a pretty safe work place. We had safety meetings every shift, 10 or 15 minutes every shift before you started, that was safety. All safety related questions were brought up, and this is every single day.

And that was actually a chance that you could vent yourself if there was something that was going on that was a potential hazard.

RH: That's correct.

Thank God for that, that the people who came in front of us had the insight to do those things.

RH: That's where you have to give them a pat on the back.

It's unfortunate down there at the monument off the Fahy Bridge that there's this list of close to 900 people who never made it at the Bethlehem plant, and you know, when you mention that to people and they say things like, just like, if you would have done a little work down there, you know, maybe the place would still be there, and I always used to say to them, you know what, did you ever carry one of your buddies to an ambulance? Did you ever go to a viewing that someone got killed at work? Because if you haven't done these things, you should just shut your mouth. And that's just the way I felt about it.

RH: And I would agree with you. Well, I was in the dispensary a few times. I got burned in the BOF and actually I finished pouring the heat, and then one of my buddies called an ambulance. I was burned a lot worse than what I had thought. You never think you're, you know, you just want to get through it and get it over with.

Get it over.

RH: And he was just saying, "Nah you're burned worst than you think." I took probably four or five ounces of liquid steel right underneath my chin and it went right down my chest.

Lord, how long did that, before you were like back to normal?

RH: I missed work three days, fourth day luckily it was a long weekend, then the next day I was back on my job. They had some pretty unique medicines back then, especially for burns; stuff called silver dean and, I guess I don't know if they still use that stuff today.

Well, you know, they used that on me. I had a 600 amp crane switch blow up in my face at the electric furnace, melted my safety glasses, it melted my hard hat, gave me second degree burns, it took the hair off underneath my hard hat, like a pot cut, like with the razor blade. I mean, and I'll never forget we were sitting down at the meeting and one of the foremen said to me, "What do you think you did wrong", and I mean, I really lost it. I said "Listen, if I even knew what happened," I says, "I would tell you,, but I know I didn't do anything wrong." You know what they found out? That those switches had been wired improperly prior to World War II, and they had functioned all that time without any accidents. I was the first accident. Then they went and found out the rest of the cranes were wired wrong, and they had them all completely rewired in that circuit for the main control. And I'll tell you what, I always considered myself lucky to be alive. Did you know that the average person on the outside, they don't know that. All they know is what's been in the newspaper, the Express Times, the Morning Call, or what Bethlehem Steel announced. This is why this book is being written, to get the real story about what it was like working at Bethlehem Steel. Now, here's something Bob, I want you to think about this. And this is, if there's something you've always wanted to say about the company, this is the time to say it. Let's say you had been in a position, okay, you're calling the shots, and you wanted to do all that you could to save the company, about what year would you have had to started and what would you have done?

RH: I think it had to be like mid-70s, late '70s. They started giving us some training along with management in Juran, and I'm trying to think of some of the other propaganda, as what most of the people called it.

Partners for Progress.

RH: Partners for Progress, very good.

Well, you know there were some people with the union that referred to Partners for Progress as something other than the phrase seems at first to mean.

RH: Yeah, they were trying to eliminate more of our jobs

"People blanking people" is how they referred to it.

RH: Well, that's what it was all about. They wanted you to rat. I guess that was their way of looking at getting you to tell the people that were sleeping, the people that would avoid work. You know, there might have been like 10 percent or 5 percent people that probably never lifted a shovel.

But in any large corporation you would still have that.

RH: Oh, I'm not saying you wouldn't. I know people that still work at Mack Truck, and I still hear them talking about, oh yeah, they get 15 minutes or a half an hour lunch and then they go to sleep for an hour. It's like, okay, well, we didn't have that. At least I never experienced that in departments I worked in. I've seen people that would spend a good portion of their day trying to hide. But …

Are you saying that cross training and things like that is something we probably should have had more of?

RH: I think if they would have done what they said they wanted to do with it, like you said, they used that more for their advantage for eliminating union jobs.

And that's why there was no trust there?

RH: Exactly. They lost the trust of the union back in the late '70s. The union and the company, if they had been working together, I think you would have seen a lot more people losing their jobs on the other side of the fence, not the union side of the fence. I think the working man could have produced more, especially, we were using a mill that was built in 1908, and we still were setting records with it in the '70s, '80s and '90s. That has to be the workforce, not the equipment. I mean, that stuff was held together with bailing wire and duct tape.

That's right. I always wondered what could we have done with state of the art equipment, with the expertise our people had?

RH: We were competing with…

And the work ethic they had.

RH: And I still hear that today. People don't realize the work ethic we did have. There were guys risking their lives.

Well, you know the Bethlehem plant was the number one plant in the entire corporation for sick days, they had the least number of accidents, the least number of worker's comp claims. And you know it almost broke their hearts at

negotiation, tell us that one year.

RH: Well, I was in on negotiations. And that was one of the other things that used to kind of get you going. You'd have five or six of the upper echelon, vice presidents and presidents, and I'd say 10% of the upper echelon knew what they were talking about. The rest were there because they graduated from Lehigh University.

They had "relative ability," a relative in a high place.

RH: Relative ability, there you go.

Relative ability for us was part of our seniority provision.

RH: I heard that from Bob Hussar back in the '70s. He was one of my favorite people.

Yup. I used to go fly-fishing with Bob Hussar up the mountains every year. We had a great time. What a great guy.

RH: He was one of my favorites.

So let me ask you this, do you think the company had enough foremen?

RH: Uh, I would say that they had way too many foremen.

I don't think they ever believed that though, do you?

RH: We proved it at the end with the BOF. Teaming people, we didn't have a foreman. When they eliminated the other parts of those jobs and they made us teaming people, they said they went from like 13 jobs, 3 of those were foremen. Then the union workers lost 5 union jobs and incorporated those jobs into the teaming positions, and we said we don't want any foremen, we'll use one of our people as a leader, and our leader worked, it was Larry Weaver, and I'll say nothing but nice things about him. I worked with him in observation. He was a very quiet guy that knew his job and knew his job well. Um, very quiet again, but I liked working with him, I liked working for him. I would do anything for the guy.

Well, Bob, I think we had a real good interview here today on the jobs you did. You worked at over 20 different areas there in the plant. We only went over like three or four of them, but I think people got a pretty good handle on the areas you did work in, what you did, what you were confronted with, you know, the products that were made, what exactly you were doing. And I want to thank you, you know, for granting this interview, and I wish the best for you and your family.

RH: And same to you Frank.

Thank you.

KAMAL ABBOUD

Blast Furnace

When Kamal spoke it was always with conviction. His sincerity was evident to all who knew him. His loyalty to family and friends is known to all. I am proud to call him a friend.

* * * * * * * * * *

We're on the record with Kamal Abboud. Today is May 22ⁿᵈ 2008. Everybody had a nickname down at Bethlehem Steel. Did they call you Kamal, or did you go by any other nickname?

KA: They called me all kinds of names. Camel jockey, Kamal, I don't know, Abboud, different names. But most of the people I worked with just called me by my first name.

Okay, I see here that the last job you worked there at Bethlehem Steel was as a pipe fitter, and you started in April of 1968. Could you tell me how you became a steel worker?

KA: Well, after I came from overseas, from Syria actually, in 1967, I work for Phoenix Clothing as a presser, and the opportunity came, Bethlehem Steel was hiring. And uh, after I went in, they assigned me to electric treatment, which I worked as a loader.

So we had furnaces that were operated by and that involved actually a little bit of tweaking the metallurgy so to speak. That's why we used an oil bath. Did you ever use a water bath?

KA: We use oil bath. Most of the time oil bath, yeah.

I was talking to some guys that were taking the electric treatment apart, and they said there were some induction coils in there. There were tons and tons of copper inside those furnaces. He says whoever bought that, which was, you know, Brandenburg, he says they really reaped the profit out of that electric treatment. Now how long were you in the electric treatment?

KA: I was there for about year, year and maybe two months Then I was laid off for two months, then Blast Furnace opened, then they call me, I have interview, then I went to Blast Furnace.

Okay, now when you were in the electric treatment and three track, you were part of the alloy and tool steel division?
KA: Yes, I was alloy and tool steel.

I see you have marked down here Power House. How did that enter into the picture?
KA: Power House, you know when the work got so slow in the Blast Furnace they used to ship us to a Power House.

But it was always better than collecting unemployment, right?
KA: Absolutely. Was much better for me. I felt, I felt better being working then going to unemployment and standing in line.

So you went to the Blast Furnace around, what, 1969, early 70?
KA: 1969 on May of 1969.

And the Blast Furnace, for those that don't know, the Blast Furnace does not make steel. It makes iron. Tell us exactly what you did there, your first job at the Blast Furnace.
KA: Well, the first job I work labor to start with. Then after that I start to fill in like first helper, second helper, cinder man. First helper.

Now what does a first helper do?
KA: First helper, it's a very, very hard job, and dirty and smelly job. They fill up the furnace, when the furnace get full of melted iron, they used to open, the keeper go and open the furnace.

That would be called casting the furnace, right?
KA: Casting the furnace. When we cast the furnace, my job is to stand by my baker dam.

So it was a continuous process. Was about every two hours and fifteen minutes or something like that?
KA: Absolutely. Yeah, about two and a half hours, until you clean and you ready to, you ready for the casting, it took me about 45 minutes to an hour to clean the runner and dry the baker dam.

This is all hot work?
KA: Oh my God, you're talking about 3500 degrees. Maybe I have ten minutes to drink a little bit of water and come out for a second cast.

You mean to tell me you weren't sleeping on night shift?
KA: Sleeping? Yeah, yeah, we are sleeping. Sleeping, where do you think I got the iron from, from heaven? No!

Well, you know that furnace wasn't very forgiving.

KA: 24 hours operation.

It was like burping a baby, you had to do it every so often or it's not going to work right. Now, I guess you, because of the close quarters you worked in and the time frame you worked on, I guess the people on your particular shift you got to know them pretty good?

KA: Absolutely, yes. I knew most of them.

It was a true team work.

KA: Team work. You have the keeper, keeper who load the gun, who checked the iron inside the furnace from the side, and after that you have the first helper. You have two second helpers, and you have two cinder men. Cinder men take care of the cinders coming on top of the iron. They have to do their job too, I mean. And you have the blower, the blower who opens the furnace, and he's a foreman most of the time. And it was team work, you had to work together.

How important would you say safety was in that job?

KA: It was very important, to be honest with you, it was very important. Like you have to have your leggings, you have to have your hat, your shield, your coat to protect yourself from burn, because it's hot. If any of the spark comes to your body and burn, I so many time I had my hand burned, my legs burned from sparks.

So if somebody was looking at a picture of Bethlehem Steel and they were looking on the cast floor they would see bodies out there in silver suits with hoods on, that was you.

KA: I was one of them.

I remember the first time, and you probably remember, that the picture of the C Blast Furnace was on the Steel Labor, the United Steelworkers magazine, remember that? I remember that one of the guys, one of the guys was Louie Melendez. That had his hood up, that you could actually recognize him.

KA: Yes, he's gone. Louie's gone. He died.

I didn't know that. I'm really sorry to hear that.

KA: Louie Melendez, I heard he's gone. Yeah. Louie Melendez was one of, a friend of, I mean he was co-worker. We worked like team. We worked like friend and brothers, believe me. I mean, we have to worry about the craneman, to getting the sand, and lot of stuff for us. You work with the crane, you work with the hot iron.

You know, may he rest in peace. I hope he goes to the big Blast Furnace in the sky.

You know there's a lot of guys over there that you know from sucking up all of that crap that came in the steelmaking.

KA: How about the sulphurs you eat? How about the stink, the sulphur, and the graphite, oh my God.

Yeah. I mean, and you know when guys went over to the lawyer, Peter Angelos, with the asbestos, a lot of the people.

KA: I'm one of them.

They discovered they had problems, not asbestos problems. They had other problems from the other stuff that was throughout the plant. And you know, I can't say with any certainty, but I heard that 68 percent of the people tested had lung problems. Now, not all of them needed immediate care or were eligible for benefits, but you know what I say about that, "60 Minutes." Why didn't they ever come to Bethlehem Steel right after it was down and do a story on that? That would have been some story. But you know what? I always felt that the captains of industry weren't interested in airing out their dirty laundry. Because you know it wasn't a safe place to work. Could you have worked there without the union?

KA: No, no. That's only protection we had, the union. If we don't have union, I don't think some people could work there, because it was hard work, and sometimes if you don't, if you don't have the union looking after your safety.

You know, when you talk about safety, when you just stop to think about all the people that were injured.

KA: Remember that accident we had in the Blast Furnace? I was there.

With the pot?

KA: With the pot. I was there. I saw the guy, it took his shoes off, and there is nothing except piece of bone, his foot gone. And how about that guy become crazy, what his name? One of the guys become crazy completely, he couldn't function.

Yeah, I talked, I talked to Eddie O'Brien about that, and he says if that's one thing he can never forget about Bethlehem Steel it would be that day.

KA: Yes, yes. I mean, I was working that shift, I was with the group when that accident happened.

Now you left there in 1992, but around that time and prior to that time, when did you actually come to the realization that that Bethlehem plant was in trouble?

KA: When we have only two. We start to operate one furnace. I know there's no way. We had five furnaces on Bethlehem Steel plant, and when we start to operate only one furnace, this is big sign, big sign in front of it, we're closing. And when they offer 500 people just to get out, this is sign. For that, I was one of these 500 people who went out. I did not wait until it shut down, I went with the 500 people.

Now what were the most furnaces ever operating when you were working there? It had to be three or four.

KA: I tell you, yeah, three.

Now, you're scheduled, how did you work?

KA: Oh, you have, from week to week, you work night shift, middle shift, day shift, Saturday, Sunday, any day.

Every holiday.

KA: And they could hold you. If there is an emergency or if there's no people living so far, they'll hold us to stay at work

Well, I used to tell people, they used to say to me, "Oh, you lucky dog you get paid double time and a half for the holiday." I says, "Oh, you lucky dog, you sat at the edge of the swimming pool drinking beer and eating food all day while I sweated my ass off at work." I says, and that includes freezing my butt off in the winter time and Christmas, New Year's. I says, but you know what, everybody seems to have a tendency to forget about that, as long as they're fat, dumb, and happy. So what would you say is your best memory of Bethlehem Steel, was it the men?

KA: I tell you the men, absolutely the men, the beautiful people, came from all over the world. I came from Syria. I met people from Hungary, I met people from England, I met people from France, I met people from Brazil, from all over the world.

You can almost say the Blast Furnace was a melting pot.

KA: That's true, and you have people coming from Western Pennsylvania, I'm sorry from the mountain. You have people coming from all over. And it was like melting pot for us. We really enjoy ourselves as friend and as a family.

When did you realize things weren't going quite right, what would you have done that you think would have helped, like immediately?

KA: I believe I will call the worker. I will have some kind of organization between management and worker.

In other words, we should have started this a lot earlier than we did?

KA: Absolutely, and start to look for avenue, how to save this plant. We should, actually if I'm in charge I would put saving the plant priority above anything else.

Well, it seems as though the management had the golden parachutes, and the only

thing we had golden was the trickle down, and that was the stuff that turned the snow yellow, so you know what I'm saying here. I would have preferred to see Donald Trautlein come in in 1965 instead of 1980. And I think we would still in operation today.

KA: Yes sir. I believe so.

Do you feel like I do, when writing this book, in that had there been more cooperation sooner we'd still be in real good shape?

KA: I have no question in my mind this plant would be operating right now, instead of making casino out of it.

I'm going to ask you something that I haven't asked anyone else? Do you think we needed more guys like Frank Anderko? There was a guy that has a hands-on attitude with everything, but he knew everything that he was doing. He knew all the employees.

KA: Yes sir.

I don't think there was a guy that ever worked in there he didn't know him by the first name.

KA: I know Frank Anderko, I work with him, and I came to him with a couple things I needed, and he did not turn me down, he just look the way how we could solve this, and he solve any problem.

So Kamal, I want to thank you for granting me this interview, and I wish the best for you and your family.

KA: Thank you Frank. I wish you luck, and I look forward to see this book coming out.

And another thing I want you to know is that when we shoot the picture, which Chris over here is going to take, we want you to show up to be on this jacket cover. We're going to stand in front of the Bethlehem Steel logo over at Martin Towers and shoot the picture.

I expect you to be there. Okay, thank you.

KA: No problem, sure.

JEFFREY HOFFERT
29 years, 11 months, 22 days of service

Blast Furnace

Jeff worked many jobs in the Blast Furnace. Forced to transfer to the Sparrows Point plant in order to accrue time towards pension, Jeff missed his 30 year pension by 8 days. Jeff served the union as a grievance committeeman and a trustee.

* * * * * * * * * *

Today is June the 2nd, 2008 we're here with Jeffrey R. Hoffert. Jeff, did you have a nickname in the plant?

JH: I don't think so.

They just called you Jeff? Okay, I guess not too many people called you Jeffrey, right? Okay, good. So for the purposes of this interview, we're gonna call you Jeff. I'm really interested in how you became a steelworker, could you tell me how that happened?

JH: Well, I was a third generation steelworker. My grandfather worked there, my uncles, and my father worked there, so that seemed to be the place to work when you graduated from high school. I applied in1971.

Did you have your application on record all that time?

JH: Yes. I kept on updating it.

Kept updating it, okay. So, at the earliest actual opportunity, they actually did call you? Now I see here that you worked in the Blast Furnace, was that the first job they offered to you?

JH: Yes, they offered me - when I started there they offered me the Coke Works, Iron Foundry, or Blast Furnace, and I chose the Blast Furnace.

Did you have people in your family that worked in the Blast Furnace?

JH: No, I had people that worked in the Coke Works, and they said to stay away from it, and I did. I picked the Blast Furnace.

Now, when you got into the Blast Furnace, your first day your first week, you must have been sort of like awestruck.

JH:　　It was like walking into a different country because everything was so new and everything was so, sort of like enormous and different than you ever saw before. Uh, when you go onto the cast floor, it's something like.

And what was the cast floor?
JH:　　The cast floor was where they tap the furnace. Where the iron actually comes out of the furnace. When they are casting it goes up to 100, over 100 degrees on a cast floor, and uh, with sparks flying all over the place.

And you wore protective equipment. And what did that consist of?
JH:　　That consisted of heavy asbestos coats, gloves, heavy asbestos gloves, leggings, uh facemasks, shield and a hard hat, but nothing would protect you from burning up, that just slows down the process.

People were still injured wearing that protective equipment. Well, I can understand that happening.
JH:　　Iron still goes through the asbestos.

And when you were standing up there and everything is running pretty smooth, you have hot metal going down one runner, and then you'll have slag eventually. How does that process work?
JH:　　The iron comes first, is heavier, then when the iron gets down to a point in the furnace when they're casting, then the slag will start to come out the top and go down a different runner. They split it up with what they used to call a baker dam, which is a uh piece of cinder block, and it has sand around it. It diverts the cinder from where the iron is going. And uh, and you have to make sure that's all dried out, the sand is all dried out so that it doesn't blow up while you're casting, and uh, and it splits it and goes into the two different, one goes in, the cinder goes into the pots, the iron goes into the ladles.

Now, here's something that's really off the wall, but a lot of people don't know. How exactly does a Blast Furnace operate?
JH:　　Well, it starts out in the Blast Furnace where they fill the furnace with the raw materials, which is the iron ore, slag, I mean the iron ore, cinder, coke, uh stone and manganese, all different types of material in a series of, a set series of how to put it in, and uh, then you got the furnace, the uh, stoves, which heat up the slag and the, I mean the raw materials. It, uh, it heats up, yeah the furnace.

The material is already on the top of the furnace, right?
JH:　　Right. And then it goes into the top through the bell system, and then the stoves heat up the raw material that going into the furnace.

And the raw material is called a burden, right?

JH: A burden, right. And they uh, once the burden is heated with the stoves that they blow the uh hot air through it to make it…

It's the hot, actually the hot blast, it's the heated air from the stoves and it's being sent up there by the actually the gas engine blowing house where they're sending up a column of super heated air. 90,000 or so cubic feet of air.

JH: Right.

About what, 36 to 38 PSI, and once that stuff starts melting, it drops down to the bottom because it's heavier.

JH: Right, and then it just cooks in there until it reaches enough temperature, and then they have to cast that furnace every two hours.

Yeah, so that's just like a continuous process. What's the longest you remember a furnace going without a reline?

JH: Uh, probably about six or seven I would say. They'd try to switch it as much as they could

And there's some work done to those furnaces in between also. So when you first started there, you were in the Blast Furnace. How was the scheduling?

JH: You worked uh, four, you worked, if you get, once you get on a regular schedule, you worked four days, four middles and five nights, and you switched every four or five days to a different shift, and you had off different days each week.

So you were like married to a schedule because technically you were part of a crew size. And your first job when you got on the furnace as steady was what?

JH: Uh, sinter man. The sinter man takes care of the sinter runners. They clean them out after the cast.

Now a sinter runner does what?

JH: It's where the uh, where the baker dam just puts it and the sinter goes down to the different pots that are underneath the floor.

Okay, so if we were at the end of the cast floor looking at the furnace, what would we actually see before the furnace cast?

JH: You would see the two different runners going two different ways.

Okay, and one would have iron right?

JH: One would be the iron and one would be the sinter. Then they have different gates, different gates that you have to lift up so that you're running into the first pot, you have a gate there so that doesn't go all the way down to the, you know, the next pot. And then you fill up that pot.

So, when you're talking, these runners are going to slag pots or they're going into the submarine one or the other. And the submarine was basically a hot metal carrying railroad car, looked exactly like a submarine. Yup, and that stuff, now Blast Furnaces do not makes steel, correct? They only make iron.

JH: They make iron.

Okay, the iron went down to the basic oxygen furnace or to the open hearth. Before the BOF.

JH: Or the uh Ingot Mould.

Yeah, and they go down there and they, you know, use the various processes either to make steel, make cast iron, or you know, whatever they're doing, and it's an awesome process if you ever get to see it.

JH: Definitely.

You know, do you remember, do you remember in the 80's when they had the tours coming through? Did they ever have any tours in the Blast Furnace?

JH: Yes they did, but you were never allowed to get off of the bus. That's one of the places where you couldn't get off the bus. You just went around and looked at the outside.

The closest thing that you could see would be the metal going into the submarine that was it.

JH: Right, from the bottom, they would never let you on the cast floor.

No, that's just too dangerous. In fact, that was really dangerous. You started there in 73. You had some fatalities even while you were there. I'll tell you what, those are things that you just wanna forget about. In fact, you know, most people that don't know that between when I started in 65 and when I left in 97 there was 31 people killed in that plant, that was the most dangerous steel mill in the United States. And you'd never know it, because I'll be honest with you, Bethlehem Steel had complete control of the press, and you know even though all these incidents were reported, it isn't something anyone lingered on. And thank God for that, because nobody wanted to be reminded anyway. So during your period at the Blast Furnace, you experienced some layoffs.

JH: Oh yeah, definitely, almost every year.

I see you worked at the sinter plant. What do you do there?

JH: When we went to the sintering plant we usually were just pool laborers.

And then probably one of the cleanest jobs you ever had was in the Beam Yard?

JH: Yes.

Okay, I saw here unfortunately you ended up at another plant, but we're gonna talk about that later. When exactly did you come to the conclusion that Bethlehem plant was in trouble, about what year?

JH: Probably in the early '90s.

And was that a result of the restructuring?

JH: Yeah, they were asking us for give backs continuously from the union, and, uh, with the reconstruction of different things, but you could see the writing on the wall back then. Some people would not believe it or didn't want to believe it, even until the last day.

What would they had to have done in order to have that place running today?

JH: Well, they needed to update more of the equipment. If they just would have kept on upgrading the things that we had to work with and use, uh, probably would have helped to save this place.

Okay, and uh, what was the last day that you worked there? What was that like, November 18th, 1995?

JH: The last cast. Did you see that picture that was in the, uh …

Yeah, I saw that. Were you in that?

JH: I was on the other side of the door. I was the guy in the shadow. I worked a double that day.

Okay, uh, you ended up at another plant, Sparrow's Point. Tell me about that experience. And you know, don't hold anything back, because there's nothing to hold back here.

JH: Yes, we, we were down there, we went down there to Sparrow's Point. We had a choice of either, I put in for Sparrow's Point, because I didn't want to go to Lackawanna. Lackawanna was too far. And we put in for Baltimore. When we got there, the uh, everybody down there didn't want us to be there. It was almost like back in the '70s and '80s when you started at the steel; people thought, hey you're taking my kid's job, you know, so that was their feelings toward us.

Okay, so you're down, you weren't well received. And what about your living arrangements? How did you guys do that, I mean …

JH: Well, we found different guys to share an apartment with.

Mostly Bethlehem guys got together, yes.

JH: And so I found one other guy to go down there with, which was Harry, and we got an apartment to share the rent, because now we have a house up in Bethlehem, now we gotta live in Baltimore, we didn't know how long. We knew it was gonna be at least four, five years, so we went down and, uh, our families stayed here, and then we went down there, uh, came home on our days off or the weekends. Of course we were …

We talking about a four-hour trip, huh?

JH: It was a 3-hour, two- and a half- to 3-hour trip on 95.

You got to know the highway real good, huh?

JH: Oh definitely, we knew everywhere where the cops sat.

Now, your scheduling? How did that work out?

JH: In the beginning we were Monday through Friday, weekends off, because we were just …

Learning your way around.

JH: Right we ended up in the sintering plant or the Blast Furnace area, they called it, but I got a transfer within two months after we were there to the tin mill. And I was, I went into the coil pack area, , uh, worked there, and there they had, they had it where you worked 6, 6, and 7. So that you had a really long weekend every month from, you finished up on a Thursday morning, you didn't have to come back until, in other words a Friday morning You didn't come back until Tuesday afternoon middle shift, so then we would go home that length of time. Other times you'd have two days off. So, but, uh, it wasn't the easiest thing to do.

No, I would imagine, you know, that there's, how old were your children at the time?

JH: Well, one was a senior in high school, one was already graduated, one was, my middle one was a senior, and then the youngest was in eighth grade, so we stayed, we let the oldest, the one that was a senior, he finished and graduated there. My youngest was just, had started, had went to ninth grade, but then after two years of being down there and driving back and forth, we decided to bring my wife and my daughter down to Sparrow's Point, because I told her, I didn't marry this guy that I'm living with, so I said you either come down or I'm coming back, so. they came down.

How about Harry, your buddy Harry? I mean, did he find another Bethlehem guy to get in with?

JH: Yeah. He moved in with another guy, and then we ended up, all of us ended up down in what they call Beacon Point, which was down in Edgemere, and they loved to see us there, because they knew they were gonna get paid as far as rent, because down there people come and go without paying, it was an apartment complex.

What kind of rent were you expected to pay down there?

JH: We got a townhouse for $600, we started out at $640 a month, in

1997. And we figured it out, and the amount of time that I was down there, I worked one year down there just for living expenses in seven years. We figured it was probably about $40,000 we spent.

Yeah, how much, how was the overtime down there? Were they liberal with it? I mean, was that something that could easily be had? I talked to some guys that were telling me every Tuesday, Wednesday, and Thursday they'd work a double shift.

JH: Yes, well I worked, I averaged a hundred extra shifts a year for five years, so that's like an extra three months a year. So, I worked in the coil pack area where the finished product gets packed and sent out to the warehouse, and, I got overtime in that department, and I also got more overtime in the tractor department running the big tractors, the forklifts that pick up coils, more than I did in my own department. There was some stretches I worked two weeks of straight overtime, double shifts every day, 7-3, and 3-11. So, I made more money down there than I ever did here at this plant.

But the first two years you were actually uprooted until you got the family down there. How did they, how did they take to the Baltimore area?

JH: Well, they weren't crazy over it, but they, we got used to it. My daughter, uh, fought like crazy because she had to go down there..

What happened down there that you came back?

JH: Well, the International Steel Group took over, but first the PBGC

Pension Benefit Guarantee Corporation.

JH: Right, they closed the door on us getting our pensions down there or anywhere, and, uh, so there was no point in staying down there anymore. I mean we could've stayed down there, and uh …

The company would've been glad to have you right? Because they knew what they had by then.

JH: There were people trying to talk us out of leaving. Out of taking the money they were gonna offer us as a severance type thing, but, uh, they didn't succeed in most of us, because we would have had to work under their contract an x amount of years before we could be eligible for the pension, and they would have, they would have, uh, well how should I say, added the Bethlehem Steel years, and our time with that company, but I told the guys down there when that ISG was gonna take over, I says he's only going to own this thing for a year, and they wouldn't believe me.

Well, you know the local press here in the area did not pay a lot of attention to guys like you. But the real story was the guys that had to be uprooted and go into other plants, and you know it was like starting all over again at day one. In your

case, like you said, you ended up making a pile of money; you had to put up with a lot of crap. Would you say it was about the time your wife came down that they more or less knew that hey, this Jeff is really a nice guy, we can count on him?

JH: Sure, oh yes.

Yeah. And then I guess after a period of awhile you were just like any other steelworker there?

JH: That's right.

Well, that's a good thing to hear that. But, uh, I think people are interested in knowing after all of that time you finally left, what kind of severance did they give you?

JH: They gave us $2,000.00 a year.

For each year you were there?

JH: Each year, but no more than $50,000

So you ended up probably with the maximum amount but no pension?

JH: Yes, $50,000, but no pension.

When can you expect to see anything pension-wise as a result of your years with Bethlehem and working down at the Sparrow's Point plant.

JH: The first chance I have is at age 60.

Age 60, that's another five years.

JH: That's another five years. I can take it then, then you lose $200 a month if you take it early.

But you're gonna get something; I guess you're looking forward to it.

JH: Oh yes.

Well, you surely deserve it. I'll tell you what; this is, you know, a real heart rending story. I hope it has a happy ending. I see now that you're working at the Lehigh Valley Airport.

JH: Yes.

And uh, I want to thank you for coming over here, and I wish the best to you and your family. Thank you Jeff.

SADER ISSA
27 years

Electric Treatment, Blast Furnace, Electric Furnace, Saucon Maintenance, SSY Maintenance

One of the smartest electricians I ever worked with. Had a quick wit about him and an amazing capacity to find answers in the field. I am honored that he calls me friend.

* * * * * * * * * *

We're on the record with Sader Issa, Bethlehem Steel employee; today's date is the 17th of February, 2008. Sader, when did you start at Bethlehem Steel?

SI: I started in April 8, 1968.

What was it like when you first started there? I mean, explain your first couple days and where were they at, what shop?

SI: Well, it was at the electric treatment.

Electric treatment. I spent a little time in there myself as a motor inspector.

SI: I was, yeah, I was a chain man because the trucks brought the steel and then they, well, you know, the crane brought it and put it on racks and we unchained it. Then they take the steel to put it in the furnace, they treat it, they heat it, and then they cool it in different ways. Some of it cooled it water, some of cooled in oil, and after it's treated, they ship it out.

So in reality what we're doing is, we're treating steel by various methods in order to actually temper the steel. To get to a degree of hardness so that it can be used by the customer. Okay, what did you like about that job?

SI: No, I was in America, and I had a good job.

Okay, now you say you're from America, and you came over from Syria. What year did you come over here to the United States?

SI: I came in February 13, 1967.

1967. Okay. That was a good time to be getting out of the Middle East 1967.

SI: Yes, right before the war.

All right. That's good. Now, when you first started there at the electric treatment, what did you think of your wages?

SI: I think I started, if I remember correctly it was $2.49 an hour, uh, but that time I came from Phoenix Clothing, and they were paying me $2.00 an hour, so hey, that's twenty percent increase, that's wonderful.

That was great. Were you married at the time? Any children yet?

SI: Yes, I was married. With Mark at home, my first born.

Okay. Now, how would you say that you did here in the Lehigh Valley with your wages compared to, like, the standard of living in the area? Did you feel as though you fit right in?

SI: To feel comfortable, I mean where, here you have to work. And I, Frank, I told you before, I had two or three different jobs. Uh, I work at the Bethlehem Steel. I was an electrical contractor and also I had apartments I took care of. and yes I lived comfortably, I sent my kids to college, three of them went to college and graduated, and I still feel I live comfortable now.

Well, that's really good. As far as that job went, scheduling and things like that, was there something that bothered you about working there? A lot of guys had problems with schedules.

SI: Well, with my case, I wanted to do something, I repeat because I came from Syria to America, I want to learn the language of the land, so I went to night school. I ask my boss at work to give me day shift, steady day shift. They gave me steady day shift. but after two or three years, my boss came to me; he said, "You want an office job?" I said, "No." He said, "Then stop going to school and do something for your family." And I had two children at the time, and I know he made sense, and that's exactly what I did.

Okay, okay. Now, you didn't stay there that long in that shop, did you? When did you leave that shop?

SI: I left it, I think, about two years later I went to the Blast Furnace.

Okay, and at the Blast Furnace you did what, electrical work?

SI: No, at the Blast Furnace I worked as a second helper..

Okay, so you were actually out there on the cast floor?

SI: Yes, yes I worked on the cast floor.

Okay, an absolute hot metal job with the iron coming out about every two and a half hours they'd be tapping the furnace.

SI: Yes, and the temperature of the metal was about 2600 degrees.

Okay, and now at the time that you were there at the Blast Furnace, how many Blast Furnaces were in operation?

SI: Uh, at one time there were four of them.

You were actually there under a four furnace operation?

SI: Four furnaces, yes.

Okay, that would be about right, you know. I think the last period they may have had of a four furnace operation was in the '70s. Okay, now at the Blast Furnace, how was the schedule up there?

SI: Oh, at the Blast Furnace I worked three shifts, whatever they offered, I accepted and I uh, and I did, I worked, whatever they offered me. You never knew basically from week to week how you were going to be working. How about your vacations or getting days off? Did you have any trouble with that?

SI: No, I enjoyed my days off, and I actually enjoyed vacation that Bethlehem Steel gave me once in a while.

You know one wrong move, and you know, people could be in trouble. Did you find that to be true?

SI: Yes, that was true. We took care of each other.

That's great. Now did you ever socialize with any of these people after work, or?

SI: Uh yes. We used to have to go, we used to go picnic or a clam bake, and I used to be with them that way.

How about during this period at the Blast Furnace, did you have any lay offs?

SI: At the Blast Furnace yes, they laid me off one time for a whole year. Uh, actually one year minus one day.

Wow. Okay now, because the Blast Furnace was a dangerous place, safety played a big part in what you were doing

SI: It depended, it really, it depended on the safety representative. Some of them cared, some of them didn't care. I know many people died in Bethlehem Steel, died working.

I've had people tell me, Frank, the only reason they paid us the way they did was for the hours we worked and the conditions we worked under. Do you agree with that?

SI: Uh, no. They paid us the way they did because of the union representation.

Well, that's refreshing to hear. Okay.

SI: If it was not for a union, they would not have paid us what they did.

Do you think the union fought a good fight there toward the end, or do you think they were in a no-win situation?

SI: I think they were in no-win situation, and truly, I like to defend the union because we needed the union, the union were our lawyers, they were our defenders, they are the one who increased the wages. Of course not.

You know when I was on the grievance committee, people accused me all the time: all you take care of are the foul balls, and you know they were right. And I said to them, I hate to tell you this, but I spend 90 percent of my time on 1 percent of the people, and it's just unfortunate, but you know if you don't do that, you put yourself in a position where people are being taken advantage of.

SI: Exactly, exactly. Uh, I appreciated the union very much.

Now if you could go back in time, when did you first realize that the company was in trouble?

SI: Well, that's fine if I tell you before I started in Bethlehem Steel I had relative working there, and was told as early as 1965 it was going under. During the time I was there I was often on layoff..

Now, I understand you worked at, besides the Blast Furnace, you were in the electric furnace for a while too. Do you wanna tell us a little bit about that?

SI: Yes. Well, in the electric furnace I became a motor inspector A. But it was hot, hot, very hot.

So now we've had you so far in the electric treatment, we've had you in the electric furnace, we had you in the Blast Furnace. You also spent some time in the sintering plant, didn't you? Ore handling.

SI: After the electric furnace there was a posting at the ore handling, they needed a motor inspector, and uh, I went there, and I don't remember what the year was, and I worked as a motor inspector right there.

Well, I worked down at the sintering plant, ore handling too, and I tell people I never worked at a place where the guys went out of their way to get the jobs done because of the noise and the dirt." They wanted to get in on a job and out, okay. You know, I had guys tell me in the supermarket, Frank, Bethlehem Steel would still be going if you wouldn't have been cooking on middle shift and sleeping on night shift. And you know what my answer to that was? Your uncle is a fireman isn't he?

SI: I guess you told them. Frank the reason we had time to do what we wanted to do, uh, lots of time we were motor inspectors, we were on calls. When something breaks down, we went there, we fixed the machine as fast as we can, and we came back, and if we were cooking, we would cook. That's the truth okay?

I can remember in the electric furnace cooking on middle shift where the superintendent, Dave Keiper, came in and he said, "Do you have any extra clams tonight, Frank?" I said, "Yes, Mr. Keiper, we do." He said," I wouldn't mind joining in on this." I says, "Well, we have plenty of clams." He says, "But remember one thing, if that whistle goes off, I wanna be the only one sittin' here at this table eatin'. I says, "That won't be a problem."

SI: Exactly.

And I'll tell you what, we really appreciated the fact that the top guy in the shop could talk to us like that.

SI: Well, look Frank, to agree with your story. There was a superintendent of the Blast Furnace, his name was Frank Anderko, I heard that he said this. Uh, he came one time to the furnace, you know after he done casting and the employees done what they had to do and then they went and laid down on the benches. So when Frank Anderko came up, the foreman ran to wake the guys up, and he said, "Leave 'em alone, their job is done. If these guys are sleeping, the job is done, we don't have to worry about it." And I liked that. But they used to say about Frank Anderko, I don't know how true it is.

I've never heard anyone say anything bad about him. In fact, I remember Eddie O'Brien who was the President of the local and a staff representative, and the assistant district director with the United Steelworkers told me that during the course of grievance meetings Frank Anderko never once opened the contract book, and they asked him about it, they said, "Frank, do you know what's in there?" He says, "Listen, I know what's in here, and he pointed to his heart," and he says, " and I know what my guys will do for me, and as long as they're doing it, I'm gonna give' em the benefit of the doubt."

SI: That is Frank Anderko.

That was him. Well, okay, we just about went over most of the things you did in the plant there. Coke Works, you're in the Coke Works awhile?

SI: Yeah, I was labor.

Labor, what were you like in between at the time or?

SI: I was laid off and then they moved me to the labor gang. Frank, to me I feel Bethlehem Steel was a blessing to guys like me who did not have the experience, who did not have the knowledge of the English language, and yet I, after one year of being in the United States I got a job in Bethlehem Steel, and through that job I have what I have. I do appreciate Bethlehem Steel. You know sending my kids to college was Bethlehem Steel pay check, working the overtime. And I thank God for Bethlehem Steel.

Well, I'd like to thank you for your candor in this matter, and that concludes our interview with Sader Isa.

CLAUDE BUSKIRK
41 years of service

Beam Yard

Known throughout the Beam Yard as a die hard union advocate. Was an officer in Local 2599, a period in which by his own account were the happiest days of his years at Bethlehem Steel. Also known as the man who "wanged" you. He'd greet you by saying "wang" and they guys would reply "ricket"—it was a Bethlehem Steel thing that only Beam Yard people could fathom.

* * * * * * * * * *

Okay, today is the 14th of November, 2008, and we're here with Claude Buskirk. Claude, did you have a nickname down at the plant? And what was it?

CB: Wang

Wang. And what should we call you for purposes of this interview: Claude?

CB: Yup.

Okay, Claude here we go. I see you started here in the plant back on August 1st of 1955. How did you get to become a Bethlehem Steel worker?

CB: My father worked there.

Most of the time down there you worked the Beam Yard? Is that where you started on your first day?

CB: No. My first day I started I was down in DEY.

The Merchant Mills? That's where I started in the plant. Lot of people, huh?

CB: Lot of people, and dusty and dirty.

Yeah, and you had a hard time finding a basket I bet when you got in there? But let's get back, what was your first job in the, up there in the merchant mill?

CB: I was a craneman.

And the main product up there was alloy and tool steel, correct? And that was the Cadillac of steel that the steel company made. It was like the highest grade that they put out. Came from the 35-inch mill, right?

CB: Right.

22-inch mill? 18-inch mill? 3-and 9-inch mill? 12-and 14- inch mill?

CB: Right, right, right and right.

The 8-, 10- and the 12-inch mill?

CB: Yup.

And you were there when those mills were operating, the small mills, the 8, 10 and the 12, weren't you? What was that, the Hunky, the Dutch and Slovak mill, right?

CB: You got it.

That, that was really something. I remember I went in there, and I said to the foreman, I says, "Do you think I'll ever work there?" "Kid," he says," if you don't have forty years, you're not gonna touch one of them jobs.. Did you ever work the 12 and 14 or were they just building it when you were there?

CB: No, that was down in East Lehigh; no I never worked down there.

So, as you progressed down there at the mill, did you ever do anything other besides chaining up? In the Merchant Mill.

CB: Merchant Mill, no.

Okay, when I was down there I worked in the bung furnaces.

CB: Oh yeah, I worked the bung furnace, pardon me. I did work, and that is something, something to behold.

Yeah, that's where the steel was taken off the 35 and the 22 and it was placed inside. It was a controlled cooling situation. So now, eventually you go down to the Beam Yard, how did that happen?

CB: We went down to the Beam Yard in October of 1956; only lasted a little, about a year and a half down in the merchant mills; that was due to the lack of orders. That's when we went down to the Beam Yard on a temporary basis, then after awhile they said, you are not going to go back. You can elect to go back, you can work here, if you have a recall elect to go back. But what they told us there in the Beam Yard, we don't think you'll ever get back there. So naturally we went and signed off, and that's how we got to work in the Beam Yard.

Yeah, that was one thing that they did do back in them years, but that was also back in the years where if you were going to bid to another department, the superintendent didn't have to let you go. You probably remember that. There were guys that were held in departments, and they could hold them indefinitely, and the consent decree came along and limited what they could do. So you get down to the Beam Yard, now that has to be like a completely different operation.

CB: Like a foreign country.

Yeah, it was big too, wasn't it?

CB: Absolutely.

No, I think that was because no matter what it was doing, you were working. The only thing that held you back was an ice storm, where you actually couldn't get out there and move around. It wasn't safe. But I'm sure there were days when there was ice that you worked anyway. But, talk about the Beam Yard, it was in the process of shipping steel. It was the biggest structural shipping yard in the free world.

CB: That's right.

And there was that one time, I would imagine you probably lived this, 2,200 guys working down there. That must have been like a three ring circus.

CB: That was before the new yard was added on to the original yard. Man, I'll tell you.

And the new yard actually effectively increased the size of the yard; it doubled it, didn't it. And the auxiliary yard that was located about a half mile away, that was what? What year did that go in?

CB: 1953.

Okay, '53 they put that in. So when you went down to the Beam Yard, the first time the auxiliary yard was already there?

CB: That's correct. Matter of fact it was there before I started steel back in 1953.

Yeah, yeah, and when that was first put up, that didn't have, that only had a roof over it, right? The sides didn't extend down? How was it?

CB: They had an open roof. I remember working there and one day when they were hooking up the steel and putting it on the trucks and then the rail cars, on the midnight shift when you're talking about it never rains in the Beam Yards. I'll tell you what; I worked under that without a roof. It's only 11 years that they put a roof on. We were out there when it was pouring rain, and the water was, it was like me, or a fisherman, standing in the Little Lehigh fishing. That's when water went into my shoes and there it stood. Didn't make a difference if you wore rubber, it was pouring down, and you kept right on working.

Yeah, well, see that's the part the average person in the Lehigh Valley has no comprehension of that. But, by the same token you could go in there as a chain man for years and years and years, and every day was different, correct? And that's what kept people coming back. They loved the idea of the variety.

CB: The guys.

There you go, the guys. And the guys were a tight group, weren't they?

CB: They were.

Everybody had their watering holes after work. Everybody had their, the guy they played their numbers and their horses with and their football tickets, and it was, like, I would say like going into a club but in order to maintain membership you had to work. That's the best way to describe it. And we had hard workers and we had hard players too. And Lord have mercy, thank God for the union. Do you think you could have worked down there without the union?

CB: No.

Why's that?

CB: Because there was too much, one thing, too much favoritism from the overhead, the foreman that you worked under. If they didn't like you, you would have been out the door.

Yeah, I'm sure you heard this from your father.

CB: I not only heard it from my father. I remember the strike in 1941 when the union was in, how things were; they called in the state troopers, they brought them in box cars from the outside, and they unleashed the horses on the people. And those state troopers, the people were out on strike, the employees, and were sitting in a bar room enjoying themselves, having a few drinks, they went in there with horses and clubs on Third Street, especially on Fourth Street, and beat the people over the head with their clubs.

Now what do you think would happen today if they did something like that?

CB: I think they wouldn't get away with that.

You're exactly right. Back in them days Bethlehem Steel controlled everything. I mean it was absolute control. And in fact after the '41 strike, I don't know if you're aware of this, Eugene Grace had the main gate moved to the other side of the west office building so in case there ever was another strike he didn't have to look out his window and see what was going on. Did you work on crews.? And were you part of a regular crew?

CB: Oh yeah.

And what did they call your crew?

CB: I can't answer that, I don't know.

Well, all right, you were just, I thought maybe you were a can't-locate crew.

CB: No, we were a regular loading crew.

The loading crew had what, how many people?
CB: We had cranemen, and the expeditor and let me see, it was two chainmen.

And so that was it. "Hey, how the hell did you get away with sleeping on night shift? They said, "Well, here's how it worked. We would come in and there'd be a straight length of maybe W8 31s standard house beams for you know the outside construction and we've been rolling 'em for a couple of shifts. We would pick up the phone, the expeditor would pick up the phone, or the cutter, and he'd call this phone number and these little guys would come out of the river, like these gremlins, we'd go to sleep and the gremlins would do the work all night and then wake us up at quarter after six. That's how we were able to sleep on night shift." And the one guy says, "And if you believe we slept on night shift when there was work, you believe the cow jumped over the moon. He says we worked all night long. He says, and on middle shift if that cutter didn't make hot dogs and sauerkraut, we didn't eat, because we didn't have a chance to get to our lunch. So as you progressed there, tell me some of the other jobs you did, other than chain man.
CB: I was roller line operator. That's where they transferred the beams on the roller line, and you would control the flow of the steel.

There was a time when there were 25 runs there. When that place, when you first started there were what, 13 or 12? Thirteen when you first started. And then they added on the other ones in the '60s, right? So, I believe there were like 105 cranes total in the Beam Yard area? That included the AY. That's a lot of cranes. So it was real easy to get injured at the Beam Yard, wasn't it?
CB: Yeah. As a matter of fact, can I comment on that. Back in April of 1959 it was on 10 run I think, I was back chainman. That was before that big strike .I had a serious injury. There were two pieces of steel involved, and the one hit my right knee and it overlapped, luckily, it overlapped the other beam the way it was. I had smashed my muscle on the upper right leg. And they took me out and they took me to the main dispensary, and I still remember that. And the nurse that was tending to me, she told me, she says, you have a guardian angel, because my leg could have been cut off. And that is the extent of working in such conditions in the Beam Yards. That was just one incident.

Yeah. One wrong move and you're in trouble.
CB: You're in trouble, yup.

Unfortunately, one wrong move for some guys at the Beam Yard was their last move.

CB: You know, Frank, let me comment on that, on my injury. Now that's going to be fifty years in April, and to this day I still have pain in that right leg. And when I go sometimes, my leg used to give out on me. I had no strength; it looks just like it was dead, going to sleep. And I still suffer through that. And as a result of that accident, you wouldn't have believed they tried to get me out of there, transfer me out of there. I says, "Try it."

Well, that's the way everything didn't always work out the way you wanted it to. So when did you actually come to the realization that that plant was in trouble? This is just your own opinion.

CB: My own opinion, one year after I started at the Steel in 1956. Foreman told me around 1960 the hot end was going to be history on another 30 years. And the reason that happened is because your imports after the Second World War were coming into the country, and this is how they foresee in the future. So when they plan something, they know what's coming.

You think our government had their head buried in the sand all them years when those imports were coming in?

CB: Yes

No doubt about it, because you know those foreign producers that were dumping steel in this country, they were doing it because they were subsidizing their own steelworker. About the only protection we ever had was the ERISA Act, you know to protect our pensions. And without that today, where would we be? So, you know, that's just the way it was, and that's what you had to live through.

CB: You did have a guaranteed pension. Happened in 1974 that was signed into law. Yup, and when you were mentioning government that knew, had their heads into the sand, in other words they had knowledge of what's going on. I remember a certain president when the steel companies asked for help, what did he tell those steel companies? That was tough shit in Washington, swim or sink, do it on your own.

Yeah, well, you know, we're into a different type of an era now, and lord knows what's gonna happen. So Claude, if there was anything, if you would have been in charge in your later years at Bethlehem Steel, is there anything that you would have done, like immediately, to help save that plant?

CB: My main concern would have been modernization and new equipment. And this is one of the biggest reasons, I believe, that it did shut down.

While we were working with stuff that was built in 1906. I mean, it was amazing the amount of steel that came out of that plant with the equipment we had. And were you aware, Claude, that in 1994 there was a group of men that were willing to buy the Bethlehem Steel? Very few people know that. Had that been sold to them, the chances are I'd be retiring in two or three months and you would have been out of there ten years ago, and things just would have been so much better, but you know it didn't happen. And I think we all know why it didn't happen, because people were afraid they were going to look bad. Well, okay Claude, it was pleasure talking to you, and I wish the best to you and your family.

CB: Can I add something onto what you were just talking about? That group, after the shutdown, I think are you referring to Jack Roberts.

Yes, every indication is that the people fell asleep at the wheel and let the ship run aground. Okay, Claude, thanks for adding that in there.

CB: Thank you.

The best to you and your family!

STEPHEN NEMES
30 years of service

Beam Yard

Without a doubt, Hector Nemes played a major role in the extension of seniority for better than 50% of the employees at the Bethlehem plant. Without his leadership, many of these men and women would have never received a pension. To know him was a true honor.

* * * * * * * * * *

We're on the record with Steve C. Nemes, otherwise known as Hector. Today is March the 10th*, 2008. Steve how you doin'? Now, do you mind if I call you Hector for this meeting?*

HN: Wonderful, Frank. That's fine, everybody does.

Okay, so we'll refer to you as Hector. Now Hector, how did you come to be hired at Bethlehem Steel?

HN: Well, Frank, going back, I was 18 years old. I had did a short stint working at Durkees, and I can remember well. I worked nine days, and I got, I walked the picket line, they were out on strike, so what I didn't know at the time after the strike was over, they called me in and fired me because I wasn't in the union. You had to be in there for 30 days. So my short-lived experience at Durkees, which come to pass, I ended up back there as a representative of the union, which was really funny. But that's how it started, and I lost that job, and I went to the IBM school for six months, and I came back here hoping to get into the Steel, in the IBM department. Well, I tried, tried, tried and I couldn't. So I finally, at 18 they offered me a job in the Structural Shipping Yard, the Beam Yard.

Okay, and I see here you started in July of '64. Now, I would imagine that in July of '64 there was a hell of a pile of people working in the Beam Yard?

HN: Correct. Oh, every month they would be bringing, every week they'd be bringing new people in. I started early in the month. Yeah, I think it was, I want to say it was the 11*th*. I think somewhere around there.

But I mean, and back then they were hiring so many people and bringing them in day by day. As you would know going through the 30 years that I was there, that one day made a difference in your seniorities.

Oh yeah, oh yeah. I was talking to a guy that, they needed people so bad, they asked him to come in on a Friday night for a Saturday, and because of it, he had seniority over 52 other guys. And you know, he was really proud of that, that he was smart enough to do that..

HN: There ya go.

There was like 2,000 people there then, wasn't there?

HN: Oh, at least, yeah, at least 2,000.

So they were really recognizant of the safety. Right from day one

HN: Oh yeah, you were pretty much thrown right out there onto the job.

Right into the fire. So what was your first job?

HN: Okay, my first job was I was sent to the 28-inch mill, which made channels and angles, but I worked at what they called the gag. Now, the mill would roll the steel, these angles and channel, and then they'd cool off in a hot bed, and they'd ship it down to the gag, and the gag's job was to pile it up in piles according to orders. If somebody ordered ten channel, you would pile 'em, one with toes up on it and one on top of it toes down, and then you'd make a pile of ten, and then you'd get it ready to be stenciled and shipped out in a truck load or a car load.

Now when you talk toes up and toes down, what do you mean by that?

HN: Well, on a channel, uh, a channel is exactly; it's got one flat piece, and then it's got sides to it, little sides, small maybe only an inch high or two, depending on what size the channel was, and so your first piece would be laying down with the toes up, and your second piece would come out, and you'd pile it on top; you'd have to flip it, cuz they'd all just about come out toes up, so you'd have another guy there with a wrench that would turn the piece upside down.

An actual turning bar?

HN: A turning bar, yeah. It's a big bar with a hook at the end, and you know, and you just flip it over.

So it was actually metal on metal.

HN: Metal on metal

That was creating a situation where, when you could obviously see the bend in the bar, you could actually straighten that out by pushing in the opposite direction?

HN: Right. The guy that I worked with was the straightener, and I would be what they called the gag labor. And it was quite a job. The guy I worked with had 50 years when I got there.

Wow, I guess he knew what he was doing?
HN: His name was Mockeye, yup. I think I worked there two years, and he retired.

Yup, that's a lot of years of service. I'll tell you what, 50 some. How long did you do that before you moved on?
HN: Uh, I did that until September of '65, and then uh, I got married and I got drafted all at the same time.

How about that, it was a bad month huh?
HN: It was a bad month. I went on my honeymoon, I came home, and my father gave me my draft notice.

Did your dad work in the plant?
HN: Yes, he worked down at the Blast Furnace.

How about his dad?
HN: I'm not sure about his dad. I don't think he did. My dad worked down at the Blast Furnace, they used to call him Bougie. Uh, he knew everybody in the whole world down at the Blast Furnace.

No kidding; well that was like a big family down there.
HN: Well, any place you worked in that plant, you probably ended up spending more time with those people then you did your own family.

Oh, absolutely, no doubt about it. Because you never knew what was next.
HN: Well, I think from there I went, uh, it's a long time ago, Frank; you're talking twenty years.

I hope you can drag your memory back that far.
HN: I think after I came out of the service, before I got back to where I was at the gag, I did go back there for a while, um, I ended up at the 12- and 18-inch mill, which made little angles and little channels. The only difference at this mill was that they were 60 foot long like the other ones, but you had to pile 'em by hand, so they called those guys cradle men. I did that for about a week, and I got off of that job.

It's a good thing you got off of that, because I hear nothing but horror stories about people with back problems that worked cradling. And still to this day people talk about it.
HN: And there were some guys that were very good at it. They had the

routine down.

Well, you know, there wasn't a lot o training, it was all on the job training just about, and you know that and I know that. But you know the people that are going to read this book don't know that.

HN: And you know as well as I, when you were the new guy, I didn't tell you when I first started down at the three gag at the 28, you come in, the guy told you where to sit, that's where you sit, that's where you eat your lunch, and being the new guy, you always walked to the bottom to get the coke to bring it up for the fire, which you never got a chance to sit by, but that was your job.

Now you talk about the coke and the fire, and they used to have what they called salamanders. Okay, and those devices were nothing more than a rudimentary heating device, because you worked in all kinds of weather down there at the Beam Yard. Now, what's one of the first things you learned working at the Beam Yard about the weather Hector?

HN: Weather was never a factor.

And wasn't it ironic that our friends who never worked there will always tell us, "Just think, you'd still have a job if you wouldn't have been cooking on middle shift and sleeping on night shift," and I would say, "How the hell do you think that steel got loaded and shipped? I mean, do you think somebody picked up the phone and dialed the Blast Furnace and said, send down a finished product, we don't want to work today." It didn't quite work that way.

H.   No.

So after a period of time I guess you started gaining a little bit of seniority, and what happened then?

HN: Well, then they opened what they called a new part to store the steel where they would be loading railroad cars and trucks and bolsters and carriers and all that. It was called the new yard. And that's where I ended up going for a while for a number of years.

Okay, the new yard. And then you know, there's like ten different jobs down in there, but they all involved the same thing, finding steel, getting it put together, loading it into the car around to the truck. And you had some real characters down there, didn't you? You had a guy running around in a clown suit, didn't you?

HN: Oh yeah, John. John used to run around in a clown suit.

We'll be talking to John later on.

HN: He ran around with no suits on sometimes. I remember that quite well.

You know steelworkers were great for horseplay, but you know the horseplay that we were involved with was more or less like child's play more than anything else.

HN: And I can't recall exactly, but I think even when I was down there, there was at least two or three people that were killed on what they called the roller lines.

Dangerous operation. The roller line actually went from one end of the yard to the other.

HN: Which was a long distance.

Which was long, you know, over a thousand feet. And, this steel would come down there, and a lot of times the steel that was coming down the roller line weighed, you know, sometimes ten to fifteen tons, and it didn't stop right away, did it?

HN: No, it didn't stop right away.

You had to have a knack on how to run this. There was a lot of safety involved with the walkways and things like that, but still, you know, one, one wrong move, and you were in trouble.

HN: Well, the difference even that they made from the years before when they lost so many people, I think back before we got down there.

It was worse.

HN: But when you walked on the roller line, you walked, there were no steps or anything, you walked straight; in other words, your hip would be, and your waist would be level with the roller line. Whereas, when they made the new yard there, it was like two steps, and you were always standing on top of it.

Yeah, big difference.

HN: You could imagine walking through a roller line and a steel beam come down.

Yeah, yeah. Now, how was it with the bosses? Did you have some good bosses you worked with?

HN: I had a lot of good bosses and a lot of bosses that thought they were bosses.

Yeah, in other words they, they were a little lacking on knowing the job, but I guess that's no different than anywhere that you would work.

HN: Mostly anywhere you'll run into that situation. They got what they called them the green helmets. They got their green helmets and they thought, as soon as they put the helmet on they knew everything about everything.

They thought they were Superman, huh? When I ask, I'm going to ask you one,

give you a term; you tell me what you think about this term, relative ability.
HN: Relative ability that means that if you got a friend or somebody, they're going to end up getting the job, that's what it means.

Although when we worked, as we worked with the union, relative ability meant something else. It meant the ability to do the job
HN: Right.

Okay. We always used to joke about that, "Well he's got relative ability; that's why he's got the green hat.
HN: That's why he's got the green hat, yeah.

God bless him. It's the same as any other place, though. You know we had good guys and we had bad guys.
HN: A lot of relative ability came from kissing ass.

Oh yeah. Did you have a favorite job you performed down there?
HN: Uh, I had a couple good ones. The loading gang was one of my favorite jobs.

Oh yeah?
HN: Yeah, that was just like an 11 man crew that worked in the old yard where the cranes were lower and everything else, and back then they weren't making much money until we got there.

Yeah, now because you were down there and you didn't have a lot of time when you first started; how long was it before you could get a vacation in the summer time?
HN: Oh I don't know maybe 15 years, Frank. Yeah, it was a long time. I mean the only good thing, bad for us, but the company used to shut down too once in a while, and if they shut down in the summer months that's the only way, but then you were forced to take vacation.

You were forced to take that.
HN: You had one week; you'd have to go whenever they shut down.

Yeah, it wouldn't be for that, you'd probably never get a chance.
HN: No

To go anywhere with the family or anything like that. Now you worked every shift there was, how about it?
HN: Days, middles, and nights.

In every location?
HN: You have to remember, we were like a family. You worked with

those guys eight hours, sometimes five, six, seven days a week, depending on how much work was there, and you'd always spend the time. You'd go out after your 3 to 11 and there was a little bar right outside the bar called Hofriges. You'd stop in there, you'd get your shot and your beer, you get something to eat, 11 o'clock they'd cash your check for ya, and you leave there at 7 in the morning.

And get ready to go to work middle shift.

HN: And of course, you'd be telling your wife that you worked a double when you got home at 7. You couldn't go early; you'd have to wait until 7:30.

Yeah, so you might as well drink all night, right? Just don't get too close to her so she can smell your breath.

HN: Well, you try to sneak in, if you got caught sneaking' in with your clothes, you'd say, "All right, I gotta go, and I'll be back in a couple a minutes," and make like you were just leaving.

Unbelievable. You know when I first came down there, I didn't get down into the yard until '88, but I was sort of like taken aback at how easy it was to get a bet in, get a football ticket, how did that work down the yard?

HN: Oh, there must have been a dozen bookies down there.

Oh yeah?

HN: Yup, if you wanted to get a number in, you want to get a football bet in. There was always football tickets all over the place. It was all part of, you know, the whole family thing.

Yeah, I remember one year I saved all of my drawing tickets, and at the end of the year I added them up, and I think I spent $878 one year just on drawing tickets.

HN: Oh, I can believe it.

Because everybody sold tickets to everybody.

HN: Everybody had tickets.

Pension parties five dollar tickets, ten dollar tickets, twenty dollar tickets on the Super Bowl. I mean it just went on and on and on.

HN: That's how it was. I mean, you might spend your whole pay check on tickets, not to mention there might have been a few card games down there once in a while.

Every now and then there'd be a card game.

HN: Well, I mean even though we worked through the bad weather and all, when you were getting, back then you'd get eight, ten inches of snow, it was very difficult to find any steel, and it was the most dangerous time to be out, and I don't have to tell you, you're the maintenance guy. You got trouble with the crane, you're up on top of the crane looking for what's wrong with our cranes.

We know about that. I remember one of the first jobs I got when I got down to the yard, the foreman told me, he says, "Hey," he says, "I'm gonna come over with the shovels," he says, "Shovel the crane run off." I says, "Well, what are you talking about, shovel the run off? You mean to tell me we're going up there?" "Oh yeah, we gotta change that crane wheel". And I went up there and shoveled the crane run off, and when you think about this when you talk about shoveling the crane runoff, here's an area that was about five feet wide from one side to the other, it had a crane rail like eight inches from each edge, the outer edges, full of oil, because all of these rails were oiled constantly to allow the crane to pass back and forth, it had to have leeway to move back and forth, and I'm up there shoveling this stuff off the side, and people are looking at me like what the hell are you doing? All of a sudden, here comes the crane car and everything, and these guys are sitting down there at the combo saws, they said, "Can you believe that? Those guys from down at the maintenance group are going to change a wheel out here in the snowstorm?"

HN: Absolutely.

You should have seen it when it rained.

HN: Oh, that was more miserable.

We had a foreman that never looked at the weather report. If it was going to rain on Tuesday and be clear for the rest of the week, we changed wheels on Tuesday. I mean that's just the way it was.

HN: We had foremen like that, too. You mentioned about the foremen. We had one on the loading gang like that; we straightened him out real quick.

Now over the years because of the, you ran into so many people over there, you did get involved with the union?

HN: Yeah, after I came back, one of the first jobs I got I think was, involved with the union, was Nick Kiak. I think was President at the time, and he appointed me as bible committee chairman.

Somebody had to do it. What did the bible committee guy do?

HN: Whenever somebody would die in our local, it was my job to deliver the bible to the widow.

Well, somebody had to do it.

HN: Yeah, it was, you know, and a lot of times I wouldn't know the person, other times I would know him, you know that I worked with him, and you had to do it.

What was the first union office you ever ran for?
HN: I think the first office I ever ran for was, I think I ran for vice president first.

Okay, what year would that have been?
HN: I think it was '76.

I remember one time you were running, I believe with a guy by the name of John Czipoth.
HN: Right.

And I don't remember the other guy, but I remember that you put out the most memorable piece of campaign literature that I ever saw in the history of the plant, and it had the name of your ticket on the front, which I think was the Czipoth, I don't know what ticket. Was it the Czipoth what ticket?

HN: Czipoth-Nemes ticket.

Czipot-Nemes ticket. And it said, "What the other two guys running for office were going to do for you," and when you opened it up there was absolutely nothing there. I'll tell you what, to this day people still talk about that.
HN: I think if I look through my drawer, I could probably find one of those.

I'm telling you right now that when I first saw that, I was running for office up at the other local, and I said to myself, "I just got to get to know these guys." And from running around over in the hall, that's where I first ran into you. In fact, the first time I ever talked to you at any length was the first time you ran for grievance committee. When would that have been?
HN: '79.

Yup, I remember you sitting over there in the old wage and equity room. Right, you were sitting in there with John Czipoth, and you were talking about oh boy, and you were like a nervous wreck, one cigarette after another. You were so nervous you couldn't even drink any beer. And that's when you were really nervous.
HN: That's when I was really nervous was right, Frank.

But you did win that election, didn't you?
HN: I did win in '79.

And then you continued on for quite some time.
HN: Right, in '86 I think I became chairman of the grievance committee, and then in '89, um, I think, uh, that's when I was appointed to the staff of the international union.

Okay, we got started in '79, and we made a progression up the ladder. Now, who would you say, because you moved up, like sort of took you under their wing?

HN: Well, I have like four mentors, starting off. Like you mentioned, the two most popular guys and guys that knew about the union were Chico Curzi and John Czipoth when I worked in the yard itself.

Okay, so they were like the big brothers?

HN: They got me to be a shop steward, and they brought me along. They used to call me the hippie shop steward, because I had long hair down to my shoulders, and yeah. So as I ended up running for office and I got over there, Vince Zoppi was, I think, the chairman of the grievance committee at the time. And till this day I really love Vince. He's a great guy, and probably a lot of my union activities as a grievance committeeman I owe to him. Because when I got on, now remember I'm familiar with the Beam Yard, but you know as a local representative, you had to go into all the shops.

Yes you did.

HN: And what he did was he gave me every shop but the Beam Yard. He gave me the machine shops, he gave me Ingot Mould, and I didn't know at the time, I thought he was really stickin' me, but what he was doing was giving me an opportunity to learn more and more about the steel and all the different shops, and as it turned out it was the best thing that ever happened to me.

Okay, and you know the people that you actually touched base with, that was priceless down the road, as far as moving on with the union. Because trust was everything.

HN: Absolutely.

Particularly with the union people. You know, I was down one time, down in the yard, and you know, I've never heard any grievances in the yard, but you know I was on the grievance committee from 2599, and I said, said to a guy down in the yard one day, "I just stopped down in the noon time, you know, down the car blocker shanty," and the guy said to me, "What the hell kind of an idiot must you be to be on the grievance committee?" "Right, I mean you just take such a beating." I says, "Yeah, but you know," I says, "I got something going for me no one else has," and he said, "What's that?" I said, "I got 100 percent approval rate." "You gotta be crazy," he said. I said, "No, from what I hear 50 percent love when I show up and 50 percent when I leave, 50 and 50 is 100." The guy says, "Get the hell out of here, you are crazy."

HN: You always had a way.

We had fun with that. Now, you were over there in that period of '79 to '86, were some really tough times, particularly around '82 and '83. Do you remember any of that? And a lot of layoffs.

HN: A lot of layoffs, but prior to that was, you know, the whole deal about the Japanese steel, knocking us out to foreign steel. Because in '82 I was sent over to Japan by the steel company with three other union representatives and four people from the company.

And what did you see over there?

HN: I saw six modernized brand-new plants over there making steel.

Yeah, sort of like took your breath away, I guess?

HN: Well, it sure did. I mean, you know better than I what it took to keep the plant going, those machines, because you're the maintenance guy and how long we produced steel with that steam engine that we had. Over there it was all brand-new. We went to six different plants. We were over there for 19 days. I wrote about, I'd have to look, I wrote, I don't know a 10 or 12 page report about all my time over there. But I could tell you this, in '82 already the Japanese were feeling the crunch in the Third World nations.

Okay, so you more or less knew then the time at Bethlehem was becoming numbered?

HN: Yes, not only because of them, because right after that coming back in '82, and we did our report on that, then I think it was the end of '82 or '83 we started visiting. I visited these places in Texas, Chaparral, and Nucor, which are mini mills.

Yeah, also new operations.

HN: New operations. Right here in the United States, non-union. We visited those. Those were the most horrible plants you'd ever want to walk into.

Okay, tell me why.

HN: Well, first of all it was dark, dingy, they didn't have any unions. They didn't, there was absolutely no concern for the workers. And I can say that from what I saw, and this is my opinion. Uh, you know as well as I down the yard you had a safety guy, you had a safety committee, you were involved. They didn't have any of that stuff down there.

But the bottom line is they're still there and we're history.

HN: Well, at the time the only thing that kept us going was we, see they usually cut 40, 60, and 20 length. And that's what they would cut. In the beam yard, we'd cut 42, 1 and ¾, 44, we'd cut anything that they ordered, whatever the customer ordered and what they ordered, that's what we cut.

Were we like the only ones that did that?
HN: Yeah, that was it.

So that was a plus for us?
HN: We cut the length, yup.

It was a plus for us, but we really couldn't get the economy scale of straight runs by doing that? Do you remember when they finally opened up the auxiliary yard as a service center with John Eckert? That was a raging success.
HN: Yes.

I mean, I think we all know that.
HN: Yes.

I don't know if this is true or not, but John told me that he personally presented that plan to Walt Williams when Walt was the top dog for the plant, and Walt Williams looked at it and called him the next day and said, who's gonna run this? Well, you know John is never bashful, he says I'll run it, and the rest was history.
HN: I think I got called in on that, and I recommended John on top of it, but …

Well, thank god for John
HN: Well, that was the problem with most of the management down there. And you had to be sharp enough to get them to think it was their idea.

That's right.
HN: But it was your idea.

You'd have to play both sides against the middle.
HN: Right, and try to get them to implement, because the most important, I implemented down the beam yard, uh, we got called in, and they would always discipline somebody. If you'd send steel out to a customer and a flange was bent or the steel was bent or something, uh, they'd give our guys a day off, three days off, two days off, they'd give 'em discipline for it, so I came up with the idea, I think MacGavern was back there, was the superintendent, I said, "Why are we doing this?" The guy don't really give a shit, he's getting a day off. If it's a Saturday, he's happier than shit. I said, "Why don't we send these guys to the customer and let them see what's going on? Well, not only was it an awakening for our guys, but it was for the company, because they started seeing when the customers were moving the beams around, they were using these flat hooks and picking up

10 to15 at a time, and they'd be the one bending the webs and bending the material, not us.

Yeah. And they were turning this in in order to get a rebate.

HN: Rebate and get a claim, and then we'd have to pay for it and then send 'em new steel. Well, when they started doing this and these visitations they saw a lot of things that they could go after the company. Just imagine a forklift going to pick up 60 foot long steel, thin, light steel? Well, you're gonna bend it, it's gonna bend. There's no, because when our crane men would pick up the steel, we would have to help. Well, when you were looking at a 60-foot piece. They'd pick up the ends, we'd put what they called a spacer, a little metal thing across, and then moved the chains in on the other side, so he would pick up the steel that maybe he had 20 on this side of the chain, 20 on this side, 20 on the other side of the chain, so you wouldn't bend it. Where they were just putting two hooks at both ends.

Opposite ends, and…

HN: And pick it up.

It's like your grandmother's bay window, huh?

HN: There ya go.

There ya go. So you know, after all this, going into all these shops and seeing all these operations and hearing countless grievances, the time finally came when the international union says, "Hector, we want you to work for us." Tell me a little bit about that.

HN: Well, it was, the staff guy at the time was Marvin Peters. And I have to say, if it wasn't for Marvin Peters, I probably would have never been a staff man, because he's the guy that suggested to the international. , you must remember, there's only a couple hundred staff guys, and you know the numbers. Back when it was over a million people, they're represented by the steel company, I mean represented by the union that were only chosen to be staff guys. And I had an interview with President Williams at the time, and he interviewed me, and they made me a staff guy for the Bethlehem plant to go on later on, and I represented the Steelton plant too.

Yeah, that was in 1986?

HN: '89.

1989, and that's when you really …

HN: That's when the shit really hit the fan, too.

Because that was at the stage of the game where people were starting to realize what is the most honorable thing we can do by our steelworker members? And that was keeping places open as long as possible. And is that the prevailing thought the whole time?

HN: Uh, save the plant itself?

Yeah.

HN: I don't know if they thought they could save it, because they knew. I mean, both sides knew exactly what they were up against, unless we could do something to fight off, no longer was the foreign steel we had to fight off, it was the mini mills, the domestic mini mills right here in the United States. And you know as well as I do, it came to the point where we negotiated, and I was the lead on it, uh, get rid of 500 jobs, and they were going to put an electric furnace in the Bethlehem Steel, which you remember, and save what we could out of the place. We signed that, big pictures in the paper, Hank Barnette, and everybody there, the three presidents, myself, at Hotel Bethlehem we signed it, and then six months later they came back to us and told us they weren't gonna do it, I think it was 180 million or 190 million at the time, they were gonna invest in the plant.

Well, there was, over the course of your union time, you were quite the guy when it came to writing letters. You did your best work when you were really fired up. Tell us a little bit about the big march we had over at Martin Tower? How did that come to be? Wasn't that your friend, John Czipoth, more or less organized that?

HN: Yeah, they took it to heart, I mean you were there.

Well, hey everybody took it to heart. That was a spontaneous outpouring of love is what it was.

HN: Right. And there was a lot of people there.

You better believe it.

HN: And we tried to do the best we could, and it was all about the people.

Sure it was.

HN: That's all this was about. I mean the union, say what you want about unions, the unions cared about the people, and that's what they were trying to do, protect 'em as long as we could. I remember when we were negotiating a contract one time, Marvin took out, it was 3 o'clock in the morning, and we had like a little break. You might have even been there, when he went on, what did he put on, what strike was it? He showed the film of the '59 strike? He pulled that at 3 o'clock in the morning, the company went out for a break, and he puts this film on the '59 strike and showing the guys out there fighting to save the jobs of the steel company. Oh my God it was, you know, and you get all pumped up and everything else.

Oh yeah. Yeah, I'll tell you what, that was really, well it was a way of life. Let's face it, you take a guy like me, four generations, my great grandfather, my grandfather, my dad, myself, we all worked down there. And you know, it was a good life. I mean, who cares if we worked days, middles and nights in the same week, and we all did that.

HN: And it was the operation. If we …

And you know nobody could believe if you said if you took off you were subject to discipline. They thought we were crazy. What do you mean if you took off? "You just worked the last 10 years in a row Fourth of July." I says, "And guess what? This year is number 11..

HN: I don't ever remember a day at work where any of the steelworkers said let's figure out what we can do to screw the company.

Yeah.

HN: That was a way of life.

Now, Hector, through all of this, and I see you retired up there in '94, through all of this time that you had there, when was the first time you actually came to the realization it wasn't gonna be saved?

HN: Personally, me probably around '89. Yeah, 89. Because the things we started to do. If you can remember the international semi, we had to get, part of the whole negotiations was to take us out of the basic steel agreement, which means it's the, that's the main agreement that covers all the plants. And they wanted us out, and I had to write up contracts for us, and we were going to be removed from there. Now, and that was held at Martin Tower, and I can remember that negotiations like it was yesterday, because the only, I knew it was the thing I had to do to keep us going for as long as we could, because the theory in my mind at the time was the longer I can keep this place going, the closer everybody gets to pension. The more guys we can get covered in pension, the more guys won't get hurt as much.

We're talking about what? 1990, '91?

HN: Yup. So what we did was at the time was they took us out of the basic steel contract, took us out of profit sharing and all, and you must remember this time Burns Harbor was making tons of money and everything else, and probably by having us in the contract, instead of them getting $2.20 an hour for profit sharing, they were down a dollar and a quarter or something. So when I agreed, and then we had to go back to all the people up at Stabler Arena and explain all this to them that we would come out, the only thing I did at Martin Tower that I asked for was to put in the word called snap back, that if they failed to modernize and put the 180 million dollars in the plant, that we would snap back to the agreement. Well, six months later they balked on their 180 million, and we snapped back to the basic agreement. You gotta remember all that?

There's a lot of people that did understand you know what the name of the game was, but you know when you look back on it now, even though we're looking back as Monday morning quarterbacks, everything is like falling into place with what you said about we had to keep the place open as long as we can to get as many people eligible for pension, and there's a lot of people who understand that, and if I had a dollar for every guy that said, thank God we have Hector Nemes at that time, you could retire right now, you wouldn't have to work for the Parking Authority. But you know, I'm just doing that to inflate your ego a little bit, but I want you to know that that's what I hear all the time, and when these guys went off and you know that these people that had to go to other plants, and this is a very hard thing for me to say, but I'm going to say it: they would come back and say our union people here in Bethlehem have already forgotten more than these other guys know. And I said, "Well, those are pretty harsh words." They said, "Frank, they don't know the basic things. All they know how to do is go in and argue with the company. I'm not saying they're not doing a good job, but the things we take for granted, he says, " they just have a hard time with it." So you know, so finally the day comes, okay, where you're finally deciding do I wanna keep doing this or was that because you were just had your fill of it?

HN: Well, to be quite honest with you, I was, at the time then I was removed from the Bethlehem plant as the staff representative, and you know, I probably got myself in a whole bunch of trouble fighting for the guys, because I always put them ahead of everything else. And basically right up until the day I got relieved, I was pretty close to negotiating and trying to cover some of these people that were transferring to other plants, and then I got removed, and then that all fell by the wayside, because like you, my whole goal from '89 on was to keep it going, to do whatever I had, face the people knowing that I was trying to do the right thing by keeping it going so more people, you know '89, did you, you didn't have enough time for pension. I didn't have enough time for pension.

No, I didn't have enough time for pension.

HN: And I knew as long as I could keep going, we'd be covering more people. And I'm telling you, it was a, I mean I feel real bad for the guys that I couldn't help, those last couple guys that had to go, but it was a miniscule number that were left that weren't covered under the 20 years or anything else.

Yeah, that did not get a pension.

HN: That's right. I mean, that's how many guys. By us staying open till '94, '95, '96, '97, '98.

HN: Yup, it just, it helped. I mean, boy you gotta think, all the guys, I mean the guys that were hired between '64 and '66, Frank, were unbelievable the numbers, and they all ended up getting. I never ever felt bad of anything I had to do. Fortunately, I got along real good with some big time guys in the company, and because they trusted me and I signed agreements when, you know, we cut, I had to cut jobs, I had to cut incentives, I changed practices, I did whatever I had to do at the time. We were lucky, though; we got some reverse layoffs to the point where they would lay the senior guy off and keep the young guy working.

Well, you know what, they never really believed that at the other plants; they always thought that was a myth, that it never happened.

HN: Oh that was true.

That 20 year guys could take a layoff.

HN: Yup, well we signed the papers. We ...

We had a lot of guys; they loved that.

HN: Oh absolutely.

Oh, they foamed at the mouth.

HN: And then when you had the guys, the younger guys working, that was great for them because they were adding years of time to their service.

Sure they absolutely were. A lot of 'em were there that wouldn't have been there any other way.

HN: No.

And you know, I'll be talking to those people, too. So finally you do retire. What became of you after that? You had a party and everything didn't you?

HN: Yes, the guys threw a nice party, a retirement party at the union hall for me. I got golf clubs and a watch, and a lot of nice words more importantly than the golf clubs and a watch.

Well, that's good, that's good. And how did you get involved in the community after that?

HN: Well, after that there was a young guy, I worked, I was friends with his father for 30, 40 years, Don Cunningham, and his son was gonna make a bid to run for City Council in the city, and I knew him since he was a little guy, and he asked me to help him with his election, so myself and a couple, just a few other people, worked on his campaign, and he was elected to City Council. And after that he, one term I think he served, and then he ran for Mayor, and he was elected to Mayor, and after that he asked me to come work for him as his Assistant to the Mayor for Customer Service, because he knew me from over the years about handing problems and handling people, and he asked me to come.

Well, that was the big thing, handling people, no doubt about it.
HN: It was only about $22,000 a year, it wasn't a lot of money.

It wasn't a lot of money, but it was a foot in the door, huh?
HN: Well, I figured it was. It was a good job. I liked the kid; he made a good Mayor for the city, and I didn't mind doing that. It was fun.

And what are ya doing now?
HN: Well, he was leaving, so he was going out to Harrisburg to work for the governor, and a position came open here as director, and I put my hat in the ring to become director of the Bethlehem Parking Authority for the City.

And they did pick you?
HN: Yeah.

And that's what you're currently doing now?
HN: And I've been doing it going on seven years, six years.

Well, Hector I'm gonna tell you something that I haven't told a lot of people, but over the years they could have paid a guy more money but never got a better guy than you.
HN: Well, I appreciate that Frank, thanks Frank.

Thanks a lot.

CALVIN W. RESZEK
32 years of service

Beam Yard

Cal started in April of 1964. His grandfather and father were also steelworkers. Cal started at the Beam Yards and put in 32 years there. A man who truly understood the value of the union as he was one of the highest paid men to ever work in the Beam Yard. Was a master of all the jobs he handled but excelled as a cutter. The first man who ever told the author that controlled cutting was killing the company.

* * * * * * * * * *

Today is March the 7th, 2008, and we're talking to Calvin W. Reszek. Is it okay if we call you Cal? Tell me something, how did you become a Bethlehem Steel worker? How did you get hired?

CR: Well, through word of mouth, I got hired early in '64, 1964. Work was tough to get, good work, and I'm a third generation steelworker. My grandfathers, my father, both were employees of the steel company at one time or the other, so I went right in after. I was looking to get in. I looked there for the opportunity.

All right, because you heard stories at family picnics and being around the family, it's not a bad place to be. That makes good sense to me. So when you went into the employment office, is this the first job they offered you?

CR: No. What happened was they also had an inspection job open, and my father, knowing his way around the plant and knowing Julius Baylas as you know, and Bob Gallagher, they advised I get out of the small department and go someplace big. The mistake was I ended up in the beam yard, and they called that the, uh, where everybody got crippled up and didn't come out so good. They didn't like that either, but I took it. And I was advised that the weld bed was a high paying job. I had a family already, a couple of children, and weld bed would pay well, and I took it. I connected with that.

Well that's, that's, I would say, pretty representative of what I've been hearing from people.

CR: And we were also tested for aptitude. It was a four-day test. Started with the employment bureau for the State of Pennsylvania you tested, and then you went to the Bethlehem Steel main office and tested for three days. And it was a placement thing, according to that also.

I'm sure they looked at that, because that was a big thing even when I started in 1965. Now, one of the things everyone wants to hear is what was it like when you first got down there? Try to describe your first week to me.

CR: Okay, my first night was a nightmare. I went in night shift 11-7. It was a Saturday night for a Sunday. It was the 10th, May 10th, 1964, and the safety man took me down alone; there was nobody else with me. Took me down, it was pitch black and the sparks were flying off the saws, the screaming noise, the water flying around, I was warm because it was a May night, but it was about what was to come, and that was working out there in the winter at the same time, you know when it was cold. But I took it. I went around, and they made me comfortable in the different areas, made sure I was, you know, I wasn't walking into an area that was unsafe, and then they took me over to what was going to be my job, the weld bed. Okay, and there I met my co-worker, who happened to be Frank Hepner, and we started the same night, the same time I met him, and they introduced us to the people that worked the bed. And the first thing was safety. The first issues were safety, and I got a ring on that because it was something that went over and over no matter what you did down there, safety was a big thing. And they told us what our job basically was going to be, chipping, grinding, and welding, okay, reconditioning beams that would go out to the customer, and they had to be polished up and look good, presentable.

Why were they reconditioning these beams, Cal?

CR: Okay, to save tons of money. The stuff would come out with scrap on it. Ovkay, maybe it only had a few feet of defect, but it could be repaired, weld repair. So what we would do, gouge out the bad steel. In some cases it wasn't bad at all; it was just a fill in with a weld stick and make sure the tensile strengths matched up and, you know, the right heats, and then we would apply this weld puddling, it was called, no big skill, okay. And then we'd grind this off to a shiny finish, and it was accepted. And we did this on all kinds of scrap.

So there was no shortage of people willing to buy beams that were reconditioned at a lower rate? But that was still way better than buying the new beam price-wise.

CR: They even weighed it. They'd line it up for the good heavy section because they needed it.

That's great. Now, I'm really glad that you brought up the part about safety. Let me hear some more about why safety was so important down there.

CR: Well, because it was a place where you could be dismembered really quickly by making a wrong step, put your fingers in the wrong spot, even sparks flying from a simple grinder, which was very heavy, and had a lot of danger to it, but if you ground into somebody, you could have blinded them or maimed them for life. You always ground away from your buddy. Your buddy ground one way, you ground the other way, and this is with the grinder, a high speed grinder, and it was air driven by hundreds of pounds of pressure

Now, I would imagine that in an operation like that where it was work where you didn't want to make mistakes in close confinement, your crane men were usually the cream of the crop, weren't they?

CR: Yes, they were; they were very good crane men.

I'm going to be interviewing some of those guys later on. So how long did you work at the weld bed?

CR: First, on and off, probably the first seven years I was there.

First seven years. Did you have a family at the time?

CR: Yes, I did, and that was the hardship, that it may pay good money when I worked, but we were down to 30 hours a week. Now, for two hours I'd collect unemployment compensation through our SIP plan, if you recall that we had a plan that would pay us a little supplement, okay, wasn't much, but it was there. But the thing was I was only getting 30 hours a week. Now you know if you make good enough money in that 30 hours, you could live on 30 hours. What happened was it was always just a little short, you know, just a little short. So for the first ten years down there we scrimped and saved, and you know, just made it through. It got better as I went on.

And so it wasn't always a bed of roses financially?

CR: No, boy, especially the first ten years, twelve years.

Okay, so that was my next question. How long was it before you turned the corner and things were getting a little bit better?

CR: Ten to twelve years, and then what happened was it got a little stagnated, it started slowing down, and right around the holiday Thanksgiving and Christmas. So we had those ups and downs in the plant.

So right at the end of the '60s things were, I mean the end of the '70s, things were slowing down.

CR: That's right, '76, and then they had a hiring, and '79, and then it went flat. Something happened and bang, we were all back to almost starting routes and short hours again, you know. And the other thing was that you worked with what was available to you, and sometimes they were dirty, grungy jobs that you didn't want to get back into, but you took them because you had to stay.

That's it. In other words, you're saying that you weren't there every week at the weld bed. You were there when business was good and as it tapered off, you like slid down the ladder a little bit.

CR: And took what was open.

You just grabbed what you could and you're hoping to hang onto the ladder. Did you ever get laid off?

CR: Never.

Wow, you're the first guy I ran into that's able to tell me that.

CR: I took a preferred lay off; that was about two weeks; that worked. Well actually, Gil Leesburg was our assistant super at the time, and then he stopped it because too many guys wanted to do it. Because actually it was paying more money to be laid off than if I stayed. That's how it worked with me, because I got the supplement, I got the state unemployment compensation, and it was better on the top than it was. It was right around the holiday, Christmas, and I took a preferred layoff, two weeks, that's the most I ever got out of it.

Cal, I'm not bragging, but I haven't run into too many dumb steelworkers. I mean, they all knew, you know, how the game was played, and I'm glad that you brought that up. Now, after that period of time, you know, like into the late '70s, we got into that period around 1979 where they hired again. Tell me about that.

CR: And it was a short-lived period. A lot of young guys came in. It was like the bloom of spring. We loved it, you know, because we were moving up as these young guys were coming in, and they were taking our place. And it was short-lived. It lasted about nine months, and that was one of the biggest hardest times we went through. Yeah, beam yard, by hundreds they were out, and a lot of them never came back. Uh, most of them didn't come back. They were hired in that period. And some of them lost really good jobs, because they left jobs that were probably good in the way they performed, day shift, things like that, but we made more money, so they were happy with the more money. Now when they lost the Beam Yard money, or what happened at the Bethlehem Steel they got laid off, they couldn't get back to the job they were at before that, you know on the outside. It hurt 'em, because we were known as steelworkers, there was a possibility of a recall, and nobody wanted to take that chance, you know, recalling people.

Now, those people that went out, I'm looking at the end of 1980, beginning of '81, uh, most of them had opportunities to go to other areas of the plant, but the rest of the plant wasn't doing that well either.

CR: That's correct, that's correct. And if you didn't have a skill, it hurt you more yet. You know, machine shops, things like that, you could possibly pick something out. Without a skill, you weren't going anywhere.

So during that period up until they had that hiring in '79, what was like your favorite job while you were working there?

CR: Operator in the combo mill. Saw operator in combo mill. I cut the stuff up for the customer, you know, through order. We had a pretty good system, a somewhat computerized system. The customer would come over and I'd cut the length for him, push it out on a bed, we had an inspector look at it, and then the chainman of course cleaned it up and the markers and the, we also had a leader on the job, which I become later, cutter, that was the title for that job, was cutter, and I become one of the people that led, you know was in an area where I would receive the orders and I'd apply them, and everybody else did the work. We all worked, but more or less there was labor out on that bed, and as you know, you worked in them areas. You seen the people toiling with turning wrenches and what other tools we had, and some were too heavy for the people to even lift, and we had wrenches, turning wrenches, that probably weighed about thirty pounds.

And that was also an area which had a high incident of injuries, didn't it? What type of injuries?

CR: Mostly minor, mostly fingers, toes, knees, uh scrapes. We had a couple where, actually had a guy on my crew lost his fingers, three fingers. I had another young man, I don't want to give his name, he was rushing, it was the end of the shift, and he tried to nest a beam that was twelve inches wide, and he lifted it in the front, it came down in the back, and it took his finger right off.

Well, that's one thing that we always used to emphasize to people that were new in the area, you know, that you don't get too many chances to make mistakes around here. They usually bite you immediately. But you were a saw operator, right? Tell us about the size of those saws and exactly what they did.

CR: Okay. It was a huge saw, it was 300 horsepower. It was driven by two 150 horsepower electric motors. It had a huge frame. The blade was six foot in diameter, okay. It was a six-foot blade, probably about anywhere from three quarters of an inch for a thin blade up to maybe seven eighth of an inch for a thick blade. They had various size blades for various reasons. Now, that thing would cut into a section. If it's six foot diameter, the saw probably would cut in as deep as, or I should say in width probably 24 inches. I don't think we did too much over 24 inches. We had sections like PZ36, 27 and 36, but that would be compacted somewhat on the roller line. Our main rolls were 36 inches, and that was stretching it. And the thickness of the material, I would say up to about on that mill, probably 150 pounds per foot, okay.

So when you would talk thickness on a beam that might have been like a W12, you would be talking about …
CR: Maybe an inch, inch and a half thickness up to, like I said, about 150 pounds per foot. We didn't have too many sections like that. I'll tell you one big heavy section. We used to cut motor heads for General Motors, it was a GM product, and it was unusually thick, it was a couple of inches, and they made engine blocks for diesels out of that. They actually rolled a section that they could later on grind and finish off, polish, and put two sections together, two sides together, and make an engine block, where the pistons and everything would, that was unusually heavy material, and them saws worked to get through that material.

Now can you describe the noise that was generated by these saws?
CR: You know I'm guessing at this. I may be even going over the top here, but I think it was as high as 150 decibels. A jet engine is around 125/120 okay. Now, I really emphasize this. I used to go home, I lived approximately two miles from the plant, two and a half miles at the most, on middle shift I'd go out, sit on my back patio and hear the saws at my house, and I would know what sections they were cutting by the noise of the saws, and this is in the combo. Now the people in Miller Heights and Freemansburg also heard this come over the river, and they complained at times, you know, that there was too much noise. The other thing was the four and twelve saw cut huge material, I don't want to get off the beaten path. But they cut huge, they cut 14G, 734 pounds to the foot, and that would wind through, some of them cuts would go through for thirty minutes, the saw trying to go through. Ours were a reciprocating type in the combo in the other finishing end on the cold saws. For 4 and 12 they were push type; they pushed through the material with relief. The operator would relieve the cut and go into it again, relieve and cut, and it would grind and holler and scream. But I'd hear that. That was on a Friday

night usually we cut it, they'd roll it early in the week, it'd cool down and by Friday night they were cutting that section into the weekend, so all the neighbors put up with it, you know. You had to hear it.

So that was W14G, that was about I believe 823 pounds.

CR: That was 734. That was the big; then they cut it down four pounds. And then under, that was probably the biggest, heaviest. It was only 14 inches each section, okay. They had 'em, all the way down, 500 pound, 400 pound, you know, with odd increments on the end. I don't remember exact depth anymore. And then you also had your 14, that was 14E. Then you had your 14D's. You know 14G, 14E, 14D, and you get the point coming down it got lighter, the section got lighter and less noise, but it was permanent ear damage no matter how well you were protected. Bethlehem Steel they give us enough protection. There was no other way around it. It was ear muffs and ear plugs, and then it was loud, and then again you're losing your senses, because you depend on your hearing to be safe, your eyesight to be safe, and without those qualities of life, you know you're hearing's blocked to block the noise out, it could be detrimental to your health or your life. Somebody could be hollering at you you're in harm's way, and you don't hear it. You'd get hit before you realize what was going on, and that happened to a lot guys because of hearing protection. I'm not saying it was wrong, but it was the only way, and it was the way of the paycheck, you know.

And these 14G's, this was the same material used as the anchoring foundation for the World Trade Center and big buildings throughout the world.

CR: That's correct. And the first ones I worked on on the weld bed, I didn't cut em at the time, I retraced 'em and made good steel out of 'em. It was the, it was Cape Kennedy then, which turned into Kennedy Space Center later, but Cape Canaveral. They planted these 14G's into concrete, embedded in the concrete for the blast area, the blast pad, because that was the only thing that could really hold the pad in place, and they flew them down at time with planes, maybe one piece in a plane, forty foot long, that's how heavy it was. Well, you can compound that, you know. It's forty foot long and 730 pounds in a foot.

That's 28,000 pounds at least. That's a good load for any plane.

CR: That's right. If they needed emergency fix up, we'd repair them bars on night shift on the weld bed, and that's getting off the saws, but the weld repair, they took it to the airport, transported it to Florida. But that was the start of the space center and the first big blast offs, you know, our moon shots and everything else. We were instrumental in almost everything that went on in the world, okay. We were the first ones to go to the moon, of course you know that, and we were instrumental in setting up that platform with our steel, and we were proud of that. You know it was something that you carry, the star, you know, it was a, a lot of times just an atta boy, but it worked.

That's true, you know, uh, that was a different time and place back then. Did President Johnson make a call on you while you were working at the Steel?

CR: No, as a matter of fact, when they did, they gave out little pins, and I wasn't present at the time, I missed my pin, but I didn't care. Everybody got the same condolence, because also we made stuff for Vietnam.

But I want, I really meant: Were you drafted?

CR: No.

No, okay. You were married with kids.

CR: I was married with children when I started at the Steel.

Plus you were working at Bethlehem Steel on top of it. Okay, now I see you were also a main yard loader. What period are we talking about here?

CR: That was in between the weld bed, because what would happen…

The weld bed and the saw job? And what did the main yard loader do?

CR: Okay. Main yard loader would assemble the steel off cut slips, okay, raw cut slips. It was customer orders. And the customer relations would assemble these loads. It was supposed to be maximum of 40,000 on a truck or 180,000 in a car, railroad car. You did mostly railroad cars.. You were in that car a lot of times with the crane man, you know. You depended, you put your life in front of that crane man.

And for what period were you actually a chain man down there?

CR: Okay, mostly every job you start, you start as a chain man, either front or back, mostly in the back if you didn't have the time.

Why would you have two chain men?

CR: Okay, because there was two ends to that crane. Believe it or not, some of them cranes were over a hundred foot long, and you had lifting equipment on both ends.

In other words, you had, they would lift from two different locations.

CR: That's correct, at the same time, simultaneously you'd have two hoists, two blocks, and two trolleys.

Working independently of each other.

CR: Independent. But the crane man would be in control of all of it.

Well, he must have been some sort of an operator that crane man.

CR: He was. One of my good friends always gets credit for that. You see him from time to time, and he always asks me, he says, "How was I?" And I said, "Well, I can't really answer that, but I'll tell you what, you never hurt anybody, you were always there when I needed, and you never made a mistake when I was with you."

Well, that's great. Now, I'm looking down here on your sheet here, it says you were a gauge man, what was that?

CR: Okay, what you did there, that was on the big saws. Our combo saws all had automatic computer gauges, okay, dial it in. These things were manually operated, okay, and some of those gauges probably weighed a ton, and there were probably four on a run, and you cranked them by hand with a big paddle wheel, okay. You cranked this gauge, it had teeth in it, and this paddle wheel would catch the teeth, brass normally, and you would set it, and then there would be a scale in front of you, a rule, and you would say you wanted forty-foot-eight and a half inches, you would set it to forty foot and then the eight and a half inches you'd roll up until you got it. And you had to know where your marks were, because they weren't very accurate. Some time you could be off three quarters of an inch. You had to know what that particular gauge represented. It could be off an inch minus, it could be off an inch plus. You had to know where that laid, because you couldn't afford to make a mistake with that.

You couldn't be short could you? It wasn't quite so bad if you were over.

CR: You couldn't be short, but the customer didn't always appreciate the dividend either.

Yeah, because they had an extra step to make.

CR: That was something to deal with. You know, if they couldn't fabricate it at the time because it was an inch long, they didn't want that either..

And what's one of the first things you learned about working in the beam yard? What's something that it never did in the beam yard, Cal?

CR: Never rained.

You guys were just fortunate.

.CR: Any kind of weather. I worked a Thanksgiving down there, and I'm not going to say rain, wet, high humidity on Thanksgiving. It was a middle shift on Thanksgiving, and we worked. You were driven by the incentive on a job.

Well that was the absolute worse shift to work on a holiday was middle shift.

Because you could just, no telling what you could miss.
CR: Family and friends.

How about vacations and stuff? How long was it until you were able to get a week with the family in the summer?
CR: Probably fifteen or twenty years.

Yeah, wasn't until the '70s then, late '70s, early '80s.
CR: '86. I'm gonna tell you what happened there. The consent decree, tell me if I'm pronouncing that right, it was a ruling in favor by the arbitrator of the older worker who was displaced, and what happened, they were able to come back to all these jobs and move right in where there was an opening. They couldn't take your job, but if there was an opening, they could move in.

It was plant seniority instead of shop seniority.
CR: Exactly. And I got knocked back a thousand numbers.

A thousand numbers.
CR: I went from 1054, that was my starting seniority number, I was all the way down in the four hundreds and went all the way back to like 1500. Higher than the number I started.

Well, how many people you figure were there, the maximum number any time during your entire time?
CR: 2,250 men. That's a lot of people. And the war broke that up, Vietnam.

And how about the scheduling? How was the scheduling?
CR: Scheduling was terrible.

Give me an example of that.
CR: Okay, start days, middles and nights in one week, in one week, and then maybe you just finished up middles on Saturday and they needed you Saturday night for Sunday, you were coming out already night shift. And holidays, there was no such thing as a holiday. You got a premium pay for a premium day. That's what a holiday was to us. If they, it was a 24/7 operation. We never stopped. That place never slept, and I don't care if it was on what holiday it was, with the exception after first five years we start knocking off on Christmas Eve. We'd work a short shift Christmas Eve and maybe be off for eight hours, okay. That was in general for the yard, for the Beam Yard itself. Guys would start coming in day shift, okay, Christmas Day maybe some guys worked stuff like that, but by middle everybody worked.

Now an interesting thing about the way the scheduling is going, the prevailing attitude was we're going to pay you a premium, you just come in and work, but didn't this really wear on some people? It must have had an effect on marriages; it must have had an effect on everything.

CR: Well, the thing was everybody, you know, your Fourth of July or whatever, it was a hot stinking day, you're going in there middle shift, the picnics just start.

I'm looking here and I see that actually your main job and the job you retired from was cutter. When did you first get onto that job? And what is a cutter?

CR: Okay, he's the guy who takes full responsibility for his crew. Okay. What he is, he lines up all the cutting that's given to him, probably off a computer driven program, okay. It comes from the customer to the office, from the office to the cutter. Cutter lines it up, gives it the saw operator, which I done earlier I told you. Saw operator would cut it to length. It would go out on the bed, on the placement bed, okay. Then your chain men and your marker are responsible at that point, they'd be given sheets off the computer to follow and stencils to be made, the stencil material so it had nice legible markings on it. The marker would apply that stuff, mark the beams with a nice marking ink, and then the chain men would pile it up and put it by schedule, okay. When it was all piled and assembled, then it was a final lift for that customer. Maybe we were working three, four, five customers at one time, and these beds weren't huge; they were, these beds were probably sixty foot wide, if that. A lot of the smaller beds were less, and the depth of the bed could be anywhere from seventy foot to maybe 109 foot or 110 foot on the big beds. And what happened, you assemble this stuff. Now it comes time to clean the bed off, because at some point you become saturated with all the steel you just cut up and applied and piled and it has to go out. And it goes out from assembly into a yard, a storage yard, a storage area. And then we'd have either crane men, a helper crane man come in, your same crane man that just piled all this material with you, he put chains on, take the hooks off with chains on and put the stuff into a run or possibly on a roller line that went to another yard, so to speak. All in the beam yard, but to another area. And from there it would be put into areas that were easy to load from for that customer. There were mostly customer runs, okay, so to speak. When a railroad car come in, a truck come in, that was that run, okay. And that went on continuously. We had no lunch in the combo mill. When we're referring to me cutting in the combo mill, my men out there, five men, we had no lunch. Your lunch was your incentive on that job, other than making the dollar, was to try to get enough time to eat, okay. Or you ate with one sandwich in your hand.

You know Cal, there must be something wrong here, because my friends that didn't work at Bethlehem Steel told me that I'd still had a job there if I wouldn't have been cooking on middle shift and sleeping on night shift. I mean, tell me some more about this job.

CR: Do you know how many times that reference was made, and you end up eating it at the end because you'd be in trouble if you went after everybody that ever brought that up, because I hear that today at McDonald's. Well you guys slept all night. Well, I'll tell you what, we worked all night, that's why a guy like you didn't stay there. The guy that, the same guy that has this reference to me sleeping all night, why didn't you work there, and he would say, oh well I had a better job. Then don't complain. We didn't sleep all night. I have what you have, you have what you have. We did work all night, believe me.

I'll tell you, if you didn't work, you didn't make any money did ya?

CR: Well, not only that, you'd go home. Your foreman wouldn't tolerate that.

They didn't fool around. They didn't fool around. And I remember, I can tell you what. You know, I was involved with the union a lot, and a lot of times the guys would say to me, "Bamie, could you come over the shanty," when I used to work with Wally when I was the motor inspector for the combo mill, "you would come over with Wally and get these hot dogs and sauerkraut together for us? We got, we're buried in work, and we can't handle it." We'd go over there and we'd actually do that ourselves, because we were the maintenance people, we didn't have a specified job. Or they'd say, "Could you do this?" Sure we can do that. It didn't happen often, maybe once every two three months, but you know we were always glad to help out, and those guys really appreciated that that they had somebody there, because they ate on the fly.

CR: And there was a lot of camaraderie, I'll tell you that.

Oh yeah, and there was a lot of going out after middle shift and breakfast after night shift and things like that. That's probably one of the hardest things that any steelworker misses about the place.

CR: Walking away from people like that.

And these are the same type of people that if you were in a fox hole you'd want 'em right in there with ya, and you knew that they were gonna cover your back.

CR: And I'll tell you what, when Pauly Shinsec, and the other guy, I can't even think of his name right now, I'm lost for words, but those guys always backed us up. They were there. Something went wrong, boom they were there. They fixed it, and they didn't make the big incentive off that. They were just to repair it and help you out. And they helped in other ways, too, if they could, you know. So yes, I had a lot of good close friends that didn't even work in my department.

Now what was the first, like, full year that you had as a cutter?
CR: Uh, that was in the '80s, I would say around '86, '84, '84-'86. Yeah, we just started making a comeback. We had big layoffs up to then, and started, and I bid the job because they put a third unit on. That was another thing. It was 24/7 with the exception of a repair shift that came on a Wednesday, and you're well aware of that because you probably worked a lot them dirty rotten jobs on the down shift.

Because the incentive was all derived strictly on tonnage versus man-hours.
CR: And a continuous operation.

That's right. Now when you started, you were running long periods on certain sections, sometimes days at a time weren't ya? Give me an example of that.
CR: Okay maybe three days in a row. Now you know.

And what type of section would that be?
CR: Maybe 12L, 8L, 6L.

Okay, these are all structural shapes right?
CR: Yes, light structural. Let me say 6L what it was used for. You seen many of them if you travel the highways. They're the guard post for the guardrail, and we used to cut them by a thousand in one shift, one turn. I mean one unit. There were four units operating. So that'd be 4,000 pieces in one shift, and then you had three shifts around the clock, 24 hours.

And this is the stuff that was pounded into the ground and then they attached the guardrails to it.
CR: Yes, that's correct. Some of it was galvanized, it was sent to a galvanizing plant. You know, they pick 'em and galvanize it. Others were sent to a different type of applications along the highway, but basically that's what they were cut for, and what would happen, as you know, a car would go over the guardrail or truck, or tractor trailer would take out 1,000 feet of that guardrail, that was replaceable. So we made more, you know. And as the years went on, we really, we out-priced ourselves for the product. The product that was out there, somebody else sold it to them cheaper, a little different, okay.

But in your opinion, they never got better quality than what we made.
CR: Never.

I heard that from everyone I ever talked to, and they weren't just Bethlehem Steel employees. I heard that from people in the construction business. Even such a small item like Bethlehem Steel nails, the carpenters in the Lehigh Valley still talk about the Bethlehem Steel nails.

CR: Well, we were proud of our brand. Our brand was our pride, and you looked at that stamped into the beam, you knew it was yours, you knew there was no garbage in there. They're not making it out of recycled steel, cuz they don't know what the heck's in there. There could be razor blades.

Well, Cal, now we've actually gone effectively from a period from like 1964 to 1988. Now some big changes came in, we had what was known as control cutting. You want to tell me about that? And I want to hear your opinion about this, because I want you to know this is a very controversial thing.

CR: This was probably the demise of the Bethlehem Steel as we knew it back then, from the good Bethlehem Steel to what happened. They tried to shove something down our throats, and it was computerized cutting. They wanted to control the factors, whether it was for profit or. It was not for quality, we could tell you that right now, because we judged the quality of that steel. We knew where to cut it off, where to end it. You know there were bad marks in the steel itself. We knew where to terminate that at. When we went on computer cutting, we didn't have that advantage, we didn't have that leverage. We had to cut what was there, and it would get so jumbled up, it just, it was something that nobody understood, including the people that presented it to us and made us work it.

And who were those people?

CR: Well, that was mostly your main office people and your computer geeks, you know, that wanted to get into the computer world. And you know, God knows we didn't understand a computer back then either, like we have today, the little . . . we had main frames back then. Today we work with these little pc's, but everything was in there, but according to rules one little thing messes up and the whole program's messed up for the day. You know one little thing, one variance, and they never considered this. They, everything was worker resistance; it was not worker resistance; it was a company trying to shove something down our throat that would not work. Everybody realized it, but the people out there that wanted to push it.

Cal, I'm going to give you something that I had a couple people mention to me, and they said when you talk to Cal you gotta ask him this one question. I said, "And what would that one question be?" He says, "Is it true the men could make more money by changing rolls than they could by rolling steel?"

CR: That's correct.

How on earth could that be? I mean, that is counter productive to anything that any employee would even want to do to their own company. It's like cutting your own throat.

CR: Okay, by design, the original plan was okay for the company, because the rollings would be three days like we discussed earlier. You could have three days/three shifts of that rolling, okay. What happened was the orders become less and less. We were having more roll changes to the new section than we were rolling section. And in that balance, what happened was we get paid so many minutes to take so many things apart and replace them.

And rolling section was actually changing to different sizes of steel bars.
CR: That's correct.

Okay, go ahead continue.
CR: So then what happened was up in the mill they would have the down time; up in the mill they'd be getting paid for it. We'd have down time where we were, but that's non-productive. It no longer was an advantage to the company to even roll that section. There was so much time lost that we'd be sitting waiting for the steel. We made a little money on it, the mill made a little money on it. Outside of that, it wasn't feasible. It was like you said, more down time, more roll building time that we get paid for than product being pushed out.

Cal, were you aware that not the Bethlehem steelworker but the American steelworker per se was more productive per man-hour than anyone in the world?
CR: We were told that even by upper supervision. We were told we were the most productive people in the world when it came to making steel.

We just didn't have the modern equipment to compete.
CR: That's right. We worked with antiquated equipment; even when that mill was new, they didn't take the prescribed machinery. They put used stuff in there. They put stuff that was antiquated, should have been updated. You know, they blamed it on the company itself that produced the machinery, and Westinghouse was one; they were known for their electronics, or electric. But we got the old stuff. So you can't blame Western Electric or Westinghouse; you had to blame the people that bought the equipment and put it in there, the cheap way, the cheap way. And uh, you know the handwriting was on the wall the whole time.

When did you first realize the company was in trouble? When you knew then that the end was coming?
CR: In the '90s. It was definitely on the wall.

It had to be a sad point in your life.

CR: It was one that you only hoped that you could have enough time. The big thing was down there is years worked and your age, your seniority, and they would bridge that time, and they would come up with a magic number. That was what everybody was looking for their magic number. You got that 30 or you got that.

Well, if you were age 55 plus your years of service, you had to hit 70. If you were younger than 55 it was your age plus your years of service had to add up to 80. Like in my case, I had 29 and three quarter years of service, I was 50 years six months old when I got out. I met the rule of 80 and you know I got out. But how was it working with your foremen?

CR: They were okay at the end. They were more sad than we were. They knew they were losing theirs

But then at the end, too, there probably wasn't a person there that didn't have at least 25 years seniority. So that made things a lot easier for the foremen didn't it?

CR: Exactly right. Foremen didn't even have to be there. Safety-wise. Everybody was old enough to know the rules, okay. And what could bite you and what wouldn't bite you, okay. And for most part, they really had cut back on foremen. We had very little supervision at the end, the way it should have always been. We were so outpaced that we had probably for every man worked, say we had ten men, we probably had two supervisors. What was the sense in that? Every ten men and two supervisors that were doing nothing but filling out time sheets.

Well, you know most people don't even believe that, Cal. I'm glad that you brought that up. I mean it's not as a reflection on foremen;, they needed a job too. It's a reflection on upper management. What would you have done?

CR: Okay, I would have taken some of them foremen and put them into the units. Uh, not against their will, you know, you don't want to start something like that either. But some of the foremen should have been put back in the units. If they were that bright out there leading us, then they should have been that bright leading us under the union flag, okay, where we needed extra workers and not more supervision. We didn't need people to tell us what we did wrong, we needed people to tell us what we should be doing right. Most part, the guys that worked knew more than a foreman. A lot of them foremen hid behind their paper work.

Okay. Now you've really given me a great rendition of all these jobs you did there, you know, how you could have run things had you had the opportunity. I want to thank you for all that, but right now I'm just going to let you talk about anything you want to say about Bethlehem Steel and we'll wrap this up.

Go ahead.

CR: Okay, I mean from the very beginning it was a job, and I needed a job. I already had two children on the way, I had a new home, and you needed everything. Like I says, third generation steelworker, it was in our blood, our lives, you know, our families. Most of the good times came because of the laughter with the men, you know, a joke here or there, somebody screwed up, you know, and for a week you could ride this guy, you know, how he screwed up, and that comes back to the camaraderie part, and then there was also, you know we had our little guys we could pick on, and there were guys that had their peculiar ways, so that carried, you know everything was according to the day you were going in there.

It was all part of the shift.

CR: You didn't know what you were going to be up against. I've gotten hell for doing too much work down there, and this is a true story. I don't want to mention the general foreman's name, but he said, I'll tell you right now if I catch you loading one extra car tonight, he said tomorrow you'll have none, you'll go home for loading too many cars because the incentive, the incentive was there. We did it anyhow. And this is gonna come back to bite me, because this guy is gonna know who said it, and that's the way it was.

Only if he buys the book, Cal, only if he buys the book.

CR: Well, he'll know because he's a good friend of mine. I consider him a friend.

Well, look I want to thank you for your dialogue with us today, and you know sharing these stories, and you're very informative, and I'll tell you what, I believe we got some information out of you that we didn't have before, and thanks a lot.

CR: Okay, you're welcome.

RAYMOND F. ROSATI, JR.
31 years of service

Shipping Yard Maintenance,
Coke Works Maintenance, Riggers

A dedicated worker, this man was never paid enough for what he did for the company. He was a one man engineering and layout man. He could also design and retrofit. He designed and built the Steelworkers Veterans Memorial located at Third and Fillmore in South Bethlehem.

* * * * * * * * *

Today is April the 3rd, 2008, and we're here with Raymond F. Rosati, Jr., and is it okay Ray if we call you Ray?

RR: Yes.

Good. Okay, Ray, we're ready to go. I see you started back in June, the early part of June of 1966. You worked there almost 31 years up until the middle of April of '97. Tell me about how you became a steelworker?

RR: My father was a steelworker, my grandfather was a steelworker, got out of high school in June, Steel company opened up, I put in an application, and was taken in June. Right out of high school.

There ya go. And you had a family history, so you had a little bit of an idea of what you were getting into. And you started at the Coke Works didn't ya?

RR: Very little. Yeah, very little idea.

Very little idea. Now I would imagine that when you started down there, seeing how it was the Coke Works, you must have thought you walked sort of like into some sort of an annex of hell.

RR: They used to have a sign on the parking lot going up to the batteries: "This way to hell," and they weren't kiddin'. No kiddin'. I'd seen grown men cry teaching them how to push lids on those batteries.

Okay, now when you talk about lids on batteries. What is a coke battery Ray?

RR: A coke battery is where they pour in coal, seal it up, cook it at about anywhere between, I guess, 1800 to 2200 degrees, and they call it coking off all the gases, and the gases go, they're sucked up into a main, and they're taken over into the distillery. After it cokes for about 18-24 hours, and then they push the coke out into a quencher car.

And it's the same as like pushing red hot coals out of a fireplace.
RR: Oh, it's red hot, all right.

Oh yeah. In fact, I have a guy I'm going to interview before this is all over by the name of Manny Pinto who unfortunately had a coke oven pushed right on top of his larry car, right on top of his buggy, and he lived through it. And it's gonna be an interesting story.
RR: They screwed up down there all the time.

In other words, you're saying it was a dangerous place?
RR: Very dangerous place.

Okay, now when you first started there, how did the guys treat ya?
RR: They wouldn't even talk to ya. You had the Pennsylvania Dutch speaking Pennsylvania Dutch, you had the Portuguese speaking Portuguese to one another, you had the Puerto Rican speaking to them to one another, and there wasn't a whole lot of Caucasians there.

When you started down there did you still have a core group of Mexicans?
RR: Oh yeah.

Oh yeah, because there's a history behind that also. I mean they actually recruited Mexicans to come to the Coke Works.
RR: There were Spaniards there also. And Portuguese, a lot of Portuguese.

Yup, I know the Portuguese community was right down there outside the Coke Works' gate for a long time, they lived in that neighborhood.
RR: Oh yeah, and Brancos Lounge down there.

And these were people that were hard workers and dependable.
RR: Absolutely, never missed a day's work most of 'em.

And that's just the nature of the Coke Works people. I mean, when you worked in an environment like that, you had to work, because people would let you know. If you weren't carrying your end of the deal, you knew about it immediately. And because of the situation you had down there working in all that heat, and the heat was constant, I mean it wasn't that you'd get away from it in the winter, it was just a little bit cooler. I would imagine you guys really got close to each other as far as you know, getting together afterward, getting together before, you know socializing and things of that nature. How was that at the Coke Works?

RR: It was close.

The guys were pretty tight, they helped each other out? It was sort of like a family?

RR: Yeah.

Okay, and uh, how long were you down there Ray?

RR: 13 years.

13 years. How was the scheduling?

RR: 6 days 7 middles 7 nights.

In other words, you were on a swing shift most of the time? And I see that somewhere towards the early '70s you actually became a maintenance man down there. Tell me about that.

RR: Well, I was working five battery lids, and I was in the middle …

What is the lid job? I hear so much about the lid job.

RR: That's when they, after they push an oven, it's empty, put the doors back on, larry car comes down, drops its hoppers, opens up, and coal goes down inside the oven, okay? After they got done leveling up, they had to put a leveling guard through to make sure it was open all the way through. The lid man would come along and push these lids on with like a 14 foot broom, a big heavy metal head, metal bristled broom that weighed probably around 20 pounds, and the lids on five battery were about three foot in diameter weighed about 150 pounds a piece easy, and you had to push these on and close off the gases from coming out of the oven, because if you waited too long it would catch fire. And if you had a windy day, that's why the lidsman always watched the direction of the wind so he can get upwind after the larry car moves up to push his lids back on. You know, five battery you had to seal the lids back up with a mud mixture, mud made from coke, you know, and they'd ground it up in the mud mill and you'd pour it around the lids, and it would seal itself up and leave gases into the atmosphere. Hot job.

It wasn't a job you wanted to get, you wanted to do it and get out as fast as you could.

RR: You had six ovens to do in a row, sometimes seven, and uh, I think the first year I was there in '66 I did a thing called cooling out; that's when you get heat stroke; you're starting heat stroke from the heat, and you don't sweat anymore; you sweated to the point you can't sweat anymore, and I wobbled to the end of the battery and down I went, and they rushed me off to the dispensary feeding me sugar and salt water until I recovered.

You got both sugar and salt water?

RR: Yeah, plus they fed you salt pills like they were candy, you know.

And isn't it ironic that 15 years or so after that, after you started they stopped using salt pills altogether.

RR: No wonder why I have high blood pressure, don't you think?

When I started in the Alloy Division in '65 there were salt pill containers everywhere. Every drinking fountain had salt water, and foremen used to remind you at the beginning of the shift, make sure you take your salt pills. I also have high blood pressure. I don't know what it's caused by. 'Course I do like to eat, ya know, and I could afford to lose 50 pounds, but anyway, that's neither here nor there. So, you did these jobs at the Coke Works. I mean what other jobs beside lidsman did you do when you were in the operation department?

RR: I ran larry car.

Okay the larry car is actually used to take the material that's gonna be turned into coke and load it into the oven.

RR: Right.

What about, what about when the ovens are pushed? What is that piece of equipment called?

RR: Well you have, you actually have three pieces of equipment. You have a pushing machine. Okay, and then on the coke side, pusher side you consider, pusher side, is where the pushing machine is, coke side where is the door machine's at. Door machine goes up, takes a door off, moves a coke rack up against the door electrically engages the rack into the oven, and then a quencher car comes by and he catches the coal, the coke, and he takes it down to a quenching stack where they spray water on it and put it out so it doesn't burn apart; it would just burn up, and if they lost power and they couldn't quench, they'd have to dump that or it would melt the larry car down, not the larry car, the quencher car.

But you performed all of those jobs.

RR: I never ran the pusher, I never ran the door machine.I did loader man couple of times, that's when they mud up the door so they don't leak.

Okay. And then you actually came into maintenance. So I understand with the maintenance job there was a little bit of controversy involved there because you were sort of like the new kid on the block. You wanna tell me about that?

RR: Well, first off, I'm gonna give you the reason why I went into maintenance. I was lids man in five battery working day shift, I was in the middle of the oven, battery up on top, when all of a sudden gases started pouring out of both ends through the lids pushing up through catching fire, 40, 50 feet in the air coming toward me, battery, each oven lit, and I was in the middle like a rat trapped, because it was 40 feet down one way and you couldn't get out the other way. By the time it got to me, I jumped over the safety railing, grabbed onto the beam, and slid down to the door machine, and I hit hard, rolled, I almost rolled over into the quencher car tracks, or I would have been burned to death back then, and that was, it's right back from Vietnam and I'm almost dying at the Coke Works.

Ray, are you telling me this was worse than anything you went through in Vietnam?

RR: When you were shot at, at least you could shoot back. This, I was trapped like a rat.

You were a ground grunt over there; you were actually out there in the jungle weren't you?

RR: Yes, I was a radio operator.

You come back here to the states, you know, all that behind you and almost get killed at Bethlehem Steel. Almost enough to drive you to drink, Ray.

RR: It did.

Something like that you'd have to dump down a couple just to try to get it out of your mind. Well then how did you get into the maintenance then?

RR: Well, they had an old guy that was the head of maintenance, called a master mechanic, and after I got out of the dispensary, I went over to see him and I said, "That's it. I'm done with operations; you need a maintenance man? He said yeah, that was it.

Wow, boy that was nice. Did you know this guy, I mean?

RR: I heard of him, I never went to see him. I can't remember what his name is for the life of me. And you had, Joe Callaman was one of the bosses over there, and he thought I was a good guy.

So you actually became a maintenance guy, and you moved up through the ranks pretty quickly didn't ya?

RR: Very fast.

So tell me a little bit about that.

RR: Well, I was 19, I believe it was 1971 that I went over there, because I got out of the Marine Corp. in November of '69, so it was probably '71 that I went over to maintenance and by '73 I was an A man, made a lot of people angry.

Why would anybody get angry because you became an A man?

RR: Because I was young. A lot of these guys worked their whole lives and couldn't be an A man.

And you were an A man because you either passed the test or you demonstrated you could do all these jobs, or both.

RR: I passed the test. And both, and do all the jobs.

Plus you did all the jobs. So there was never any question as to whether or not you were performing the duties of a millwright at the time? Did that include welding at the Coke Works?

RR: Yes it did.

I understand they did a lot of welding down there without official welders. I mean it was sort of like part of the job, I understand.

RR: I worked on the gas mains, welding gas mains. With Marvin Sisinsky, the senior A millwright at the Coke Works and we'd be out on two board hanging over those, over the edge of those batteries welding these seams of these pipes because they were riveted, and through years of contracting/expanding they would leak, so we started welding 7818 all the way around these seams on these pipes.

That must have been quite the job huh? How long did you do that? Was that something you did at a certain time of the year, or you just did it as needed?

RR: Well, it would have to be in the Fall and Winter, Summertime you couldn't handle it. You couldn't stand the …

No, too much heat.

RR: Oh my God, yeah, you'd die out there.

So were you ever injured down there?

RR: Hurt my back down there pretty good. I was working on a door machine when I hurt my back.

Yeah. Well, you know there's a lot of people, particularly sinter plant people. Sinter plant people always say if they were gonna give the plant an enema, the hose would go there. And whenever I'd mention that to Coke Works people, they would always say, evidently they never worked at the Coke Works.

RR: They never worked at the Coke Works.

But that was quite the place, full employment, not too many lay offs down there how about it?

RR: Not too many, except what year was that the BOF blew up, then there was lay offs down there.

So after this happened, I see you spent a little time at the riggers; was that, how did that come to be?

RR: I was trying to get out of the Coke Works and I took a posting.

And how long were you with the riggers?

RR: About three months. The reason I left the riggers is because we were working about I would say 75 to 100 feet off the ground, and there was a boss standing there watching us the entire time with his arms folded looking up in the air while we worked, the whole time, and you'd have a safety sling on your waist, and uh, as you're walking across the beams, this thing, you had nothing attached to anything, so if you slipped you were gone, and ...

In other words, it was the type of job you really had to get used to and you never quite got used to it.

RR: Well, there was some horseplay going on, and somebody was spudding a bar while I was walking across it, and uh, I figured enough was enough of that crap.

Yeah. I remember there were certain riggers, and they were like legends in the plant, I mean they'd actually walk across railings on cranes, safety railings, while the crane was in operation.

RR: Yeah.

And they did it regularly without a problem, like nothing was going on. And I asked the guy one time; I says," Charlie, how come you do that?" You now what his answer was, "because I can." I said, "Oh my God." He turned out to be a real dandy guy. I'll be interviewing him later on too. Okay, so now you go down to shipping yard maintenance. How did you get tipped off to go to shipping yard maintenance?

RR: Richard Sterner. We were working up at coal handling, me and Richard, and he said he had to go.

He had worked in the Beam Yard once before, hadn't he? So he knew a little bit about it.

RR: He was a crane man. He went and filled in a job application for shipping yard maintenance, come back and told me about it, and I says, "How many openings are there?" He says, "Two, you have one, I'll have the other." I went down there filled out, and I was gone.

And that was it, down you went to the Beam Yard. The beam world. Down there we had I think 108 cranes and plus we had four roller lines, one in the combo mill plus three more over in the main yard and the new yard, plus the roller lines in the auxiliary yard, and all of these were driven by gears and gear boxes. *They all required maintenance for the aprons which were the safety plates that were built up so that you could not walk between the rolls. They had, all had safety gates so that the rolls couldn't move when you crossed the roller line, and you worked on all that stuff.*

RR: All of that stuff.

Plus, that doesn't take into account the work you did on the saws.

RR: Oh, I did a lot of work.

Tell me a little bit, give me like a classic week at the Beam Yard in maintenance, some of the jobs you would do.

RR: It could be anything from working on a gag.

What was a gag?

RR: A gag is where they straighten bars; one side oscillates about a, makes about a half-inch movement back and forth, and the other side has ambles; well both of 'em have ambles that go up and down, but the gag, one end moves in and out, so they can bring it in up to the bar, and as this bar is going through, this thing's about I would say about 18 feet long, and what they would do, it was a bar bender. And he looked it up, it would look down this bar …

You'd actually eyeball it.

RR: Eyeball it, cuz he sat right over the bar, and you'd look straight down the bar, and you could actually straighten that bar out no matter how it was warped, he'd flip that thing over, they had these tilters that used to flip the bars over, it was bent one way he'd gag it one way, if it was the other he'd gag it the other way, gag all four sides, and straighten that bar out, get it as straight as can be.

I talked to Don Trexler and he told me that some of our guys went up to the Lackawanna plant, and they were complaining about they couldn't make any money with the incentive plan, and they found out it was almost the same incentive plan that Bethlehem had. So the one guy, I guess it was Jimmy McGinley, said, "Hey, let's see ya operate here", and the guy was operating and operating, and he says, "Can I try it?" And he sat down, and he said the bosses up there were like, their jaws just dropped down to the ground; they never saw anything like it, and privately the one guy took the guy aside from the gag and said, "This is why you're not making the kind of money we're making at the Bethlehem plant. The company don't care what they pay ya; they just want the steel out the door."

RR: Absolutely.

And that was quite the job. When something went wrong on one of them gangs, that was a big greasy dirty job wasn't it?

RR: Could be dangerous too.

Yeah, because of the sheer size and the weight involved, and the grease.

RR: Oh, grease everywhere. And, say if they had a real expensive bar and they jammed it in the head, you had to get between that thing. I remember one time me and Eddie Kemmerer were working on it, actually lifted the moveable head up off the shoes, and this thing's, you're talking 30 tons, actually up in the air, and we had to burn the anvil blocks away, not the bar, the anvil blocks away, and you hear this thing creeping and groaning, and you're afraid what the hell's this thing gonna do? Is it gonna snap in half and you're up there in between it as your buzzing this thing apart. There were a lot of hairy jobs in that place, man.

Now you know in like the last ten years that the Beam Yard down there was in operation there was a lot of improvements made as far as crew shanties, safety devices, specialized equipment, and the guys in what they call the 18-inch mill did a lot of layout and fabricating on their own. They, you guys actually made parts that couldn't be bought anymore. Tell me a little bit about that.

RR: Well, we designed and built a lot of our own stuff. Like the saw doors, okay, because first we'd wait too long to get 'em and all the changes we were making on the prints because we would fab 'em up right away, but we started making small in-roads like uh spray blocks just for one. They used to have where they used to spray the water on a blade and they would say maybe get 5,000 cuts, so what we did we got together and we made up a spray block and shot the water in a way onto the blade itself that it no only cooled the blade, but it flushed the chips out of the blade, and their cuts tripled per blade.

Wow.

RR: If not more, tripled.

This was something that the guys in the Bethlehem plant came up with on their own. I guess the guys in the saw shop didn't really appreciate that.

RR: Well, the guys in the saw shop didn't mind at all, it was weld men that mind it.

Because they were making the actual blanks.

RR: Well, yeah, the one time we got a cutting block, well, it was a part of a cutting block in and we had to revise the prints four times already by the time we got this back from the, and the thing was totally changed. We had a guy named Donald Yelsits that worked in the gang and came up with a chip ejector, and we used to get these chips from the cuts, they used to get stuck in the cutting blocks and it would take hours to burn em out. Well, he came up with a rig that hooked onto the pusher where they pushed scrap off, and mounted it onto there, and we used to push the chips right out of the cut.

Wow, I bet that was a big time saver! That was also a moneymaker for the operators and everybody on the crew, wasn't it?

RR: A big time saver and a moneymaker. And we used to have the doors that, they used to swing open, but because of the vibration from the saw, the big heavy four inch pins would actually wear into the knuckles, and the guys couldn't get the door open. They used to have to use a crane to lift the door open and lift the door close. So we changed it so they could actually just lift the door off and get it out of their way, cuz it was always in the way when they wanted to change a blade anyway.

So in the early days when you went down there to the Beam Yard, did you work all three shifts, or did you work mostly with the day shift guys?

RR: It was mostly day shifts, but I did work shifts down there.

Yeah, you did work shifts? And ya know, the amazing thing about the Beam Yard that anybody that works down there, we all know one thing for sure about the Beam Yard, and you know what that is? It never rained in the Beam Yard.

RR: Never, Harold Amey, it never rained in the Beam Yard.

Nope, never rained. And another thing, uh, what used to happen was it didn't matter what was going on, those cars and trucks had to be loaded. It was in constant movement.

RR: Never stopped.

But yet we still had people that said all we did on middle shift was cook. What do you say to something like that?

RR: I don't remember 'em ever cooking on middle shift. We brought our lunch.

A lot of times the guys threw something, a lot of times the guys threw something in the oven at the start of the shift, went out, and when they came back it was done.

RR: Absolutely, cook on middle shift.

But you know what, I'm just saying that to be a little facetious, because the rumor always had that you know you cook on middle shift and ya sleep on night shift. But ya know one of the things that I have to ask you is when you got down to the Beam Yard, now we're talking now it's the '70s, how long was it before you actually realized the company was in trouble?

RR: 1980. When the air traffic controllers were squashed and fired. I knew this country was in trouble, and I knew the Bethlehem Steel was in trouble. They were breaking the union. They broke that one, they can break any union.

Do you think you could have worked at Bethlehem Steel without the union?
RR: Never. I would have been fired.

You would have been fired, why's that?
RR: Back from Vietnam.

In other words, you were like a wild and crazy guy, but a wild and crazy guy that absolutely came to work and did your job.
RR: Absolutely.

And I would imagine you run into a lot of people that were, how would you put it, felt the same way you did about it?
RR: Oh yeah.

If Bethlehem Steel was running right now and hiring, would you go back?
RR: Absolutely.

And why?
RR: Cuz I loved that job.

There ya go And what do you miss most about it?
RR: The camaraderie.

Being with the guys.
RR: Absolutely.

Thank God for that. Now here's a question, and then we're gonna be done. If you had been in a position any time during your Bethlehem Steel time to do something at that plant to make it better, what would you have done?
RR: Not only what I would've done, I did. The Homestead project they could only use one saw to get those piles out, remember? The maintenance gang got together with the operations and built a drop in roller table, okay, so 14 saw could get out the steel, and we put our own roller table in 15 run, motorized with big dogs, I worked with an engineer, and we devised these big dogs, so they, we were pushing out twice the amount of product as they would have gotten. They used to pull these bars out with a car mover and a cable pulling these bars off the bed. It was so dangerous they had a cable like 250 feet long stretched like a rubber band. If that thing would have snapped, it would have killed anybody that was anywhere near that. So we came up with our own process of doing this, and what'd we get for it? The

yard charged us for the scrap beams we used to make the rig for 'em. They charged us. It was scrap, they were gonna throw it away any God-damn way, and they turned around and fucked us for helpin"em. They absolutely fucked us.

How did you find the foremen to be down there in the yard, overall?

RR: Overall good. Good compared to the Coke Works.

Yup, well with Coke Works, you know, I think the nature of the work really goofed things up at the Coke Works, because of what you have to work in. The one thing about the Beam Yard because it was, most of it was in the open, most of it was a lot cleaner to work around the jobs you had to do.

RR: A lot cleaner and a lot colder in the wintertime.

Yeah, well I guess you're right about the wintertime. Well, okay Ray, we want to thank you for taking part in this, and we wish all the best to you and your family.

RICHARD G. STERNER
32 years of service

Shipping Yard Maintenance, Coke Works, 42" Mill

"Big Dick" had a smile and a handshake that was known to all who knew him. He was active with the union as an officer, safety representative, and shop steward.

* * * * * * * * * *

On this May 22nd, 2008, we're interviewing Richard G. Sterner. Mr. Sterner, what did they call you at Bethlehem Steel? Did you have a nickname, or you were just Richard?

RS: Big Rich.

Big Rich, okay. Big Rich, for purposes of this interview, we will call you Richard. Okay, great. Now, Richard, I see January 25th, 1965, tell me how you became a steelworker?

RS: I was told by a friend who was a steelworker they were hiring, and I was laid off at the time from being a carpenter's helper at Dries Building Company. Walked in on Friday, hired on Monday. They took me in and sent me into the shipping yard.

Did they give you a choice or did they say we have openings right here?

RS: They were trying to get me into maintenance right in the beginning. But I said, "I really don't want to get into maintenance, I don't want to do maintenance; uh, what other jobs," and they said the shipping yard and I says okay I'll work in the shipping yard.

Do you remember who the guy was that hired you?

RS: No. I can picture him, too. It was cold as hell. And it was noisy as hell. I thought to myself, what am I getting into? But I stuck out the day. They had a little orientation, and they sent me to chain school, which was a farce.

And chain school, what did they do in chain school?

RS: They were trying to teach me the proper way to hook up and pile beams.

They want to make sure you weren't gonna kill yourself or somebody else. But there's nothing like on the job training, right? This was just like preliminary, the bare basics.

RS: This is very bare basics. And of course they, the first thing they, actually the first thing they make you do is get a pair of safety shoes, I remember that. They set you up, you got safety shoes, you got your safety glasses, you got your hard hat, you got your gloves, then next you went to chain school, and uh, it was different. But with gloves it was tough to chain with gloves with hooks, but you did it, and they taught you how to put chains on and hold your palms open so you don't get caught in the chain. It was different, and it was a very cold day.

How long would you say you were chaining before you felt comfortable doing it?

RS: Honestly, I would say at least a month.

Yeah, it felt, after about a month it was almost like you know something you did every day.

RS: They sent you to chain school, but that's not what they did; the first thing they did is they put you on labor gang. And you were emptying out sluiceways underneath saws and working on the 42-inch mill, and working the 48-inch mill. You got all the dirty jobs the first couple of weeks that's what I got, but then they hired more guys.

Yeah, now how was your schedule? Cuz a lot of people can't envision not knowing your schedule until Thursday. Tell us a little bit about how that was.

RS: You never knew how to plan your life at all. Working all the time. Because your body just didn't adjust to that swing shift constantly with all these changing schedules. And being a young guy, during the summer time you get stuck on a lot of shifts that nobody else wanted, of course they were night shifts and middle shifts, that's what you got, and until, it took quite awhile before I got enough seniority to change that.

And if you were chaining and you were on a crew and you had six trucks to load, you loaded six trucks. See there's people out there Richard, I'm asking you this question because they think that everybody that went in on night shift just went to sleep. Well, I want to get this out in the open, you know, that people understand this.

RS: If you had six trucks to load and you didn't load those six trucks, they wanted to know why you didn't load those six trucks at the end of the shift. Some of 'em weren't, we had some general foremen that were not exactly what I would say polite when they talked to you. They would talk down at you; they wouldn't talk to you; they would talk down to you.

Would you say these were like the old time foremen or?
RS: Yeah, the older ones yes, yes.

Well, they were used to that; I guess a lot of them started before the union was even in there. Do you think you could have worked there without a union?
RS: No.

Why's that?
RS: No, because I couldn't have 'them sleepin' with my wife first, and given them a chicken for supper, and things like that. I don't want to get into that, because I was told by these older guys some of the things that they actually tried pulling.

Well you know right after the plant closed down, we had a guy, Jay Callahan, who was a professional storyteller, and he was being paid on a grant, a lot of money, and he told the story of John Waldony, and his time at Bethlehem Steel was tremendous, it was almost two hours long. He talked about all those things, and I'll tell you what when the people walked out of that auditorium at Lehigh, they had a whole different outlook on what it was like in the early days at Bethlehem Steel.
RS: The older guys, when you talked to them they really didn't say it in front of the bosses; they would talk to you on their own, and on a job or stuff like that, and they would tell you how it was, and the Beam Yard was called the slaughter house, because it was very unsafe. People were always getting killed, and when I was there people got killed.

When you were there originally when you first started, that was before the aprons and everything were around the roller lines, right?
RS: Well, there were some aprons in, but not everything was, the gates weren't in. There's a lot of things that weren't there.

Well, explain to us about the, what is an apron and what is a gate? Because people don't know about this stuff.
RS: Well, aprons are like a stepping area to step up onto the roller line and get between the roller, that you weren't standing exactly inside the roller line. In other words, there was a little platform built in and around the roller line, and they had, then they had, then they finally, they were putting guards in the gearing area, and the gates, the gates were something that would, you would close the gate and you would keep the gate closed so you couldn't walk into the path of oncoming steel., because there was no breaks on those roller lines. Once that steel was moving, it moved, and

the only way to stop it from moving, you had to plug it, and that was called where they reversed the motor and it would stop, but if it was cold, wet and icy you could plug it and it would just keep sliding; of course it was on ice, and it just kept sliding right toward somebody, and I actually seen it, that it was over a person, and the only way to get it off they ran it back over the guy. The guy wasn't, you know he got panicked, and he ran the load back over rather than lift it off him. The poor young fellow he died before they even got 'em out of there. It's not a pretty thing to see.

No, and uh, you're the first person that's actually referred to it as the slaughter house, but I think that maybe you're the first person that could actually talk about this. A lot of guys, you know, they like hide from it; they don't wanna talk about it; you can hardly blame 'em.

RS: It was a very dangerous place to work, it was very dangerous.

Now, you were there for how long at the Beam Yard when you originally started?

RS: I started in the shipping yard, like I said January 25, 1965. I stayed there until 1969. When they laid me off from there, they moved into the 42-inch mill. Then I was in there for about six to nine months I was there. And then I went back into the shipping yard. And I stayed there until 1976 when they had the gasoline crunch. I think it was some place around there? And then I saw an opening; rather than take another layoff with three kids, I went to the Coke Works, and I worked there for three years.

Yeah, and what did you do at the Coke Works?

RS: I became a maintenance man, I was a maintenance helper.

Okay, everyone starts somewhere.

RS: Until I found out that they had some what they called temporary C's, temporary maintenance men, and they were all junior to me, so the first thing I said is pardon me, I have seniority in these, you know, I should be a temporary C. Well, I can't do that, well, they could do that, so they wound up from day one I was no longer a maintenance helper, I was a maintenance temporary C.

In other words, you ran into a situation where everything had gone the way they wanted it for years until you came along and told them the proper way it had to be done? Thank God for the union right? Okay. Now, how did your co-workers look on that.

RS: Uh, they weren't exactly happy that I was getting a C and I'm a greenhorn. I was a newbie on the block, you know?

Well, that's the nature of the temporary vacancy though.

RS: But it was a temporary vacancy and I filled it, and it was, after six months they sent me for a test for the C, and I passed it with flying colors. I had one more test, if I could have passed one more I would've had a B, but I didn't get the B and held back on that for a slight mistake which, they had the right to, but it seemed like they knew how far they wanted to let me go.

Yeah, yeah. So you were there for three years, and I'm looking here, and I see, lo and behold, if you didn't come back to the beam yard, but to maintenance.
RS: Yes, I came back to maintenance in January of '79.

Wow, boy you picked a good time to come back, huh? Actually back home again
RS: No, I was used to that, cuz, the same thing out the Coke Works, it was atrocious out there to work with all the, you know, every place there was signs, uh, possible cancer hazard, and you had to wear respirators, you had to wear crappy suits, and, one minute you're warm cuz you're by an oven, the next minute you're freezing your butt off.

Yeah, so it was something you know. It wasn't a bed of roses, but you got a paycheck every week or two, right?
RS: Yeah, well, when you had three kids though, you …

You did what you had to do you were in a place called 16 run weren't you? Yeah, that was like your office and your tool area, welfare facility.
RS: That's where they'd set up the job where you had to go, and you would go into wherever, whatever equipment was down at the time. You would set up all your tools, you would go up there, and you would be changing broken rolls, you'd be putting new gears in, changing motors, and uh, it was all greasy, grimy, disgusting jobs, but somebody had to do it.

Yup, but one of the benefits I guess to the Beam Yard is as far as the filthy, fine, powdered type dirt, they were like minimal at the Beam Yard compared to the other areas of the plant, because they were exposed to the elements.
RS: Well, when I went down there after about six months or so I stopped coughing up black shit from the Coke Works. And, I was doing that in three years, I was wondering what these guys did that were there, lifers.

And you did something else; you did something else when you came to the beam yard. You got a hold of one of your buddies and you told him to come over. Who was that?
RS: Oh, Ray Rosati. Because when I was up there, I was working with Ray at the time, and he says to me, it was funny when we went onto the job that morning, I got on the job.

Both of you guys are Army veterans too, right?

RS: He's a Marine, I was Army. We were both in the service. But he was funny because I got up on a job, uh, as usual right, and I'm a minuteman; I was right on time, and he says to me, did you see that posting, and I pulled a piece of paper out of my pocket and I showed him that I already applied for the posting for the shipping yard maintenance. He dropped what he had, what he was doing, and went straight over to the office, and he applied also. So it just happened that Ray Rosati and myself wound up going to the shipping yard together.

Did they have long faces at the Coke Works or were they glad to see ya go?

RS: I was a troublemaker; they were glad to get rid of me. When Ray was a shop steward there, and they did not want him around anymore, because he would fight all the time for the maintenance guys.

Yeah. So you guys actually sort of like found a home for yourselves then?

RS: Yeah. It was the last stand, that's where we were. That was Custer's last stand.

So you did every job there was there, roller lines, you worked on cranes, you were actually a welder in later years also, weren't you?

RS: Yup, I wound up getting a welding rate, and I did welding, some tricky welding, too, at times. I learned how to weld with a mirror behind machinery that didn't want to move. It was tricky, but it's possible. I found out there's all kinds of things you can do.

And all the time that you're doing this, you're working swing shifts, right?

RS: Yeah, I was working a lot of swing shifts.

How did that impact your family life? Vacations, days off, you know getting …

RS: We didn't get along real good with the bosses on me taking off or leaving early, because my children they would be doing something, they'd have a football game on a Sunday, and I would leave at noon to go see them. They did not like that. And they tried disciplining me a couple of times and stuff like that. I said, "Yeah, no problem, do whatever you want." I says, "There's a few things that work in my life, and uh, God and family are first." I says, "And everything else falls after that."

Now, I would guess, I would guess if you said that enough times to 'em, they'd finally realize that you were serious.

RS: Well, I have to admit I finally had a boss, well, at the Coke Works I had to switch with somebody constantly, and I would always find somebody to switch, and then I would wind up getting some real shitty shifts so I could see my kids do their thing, but uh, when I came down to the shipping yard, I couldn't do that. Well, my boss, my general foreman, named John Chunko, finally he says when it got to the point, he says, "You're always doing this, you're always taking off." I says, "Well look, I'll work all the weekends in the summer or whatever you want, but when my kids are playing football in the Fall and they're wrestling in the Winter, I'm gonna see them." I says, "This is one thing I am going to do. My family is first." John Chunko was a fair man; he went and said, "All right. Well, just tell me when it is." When I found out, the kids got older, he'd ask me what the schedule was. He would try to be fair all the time.

Now, there were some people down there who I talked to, you know, that were down there with you that said, "Hey, John wasn't always a saint with us, but he found out somewhere around the mid '80s right around the restructuring period that the best thing for him and the best thing for us was to work together," and they said, "He was sort of like a saint from that point on." And that's a great thing, but don't you feel that when we had that where the company and the union were getting together being on committees and things, safety committees, isn't that something we should have had years and years earlier?
RS: Oh yeah. They should have gave us a voice all the time. Uh, if they would've gave us a voice in the business plan, their business plan would have been a lot better too. Because they did some stupid things.

Now, let me ask you something, let me ask you something, foremen versus working leaders, where does the value really lie in the maintenance-like unit? Do you absolutely have to have a bunch of foremen; what do you think working late or was the way to go?
RS: It got down to the point that they used to have, oh, they had foremen coming out of your ears. Working leaders were a lot easier to work with because we worked, and when, well as a millwright myself I liked when somebody would work with me rather than try to tell me what to do and then not seeing how it's done and the problems you run into. It's much different when you're working with a person and …

So the working leader you feel had practical knowledge?
RS: A lot more.

Okay, so if there ever would have been a point in your Bethlehem Steel career where you had an opportunity to call the shots, okay, for the betterment of the company and for the betterment of the employees, you would have gone with working leaders? Because they knew the job.
RS: That's correct.

Okay. Now, I'm not gonna say we had some good foremen down there, I'm not, you know, saying that our foremen were all dogs or anything like that, but you know, I guess like any business, you know, there's good and bad.

RS: I only ever had one that I really liked. His name was Will Reinhardt. Willard.

Willard? He was like a blessing to our department. He actually felt that his most valuable asset was his men, and everybody bent over backwards and worked their buts off for that man. And do you know what the early Evangelical leaders, the bible thumpers would say about that? Hallelujah brother. No doubt about it, Will was a, just a great guy.

RS: He was a unique individual.

I came down there, listen, you remember when I was on the grievance committee I came down there to work weekends, because people were telling me, they said, "Bamie, why don't you come down here; they need people on the weekend. You're gonna, you know, help your pension out, you're gonna make more money," and the first time I came down, Will Reinhard took me outside, he says, "Look, the guys are telling me you haven't been around here for about two years." I said, " Yeah?" He says, "Whatever you do, don't do nothing stupid." He says, "If you're not sure, don't do it or ask somebody, get help." I was really impressed that anybody would do that.

RS: He cared about his people.

And then about the middle of the day I came in, you know, for the lunch break, and he called me in the office, he says. "How're you doin' okay?" I says, "Absolutely. Everything is coming back a little bit at the time," and after a couple weeks coming down like that, you know, it was like, well, hey you know I can do this this, this, and this, and you know, Will knew, and he also knew that he could send me up to the general gang up at the mills, and I didn't really complain about that, and he sort of liked guys that he could send up to places like that that didn't give him any crap, because a lot of guys didn't want to leave; let's face it: it was very territorial. I didn't care, I went up. Of course they would assign me with Stevie Novak. We'd work on safety jobs. We'd have a list of five or six jobs, Stevie says, "Well, we'll just pick one," and then you know that's what we did, so we had a good time. I'm sure a lot of people out there that are steelworkers when they hear me say I was assigned to work with Stevie Novak, the first thing they probably say is, you probably did most of the work, but I wish I could interview Stevie about that, but I'm having a hard time getting ahold of him. So Richard, there had to come a time that you finally realize that the company was in trouble. When was it?

RS: Well, the handwriting was on the wall after we restructured. That was in '91 or '92, in that area in the early '90s when we were restructuring.

You sure it wasn't earlier than that? Most of the guys went out in '87.

RS: Well, in the '80s what they said they were gonna do in the '80s they never did. They, uh, we were working on, I think, it was called Partners for Progress, I think.

Yeah, well there were some people that referred to that PFP as something else. Partners Blanking People.

RS: Yeah, they uh, I remember working on that, and uh, that was like the light bulb was going on, like there's something going on here, because they said they're gonna reduce their numbers, especially, like, in the management area. Well, after a couple of years they actually had more people in the management area and more people standing around doing nothing, which never made sense to me, because if you actually want to make money, you have to have people producing, not people standing there watching you turn a nut or a bolt and tightening things up. I mean, uh, you could have a bird sitting there and do that, a pigeon can watch you do, tighten bolts and nuts. They're not supervising you, I mean, what instructions are there, after you've been doing the job for years; you know you're a mechanic, and you do things; you don't have to have somebody watching over your shoulders. You ever see a mechanic in one of the car places fixing a car? You don't see his service manager coming up to watch him: "Oh, are you tightening those lug nuts right now or do you have the right torque" or anything? No.

No, the only thing the manager wants to know is the results.

RS: Yeah, when are you gonna be done with it? Is it done?

So you're saying around the early 90s you knew the days were numbered. What were some of your best memories of the place? A lot of guys tell me …

RS: The guys.

Yeah, that's what a lot of guys were telling me.

RS: The guys, the guys, the guys. Well, you'd see ,em get married, you see 'em have kids, you'd see the kids grow up, then you'd be interested in what the other kids were doing and what not. It was neat; like you'd come in on a Monday morning or Sunday morning and, boy, the kid did a good job in football"; then, "Yeah well, he got his moments."

And the steelworkers never had a problem socializing did they.

RS: Nope. We had a great softball league.

How many teams do you remember at the height were involved with that? I think it was close to about 15 or 16 teams.

RS: I was the commissioner of eight teams when I took over when it was down to eight, but there was like sixteen teams at one time. And they would play each other a couple of games. It was pretty neat. Each local had their own set of teams, you know. It was pretty nice.

And then we had the printery who took great pride in kicking everybody's ass. And then you had Ingot Mould. They went ...
RS: They were tough, they were tough, they were tough. The molders are tough.

Every year, I mean every year they were just like trendsetters. And if you beat' em, that was the reason to throw a special party. Did you guys ever beat 'em? The green machine, that you know of?
RS: Yeah in a tournament.

You did once in a tournament?
RS: Yeah I think they beat 'em once in a tournament. I wasn't on the team then. I think that was before I came in. Oh, I'm sorry; I know about this now; I just realized, they didn't beat 'em, you know why? The tournament was sponsored by Ingot Mould. And they didn't play in it, and the Green Machine won. It was the year before I came there. But we did win after that, but we weren't playing them. We did win the league a couple times.

The Beam Yard had more than one team, didn't they?
RS: The Beam Yard, yeah. The production guys had a couple teams, yeah.

Yeah, cuz I remember talking to Steve Nemes and another guy, the handsome prince, Dom Strlecki, and I can't wait to interview him. That's his moniker.
RS: I don't know about handsome, that's debatable.

But everybody had a nickname, and some of ' em weren't good, be we all got along well.
RS: When you've been called everything from A to Z in your lifetime, it doesn't really matter anymore.

So, Richard if it was twenty years ago and the plant was reopening, would you go back?
RS: For the guys, yeah. I loved working with those guys. You looked forward to go to work. You actually looked forward to go to work and see what was going on, you know because ...

Yeah, there was never a dull moment.
RS: No, there was always something.

Every day was different.
RS: Every day was different.

Now I'm talking, interviewed a lot of people, you're in the low 40s that I've interviewed already, and these guys said no matter where we worked it was never the same as Bethlehem Steel. He says, "I worked at a place," one guy told me, "ten years, and no one ever approached me and talked to me." I said, "What? He says, "You heard me." He says, " and the day I retired, they didn't even say good luck." I says, "Good for you; you're out of there and you got your money, right?" He says, "That's right." Well I'm not gonna tell you who this guy is, but you and I will both be going to his daughter's wedding on Saturday, okay, and I don't dispute that he's telling me the truth. So Richard, I'd like to thank you for, you know, coming over here and giving us this interview. We want to put a face on steelworkers. We want people to know that we did more than cook on middle shift and sleep on night shift, which everybody thinks that's all we did. But I can tell you one thing …
RS: I'd still like to know how those trucks pulled out of there all night long.

Yeah, how did that steel actually get shipped and all them railroad cars.
RS: Maybe there were leprechauns.

'Cuz everybody was sleeping.
RS: …and maybe there were leprechauns that came in and put that …

Leprechauns, well, we had some Irishmen in there that were kind of, you know, had magical powers, and we had some that would come in and they would fall down because they hadn't recovered from last night, but that's neither here nor there. Thanks a lot, Richard. I wish the best to you and your family.

DONALD TREXLER
33 years of service

414 Shipping Yard Maintenance

Trex provided one of the most interesting interviews. Trex was President of Local 2599 during the darkest days of the early '90s. Taken to task by membership because of the sheer weight of the constant negotiations to save the plant, he was unfairly criticized. In reality, he saved the pensions of hundreds of his brothers and sisters by keeping the negotiations ongoing. Little did they know that he suffered a heart attack while performing the duties of President of Local 2599 USWA. This is reality!

* * * * * * * * * *

Interview of Donald Trexler, February, 16, 2008, for the book Thirty Years under the Beam. Don, tell us how you came to be a steelworker.

DT: Well, I graduated from Dieruff High School in 1963. I was only 17 years old so I wasn't old enough to work in industry yet. So I did nothing but goof off for summer. My dad started picking on me about, you know, "You better go to work." Well, I still wouldn't be 18 until Christmas, so a neighbor of mine was a foreman at a little place in Coopersburg called K&G Boiler Works. I started there painting beams with red lead. They were about to build an extension on the building. Then I painted the equipment and eventually I stayed on as a spray painter to spray paint boilers. Got laid off there in February or March of '64. At that time I didn't know it, but my future father-in-law was a steelworker, Frank Strauss, on the ore bridges. Told me, "Hey, Bethlehem Steel's hiring like crazy. You need a job; you better get down there now." And that's what happened. I went down to, you know, the Steel, put in an application, and it was such a rapid employment time that it only took a short matter of time, and I started there in July of '64.

That's pretty neat. But what really struck you about that place when you started there? What was the first thing that jumped out at you?

DT: The size. I mean I worked in a little shop with maybe 15 employees, if that, going into a business that had thousands of employees.

Yeah and how was it when you started? Would you say that it was completely different, like you were on another planet?

DT: Absolutely. I mean, I wasn't that well-prepared when I went there for a job, or I would have had a little list in my hand saying: you don't want to end up in CSL, maybe you don't want to end up in Ingot Mould, you don't want to end up in the Coke Works. It was something that I was unaware of. I just wanted a job so when that question was asked about, "Do you have a preference?" I said, "No. I'm just looking for a job." But I had a background from high school. I had general electricity as my shop, and I think they took that into account in the testing process and all, saying, "Well, this kid has a little background in electricity, let's put him in maintenance." But, for how removed it was, they gave me this gate pass, says I was going to Stoddard shop. I had to go in the anthracite gate. They explained to me how to walk down to where his office was, and to be there a certain time. Well, Stoddard was the superintendent of Saucon maintenance at that time. So I went into the anthracite gate, down behind the soaking pits, down to where his office was, and introduced myself. There was maybe five or six of us coming in that day, coming in for our first day. And he said, "Okay, let's see, Trexler, Trexler, you're going to be an oiler in the shipping yard." I'm sitting there thinking, "They make ships there?" That's what my idea of the shipping yard was. I didn't think I was going down to the…if he would have said Beam Yard, I might have had an idea, but when he said you're going down to the shipping yard, I'm thinking, "We're making ships here." But, at that time the company had a position where they had a lot of safety men. They walked around with white hats. They were salaried positions, and our safety man at that time was named Steve Lang. He put me in his car, drove me down around. The Heights were still there then, there was no BOF there yet. Drove me down to Dave Wachstetter's office at the shipping yard maintenance, got introduced to our general foreman, Dave Wachstetter. He calls John Wargo, our light man in, and says, "Take him out and find Edison Herbert. This is our new oiler. Show him around a little bit." There was no new yard then, just the main yard. So on our way up, cranes moving everywhere, carrying lifts, bells ringing, whistles, noise from the cold saws, and I for an instant said to myself, "What did I get into?" I mean, this, it was scary. I'm 18 years old and you're walking into this gigantic place and it was frightening. Took me in, finally found the oiler, he started taking me around, and the rest is history. You know, you work there and you got used to the sensation of everything happening around you, but the first time you walk into that environment, it was scary.

My experience was similar to yours except that I started up in the merchant mills. One of the things that I found out is we had a lot of people that never got through the first week. They couldn't stand the constant movement and the noise. It really bothered them. How was, was it anything like that down where you were?

DT: Oh yeah. I think, well you know Frank, the shipping yard, when the cold saws are cutting, it's loud. It's loud to the point that I have a great percentage of hearing loss, and it was strictly them cold saws.

All of us do, but you know the company always told us, "You didn't get it here." We all got it in the Army.

DT: Yeah, the Army. They fired too many weapons…

Yeah. Now, the jobs, exactly, you know, you were a millwright down there. What exactly did you do?

DT: Well like I said, I started as an oiler, and what you did then was you had a 42-mill feeding gag, also a rotary, you had a 48-mill feeding, a different set of larger gags, and it was split up into two different oiler groups. Some took care of the 42 gags and the rotary, and some took the 48. So initially I started out pumping grease in the roller line, oiling bearings, gear coating gears, doing what an oiler does. But I happened to start at a time when there was such a high percentage of guys ready to retire that my transition from oiler to a mechanical helper was faster. Some people were oilers for 18 years before they could become a helper, because there was no movement, but we had rapid movement because guys were going out. It seemed like almost every couple weeks someone else was retiring. So then I went to become a mechanical helper, get set on a crew and just assist the mill. At that time they were called mechanical repairmen/electrical repairmen. We didn't have that millwright title or motor inspector title yet. That came later down the road when the company went to that and started going to craft testing. Initially, the system was you worked so many hours at a C level, moved up to B, worked so many hours at a B level, moved up to A. That's how they ascended through the ranks. They didn't take tests; they just put so many hours on the job. But, basically, what we did was maintain the equipment in the Saucon shipping yard, which were gags, roller lines, saws, overhead cranes.

What were gags?

DT: Gags were pieces of equipment. When a beam comes out of the mill, it looks nice and straight and it's hot and it's orange, and it rolls out, and it comes across a cooling bed where this material has a chance to cool down from the tremendous heat of being rolled through the mill. When it cooled, it's a natural effect; breezes hit it from certain angles, and as it's cooling, this thing twists up. It's no longer straight. So now it has to be re-straightened, either through a rotary, which was a set of big wheels that it ran through at different pressures and guides that straighten, or it went through a gag, which was a big piece of equipment that physically crunched this thing, through the skill of an operator moving blocks up and down and hitting it at the right angle and with the right tension to actually straighten it back out. Because without that process, everything you ran out of the mill would be scrap. It has to be straightened.

It's my understanding from talking to people over time that the gag operators at the Bethlehem plant were probably the best that the entire corporation had. What do you know about that?

DT: Oh, at that time we had a grievance committee man in our local, later became a staff man, named Tony Buffo. And being a grievance committee man, I had a lot of dealings with going over with Tony and talking about cases. Told us about a trip they took up to the Lackawanna plant. A group of our union officials went up to their union officials, and part of the trip was they got to go into the plant. And he said, "Don, everything's the same. You know what a gag is; you know what overhead cranes are. They even had the same number designating the department 668, same as down in Bethlehem." He said but as they're going through the plant, they're watching these guys operate, and they have to be in the gag, and this guy was having trouble straightening this beam. He's working on it, working on it, working, just can't get it right. And straightening is an eye shot of this operator eyeballing that beam. He's the guy who determines if it's straight. Now when it gets out on the bed to be piled, there's inspectors that do more intricate testing on it, if it's squared and other things, but the operator—and it's really quite an art to have the eye to straighten it—well, as they're standing there, they said, "Are you having a problem with that?" And I think it was Julius Zavar, who at one time was a crack operator in Bethlehem, said, "Are you having a problem with that beam?" And the guy took offense to it, and he said, "Do you think you could do better?" And Julius said, "May I try?" And the guy gladly gave up his seat, not realizing, "Hey here's a guy who did this for a living in Bethlehem." And Julius: binga, banga, boonga, banga, binga, banga, boong," run it out. Tony says, "It's straight." The guy looks at him and says, "You were lucky." Julius ran it back into the gag: binga, banga, boonga. He twisted it up. "Now you straighten it." So he was getting a little testy but one of the officials from

Lackawanna said to Tony, "Hey we're not here to argue or fuss or fight or whatever, hey, you know." So they moved on, but when they moved on they looked at what these operators were straightening in a day. And Tony told me, he said, "Don, I told them, 'Don't take offense. Our operators straighten that many before their 9 o'clock break.'" So, yeah, it was a question of where we had experience. And I think a lot of in Bethlehem what happened was it was generation and generation of steelworker. Either your dad worked there, your uncle worked there. In my case, it was my grandfather who worked there before me. And discussions came over the dinner table. You know if it was a father and a son, they both worked there. "Hey, what'd you do today?" "Ah, we had this, but you know we had this problem, but if we did this..." And I think we had an edge where a lot of it was passed on in house. Ya know, not without particularly the company instructing you how. When you came in and you were going to be a gag straightener in the Beam Yard, they'd put you with another straightener and he taught you how to do it. You sat in with him, and he one-on-one instructed you. The company didn't have a program where they said, "Okay Frank, we're taking you over here, you're going to gag school, and one of our company instructors will show you how to run it." It was somebody passing it down. So in that case I had to believe that's why we outlasted them in the structural business. We were the last integrated structural mill in America, meaning we were the last company to make structural steel from scratch, from iron ore, through the process, make the coke, with the blast furnace, you know, into our own BOF and that was quite a thing. We were proud of ourselves, saying, "Hey, at least we..." Everybody else got out of this business ahead of us. You know, U.S. Steel, Republic of, whoever, Jones and Laughlin, whoever the others were who were making beams at the time. There were many. We were like the sole survivor.

Do you believe that was the work ethic of the people from this area?
DT: Oh yeah, I think absolutely.

I feel the same way, because we had people up in our area at the merchant mill where I started where they call these people actually the sacred cows. And the first time I ever heard the term, I said to the foreman, "A sacred cow? What on earth is that?" He says, "That's the guy who has so much knowledge and so much seniority, the superintendent comes to him and asks him questions." You probably had guys like that where you worked, too.
DT: Yeah, we had a little twist on it. You know, you worked in our department and the majority worked day shift doing the general repairs, and then there was a minority, some by choice but most being forced, that had to man the swing shift and the weekends and the holidays, not by

choice but because they didn't have the seniority. Well our term for sacred cows was the day shift bunch that worked days. When you worked swing shift, you said, "Oh, let the sacred cows get it."

But in reality, the sacred cows really were most of the time they were the senior people.
DT: Well, yeah.

Okay, now you know overall, you know, I can tell that you probably had a real good knowledge and had a pretty good time working at the plant. But what did you like the most about working at the plant, and what did you like the least?
DT: The most was easy: the people. When I walked in there I was 18 years old, I took part in weddings, I'm a godfather for several children. I mean, we grew up together. We were young people. We were starting out. We were getting married. It was the joy of going to each other's wedding. It was hearing about, you know, everybody at work, was hearing about their kids. "Oh my son did this, he's into that." Maybe he wrestles or whatever. It was definitely the best part of that was the camaraderie of the people. What I liked least: the schedule. I can honestly say there's not a day of the year or a time of that day that I didn't work, meaning New Year's, Easter, Good Friday, Fourth of July, Christmas. Normal times when a lot of America's workforce is off, you know, that place there was no on or off. It was, you know, 24/7, and that was literal. So when you were working swing shift, it took you seven years to rotate through one whole cycle so that, you know, you hit every day in the year at a different time, different shift. That was the least likeable thing about it.

Do you think you got paid right for what you were doing?
DT: Yeah, I think so, Frank. I think in that respect. I mean I was working for a buck and a quarter an hour. That was 50 dollars a week before taxes, after taxes and take home I used to get 30-some dollars a check a week. When I went to Bethlehem Steel to job class 4 oiler for $2.38 an hour, and I was job class 4, there were only three job classes lower than that. There were higher job classes for sure, but I thought I died and went to heaven.

And what were you able to do with that?
DT: Well, I started in July of '64 and in August I bought a '61 Corvette. It wasn't new, but it was something I could have never afforded if I wasn't there.

What did your dad have to say about that?
DT: My dad's the reason I got the car. We went to Stoudt's. I really wanted it. I looked at it, and I didn't have the nerve to sign on the dotted

line and buy it. My dad said, "Son, if there's ever an opportunity that you have in your life to get that car, it's now. You have a good job, good money coming in, you're single, you have no responsibilities. Now's your time if you want that car." So he sort of gave me the little nudge that I needed and the rest, you know, I took over from there.

And it wasn't long after that you got married.

DT: It was a little longer, because, yeah, first I got married to the Army. They called me in October of '65. I had been in the plant a little over a year. Spent two years there. Had a tour in Vietnam. And, again, I was thankful. It made it easier to go back to work. The things you went through. The conditions you were in. You know, I guess I came back and said, "Man, I'm never going to complain about if I got to work a Sunday again or if I got to work Saturday again," because I was working seven days a week in the Army, and that was endless. And, you heard so many young guys come back and had post-traumatic stress disorder and had a lot of problems to deal with. I was fortunate that I didn't have that, but I think the big part of coming back to a good job made things a lot easier. I think if I would have come back without that security, I might have had time to think about other issues, too.

Yeah, now, you know you already stated, you know, that probably the hardest part of working there was the scheduling. You were working all the holidays and things like that. How was that with the family? It must have been tough to do anything.

DT: Yeah, it, it…I mean we planned. When I worked swing shift, you had a set schedule. I knew how I was going to work for months in advance, providing I stayed on that same swing shift. So we planned vacation, outings. Things got planned around that schedule, and there were a lot of things I missed. There were times when if I couldn't arrange to get the day off and the kids had something going on, you missed it, and that was part of being there. And I think, you know it's just my opinion, the majority of people who stayed at Bethlehem Steel were looking in the future. One, they felt they had a good paying job in the present, but the future was, "Hey, some day I'm going to have a pension and I'm going to have lifetime health care." And in the '60s, the health care wasn't a great issue. I'm young, a lot of us were young; we're not thinking about having health problems down the road, so. And I don't think anybody could have dreamed where the costs of health would have escalated to, as far as the employer's obligation, our own obligation. It just escalated, you know, to the moon. But, I think the majority of the people put up with the lousy scheduling, harsh conditions depending where you worked. Even where we worked, you're outside.

And I understand it never rained in the Beam Yard. Is that true?

DT: According to Harold Amy, I think that was his quote. It never rained in the Beam Yard. It rained on it. He had some little way of twisting that around.

Unreal. Now I understand even after you came back, you were still fighting a war in the sense that you were a shop steward, and it was just something that never ended. Tell me a little bit about that.

DT: Yeah, my good friend Frank Corte was a steward. I used to play the devil's advocate with Frank. We worked swing shift together, so we had time either on the job or eating lunch to kibitz over things, and he'd say, "Well, this happened to so and so." And I would play the company part. I would say, "Ah, but Frank, you didn't this, you didn't that." And it was always like playful banter between us, but eventually after enough arguing and watching some of the good ones we had: Leo Shell, and Louis Melinko, and Frankie Vadaz. And as these guys were retiring out, someone had to step in, and Frank said to me, "Don, why don't you try it?" I got in and it was rewarding when you could help somebody, but I think, and you know this, I was the type of individual that if it didn't go right and it didn't, I didn't show it there. But when I came home, I think a lot of times with my children, it's like, "I'm home, I'm the boss, shut up, do it this way, I'm not going to argue with you." I think it took some of the patience off the home life, because you were embattled in there. But the times you happened to be able to do something positive for someone, it was rewarding.

Were you ever injured at work? Where you actually lost time?

DT: No, not that I…, I cut my hand but I was able to work. I burned my, I had a torch catch my shirt on fire, and the hot ash had burned my belt line, but nothing that kept me out of work. I mean the only time I would have been out of work was I was President of the union, I had a heart attack. But other than that, I was fortunate. I mean I had like everybody had, the nicks and bumps and bruises and breaks and aches and pains, but I never had the misfortune of having something that physical that I had to miss work.

Okay, now, when did you actually first realize that the company was in trouble? This is your own opinion.

DT: Maybe I was naïve. I never gave it that much thought until I became President of the local. Shortly before I ran for President I think I realized that if we continue the path we were on, we couldn't make it. And I was hopeful throughout my term that we could get the electric furnace, get the continuous caster, get the modernization we needed to keep the place going.

Now when you started as President, did you feel as though the company could be trusted or did you take an attitude of "let's wait and see?"

DT: Well, I think my whole life I was a wait and see guy. I never charged ahead. I believed that in an honest forthright manner we could deal with them and trust them, so I believe for the most part, because I felt they were in the same boat but in a better position. Sort of like on the Titanic, they were gonna get the lifeboats, and we were going to sink with the ship. But the whole ship was going down; they were losing their ship, too. My perception always has been, Frank, that once you got to a certain level—I'm saying like superintendent or higher and definitely the corporate lawyers—them I would not trust. Foreman that I worked for and with at the floor level, I would trust them. I think they were just a pawn in the game. They had to do whatever they were told, but, hey, many of them came out of our ranks. Many of them made that move right from off the floor and many of them were good workers, good foremen. I mean there was always an oddball here and there. But I found that I, in my dealings, especially once I became President, that the ones I sort of couldn't sort of say, "Yeah, I absolutely trust you" was the higher up they got. I mean they had an agenda, and as much as we went through Partners for Progress and although the other programs would try and get us together, I don't think we were ever accepted as a true partner. Like Marvin Peters would say, "Yeah, Partners for Progress, but remember one thing, Don, you're a junior partner."

And I also had PFP put to me a different way: people blanking people. And we won't go into any detail about that, but, Don, I'd like you to relate to our readers here when you were President out in Pittsburgh, tell us about the British deal, because that's one of the best stories I ever heard you tell.

DT: Well, when I first was elected, our local union was in the, they were in the midst of that deal with British Steel trying to make some sort a merger where we can merge with British Steel in turn for them giving us some financial backing plus us getting an electrical furnace, getting continuous caster, getting what we needed to be upgraded. So that was my first dose of being a President. We were in the midst of that, and as time went on, I forget his name was Ajax or what but, he was an annoying little Brit that sat in on all these meetings, and someone asked him one time, "What are you giving us out of this? Jobs? You'll have jobs." But eventually that started to, you know, go downhill. Found out they weren't in as good as financial shape as what they said. In other words, they weren't going to deliver their part of the bargain. And I remember one time saying to Gus Moffitt, "Hey, what are we doing here? We should be here trying to put them out of business, not trying to get in business with them." Like, can't we do this on our own? And that did fall apart.

I understand quite abruptly. How abruptly was that?
DT: I think you could honestly say you're in meetings talking about it and watch them fold up their briefcase and leave the meeting and it's over.

And you woke up one morning and what had happened? Right in Pittsburgh. They were gone?
DT: Oh yeah, they were gone. It was over.

No warning or anything? You sort of suspected it could happen now?
DT: Yeah. And that's when we said, "Hey, we're not out of the woods by a long shot. We still have problems. We're still heading downhill fast. We got to make changes." And then we went into, honest to God, day and night talks, it seemed like anyway, with the company about what we could do to keep it going. They naturally wanted the plant broke down into three plants with separate contracts, and it's funny, Frank, because everything about the modernization, and the bulk of it was getting an electric furnace, continuous caster, upgrading our mills, it was the structural end. So the people that worked for Beth Forge and other outer links of the plant were greatly disturbed, they thought we were, especially here I am a President from out of the Beam Yard. "All you care about is the Beam Yard. Nobody cares what happens to us." And, boy, we made so many provisions to make it so that they could eventually bid in, we could bid over, not that we would be locked into a separate plant and couldn't get to them. And the strange thing is, when everything fell through and we didn't get the caster, and everything went down, structural went down, and some of them places are still working under another name. The places we were so concerned about trying to bring along are still there, and what we thought was going to be the flagship is gone. It was a strange time. In one meeting, director John Repp was there and somebody from Beth Forge or something got up and challenged me about, you know, I didn't care about what happened to them. And, after sitting in all these meetings and all the arguments and all, the trying to make this possible for everybody to move. I forget what it was, but I jumped up and maybe for the first time in my presidency, I mean I'm yelling at this guy. And John Reck looks at me, and then when it's all over, he says, "It's about time somebody lit a fire under your ass." Heh, heh, heh, that's all he said to me. I mean, I didn't want to, as I would say, I think Mike Zaia once gave me this comment. The two of us ended

up in a grievance over Hugh Fisher and we're screaming at each other. And the next day he called me in. He apologized. I apologized. He said, "Yes, we both stepped out of character." And that's how I sort of looked at that, screaming at that guy that day. I tried my best to always, you know, have a level head; be compassionate; listen to what everybody says; listen, you know, to what they have to say; and take it all in and try and make, you know, the good judgment. And that day I just, you know, I thought he was way out of bounds because I did care what happened to everybody, not just what happened to the Beam Yards.

Do you think the company did everything it could to save itself? I mean, you know, knowing how Jack Roberts came in there with an offer there, like in 1995, you know, to continue.

DT: Yeah, he wanted to continue the Combination Mill and they had a group willing to purchase it from what he told us, and the company said, "Oh, we'll sell you the Combination Mill but you have to move it somewhere else. You can't operate it here. We'll sell you the equipment; set it up somewhere else." And, what the guy would have had, he would have had a competitive advantage over Bethlehem Steel itself, because guys like myself who took their 30-year pensions, and could have afforded with that pension supplementing their income, could have afforded to work for that other guy, doing what they were doing now for something less. I think they realized that. "Hey, this guy's going to get an advantage. We're going to pay these guys a pension and they're going to continue to work on the old equipment and they'll work for less."

That's amazing. Do you think the union fought a good fight, or do you think it was in a no-win situation? I mean, you saw more of both sides of the fence than most people saw.

DT: Yeah, but even we were segregated, Frank. We'd be on the fourth floor of international headquarters, we would thrash things around with Edroy and with this and that, and then all this banter would go up a floor without us. And then the staff people and the district, you know, director and the corporate lawyers, and then they would come back down with what they sort of thought, and we'd rehash what they thought. Ah, I don't…I'm not sure. I think, yes, when I got there, business was booming, Bethlehem could sell every beam it could possibly make without a doubt, the union did a tremendous job seeing that we got our fair share of the pie. It's just that when the pie was starting to disappear, I don't know what they could have done more. I think they did a good thing. I mean the organizing years were tough. Thankfully, that was before my time. I had the good fortune, and I say good fortune, of working there almost 33 years and never had a strike, other than two yearly walkouts that we did as a department. And if you talk to people and you talk about Bethlehem Steel, you know, it's, "Uh, you know, they're on strike, I'm always laid off." For every one of us that made a career there, you could probably find two or three that work there, but didn't make it a career. "I didn't like the schedule. I didn't like the job." Like you said, either leave the first day, the second day, the first week, or maybe have two years, get laid off, come back, get laid off, say, "Hey I can't have these lapses in work time, find something else." So, it's funny. It's sort of like when you talk about a sporting event and everybody says, "Oh yeah, I remember that," like as if they were there. And when you talk about Bethlehem Steel, you can find a great many people who can tell you, "Oh, I worked there for a summer. Oh I worked there for a short while."

Now, when you actually left the plant, you went to work for another company. Tell us a little bit about that. People are wondering, "Where did these steelworkers go after they left Bethlehem Steel?"

DT: I went to a company that was formed in Chicago in 1936, and at some of their plants they made different plastics at the plant I was at. We were called a converting facility. We took different types of plastics, cut them to the size the customer wanted, and it could have ended up being anything from a credit card to plastic garbage bags to the clear glass that's on a candy box, window box, so that you could see through and see the product. We never dealt with a finished product. We just converted it from one size to another for a customer. It was just a backup one step. When I left Bethlehem Steel, I had two children in college, my pension wasn't gonna pay for the college. But like the scenario with working at the mill for someone else, I could look for something of a lesser dollar value because I was getting this added. I was getting my pension from the steel. But I'm going to tell you something I probably wouldn't tell them people there. I never felt quite comfortable. It was a non-union shop, but I had things there I never had at Bethlehem Steel. We acquired per month vacation time and personal time. So if I needed a day, I could request a day, get a day off with personal time and get paid for it. You know what it was like at the Steel. You didn't have that, although we did contractually. International had agreed upon with the corporation that we could go to day-to-day vacations but they had to be agreed upon at each plant individually, locally. And it never was, because Bethlehem said, "Oh, if I had a crew of five guys and one guy reports off we don't have to replace him." And that was the stumbling block and we never had day-to-day vacation. So if you were sick at Bethlehem Steel, you didn't get paid.

Well I want to thank you, Don, for sharing this with everybody. Because you know the name of the game here with the book, Thirty Years under the Beam, is to let the people who really never worked at Bethlehem Steel know what it was actually like on the inside. It's not the story from the "Morning Call," it's not the story from the "Express Times," it's not the story from Bethlehem Steel. In this case, it's the story from Don Trexler. And at this time, I'd like you to make a closing statement and just sum up everything you said, and just let it all hang out.

DT: Well, Frank, it was all-in-all an enjoyable time. I enjoyed—I say this now as I look back on it—I don't ever remember dreading going to work. I maybe dreaded the job I was going to have to do, but going to work and the guys and the camaraderie and the horseplay and the fooling around and the name calling and all that went on with it, and you know yourself, I've never before that time been around that many characters, and I never again expect to meet that many characters. It was the best of times. I wish it could have gone on. I wish it were still going on today. It reminds me a bit of what my brother-in-law once told me, works at Mack Truck. He says all these guys walk around the plant all day pissing and moaning about the plant, but they want their kids to get a job there. And I think I would have felt that way. All my kids went to college. The first one only went for two years and then it wasn't for him and it was a waste of our money. But the other two have been very successful, and I think that's one thing I learned out of being down there was that, hey, you've got to go to college and you've got to get a degree and you can't sit back and think, "I'm with a wonderful company that's gonna be here forever, because it could happen to anybody." It was all in all a good experience. It was the job of my lifetime and I hated to see it end. What I do miss the most are the people and a good many of them are gone now, too. I enjoyed my time, thanks to you, in the union hall. All in all it was an experience I could have never ever have gotten on my own. I mean going to the company taking us to a steel conference in New York City, staying in the Trump Plaza, and getting to see the head man from Nucor stand up and talk in front of all of us and listening to what he had to say and those sort of experiences I couldn't get. It's sort of like the military. They gave me experiences I could have never got on my own. You know, flying in helicopters, seeing a lot of the world. It was a great time. It provided my family with a better standard of living than what we might have had. I noticed one of your questions was "Do you think you could have made it if another plant or a non-union plant or whatever?" And I think, yeah, as a family we would have made it but maybe I wouldn't have had three children, maybe my wife wouldn't have…and it was our option for her to give up her job. She had a good job with Bell Telephone, she was an operator, but when our first son come along, hey, it was between us mutually, be home, raise the kids, so hard to do. Either have to have day care or latch-key kids that when they get old enough they have their own key and they're on their own until you get home. And I think it provided me with the kind of livelihood that we could raise our family the way we wanted. You know, the boat, the vacations, the things that maybe we took for granted but it was all coming from that direction.

Well that's great, Don. I want to thank you for spending your time with us here and letting it all hang out and that concludes our interview with Don Trexler. Thank you, Don.

WILMER REDLINE
27 years of service

Billet Yard, Power House

"Willie the Welder" was one of the men from the short list of the avowed "proud to be steelworker" clan from north of the blue.

* * * * * * * * *

We're on the record this June 10, 2008, with Wilmer P. Redline, Jr. What should we call you for purposes of this interview? Will?

WR: Call me Will, yeah.

Okay, Will. Did you have a nickname in the plant?

WR: Willie the welder.

Willie the welder? Okay, I see right here you were a welder, too. High school graduate, did some trade school. Started in April of 1973. What was it like when you walked in there the first time into that plant? Describe it to me.

WR: Well, the size of the plant scared me. I walked in, I think they took us to the Hajoca Building first, they got our shoes and safety equipment, and some guy took us all on the bus. And he said, "Tell the bus driver where you have to get off." And they took us through the plant, and I'm looking at this plant thinking, "What did I get myself into? Oh my God!" And I got to my department entrance, at that time was called the Billet Yard. It was up at Second and New. They put me with a guy by the name of, his nickname was Hoppy. That's all I knew him by, cuz he limped. So, ah, that day we were walking around and showing me the ropes and telling me how not to get hurt and how everything worked at Bethlehem Steel, you know. So, I think the first week, it was a Thursday, I'll never forget. It was my first week working and that Saturday was the opening day of fishing season. And the boss came up to me, he says, "Do you want to work Saturday?" And I says, "Ay, I don't think so, I'm going fishing." After the boss left, this Hoppy said to me, "I want to tell you something how the steel company works, kid. When you can make overtime, you make it, cuz you can't make it all the time." I remember tracking the boss back down and saying, "Did you fill that position, cuz if you didn't, I'll work." He said, "No I didn't, if you want to come in, you come in." So I missed probably my first day of trout season in my life when I started the first week at Bethlehem Steel.

You must have been serious about being an employee then. Now how long did you last down there at the Billet Yard?

WR: I was at the Billet Yard, I was there about three weeks, and Johnny Feight was the supervisor. He pulled me in his office, he said, "I see you have some welding background." He says, "Do you know how to use a torch?" I says, "Yeah, sure I know how to use a torch." He said, "Well I want to see if we can break you in at scrap burning. Burning the pieces off the billets and stuff." I says, "All right." Well, so that's what I did, it was a pretty good paying job for a new guy to start. Most new guys you work labor all the time, but I got right there at scrap burning and I think I was in the department a year when a welding position came up in the plant at the power house. And I thought, "Well I'm going to put my name in it," cuz I went to Vo-Tech School for three years. "I'll put my name in and see if I can get this job." And I remember the guys for 30 years were laughing, tell me, "Hey kid, you need 25 years to get a welding job in this place." But I happened to go down after like 10 guys flunked the test. I took the test which took two or three weeks to take, and I passed everything, and I ended up going right into welding, down at the power house.

Wow. I'll tell you what, I don't have too many stories like that. Now, in your time there at the Billet Yard, what was the scheduling like?

WR: We worked a rotating schedule.

Yeah? So you were working all shifts? Did they use the scrap burner on night shift also?

WR: Yes, yes, sometimes.

Was it just a matter of if there was so much stuff on the laydown beds, you worked?

WR: Right, a lot of times that's how it was; cuz I was junior guy, I'd be scheduled maybe as a chain man or something, but if they had stuff to be burnt, they put me at scrap burning.

Yeah, they just pulled you right off it. That was what, job class nine, wasn't it? The chain man was five. I believe it was nine, because I did that job, too. But I did it in the '60s before you were ever down there. You know then I was in the service after that. I remember Johnny Feight; he loved those whistles and bells, didn't he?

WR: Ah, Johnny Feight, I can tell you a story. I was a heater helper one time, and Johnny Feight just got done saying to us, "Now listen you guys," he goes, "no picking up with the chains more than two rows. You can't pick more than two rows of these billets up; they're too heavy." So I remember we're taking this hot stuff out; it was so hot, I mean you have to remember in the summertime we wore insulated underwear on. You had a freaking face shield over your face and you had long hooks trying to hook the chain around these billets, and I remember, I'll never forget the guys name was Yuhasz. And we couldn't grab two. I said, "Grab three." So we could get the chain under three, we picked them up; down goes the crane with the three rows of billets and Johnny Feight sees it. He just got done telling us no more than two, and he ran into Johnny Yuhasz and he goes, or was it Steve? Steve.

Yuhasz was the heater?
WR: Yeah. He goes, "Steve, I just got done telling you no more than two rows; you gotta work as a team." He said, "Well, the team screwed up, the coach didn't," he said. Cuz he was the heater, we were the helper. So he said the team screwed up, not the coach. He came up in the furnace and told us about it laughing. And they used to have a saying on the wall, I don't know if you remember Frank. "Get out of the shade, get into the heat." Get off your ass, get out of the shade, and get into the heat.

Yeah, I used to work there with a guy, you probably remember him, Chadda Bob.
WR: Yeah, Chadda Bob, big Chadda Bob.

He used to be my heater. What a time we would have. We had a little guy named Tony, a little Portuguese guy, and all he ever talked about was Yankees baseball. And if he was talking about Yankees baseball with somebody, you couldn't get him out to take the steel out of the furnace or unload it. He wouldn't move. Ah, Jack used to get so mad at him. Boy, we had a time down there. So now you get down to the power house, what was that like? In fact, what did they do in the power house?
WR: At the power house we supplied air to the blast furnace and to the plant, to the other shops. We also took the old blast gas from the blast furnace and fired up our, we had these piston engines; they're like a four-cylinder car but gigantic. I mean the pistons, the cylinders I could walk through. That's how big they are. I used to have to go in there sometimes and they'd get a water leak in there. They were cooled with a water jack and I'd have to arc out the water jack and place it. The fly wheel was 75 ton, if you could picture it. I'm gonna give Frank some pictures of it because they're unreal to see. They tell me that when they install these, they had

to take the roof off the building to install them. And they said that the patent came from Germany. Somebody stole the patent for these engines from Germany. That was the rumor when I was working there, the old guys telling me. They ran really for nothing, because there were enough BTUs in the blast gas at the time when all the furnaces were running. Where these things would run for nothing, they'd make electricity for nothing. And then we had turbo blowers.

Electricity was used in the plant?

WR: The electricity was used ...we sold electricity to PP&L, because we had two big generators, and we sold electricity to PP&L, but then we bought it back for cheaper than what we were selling it for. So it was always a moneymaker, the generators. And with the engines, other than the repairs of them when something would go wrong, they ran for nothing, other than paying the guy's salary, what sat there and greased them up every shift.

And that was a continuous operation; they never shut down. How many engines were there? Do you remember? There had to be close to 20 some.

WR: Ah, let me see, 17, 16, 15, 14 blowers and then there's 2 or 3 missing, 7, 8, 9, all right 7, 6, 5 … there must have been 10 on each side at least. Ten electric and 10, the electrics went down early. They stopped using the electric, because they were making more electricity off the generators. The one generator we got, the Westinghouse I think it was, that was in an old battleship. The Navy during the war gave that to Bethlehem Steel, and they installed it, and that's where that came from, that came from the Navy.

Yeah, well most of that plant was owned by the government. A lot of the equipment, almost all of the cranes, they were all owned by the government. You know, the actual blowing engines, can you describe to people exactly what that blowing engine did for the blast furnace?

WR: That blowing engine, just picture a piston working. And, they always said that we made better steel with the blowing engines than we did with the turbines. I'll tell you why, if you picture a fan with the turbos, there was a continuous pressure, continuous air pressure on the furnace. But with the blowing engines, you had that shhh, with the piston working, shhh. And they would get surges, and what that really did was mix the steel, that stuff in the blast furnace better. They always said the blowing engines always gave us better steel than that constant turbos.

And you know most people that I talked to when I tell them how a blast furnace operates, that the ore that goes up in there and gets dumped in on top of the bell at the top of the furnace, that the ore is being held by air pressure until the heat becomes sufficient that it melts and it drops down into the bottom of the furnace, they can't fathom all of that ore being held up by a column of air. But when you're talking about 90,000 pounds, okay, of pressure at 36 to 40 psi, I mean, that is, no one can comprehend that. Nobody can comprehend that. And when we do the tours and we drive by, I mention this to people in the bus, they look at me like, "Is this guy really on the level, I mean, could this be true?" Luckily every now and then there'll be somebody in there, you know, one of the bosses or something, and blah, blah, blah. Like the one time when I was telling the story, and John Freeh was there. He was the superintendent of maintenance at the Saucon plant. And he says, "Everything he just told you was true." He says, "I was the engineer on some of those repair jobs and stuff like that" he says "and that is the way they operated." So you saw some, ah, many, many years there in the power house, you were a welder. Give us some sort of example of what your day-to-day routine would be.

WR: Well, if there was breakdowns, of course I was on the breakdowns because I was the only welder. And I'll be honest, and this is probably hard to comprehend, but if we had, like I said, the water jacket leaking on an engine, I would go down on that job, I would start that job maybe at 8:00 in the morning, I would never even take a 9 or 12:00 break. I'd stay on that job trying to get that engine done, even sometimes work overtime. Now there were some times where the cracks were so big it might have taken a day or two to get done, but I work constantly. I'd arc it out, I'd start welding it up, and I would stay on that job. Even my helper would go, "Yo, Willie, it's lunch time." And I wouldn't leave, I would just stay there and try to get this done because I knew we needed this air, this blowing engine to get done so we could get more air on the furnace.

And do you think that was the true mentality of the up homer North of the Blue Mountains? Right there in a nutshell.

WR: Oh, yes, right there.

I mentioned that to George Pinkey just about two hours ago, and George came and he said to me, "Frank," he says, "we had an ethic around here, a work ethic," he says, "that came down for generations." He says, "But we had a big advantage over steelworkers." I said, "What's that?" "We saw what happened when the mines went," he says, "and we were bound and determined it wasn't going to happen while we were working here." He says, "Some of us didn't quite make it," he says, "but you know what I'm saying?"

WR: I'll be honest; right now I'm 57 years old, and where I work now I get complaints. There's five welders—I get complaints that I work steady nights—complaints that I do too much work. All they do is complain that I work too much. The other welders at the plant that I'm working at right now. It's just the way we were brought up, our work ethics. And I tried to instill that into my children.

Well, I'll tell you what: it's definitely nothing to be ashamed of; it's a big asset. The only problem was, and you know yourself, I mean, it wasn't until maybe the last ten years that the plant was there that actual management and the people at Martin Tower started to realize that we weren't a liability, we were an asset. Then they tried to, "Hey, what can we do to get these guys to help us?" But it was too little, too late.

WR: Right, the ship was already gone.

We would have liked, and you yourself know, wouldn't it have been nice if we would have had the Partners for Progress and Juran training right when you started instead of in the '80s and the '90s? See because that time, you know, there was, I hate to say it, I mean, correct me if I'm wrong, there was just so much distrust between management and the union. It was sort of like a wedge driven between, and it shouldn't have been, because we both needed the jobs. This had nothing to do with, "I'm better than you and you're better than me." It had everything to do with, "Are you going to go home and take care of the family." That's what it was really all about.

WR: Most of the time, being in the power house, I can truthfully say, most of the foremen I worked for were pretty good. And at the end, Charlie Chapman, his name was, he was a great guy to work for. I was a shop steward, and if there was a problem with something, I thought he was doing wrong in the contract, me and him would go in and we'd call our union hall, and Chapman would talk to them. If he was wrong, he'd straighten it out. "All right, well what can we do, we don't want the plow here. Does the guy want to work or does he want to get paid, or …"

It's a shame we didn't have more of them, huh?

WR: Yeah, see he was a very, very good guy to work for. He passed away.

I remember when I was Vice President of the union working with him and we always had, you know, nothing but cooperation. It was always, you know, just good to be in the same room with him when you were working on a problem, because you know he had, I would say, tremendous practical knowledge. He was one of those guys that he could take a cup full of dirt and make something out of it.

WR: He was the type of guy, if a salesman came in and say, "Here I have a hat for you," he would tell him, "Go back to your car because I have ten repairmen. I need ten hats or don't give me any." That's the type of foreman. He was a coal cracker, too, by the way. He was from up this way.

Okay, now here's an interesting point here. You had good times and you had bad times. Tell me about some of the best times you ever had in the power house.

WR: Geez, just our ride to work sometimes was a lot of fun. When I started these old timers would start at 7:00 in the morning, which took us 45 minutes to get to Bethlehem Steel. We all met at 5:00 in Lehighton at the coffee place. And at 5:30 we were on the road. And these old guys, half the time I would be sleeping, but these old guys would be telling stories all the way down and all the way home.

And I guess when you were a young guy you didn't know if half of them were true or not.

WR: That's right.

Then you found out later on that most of them were true.

WR: Oh, they were all true.

Yep, and the stories went on and on and on. That was the power of the company that you wanted to go to work because every day was different.

WR: I had so many stories from the old guys when I worked there. They had a guy, they told me before I started, his nickname was dynamite, they told me. They called him dynamite because they say he was built, big arms, and a guy did, George Orzio, worked with me; he looked up his name. He played as a running back for the Washington Redskins. And they were telling me how strong this guy was that one day he came into work and he said, "Boy oh boy, do my arms hurt." And they said, "Well, what's the matter Dyno? What did you do last night?" He said, "Well, I rented one of them floor sanders. "Oh …oh," the guys said, "they're not hard to use. You just hold the handles and sand your floor." Dyno says, "No, I did my ceilings." He said he held it up and did his ceilings. (laughing)

Oh boy. I bet that brought the house down, huh?

WR: Oh my God, they would tell me so many funny stories. Oh my God.

Now how did your job impact your family life? You had a young family at the time.

WR: What worked out good for me was there was always two welders in the power house, and my schedule was a pretty good schedule. I had all the holidays off, and I worked Monday to Friday, and then the second week when we had the two welders, I'd work Monday to Thursday middles, off Friday, and come in Saturday days. That was my schedule for my first ten years at Bethlehem Steel after I got welding. And then after he retired,

I was steady days. So I always had holidays. We didn't work holidays, the repairmen.

You're one of the few guys that I've interviewed that have been able to say that.
WR: We always had holidays and stuff off if you were in maintenance at the power house, unless there was a break down or something that you had to come in.

Do you think the company paid you a good wage while you were there?
WR: Yes, yes, I thought I had a fair wage there.

Now, another thing, would you say that your standard of living within the area was equal or better than most people that you knew?
WR: I say it was better.

It was better? No problem there as far as paying the bills and stuff?
WR: No problem, you know, and you'd work overtime. You could always pick up a couple overtime shifts sometimes.

What was the number one thing you enjoyed about the plant more than anything?
WR: I think all the different guys. You had so many different personalities. You had the tough guy, you had the funny guy, you had the foreigner. And you know what? I don't think race or anything ever came into play at Bethlehem Steel. I didn't care if that guy running the crane was black or Indian or what he was. I just wanted to know, do you know what you're doing and what I'm doing? We never had a racial problem ever at Bethlehem Steel that I can ever recall.

I talked to some Syrian guys already for interviews, and I mentioned to them, I says, "You know the name calling and the carrying on." And the one guys says, "Listen," he says, "in the first month that I worked in the Blast Furnace," he says, "I got called about 40 different names." He says, "And what you might think is offensive, 'Hey, you camel jockey.'" He says, "It didn't mean shit to me because I heard so many other ones." He says, "I was never going to tell them I didn't know what some of them meant." But he says, "It was okay because we all did our job." He says, "And at the end of the shift we all stopped for a beer." He says, "So it was never a problem." And you know I said to him, "Would you go back to the plant if it was still there?" "Oh, yeah, I'd go back tomorrow," he said. He says, "And I don't have to go, I got lots of money." He says, "I don't have to go, but I'd go back."
WR: Oh yeah, we had a lot of fun.

When did you actually come to the realization, Will, that the plant was in trouble?
WR: Well, see, I wasn't a shop steward. What happened was when

they went through this restructuring we didn't really have a shop steward, because if we had a problem, we just told Chappy, "No, I think you're wrong." He'd call the union hall and we'd straighten it out. But when they were going through restructuring, the guys all said, we need someone.

Now about the restructuring, how did that restructuring work?

WR: Well, it gave us a lot more money, because we only got like $35 bonus, and like when the furnace was making $250 bonus a week. So what happened is they gave us like a $2 an hour raise to bring us up to their bonus when they did the restructuring.

Yeah, and that was all that restructuring was all designed to do: have all the pieces meshed together, correct? It's like try to get people working with each other, yeah.

WR: Right, try to save the plant. In other words we were taking, we might have had six repairmen, we were gonna decide if how many repairmen we actually really need in the power house to run the power house because we didn't have everything running at the end. Do we really need a welder? Like they asked me, "Do you weld 40 hours a week?" Which, to tell you the truth, I was honest through that whole process. In fact, when I came back, my men told me they shouldn't have sent me because I was too honest. And then when I really found out, a lot of people lied through that whole process, union people included. All they did was try to save their jobs. I eliminated my own job; I went over to the blast furnace to work after that restructuring every day. I could have lied and said "No, yeah, I have welding 40 hours a day." But I didn't. I thought I was there to try to save Bethlehem Steel and that's what I'm gonna do here; I'm not going to sit and lie about nothing. After going down to the sintering plant and seeing some of these guys, they kept more guys as a home crew then we did and they didn't need all them guys. It was different.

Did you ever have any accidents at the plant, Will? And what happened?

WR: I thought I sprained my ankle, but I'll never forget. It was a week before I was going to Disney, to take my kids to Disney for the first time. And walking over to the blast furnace I turned my ankle on some of the coke balls. What were they called? Billet? And by 9:00 it was up like a balloon. They took me up to the dispensary. He said, "You got to go home, you're done." It was all swollen They took me home. And I think one of the guys in the carpool brought my car home for me, someone I was carpooling with. And, I remember I must have went to therapy for it. We had a little therapy place at Bethlehem Steel. I remember going to therapy and still complaining about it, complaining about it, finally they did a bone scan, and here it wasn't a sprain, it was a break. But it was already healed, there was not much I could do about it, and I still get, ya know, sometimes it turns over on me. I sprain it a lot now I notice.

And what do you think of the safety program at the plant overall?

WR:　Overall I don't think it was bad; you know, you had safety guys what you could talk to. I remember I had to weld on a live blast furnace line with the gas in it and I was scared. Oh my God, I was so scared to do this. I mean the minute I struck an arc, it lit up but as long as there was pressure in it wasn't going to blow up.

You know what, the first time I ever saw that was on an outside line down at the electric furnace, and I said, "What on earth is that guy doing?" Well he says, "He's got a patch he's gonna weld up." "But that line, that's a live line." "Yeah, but it doesn't matter, there's pressure in it." He says, "By chance he breaks through, and he probably won't, you'll just have a little bit of a flame until the arcs on over."

WR:　Well, this had a hole in it, and all we'd do, we got a pipe nipple, I held it there, and I welded around it, and when I was done, we flipped the valve on it and closed it and that was the end of it. But I remember checking with the safety guy, I was really concerned, am I going to blow up on this job?

Do you think you could have worked in that plant without the union?

WR:　No.

No? Why was that?

WR:　At my shop I probably could have, but I don't think you could cuz, no, I wouldn't trust them. I have trouble trusting company people until this day.

You know I asked the last guy I talked to about the company, "Did they consider you an asset or a liability?" He says, "Well, you know what? I'd say the first 15 years I was a liability. They thought they were paying me too much money, but all companies think that." He says, "Then when we started doing the Juran and we started doing the Partners for Progress, then I became an asset, because they needed me." I says, "Well, in reality, George, they needed you the whole time, didn't they?" He says, "That's right. That's why I couldn't have worked there without the union." You know the unions are, they only exist because people believe they are not being treated right. They want to have their piece of the pie. They don't want to eat necessarily the whole pie, but give us a piece of the pie so that we can at least sit at the table. And that's really what it was about. So what time in your career, when did you realize that the company was in trouble?

WR:　Well, when you start seeing the chairman, Williams. What was his name? Walt Williams. When Walt Williams came to the plant I knew, you know, at first. I think he came twice. The first time he came he said we're gonna redo the beam yards, we're gonna do this, you know. The mill, I mean, not the beam yards.

Yeah, well believe it or not, Williams was the last guy they had as a general manager that actually had a steel background. The ones that came after that were accountants and all, everything under the sun. And, if you wanted to get on the good side of Walt Williams, all you had to do was talk about the 101st Airborne and you were a friend for life, because that's where he came from. So, as the place was winding down were you making preparations for life after Bethlehem Steel?

WR: Yeah, I knew it was going to go. Well, I have a welding background so I know.

Yeah, so you more or less had a handle on places you could go and look for work.

WR: Right, I was looking for work. I knew things were going, too. And the last day was like a death in my family. That's how bad it was.

How do you mean that? What was your last day, do you remember?

WR: My last day was the last cast at Bethlehem Steel. Them guys standing outside holding the sign, I was right inside, and they said, "Willie, come on out and get our picture taken." That's probably going to be in the archives forever, that picture of them guys holding that last cast. And I could have been in that picture, but I was just so depressed. That I'll never forget when that furnace emptied out and just started spitting. It just … uh, I get tears in my eyes talking about it now, I mean, it's … I remember walking behind the furnace and crying like a little baby, that it was over. It was very, very hard.

You know, I talked to a couple guys about this. They didn't explain it as well as you did, but I know deep down it meant the same thing. Okay, Will.

WR: Then after that, I'll never forget my first day, cuz I really didn't collect unemployment. I was one of the few lucky guys at the steel company where I didn't get laid off. I mean, I worked four days a week sometimes when things got real slow, because I didn't have a lot of time, but I was the only welder, and they always had to keep a welder with the repair gang. And I remember my first day going to sign up for unemployment, standing in line and waiting for it to open and listening to these guys complaining about the state unemployment office and these people that work there. And I remember the girl waiting on me couldn't have been any nicer than she was to me that day. And, I get choked up, I remember coming home and walking in the door crying and my wife saying to me, hugging me just telling me, "It isn't your fault. It's not your fault. Just remember that," and that we'd make it through it.

Will, do you think the union fought a good fight or do you think they were in a no-win situation?

WR: We were in a no-win situation. The company lied at the end. We gave that dollar an hour or something back to re-modern and they just lied. These accountants knew all along what they were going to do to everybody.

Well, that's one of the main reasons I'm interviewing you guys, because people don't know how the employees actually felt who worked in there, and little did they know actually what they did. I'd be standing in a supermarket, and a guy would say, "Hey Frank, just think you'd still be working there if you wouldn't have been cooking on middle shift and sleeping on night shift." And I said, "How many of your buddies did you carry to the ambulance? How many funerals did you go to?" And they would look at me like and I'd say, "Yeah, give me that dumb look, because you don't know, so keep your mouth shut." But now we're getting the real story from real people like you. It's not coming from the newspaper; it's not coming from Bethlehem Steel. But this story will be out there forever.

WR: You didn't know if you were coming out head first or feet first when you worked at Bethlehem Steel, you really didn't know. Especially at the end. We were working with dilapidated conditions and piping what was thin and, I mean we had an explosion at the power house at the end what blew every window out in the place, every window.

Yeah, you actually worked beyond that blast furnace shutting down, too.

WR: Yes, well what happened is when they shut down that we did have a junior man working on our generators. They kept the generators running cuz they still had steam water and air working, and it was a moneymaker. I mean, they made the electricity, sold it back to PP&L, bought it back cheaper than what they were paid for. And, they wouldn't let me bump him. I went to the union, and the union said I couldn't bump him cuz I wasn't trained on that job, but from the time that I was in that department which was 26 years, we never laid off a junior man. We always trained the senior man. I mean, not a junior, the senior man we always trained, whether he was ever on that job or not.

And what happened to you?

WR: They wouldn't train me. So I remember arguing with the union, and I said just give me grievance papers, I'm gonna grieve it. I signed the grievance papers, but they never heard the grievance. Well, a year later, one of the older guys retired on the generator, and they called me and asked was I interested in taking the job, and I said, "Yeah, yeah, I'll take it." So,

I got trained for two weeks, and then I was an operator. Then, which was a difference for me, I had to work all three shifts. It was different but I really never minded it. I never minded. In fact, I did both. I worked on the operating part; they asked me did I want to get re-certified for welding so that I could weld steam lines and stuff for them. So on my day off I came in one day, went back down to welding school, got re-certified for pressure welding again, and when a repairman needed a hand, I worked for them.

And, they finally did hear that grievance, didn't they?

WR: At the very end they were shutting down, and John Weiss came up to me, because he was a shop steward, and said, "Do you have any grievances?" and I handed him this one. I'll never forget. I said to the union, "I'm not worried about back pay for that year. I want to get that year's wages counted towards my pension for consecutive years cuz I had nice earnings for five consecutive years. But that one year I had no earnings. It would have threw my pension way down. And John says, "All right." He goes, "We're gonna go for everything." I had letters from people what were bumped, from older guys. I went out and got these when I got laid off. Guys what were retired. I had guys which did the bumping, letters from them. I had a letter from the old shop steward, Alex Poniktera; that's how they ran it. They never laid off a junior guy. So he took it to a meeting and I think it was my last paycheck. He called me, and he said, "Willie, are you sitting down?" "Yeah." He said, "Well, here's what you won. You won your year's wages, you won your five weeks vacation, and everything will be counted towards your pension." Which I think the check was for some $50,000.

Ha, ha. Well, I'll tell you what, I don't know this for a fact, but that may have been one of the biggest settlements we had. I know we had a guy from ore handling that was supposed to go down to the weld bed, and they held him over a year. I know he had probably a heftier one than that, but you were right up there in the top three, I know that. I'll tell you what, I remember John Weiss telling me this. He said, "You know, that Will was flying around on a cloud," he says. "And one day when he was flying around on that cloud he called me and he says, 'Hey we're going to have a little party, I want you to come up.'" Tell us about that.

WR: Oh, I took …there was only maybe five of us or four of us repairmen, so I took John Weiss and his wife, and the four repairmen and their wives, and we went up to the Power House at White Haven. A real expensive place to eat, and I bought for everybody. I said, "This dinner's on me." I treated everybody for dinner.

Wow. That must have been one of the best days of your life.

WR: It was. It was nice.

Well, I'll tell you, Will. This is a dandy interview we had here today, and I hope there's nothing but good health and the best for you and your family. Thanks a lot.

WR: Okay. Thanks, Frank.

RICHARD ADAMS
20 years of service

Human Resources Manager

Dick would have been a great umpire. Being manager of human resources put him in a position of dealing with the union and the collective bargaining agreement. My pick as the most consistent of all managers in the position. He attempted to buy the Bethlehem Plant, along with a group of investors, but was not successful. What a shame!

* * * * * * * * * *

Okay today is August the 5th, 2008; we're on the record with Richard Adams. Richard, how you doing today?

RA: I'm good, Frank.

Okay, Dick, how did you get to become a Bethlehem Steelworker?

RA: In 1964 I was in Buffalo and I had just gotten out of the Marine Corps a couple years earlier, and I did teach school for two years, and I was looking to get into a better job, so I interviewed at Bethlehem Steel and was hired as a trainee in the industrial and labor relations department, um, back in July of 1964, at the Lackawanna plant up near Buffalo.

Okay, in 1964 that was going real good.

RA: There were 21,000 employees at the Lackawanna plant when I was there.

Ooh boy. I don't even think there were that many at Bethlehem at that time.

RA: That I don't know. I came to Bethlehem in 1969, and when I got to the Bethlehem plant in 1972 I think there were approximately 14,600 people that worked at the Bethlehem plant.

Okay. Now I see here that your last job held up there was manager of human resources at the Bethlehem plant. Let's do a little climbing of the ladder here, and the first thing we want to start out with is when you're talking about the labor relations department, what exactly was your job?

RA: When I was first hired, my job was to investigate at the step 3 level, uh, which is the level between where members of the local grievance committee and the plant superintendent of industrial relations, or management's representative as he was called at the time, would discuss grievances and complaints, and my original task was to investigate those complaints and then to prepare a written story about each one so that one of my superiors could meet with the union and discuss that individual case.

So, the real crux of the matter came down to you were directly involved in the collective bargaining agreement with the union.

RA: Not initially, but, in 1964 I sure wasn't, but then I started to move forward, and I moved from what they called me as an engineer aide to an industrial relations assistant after a year. That was an exempt position, and there I had some more responsibility with meeting with the union to talk about different contractual violations or contractual issues as they came up. And then in 1967 I think it was I promoted again to assistant to the superintendent of labor relations or assistant to the management's representative, and there I had a lot more responsibility dealing with staff representatives, local union presidents, grievance committee people, and discussing the issues that were prevalent at the Lackawanna plant at that time.

And all of this time, you know, we're still heavily involved with the contract book.

RA: Well, that's the bible. You had to be able to interpret the contract and determine what, if any, provisions of the contract were violated when a grievance was filed. If there were no provisions violated, the grievance had no merit, and it would therefore either be withdrawn or would fall by the wayside at some step during the grievance proceeding.

Okay, now in your perspective, the name of the game here was in reality to insure that the company's side, okay, had all the facts and was presented accurately so that a good judgment could be made.

RA: That's correct.

Okay, and the union was doing the same thing, you know, looking at the contract, maybe in a different light.

RA: I think they were, and I think the grievance committee people and some of the, uh, shop stewards down in the various departments would notice violations, and many of them understood the agreement fairly well, and they knew exactly what it was that they needed to say when a complaint was filed by an individual employee.

Okay, now, we're up to 1967. Where do we go from there?

RA: And I stayed in the position at Lackawanna until 1969, and in 1969 I was transferred to Bethlehem, and I was assigned a position as management's representative for reinforcing bar fabricating shops for the corporation. We had thirteen shops located around the country, in cities from Boston to Miami, over to Houston and up to Minneapolis, and there were thirteen shops scattered around in that two-thirds, eastern two-thirds of the country, and I was in charge of all collective bargaining and all personnel matters for all of those shops. Some of them were represented by members of the United Steelworkers, some under the master contract. Some of them were represented by Steelworkers under individual contracts, and still others were represented by a union known as the International Association of Bridge and Ornamental Iron Workers, and depending upon where I was in the country, uh, I needed to administer the labor contracts for all of those different plants and those different unions. In addition to that, I was one of the prime spokespeople in the negotiation of all the new contracts for any of the plants that were there, and I participated in master steel negotiations for the first time in my career at that level.

Okay. So you're working with the fabricating shops. Now, the fabricating shops didn't stay around that much longer into the '70s, did they?

RA: Uh, the big ones did, but I was not involved with big fabricating shops where they fabricated the steel beams and so forth. I was not part of the Building Fabricating Division. That was a whole other division of the corporation. My job specifically was reinforcing bar shops. And what our task was, was to take bars that were rolled at Steelton and other mills, and we would bring them into the various shops, and then they would be cut and bent in accordance with specifications of contractors, and then placed in wet concrete to provide the stability of the wet concrete as it was being constructed.

Okay, I got it now, I got it now. Now, somewhere along the line there, uh, right after I got out of the service and back into the plant in '72, okay, it wasn't very long after that I started hearing your name in relation to the Bethlehem Plant Human Resources and Labor Relations. When did you take an active role with that?

RA: I was transferred from the position of management's representative at rebar to the assistant management's representative of the Bethlehem plant in July of 1972, and I was assigned the Bethlehem plant at that time, and my role at that time was primarily in the collective bargaining aspect of the business, but I also was the second in charge of the entire division over there, which included plant patrol, safety, fire, environmental, at one time industrial engineering, all employment, and then obviously collective bargaining, and union management negotiations. And I was, uh, however, as I said primarily in charge of collective bargaining activities with the union at that time.

Okay. Now, you're actually moving up the ladder, you're almost up there at the top and, what were the high points of that job?

RA: There's a lot of, um, the obvious high points are you got to meet many, many, many people, sometimes it wasn't in the greatest of situations, because we were hearing grievances and that sort of thing, but you were also in a position to be able to, also in a position where you had a lot of people that were working with us. We had a division that probably encompassed, we had a lot of people that were involved in the division, and with all the fire and patrol and safety and everybody, there probably were 1,100 people that were involved in the actual work that went on, and as a result of that, there were a lot of people that we had direct supervision over, but I had to make sure everything was okay, and when I say that I'm speaking at the 1972 time, I was the assistant division superintendent, and I was involved in all the day-to-day activity, but I was the second in command at the time.

Okay, and I don't think I even want to talk to you about the low points, because with every job you have 'em, you know. If there's anything that jumps at you, you know, you want to talk about it, go ahead.

RA: Well, obviously there were some obvious low points, and some of the times you'd think you had a very good position, and yet you couldn't get through to whomever you were discussing it with to get the problem resolved and it then went to another level of the grievance procedure. There were situations where we had outside truckers that were involved when they called FASH, if you remember those guys. Federated Association of Steel Haulers went on strike, and we couldn't ship any material out of the Bethlehem plant, because most of it was shipped by truck as it was, and we'd work day and night loading up ten trucks and try to get them out, and then the sad parts about it were that some of the truckers as they went out Route 22 at the time before Route 78, they were shot at by people from FASH, and that became a very serious low point, because you really couldn't, you really couldn't ship the product that you had because another union was deeply involved in it. And then the saddest parts of the job I think were related to the investigation, and my particular duty was to go to families in instances of serious injuries and/or death in the plant of an employee or employees, and I recall vividly those discussions with families after mortally, mortal injury and/or death that occurred to some of our employees.

So you worked hand in hand there with the, actually the safety department then, as their supervisor, immediate supervisor. Well, I'm sure that's something that you know that we all know happened. There's no doubt about it that had to be the low point, no doubt about it. I mean I talked to Tommy Petro about that, and you know he left the plant about two years before you did, and he told me right up front, he says, "I hate to say this," he says," I was involved in some of that, and I knew I couldn't do it again," he says, "I knew it was time to get out then."

RA: Well, Tom worked for me, and I know him, and he was a very sensitive guy about a lot of that stuff, and the difficulty was where I was, at the level I was, I was the one that went to the family direct, and I would be who came with the bad news, and/or I would have to present what we thought were the circumstances, and then of course we'd listen to what the family had to say, and we'd try to do everything we could to make sure that they got lined up with the right benefit programs and so forth. And then subsequent to it all, we would then have to go through a serious OSHA investigation, and that was directly again my responsibility, because I would not only investigate the accident again with the OSHA inspector, but then it would be my job to go to Wilkes-Barre and talk actively with the OSHA area director and discuss the accident and discuss any citations and to deal with that whole aspect of it. But all and all that was some of the saddest points that you could ever get involved with in the plant.

Yeah, I guess so. Now, you finally get up there to the point, you know, that you are the man in the Bethlehem plant. Did it occur to you at that time, and we're talking now about what years we talking, maybe '78?

RA: Yeah, I think in '78 or '79 they created another new hierarchy in the plant, and they created an assistant general manager for certain things other than steelmaking, but at the time then what happened was several people were moved from place to place, and I was promoted to division superintendent for human resources, and they later changed the title of that, I think in 1980, to manager of human resources, and in that position I was in charge of all of it, the collective bargaining, and safety, and environmental, and transportation, and fire control, and everything else.

Okay, after you became the manager, was there a time, either that year or soon thereafter, that you had a realization or you believed that that plant was in trouble?

RA: Well, I think if you look at the history of the whole steel industry and not only the plant, the thing that really rattled everybody's cage is when the steel for the World Trade Center was not awarded to the Bethlehem plant, and the corporation bid it effectively, and we did everything we could to get it, but the builders of the World Trade Center chose a Japanese supplier to provide structural beams that we were rolling in the Bethlehem plant.

90 miles away.

RA: That was the first major building project that Bethlehem had lost that they bid on, and you could start to see back then, and that was long before 1980, that things started to get into trouble. Uh, we could see that the demand was being spread out across the entire world now, and as a matter of fact a group of us went to Japan to study the Japanese steel industry to determine exactly how they did, what they did, and came back and tried to implement some of those ideas back here and did implement some with productivity teams and so forth. But that same time several things were occurring. One, there were still great numbers of imports coming into the world, or into the United States. Number two, um, we were seeing intense competition from other companies, and the mini mills started to kick into gear, where they were taking the cream of the crop away from the plant. Three, there wasn't in my humble opinion adequate reinvestment of monies into the operations of the plant at that time that would have yielded more efficient product and so forth, and particularly in the area of continuous casters and that sort of thing, which may very well have helped us. And all in all you could start to see a weakening of the steel industry. And then I also don't believe that we give enough emphasis to the fact that there was a time when interest rates went up to 18% or 19%, and when that happened, it also hurt the construction trades industry. But it also turned the union contracting to a very very expensive contract, because people at that time had the cost of living adjustment that was included in the contract, and we got way up in inflation, and the cost of living went way up, and therefore wages and salaries went way up, and we were never really able to recoup some of that. And through the entire process, coupled with all the rest of the things, you could start to see the plant was in some difficulty.

Were you ever part of the management teams in the early '80s that were investigating the mini mills and the possibility of turning the Bethlehem plant into something like that?

RA: It was talked about, and I was involved in some meetings with it. I talked to the unions about it somehow, and we didn't get a great reception to the mini mill aspect of it. Uh, and then it just never did occur, because there were, in my opinion, some people who believed that the mini mills were not going to be able to prosper and survive. But of course we found out that that line of thinking was not 100 percent adequate because today, outside of the major mills, they provide a great amount of the product that's sold here in the country.

Yeah, well, I'll tell you what, I think you more or less said it all. I mean after the early '80s I see you left here, left the company in 1984. Was that part of a, how would you put it, a purge at that time, or how did that come down?

RA: It was a purge. It was also a change in management, management styles, and there was a lot of things that went on in 1984, '82, '83, '84, and I was getting very restless. And I think part of the problem was we took the plant from 14,700 people or so when I came there down to 6,000, and I remember a specific time being shouted at and screamed at in places like grocery stores and department stores in town because everybody thought it was my fault. But that just simply wasn't the case. And so as difficult as it was to leave, um, I think it was a combination of consolidation of forces, it was a change of philosophy coming from the corporate headquarters where they wanted to have people with corporate experience in running some of these plants, and it was a good election for me, because I had met all the numbers for pension at the time I left. And I've been on pension from Bethlehem Steel since 1984, and I'm guessing that that's almost 25 years now.

And another thing, I don't think you, you maybe don't even realize it, but when you came from a high point of 14,000 down to 6,000 the actual output of steel from the plant did not change that much.

RA: It changed a little bit, um, but what we did was to continue to roll higher profit items, um, and we still made a whole lot of money with a lot less people. But a lot of that was the basic oxygen furnace was implemented into the plant and things like that. The combination mill came in that caused a lot more stuff to be made with, while utilizing less people. So, yes, the numbers went down, the tonnage came down a little bit, and the product lines, however, seemed to maintain, but at the same time everything else was also going down. The manufacturing division products were sliding a little bit, because we were making less steel. The mini mills weren't using ingot products, Ingot Mould didn't have a function in outside sales, and there were just a lot of things that were causing the entire industry to slide a little bit. And we still at Bethlehem didn't get involved in to trying to turn it into a mini mill, and subsequent to the time that all the mills closed down, and really the only thing that was left was the coke ovens in the plant. There was a group of us that tried to purchase the Saucon Mills Division from Bethlehem Steel, and we were backed by some New York financiers, and all of us were managers of the plant in one form or another, and I had personally met with the unions at that time trying to negotiate a contract that would be acceptable, and they agreed that we should do it.

But Bethlehem refused to sell the mills to us to operate as a mini mill, and so it just kind of rusted away to what it is today.

You are you talking about the thing we had with Jack Roberts? I was familiar with that. You know, I'm going to be honest with ya. There's not a lot of people that came out of that plant at the end that knew anything about that.

RA: That's true, because it was kept …

It was one of the saddest chapters I think of all the time I was there, because we believed at the union that that was the salvation right there. That was a chance to keep 500 to 1,000 jobs steady, and we only had sixteen or seventeen hundred at the time.

RA: We predicted at the time that we made our, that we did our planning process, and there were several guys involved, Jack Roberts, who was the general manager at the plant at one time was one, and Skip Franges was kind of the spearhead of our group, and then we had two guys from Washington, and a major financier from New York who was going to do the buying. But there are many opinions as to why it wasn't put out as loudly as maybe it should have been. Number one, but number two, uh, we guaranteed at the time to the union that we probably would be able to produce enough product there by purchasing ingots and slabs from Steelton and other plants within the corporation, which we agreed to purchase it all from Bethlehem. That we could bring it and reheat it, roll it, ship it, sell it, can keep approximately 1,200 people busy in the plant on a full time basis. And uh, it was just determined by the corporation, in their infinite wisdom, that that wasn't going to happen and they weren't going to sell it to another entity. So through demonstrations by the Steelworkers Union at Martin Tower, which ultimately took place after it was turned down and everything else, we were unable to get that thing off the ground. And it's really a shame, because we could have, I think, done a really good job and maybe kept steel making in town.

Well, you know I was going to ask you what would you have done to save that plant, but actually from what you've just said, you actually answered that, and uh, everyone that I know that was involved with that deal with Jack Roberts, yourself and the other guys, they always shook their head, and the general opinion always that the people over in the Tower didn't want to be embarrassed. I hate to say it, but that's what the general opinion had been.

RA: I heard that opinion, and I don't know the answer to it. There were not at the time any steelmaking executives in charge of the company, and I think by that time the CEO of the corporation was an attorney, and um, unfortunately, the people that we had that were going to do the deal had enough money to do it. We were backed up by the Tisch family out of New York, who owned just everything: they owned the New York Giants, they owned theater companies, they owned multiple buildings in New York, they just had billions and billions of dollars. And we were only talking about less than 160 million at the time, and they were going to support that out of chump change. We had plenty of money to do the deal, but Bethlehem was not amenable to it, either that was an executive decision or a board decision or whatever it was, we don't know, but uh, it never happened, so all it is is a pipe dream.

Well, Dick I want to thank you for participating in this today, and, uh, you were an absolute wealth of information. Uh, I love the way it just flowed from you, I mean you're a natural as far as explaining, and, you know, that's what this is really all about, to let people know, but I only have one more question for you. What did you think about the employees at the Bethlehem plant?

RA: Well, I think that every place you would ever go in major industry or major business, you're going to have good, you're gonna have some that aren't so good, you're going to have some that don't care. But I came from Buffalo, I was around the country in many plants, in the rebars. I participated in seminars and work projects at literally every other Bethlehem Steel plant, and it was just well known that the work force in Bethlehem was not only dedicated to its job, but they did the best work possible because they understood clearly why this city and this town prospered because of the people of the plant. And it went from generation to generation that the work force was always stable, was always good. We were always able to accomplish things that other plants could not accomplish because everybody seemed to see and to think that it was really a good idea to preserve the plant and the work force. And my opinion is that they probably were the best across the corporation.

Well, Dick, now you said it all, and I'd like to thank you for participating, and I wish the best for you and your family. Thank you very much.

RA: Thank you.

JEAN BRUGGER
24 years of service

Supervisor, Sanitation Services

To know her was to love her. A champion of the female workforce, she was always looking for equal rights in the workplace. Possessed a quick wit. Nobody ever got one up on her. A great fellow steelworker!

* * * * * * * * *

It's July 10th, 2008, and we're here with Jean "Honi" Brugger. Jean, uh, you go by the nickname Honi?

JB: Yes

Okay, we'll use Honi. Now you started in September of 1963. Tell me how you got hired? How'd you find out about Bethlehem Steel hiring?

JB: Well, my father, all his brothers, his entire family worked at the Steel.

So you came from a line of steelworkers.

JB: Right, my older sister, my older brother, so it was a logical place to go.

And you were a Bethlehem girl most of the time?

JB: I was always a Bethlehem girl. I started in Accounts Payable at the North Building before the Martin Tower was built, and had my daughter in '68, and couldn't come back in the six week time period, which was the law then. You lost your job if you couldn't return, and I did various jobs until Jackie Conover in Salary Employment called me and told me there was a job opening in industrial engineering in the plant and that was 1973. I came down, took the test, took the interviews, and started February 5th, 1973.

And you were an industrial engineer. What exactly do they do?

JB: Set piece rates for jobs, and I happened to be in the manufacturing section.

And piece rates are what?

JB: Piece rate is different things to foundries and manufacturing, but in the manufacturing section, uh, you set rates for men or women, machining.

So we're talking about rates of pay for performance?

JB: Right. Okay. And um, there was a small story behind that I want to tell you. Mack who used to be in the union and my dad, who used to be in the union, when they were going to start industrial engineering way back when, they wanted somebody who worked in the plant to start setting these rates, and Mack and my dad flipped a coin, and my dad, the loser was going to be the person.

And what was your dad's full name?

JB: Vincent Brugger. And Mack was Owen McFadden.

Okay, a legend at the union hall. And I guess your dad was sort of like his counterpart with the company?

JB: No my dad was union. My dad worked at the steel foundry. And they, the company themselves came down to both Owen and my father and said, we want somebody with math background to come and start setting piece rates for different jobs around the plant, we're going to start a department like this. Neither of 'em wanted to do it, and the company insisted one of 'em was gonna go do it, and they flipped a coin, and the loser would go salary, and that's how my dad got to be salary and went into industrial engineering.

Well, that's really unusual in the fact that the loser ended up being the winner, but you know, the company did some strange things, we all know that, don't we. So how long were you working in that shop?

JB: So, um, number 2 for industrial engineering I worked there from '73 to '79.

And that area was what, where at, what shop?

JB: Well, I worked all those shops.

Okay you worked in number 2 machine shop, Central Tool, Ingot Mould, 12 roll shop, sanitation. Well this is gonna be an interesting thing here, because we're gonna just drop down through these things and we're gonna ask what you did in some of these shops. Like number 2 machine shop, what exactly were you doing in there as a rate setter?

JB: As a rate setter, I went out into the shop and I told them what their next job was. What they were gonna load onto the machine, so. You took that slip.

We're talking about pieces that are going into the machines, machinists are going to work on 'em?

JB: Right. You took that slip, you went up, you had to pull the drawing, and at that time they had regular drawing people who did nothing but study the drawing, and they would decide how many cuts, what feeds and speeds they would need on their tooling, what tooling to use, and they would do an approximate what it should take. I then as a person on the floor took that estimate, went out, and gave them a time card that told them this is how the job should progress. And then it was your job on the floor to watch for all the delays, which were many, waiting for a crane man, waiting for tooling, changing tooling, having to have down time for chip pull, etc. So that was basically my job to go to all the machines on the shift, see what their time was running like, and we made adjustments for all of those factors.

So effectively, you were directly involved in time and motion, okay, and this time and motion, somebody had to record it, you were that person doing the recording, and the employees were finding out on these jobs what they could do, what they couldn't do, some of them got lucky and found probably some shortcuts and made time on these projects. And if they made time, they made money. And that was something the company wasn't really too worried about unless the product didn't come out as it was supposed to.

If it came out the way it was supposed to, everybody was happy. Okay, you did that till '79 all over that shop?

JB: All over number 2, Central Tool, Ingot Mould and 12 roll.

Okay. 12 roll shop, down at the cabbage patch, what was that like down there? That was all big pieces wasn't it?

JB: That was huge pieces, and the foundry side, I worked both. And uh, I liked the machine shop better.

Well, naturally, yeah.

JB: But uh, the foundry was interesting for me to just find it all out exactly the whole process, but uh, I would have to say the best part about working in all these shops was first of all meeting such a variety of people is still my best thing that ever happened to me down there, but secondly learning so many things. You can learn the process of steel making, but you will never ever learn it like you will learn it being in those shops standing there watching it actually be done.

Okay, so you see the good, you see the bad, and you see the ugly? And another thing, you're down there in 12 roll machine shop, you're sort of like a celebrity being a woman, aren't ya?

JB: Well, number 2 machine shop was the celebrity.

But by the same token there was always a certain percentage of guys that didn't think you should be there.

JB: Oh, absolutely.

Right? Because somehow they felt intimidated.

JB: My very first people who thought I shouldn't be there were my salary bosses in number 2 machine shop. They day I walked in with the big boss from industrial engineering, and he said, Here's your new employee," and he looked up and looked at me and said, " I don't want an f-ing girl." And I said, too bad, because I'm here and that's the breaks.

This is the guy at 12 roll?

JB: No, this is the guy at number 2 machine shop. He was in charge of industrial engineering. And then the guy who was in charge of the whole machine shop, supervisor, Footer, came out that day as I was being taken around and told me that I wasn't allowed to wear jeans, that I had to wear a flannel shirt every day even during the summer because he didn't want any hanky panky going on, and I told him, Footer, I'm really sorry you have this opinion of what girls are going to do out here in the plant, but I don't work for you. I'm a concession here, I work for industrial engineering, and they do not have these dress rules, and I will not be following your dress rules.

And how'd he handle that?

JB: Not well, not well.

But he got over it?

JB: No, he never got over it. He retired shortly after that.

So you've gone through all of these operations, okay, you've endured it all, and I'm sure you know the guys were always pulling all kinds of hijinks, what did they ever pull over on you or try to pull over?

JB: Well, I think the, there's a couple things I can say.

Well, you know, use your own discretion, because I know people who are going to read this book are gonna say, Hey, this is one of the female employees that worked in the plant, she worked in the company at the time, but yet she was like a trendsetter." So go ahead, let it fly.

JB: Well, I have to say this. I was the first female to go back into the plant since World War Two. So day one they had trouble finding me any kind of safety shoes, um, we didn't have the helmets with the industrial strap, so every helmet was huge, so we had to put padding inside a helmet, and the shoes were, I wore like four pair of socks every day in number 2 machine shop when I first started.

Just couldn't find anything small enough?

JB: Nothing, nothing, and I have a big foot.

Well, you know what, you were at the very beginning of women starting to get some rights, and I can imagine you know, here you go, you have a young daughter, you're in the plant, and you're thinking, you know what, I'm getting paid pretty good here, I got benefits, I don't want to screw this up. But now when you look back on it, you have to laugh about it, because in reality you could have said anything anytime and probably get anything you wanted. What do you think about that?

JB: I think just the opposite.

Oh no, all right go ahead, let me hear.

JB: I think just the opposite. There were definite things right from the beginning. I was told that I was gonna be paid $3.59 an hour, and in the form of a salary, and I started on the same day as two other guys who both went to a similar job, one went to weld man, the other guy went to Ingot Mould, and when we got our first pay check we went out to lunch to celebrate, and we went across the street to the little pizza shop, and we were so happy, because it was bad times back in the early '70s finding a job, it was very hard, I don't know if you remember that, but there were not many jobs, there was not many jobs around at all. And we were so happy, and they said can you believe we made blah blah blah blah blah for two weeks, and I went what are you talking about, let me see them pay checks. Big no-no among salary people at the steel, which we didn't know at that time. And here I am getting paid $2.00 less an hour than they were.

Whoa.

JB: I left, I went over, walked up to VonSteuben in industrial engineering and said there's a problem with my pay check, I started the same day as them, we had both worked the same amount of time doing the same job just at different shops, and I'm not getting paid the right amount. He said you'll take your pay or you can walk out the door, that's it. And I said I will walk out the door and I would go to the National Organization of Women (NOW) and I'm filing a lawsuit against you for equal pay. I didn't leave my other job to come here to get, not get paid the proper amount. So I went to NOW, they called on the phone.

He called your boss then is that what he did?

JB: To home office, and home office told me to report back to work tomorrow, and they would be issuing a new check with the back pay.

They'd seen the light. Well, I'm really glad to see that you did what had to be done. Actually unknown to you, unknown to you, even though you're a company employee, you actually performed like any union person would have performed, but I think that was more because of your family bringing you up the right way probably more than anything else.

JB: Well, you have to remember my mother was a union organizer for the AFL-CIO back in the '20s, late '20, '30s, she walked with Eleanor Roosevelt in Philly. Well, one day at work her boss came down and slapped her across the face, and that's what prompted her, the union people had been around, she talked to other girls and said, we're sick of, you know, why should we take this from this guy. They were earning $5 a week. They went to the AFL-CIO and they came, they organized them to come in the shop, and it was a big thing, they were locked out, people were, this was bad times you know and people were like we have to go to work, and my mother was one of those who said stick it out and we will all get a fair pay.

What business was this?

JB: This was a sewing factory in Fourth and Hamilton, uh, Fourth and Tilghman, and uh, what happened to her was the deal went down, they got the union in on the condition that she would not be able to come back to work, and so by that time she was married to my dad and had one child, and they knew they wanted way more kids, and my dad just said just leave, you're gonna leave anyway, so your girls will love it, they're union, and that's what she did. But she stayed active with the union for a long time. So we always had the point of view

So you were ready, you were ready when you came to Bethlehem Steel then.

JB: We always had the union point of view and management point of view in our house which was good.

So you could weigh one against the other, you always came up usually standing on your own two feet. Okay. Now, of these areas here, number 2 machine shop, Central Tooling, Ingot Mould, 12 roll, is there anything that jumps out at you, anything unusual about any one of them shops?

JB: Yeah, Central Tool, and I'll tell you this story which I think is hysterical. They hired a person who was going through a sex change. And they decided to use the women's bathroom at Central Tool for this female, when I was there, who was becoming a male, and I walked in, and no one bothered to tell me this, Now I was the only girl there, and I walked in and

148

there's, she looked very much like a man and talked like a man, and she's like hi, what her name was, tell me what her name used to be, blah blah blah, and said I'll be changing here with ya, and I was like, whoa. So I said, well, I think I want to check this story out. Well, she said, I don't see where there's any, I said, well, no, I think there is. And I said it's your choice what you want to do with your life, but I want to know if this is a true story, and if it is I don't want to be in here with you at the same time; that's just the way I feel, because too many people will have too much to say about it, and I'm not getting into it. So that was, I walked into the office, and they were all in hysterics. They thought this was the funniest thing. First of all, that they just did it and never said anything to me, and the fact that I was coming back to see if it was for real, they all just thought it was hysterical, and that was the talk of Central Tools for years to come. So that and, oh, a guy was running a crane, who was a bit of a druggy, and when the girls started there I had gone back to Central Tool to fill in for a vacation, and this girl was, you worked, my shift was 10-6. She came in middle shift, and she was pretty high, and uh, those two started to go at it behind one of the machines, and she was laying right across chips from the machine, and the foreman came out and says to me, you have to go over there and do something. I said I have to go over there and do something, you're the foreman, it's on middle shift, you're in charge of the shift, do what you want. Either let 'em do it or break it up, I don't care what you do, I have nothing to do with it, I'm just here to set my rates. I'm finishing up and I'm going home

Now, look I'm sitting here acting real dumb like I don't know what the hell you're saying, but you're telling me a guy came in on middle shift, and went with another employee behind a machine and was doing improper things. Okay, and the foreman wanted you to break it up?

JB: Right.

Wow. What became of that?

JB: So he called medical over, he called the dispensary. Medical came over, and they made the both of 'em stand up, plant patrol came too, and they both just had these chips, steel chips stuck all over 'em, bleeding, that tells you how high they were, that they didn't feel it. That to me was still one of the stories that I just think, oh my God.

You realize right now that you're sort of like an instant celebrity in this book for telling a story like that.

JB: Anybody could do anything down there. After I saw this, I just thought, anything could happen, I better start really watching my back, cuz before I always thought things were jokes that they did to me.

Hallelujah. Now eventually through negotiations and things like that, the company decides that we're not gonna have janitors in every department; we're gonna have a roving janitor crew, and you became part of that. How did that happen?

JB: We, everybody in management, I presume, but I know all of human resources and labor relations was asked to come up with any cost savings ideas they could. My idea wasn't about personnel, it was about putting a tighter rein through a centralized purchasing on paper products and chemicals that I just saw totally being wasted around the plant and all the shops I worked, and I just thought that if it was, because I worked in accounts payable I know, and we kept accounts payable central and didn't put it out to all the shops. It was good control on what you bought, and I just thought it would work. Well, they decided that they would incorporate that with an idea that Steelton had done to bring in outside service, and that's where the union came into play to say no, it won't be outside services, it will be with our own people inside the plant.

Okay, Now that was all actually part of, let me, you correct me if I'm wrong, that was like the beginning of Partners for Progress, where they were doing the restructuring? And the restructuring was where all the departments were sitting down between union and company and looking at better ways to do the things. How to reduce costs.

JB: Right.

Was this the first inkling that you had that the plant was in trouble?

JB: Uh, no, not really.

When did that first like ring a bell with you?

JB: I think 1980. And I think that's actually when we dated our letters. We wrote letters saying what we thought would happen to the plant, a gang of us from industrial engineering, even though I was out of that in '79. I went over to labor relations, well to human resources, I uh, I was still friends with all of them and we decided to write these letters and bury them in the yard office, and if the yard office was ever to be torn down, we would dig these letters up and see, and back then when the yard office was going to be torn down, we dug the letters up, my letter said, I felt as though the plant would not last beyond 1986. I really did think that I thought it would shut down. There was no money going back into the plant, they were deciding Steelton to get the continuous caster, they were pouring money into Burns Harbor, and they did not want to spend any money.

They didn't want to spend money to repair what we had, much less add anything new, and I just felt as though the handwriting was on the wall. We had people come in who were not steel people who were running the company, they had no ties to Bethlehem, which some of the other people who came up through the ranks they lived here, their families lived here, they grew up here, they went to school here, they had a vested interest to keep Bethlehem Steel and the headquarters open, these people didn't.

And as a friend of ours, a mutual friend of ours, James Mellot once said, we were the stepchildren of the family and we were treated as such. And I'll tell you what that's one statement I remember him making, I was thinking, wow, where did he come up with that? But that says it all.

JB: Yes it does.

It says it all. And that's exactly what happened too. They kept telling us, well Christmas is coming, and then the day before Christmas, they would tell us, hey guess what the boat that was coming that had all your presents on it got torpedoed.

JB: You're gonna go to Japan, you're gonna learn how to run the mill to make a profit, and all of you are gonna learn how to work with management. Lot of union people went, high management people in the steel went to Japan to see everything that was going on there. They promised that we're going to get a continuous caster, it never happened.

Even started putting the foundation in.

JB: They started the foundation to put in the mill. Never happened. They started a maintenance program that every department was going to get, nobody saw it, going to get x amount of dollars based on their yearly budget to do nothing but do maintenance, upgrade their tooling, fix their vehicles, whatever, never happened.

I remember one of the saddest things that I ever seen was Tim Lewis come to the union hall and tell people this isn't going to happen. They pulled the money. And I can honestly tell you, the man had tears in his eyes. He says, "This is one of the hardest things I've ever had to do," he says, "but here I am because it's my job." And actually the guys at the union hall felt sorry for him, because what they did, what they did is they laid it all right in his lap, but he had the guts to do what had to be done.

JB: Right, I felt sorry for Walt Williams. He came over and came down to the mills to a humongous opening that we were… Now, that was all cleaned up, and sprayed and whitewashed and big wigs from everybody, everywhere came, and he announced that mill was going to be started. The foundation was checked out; they were going to use the old foundation, that mill is going to go in, it's going to start next Monday, and he had to come back a month later to say the money is going to Burns Harbor.

How about that? So anyway, during all of this stuff you finally ended up in the sanitation department. Let's hear some sanitation stories, I'm sure you have a few, and some of 'em gotta be hilarious.

JB: Some are. The first and foremost thing about sanitation services, and this is something else I wrote and put away, is during the meetings with Hector and Mack and Eddie O'Brien.

These are union officials.

JB: With Edroy Adams.

Company official.

JB: Right. I made this statement, and I still stand by this statement, that you do not want this department to work, you want it to fail, and because they were going to make it a totally pool shop, made absolutely no sense. The union was busy arguing that they wanted 75 people instead of 55 people. To me it didn't matter because I had spent two years going around the whole plant with engineering, plumbers, scoping everything out, closing welfare rooms, became the hated person in the plant that I was closing welfare rooms to consolidate and to put the hook ups in for the equipment, and it didn't matter because, and I figured out all the logistics, the travel time, I time-studied the whole thing, because I used to do that in IE, so I time-studied the whole thing, I built the train delay time and everything, and what it all came down to is at those meetings, I said with a total pool shop it will never work. And they argued it will; I said it won't. It won't, it will not work. I've got to have a certain amount of people who are familiar with the equipment who will stay and the rest can be pooled, and that was the whole thing at that time is because all the jobs were being knocked down and they needed a place for these guys to work, and it wasn't just janitors, although they gave janitors the first crack at it, but they knew it was gonna be a revolving door. And I managed to get four permanent people who would then become leaders.

What was the highest number you ever had, permanent people?

JB: 75. Oh, permanent people? Four.

You never had more than four? Everyone else was a pool? And the four were working leaders because at least then you had some opportunity to have regular people that knew certain sections of the plant.

JB: Right, and who I could teach the operation of the equipment, be familiar with the safety program that I wrote and Bick, Bickert helped me write that, and uh, one thing I really am most proud of myself that I negotiated through that is that even though I had to go through purchasing, I had the say so to say exactly what products I would use and who we would buy them from. I was the person who picked the best deal. And it was a long hard fight with salary people

Yeah, because everybody wanted their piece of the pie.

JB: But everybody wanted their finger in that. And I knew that would further put that department out of work. It would just put it out of work. And when I, I honestly didn't want to go to work there, and I was convinced to take this, was "a promotion," and the way I feel is that by putting a girl in charge and making her the first supervisor of a plant out there and a shop and the way they set it up to be a pool shop, they didn't think it would have last until the end of the year, and they would be able to lay off a heck of a lot of people because there wouldn't be a department to send 'em to.

Well, for the benefit of the people that are wondering how the janitors worked, they worked out of a truck, it was a portable cleaning unit is what it was, but when you got onto the job site, you were able to use equipment that was at the washroom to assist you in what you were doing, and it was a combination chemicals, spraying, scrubbing, and just good old fashioned, you know, cleaning the toilets and urinals, and uh, it worked. What did you do for the women? Who took care of the women's washroom?

JB: The men.

The men handled that, okay.

JB: Any janitor. And we had female janitors who went into the men's.

Yeah, okay. Just checking that out. So this carried you right through basically to the end. Now, what I want to know from you, because you already said you thought the plant was in trouble as early as 1980. You actually put it down in paper, you thought it would go under by '86. Where do you think the company missed the boat? What was the last opportunity to save that plant that we didn't take, because I have to get this from the perspective of a management person?

JB: Well, from my point of view, they never reinvested into the plant, and that was long even before I came back in the '70s, but I think the people who were the vice presidents and higher up at that time, supervisors in the plant, just spent money like it was going out of style. Used plant personnel to do their homes during the day, paint, electrical work, plumbing, um, work on the Bethlehem Steel Club, work on Saucon, all day long, and you can keep your man-hours down on a piece of steel going out the door when you're charging 12 people working on a job on the outside against that piece of equipment.

Well, it's interesting, you know, that we hear something like that, but you know I've had people actually tell me that modular homes come in on the back of trailers went right out the other gate and up into the Poconos. I don't know if it's true.

JB: See, I never saw anything except lumber actually go out the gate on the back of somebody's truck who was in cahoots with whoever was supposedly guarding the gate, and that went out supposedly to build a home in the Poconos. But I know labor, because I know people, my uncle for one, who was head of corporation painting, he was the head supervisor for corporation painting, and um, actually spent most of his time down at Saucon Valley Country Club.

Now here's something, here's something. I think Donald Trautlein came around somewhere around 1979 maybe, or was it '80? Okay. I always felt, and this is very controversial, and people didn't like when I say it, I says listen I'll be perfectly honest with you. I think he should have been here 15 years ago, and we would have been way better off for it. We might still be working today. But what's the number one thing you missed about the plant? What do you miss most about not being there?

JB: The people.

Well, that's the number one answer. In fact, you know, the money isn't even in the top five. A lot of guys said even though we were listed as a particular day, every day when we went in the job was different, you could never get bored. And the people kept you right on your feet. You knew everybody's family, you went to their weddings, you went to clambakes, you went to softball games. I mean it was like a poor man's yacht club almost.

JB: One of the best things that ever came out of Partners for Progress was shops in the plant being able to have an open house and bring their families in. I think it should've been done years before, because there were women and kids, who, I don't care what their husband, and it was mostly husbands at that time, told them what they did when they came there, had not an inkling.

Not even a clue.

JB: Not a clue how hot, how dirty, how smelly some of their places were, and just the danger. I think the most things kids said to me on that tour was it's dangerous in here; my daddy works here and it's dangerous. Never did that get communicated from words at home.

I remember they started coming in the electric furnace. I think they lasted three days and they stopped it, because they were afraid they were going to damage people's ears being there when the furnaces were melting down. You know the noise was like 105 decibels. Rock music, loud rock music is like 100 decibels, and the company said oh no, you know what, I don't think we're gonna do this anymore. A lot of people felt cheated over that. But then again, by the same token they took people to the combination mill, and they put 'em on the catwalk to walk along while the mill was rolling. I personally thought myself that was the worse thing they could have ever done. One cobble, one cobble could have gone right up there and killed somebody so quick, you wouldn't even have known it happened until after they were dead. But it was still a good thing.

JB: It was, but the welding was also a hazard because of the welding flash. Well they made the people visit while people were welding. Never said anything to the wives and the children, don't look at the arc, don't be that near, it was crazy. Safety was thrown out on those days for a lot of shops, and I don't understand why. It could've been a really good ongoing program had they just taken some common sense.

Well, I saw something really funny. One of the guys, one of the first helpers brought his grandkids in, and when they came in he handed 'em all a pair of blue glasses and he says, "Now when that furnace starts to melt down, you hold this in front of your face." And when that was over with, they came up to him, his boss came up to him, and says, "You know we've been looking all over for those blue glasses, where did you get them out?" He says, "What are you talking about? They've been in this drawer for years. If you ever would have looked, they would have been there. If you would have asked me, I would've gave 'em to you." You know, they acted like he stole them for somebody, and he didn't. But anyway. I'll tell you what, Jean, it was a real pleasure interviewing ya, and you more or less came through in the clutch. I mean you were a trendsetter down there, and I can tell you right now that most of the people who ever had anything to say about you, is they always said the same thing, okay. If she would have been one of the guys, she'd be no different than she is right now. So I'm saying that probably has to be from your family more than anything else, cuz you actually were one of the guys. I don't know whether you ever thought of it like that, but you really were.

JB: I got along with people on both salary and …

Oh there's no doubt about that. You had to have a certain personality to do that.

JB: And I honestly think what my biggest thing that got me through was my father, who you don't know Frankie, but was a person who, if you were telling an ethnic or off-colored joke or something, he would walk away, cuz he didn't like them, but he would not make you feel bad about it. He would just say, he would just say nothing, and he would just go somewhere else. He was very social, did lots of things, he just didn't want to hear it.

And lord knows that plant was rife with jokes like that.

JB: And the day that I started at Number 2 Machine Shop and went out in the plant and after my salary boss said everything he had to say, I went out and some guy came up and told me the only reason I must be there is I must be a two dollar hooker looking for some extra money. I was so shocked, I really was shocked. I was still in shock that this guy yelled out what he yelled out when I got to work there, because all my interviews had gone so well. I was really like taken back. I still lived at home. And I went, and that night I said to my dad, I can't believe this guy said this.

And what year was this, when you first went into the plant?

JB: That was 1973.

Okay, when you came back the second time.

JB: Yeah, and I was like kind of like really, really upset, and my dad said, "Here's your rule, how they treat you is how you treat them, individually. Just bear that in mind. Never group people together because they're standing together," he said, "just like I walk away when something's being said I don't want to hear, I don't blame everyone in the group, I don't even blame the person telling it, I just don't want to be there or sayin' it." He said do not blame the group, you treat everybody as an individual. My very next night in there, cuz they put me right on night shift then too, uh, I guess to discourage me from staying. Uh, there was a man, who was a very good friend of my dad's in the community, came in, had no idea who I was because my name was different then, nobody knew my family at all, knew where I came from or anything, and came in and said, this is the rate I'm getting or else you will be tied down and whatever. So I, he went out of the booth, I locked the door, I picked up the intercom and said, "Mr. Stocker who works on XYZ machine, you will not be getting that rate, and you will not be tying me down and f-in me, and you will be reported in the morning for attempting to do so." I put the thing down. It was like a magnet, and I was sitting in the middle of Number 2 Machine Shop in the east end booth and there must have been 20 guys instantly at the windows trying, screaming, yellin', banging on the door. They're like, you can't do that. I just did. Just made an announcement that's all, I never reported it to anybody. Went home that night, that was that. So then the next day I come in, and everybody's all worried, "Oh my God, Stocker didn't even come to work today, he's so upset, he's gonna end up going to jail over you and lose his job, how could you do this?" I was like, "What are you guys talking about?" "Well everything that happened," and I went, "I don't even know what the heck you're talking about." So the foremen looked at me and they go, what happened last night? I go, what happened?

And that was the end of that.

JB: And that's how I dealt with everybody, on an individual basis.

Well, you were always known as a communicator.

JB: Somebody says something to me, I say something back. You were nice to me, I was very nice to you. You came in like gang busters and said things to me. During this time period my dad was at that time chief clerk of manufacturing. He had a heart attack in cost analysis, and he was out of work, and he came back and he got made chief clerk of manufacturing cuz they, there was too much time in between, to hold his other job. So he was eating in the dining room at lunch and the second day that I worked there in the dining room they were proceeding to say about the two bit whore that they hired to go out in the plant.

Who was saying this?

JB: Salary people. In the company dining room. And she did this and she did that, and my dad said, "How do you guys know any of this?" "We know, we know that's exactly why, that's exactly why she got hired to go out there, she's gotta be nothing but a prostitute" and blah blah blah, "and we're gonna have problems galore," and my dad said, I really wish some of you would just find out what the true story is and maybe you wouldn't think this. And the one guy said, "I saw her, she dresses like a hooker." And at that time, well you didn't know me then, I was wearing jeans and a big t-shirt with a jacket over it every day. I started in February, it was freezing. And my dad said, "Well, I hate to tell you but she isn't dressing like that cuz I see her go to work every day. This was my daughter you're talking about," and got up and walked out of the dining room, and he said it was like, he could hear the sucky tone, and the next day no one was in that dining room, he was the only person that came to lunch.

How about that? Well I'll tell you what, I'm sure the longer we went on here the better the stories would get. But, I think we've heard plenty. And I'd like to thank you for coming over to do this, and I wish the best for you and your family.

JB: Thank you.

Thank you.

JACK BONNEY
31 years

Central Mail Room

As the plant mailman, Jack knew everyone. Jack was a good listener and the most reliable source of information I knew.

* * * * * * * * * *

Today is June 23rd 2008. We're here with Jack Bonney. Jack Bonney was a mailman in the plant, starting in September 1968. Jack, tell me how you came to be hired at Bethlehem Steel.

JB: Oh jeez, well, basically I went down there, filled out an application, and on the application they always ask you if you were willing to work swing shifts, things like that. And I just kept putting down no, no, no. So it came back; they gave me a call, and the only place I could do that was within the corporate offices. So the first interview was, I went over to the sales office, well it wasn't the sales office, it was the home office, and the escort was Ruth Allen, she was in charge of all the escorts, and they had doormen. And I went in there, and I mean she says, she looks at me and she says, "Do you know what? If you would clean up a little bit, clean up your hair, you would make a very good corporate image." And I thought to myself, "Well, what do you do?" She says, "Well, you stand at the door, you open up the door for people, say 'good morning,' you learn the executives' names, say 'good morning' to them," and I'm there, "Nah."

Not my cup of tea.

JB: Nah. So then she said, "Well then, you're gonna have to go back to the employment office and Pete Dent. He was the guy who was doing the hiring. "Well, I got something else for ya maybe. Go over to the sales office and there's an opening in file." So I walked up there, and everybody was in suits, and I thought to myself, I mean I says, "Wait a minute; what's that pay? You know can I afford to go out and buy myself suits? And do I really want to walk around in a suit?" That kind of stuff. And I says …

Did you have your tie dye on Jack?

JB: No. No, no tie dye.

I'm just checking, but you had the long hair right?

JB: Longer, but it wasn't long. Iit wasn't outrageous compared to …

Okay

JB: And I went there, and I said no thanks to them. And I went back there and Pete says, "This is the second job you turned down."

They were like amazed?

JB: Yeah. And he says, "Well, we have one option for you." I said, "What's that?" He says, "Mailroom." I'm there, okay, take a look. So I go down, and I'm walking down into the mailroom, and I look in there and uh, there's Billy Smoyer, he's doing work in there. He sat in front of the thing, he's wearing jeans, and I'm looking at this place. I says, "This is it! This is it!" I mean, even though I had long hair, that time the supervisor was really down on long hair. I mean, and that was really funny.

But then when he found out what a dynamic individual you were.

JB: Well, no that wasn't even it; it was that, and then he kept calling me; he always called me Bonney, "Don't you think you should get a haircut?" I'm there, "No." A month later he calls me in there, Bonney, "You got a raise." I'm there, "Oh good." He said, "Can you do me a favor, can you get a haircut?" So I says, "I got a little bit of a haircut," and that kind of stopped him. Then he came back after I started letting it grow again. Six months later he calls me in he says, "Can you get a haircut. I got you a raise." I was getting raises for getting a god damn haircut. And then I started growing a beard, and this all really started off with this really stupid thing back then. He walks up he says, "How come you have a beard, you're growing a beard, why you growing a beard?" I says, "Cuz I dig Fidel Castro," which was like, he looked at me. Pretty soon, at that time Marty Gearhard was in charge of our department, as well as Ed Wamser who was a great guy, and they all come down there and they're kind of sitting me down in the office and talking to me and they says, "Well, you have some college?" I said, "I have a little," but I said, "I really didn't, I graduated high school, did a couple semesters, that's the bottom line." He says, "You aren't affiliated with any subversive groups?" I'm there, "Like what?" "Students for Democratic Society, Weather Underground or what? Yeah like that." I said, "What are they?" And they all looked at me like, "We don't know." I'm there, "Well, no." And pretty soon Ed Wamser, he actually became on my side, he says, "This is a nice guy, man." He said that it didn't make any difference; it was actually, it was funny back then. That was one of the most, one of the funniest eras that I could, cuz I just like to goof on people. I would say things to them, and I sat back and I just liked to have them try to figure out what the hell I was saying.

Now when you got hired, you were in the corporate mail room, right? Tell me about your travels in the corporate building?

JB: I was in the corporate mail room. That's when I was put up on the floors, and I was told to use an elevator, a certain one; it was a freight elevator that we were supposed to use. And on the sixth floor at that time of the home office was the executive floors. We were not allowed to take the buggies out because of the nice carpeting, well above everything else in the whole corporation. I do what I had to do standing there; a guy comes walking out there pushes every button, including mine. It opens up, he gets on. He pushes down, and I walked in and I said to him, I says, "Hey, you got, I think you got five elevators, maybe six." I said, "You've got six other elevators, why?" He just looked at me. I says, "This is for us, those are for you." I cancelled him out, and I pushed up. By the time I got back to the mail room, they're calling me in. It ended up to be Ira Sims who was the Executive Vice President of the corporation, and it was like I was telling him that he couldn't get on the elevator.

Well, you told him the truth.

JB: Well right. So then, this was not, then it was again turned back to an issue of my hair and, I didn't have a corporate image, so I got sent out into the Bethlehem plant to deliver mail, which back then they used that almost like a punishment, which was the best thing that ever happened to me.

Yeah, cuz you were like a legend in the plant Jack, and you never even knew it. Everybody liked you. Here comes Jack.

JB: I liked everybody out there too.

You know what it was? You were a direct pipeline to the corporate office, and you never knew it. And when guys would ask you questions, cuz most of the time they'd find out whatever you told them was right on the money.

JB: Well, it always was because what they were saying over in the corporate offices and what they were saying out into the plant, they always, they'd put a spin on it. And back then we had a teletype machine, and this is how everything came through in the mailroom. And the stuff we were supposed to deliver, we were supposed to tear off it, circle who was supposed to get it, but we weren't supposed to read it. How damn hard is that?

Yeah. Don't read that Jack.

JB: You know, I mean, and that's how we found out.

But you learned that in third grade, didn't you, reading? Or was it second grade?

JB: Second grade, I hope, I mean I could read in second grade. I mean, the stories that they were giving you from the corporate offices, I mean bullshit is really what it comes down to, and they were saying one thing over there, and then they were saying another thing out in the plant. Basically, you know, I mean it's like, we're gonna keep it going, we're gonna keep this going. And then they start putting in roads. Remember back when they started putting in roads and refinishing the roads in Bethlehem? I mean, I saw this as the end. They came to the Lehigh plant and they were putting in the new roads. As soon as the new roads were in, they shut it down. Then they started moving from Central Tool going east down towards the sintering plant area, and they started putting in new roads there. All along that route there, they'd say, "Oh that's nothing." They'd say, "That's nothing, we're okay, we're okay." The roads were in, it was down. And they kept going all the way through the Saucon plant, going down to the maintenance area, all along the pre-fabricated Butler building that was there, only a temporary structure, but we really tried to turn this around. Down it went. The roads were in. The Coke Works, we're good for five years yet. They started going down towards the Coke Works, roads going down there. I said to myself, "You're finished." "Oh no, no, no, no," they said, "we have five years." "No, they're putting in new roads" "No, that's for better traffic."

Jack, let me tell you something before you go any further. That is the damndest story I ever heard, but the more you talk, the more it makes sense. I remember it distinctly. It just never occurred to me what you just said.

JB: I just saw this, and I started saying, "Wow, wait a minute." I think it was actually about 1980, they had already, well, put it this way, I knew a guy who graduated from Lehigh, kind of like a friend of mine. He gave me a call. He works at Bethlehem Steel, and the gentleman's dead now, so his name will remain unnamed. I mean I have, really out of respect, he says, "Come on over for dinner. There's somebody I want you to meet." I'm there, "Oh, okay." He says, "Whatever you do, just don't tell them you work for Bethlehem Steel." I'm there, "Oh, okay, no problem." Well, this guy was from a firm, I believe it was from Baltimore or somewhere down towards DC area, and the first thing he wanted to know was where I worked, and I told him I was a mailman. I didn't lie to him. He said, "Oh, that's a good government job there." Well, I guess government jobs go along with my job.

You just smiled.

JB: I mean government, I always did government jobs, you know.

I was big in the government jobs.

JB: Hell yeah. And he started talking about it, I says, "Well, what do you do?" He said, "Well, I'm contracted with Bethlehem Steel now." I says, "Really?" He says, "Yeah, it's not doing too well" He says, "No it's not." He says, "We're here and we're looking at different plants, you know, for the plant and this kind of thing." And he says to me, he said, "It doesn't have really that long." I'm there, "Why?" That's when he started to explain to me a controlled shut down. I mean if you shut it down too quick, it doesn't look too good for the company, it doesn't look good for anything. So the whole damn thing took about maybe about ten years or more, but slowly it was controlled, every piece of that shut down was controlled. Not necessarily by him. He was one of the first people that they brought in to assess the situation, but that was probably back around 1981, maybe even 1980. They had the mini mill projects going on in the plant offices at that time, and uh, there were different people involved, Mike Zaia and all that crew, they had Mal Dominy, all those people, in a little closed room there, I mean, it was called a mini mill project. They were looking how to turn Bethlehem into a mini mill project all the way back into the '80s. And that didn't go through. And then the Brits, you know, which was really funny that they were coming in and they were saying, "Well, we might be able to …" And that was towards the end, "Well, we might be able to sell it to the Brits." And they came in there with the idea was if it wasn't union, we might be able to do something about it, and the Brits' idea was that we're not really used to working with unions, which I thought was really such bullshit because Europe is definitely a great union…

Just about everybody over in Europe is union.

JB: And that's when they sent in that crew. And they came in to look at the place. They went into the combo mill, and they came walking through and the one guy who was walking through it, he was just a regular worker, and he started singing that song by Anthony Uley, "Send in the Clowns." My thought was, "Oh, escort him out of here." It was funny. But you know, "We might be interested if it was non-union."

Well, you know, I had somebody told me that was involved with the British talks, that the British weren't interested in buying a junk yard. Did you ever hear that?

JB: Yeah. It was. Because you see what we thought was modern, even the combo at that time was no longer modern. And yet you had places like the 48-inch mill, the old Grey mill, they were great mills. These could put out steel, these were rolled by hand, these guys were up there working the levers, making it, you know, I mean, it was an amazing piece of equipment, cuz that's probably been there since what, 1923 or something like that, and they were still …

Oh, before that.

JB: Before that.

1908, 1909.

JB: Cuz my grandfather was part of that, and he actually developed this thing called a grasshopper down there, which was able to take the steel off after it was rolled, lifted off, and move it. It was called a grasshopper. And this was back in the early 1900s. He was a general foreman of Saucon Maintenance. He had like, and when he retired, they took four people on and split his job up to four different people.

Wow. Now, for the benefit of the people, Jack was a mailman in the plant. Jack got all over the plant, every area that you could think of, Jack was there. The reason we're interviewing Jack, everybody knew Jack, everybody liked Jack, and Jack is what I consider myself a dynamic personality, and we need him for this book. But, Jack, tell me about some of the personalities you ran into in the plant. You must of knew 'em all.

JB: Oh jeez, from all the way up, okay, 2- and 4-Open Hearth. Matt Morris, Superintendent. You know, I thought it was always funny because, do you remember Ricky's trailer? I would go walking into the office, and Matt would look at me, and he would say, "You going up to Ricky's?" "Yup, why not? Let's go." He'd jump in my truck, we'd ride up to Ricky's, I never paid. Never paid. He always bought me breakfast, you know, just taking a ride up there, sitting around and bullshit. He was okay.

Well, you know, there was another man in the plant, and I know you know him, Bob Burkey, may he rest in peace.

JB: Oh jeez, the sneakin' Deacon, may he rest in peace.

Listen, listen. I wanna tell you something. Bob said to me, he says, "You know, there were a lot of people that thought I was full of shit," he says, "but, you know what, every week I'd get a call from certain superintendents, Bob, what's going on? They actually trusted my expertise from being all over the plant and knowing everybody." They'd call me, they'd say, "Bob, what's going on?" And you know, unless you knew Bob Burkey, you would think he was the biggest bullshitter in the world. But he was far far …

JB: He was more, very civic minded.

He was a great guy. He was a great guy.

JB: He was, he was.

And you know, no matter what you said about him, they found stuff like water off a duck, he didn't care. He put his nose down to the grindstone. He did the things that were … he felt were important to him.

JB: I mean, I knew him since probably 19. I knew him before I even went into the Bethlehem plant. '67, that's when the old, the mills was going on down there at Monocacy Park there, the old …

Yeah, yeah, he was working down there.

JB: And he used to come down there; he was a little bit older than us, but you know, I mean he was …

But he wasn't afraid to impart his knowledge on other people. And that was the good thing about him, you know. And story telling, the man should have been on TV on HBO. In fact, they probably should have had him on with George Carlin, who just died recently, may he rest in peace. A legend in his own time. Now, now let me ask you something. Did you get a shoe allowance? Cuz man you did some hoofing through that plant.

JB: Yes I did.

You did. And what, what kind of shoes would you buy?

JB: Whatever was in the trailer.

Yeah, in other words, if they felt good, they were okay for you?

JB: Yup. But that's a little funny thing about the shoe trailer too. There was a little rumor that got started down there, and it was really, really funny, and that's when they started really screwing around with the salaried people out there. And I'd go in there and start just throwing out this little thing to a couple guys, "Hey, hey, I hear they're gonna get rid of your shoe allowance. "No." I'd say, "You better get your damn shoes." Well, within that month, and uh, Dick, I forget what his name was, down at the shoe trailer …

This was down Hellertown?

JB: Yeah! I mean, it was like, everybody and their brother were running down there for shoes, because I just threw in a couple and said you might be losing your shoe allowance there, you know.

Yeah, he was quite the character himself. He was a really nice guy.

JB: Yeah, he worked in the bull gang for the corporate offices. Yeah, that's where I first knew Dick from. And his wife worked in the mailroom.

So Jack, in your travels, because you're all over the plant, when did you get the first inkling that the plant was in trouble?

JB: Oh, it wasn't basically that the plant was in trouble, but I really thought that the home office and the whole thing was in trouble, and this was long before they even started screwing around with Bethlehem plant, but in the home offices when they had a cafeteria and it was all run by Bethlehem Steel. They got rid of every single employee from that and they brought in an outside concern, which they said, "We can do better." I said, "Wait a minute." From that time on I would never even go there, that they brought an outside concern in. I mean, they had great food before, and then it really started going down when they brought in the outside concern. I mean, I just like boycotted the cafeteria and manpower.

Well, you know Jack, I was in there before and after, and let me tell you a little story. People who know me have always said, Frank has never missed a meal in his life, and it's probably true. But exactly what you said, I went in there two or three times after the new outfit come in, it was not the same.

JB: No it wasn't, it absolutely wasn't.

And you know what? You know what the biggest part was? You didn't know anybody.

JB: That's right. And all the people that I knew for years, for years been down there, you know, you see 'em gone, and they were really good people, and they were really down about losing their jobs and things like that, and then manpower. And that really, really, really showed me that this place, when they started getting rid of people and contracting people, any corporation that does that is on its way down. And then with the salary, they would cut your salary.

So we're talking, we're talking right about the mid '80s then.

JB: Right, cutting the salaries. I mean, we took a, salary people, I mean we took a 5 percent pay cut, then we took a 10 percent pay cut, then we took another 5 percent pay cut within the corporation. I said, any company that tries to sell, they're trying to save the company by cutting your wages, I said, you're done.

Do you think they cut the top people?

JB: No. Absolutely not. After they got done doing what they had to do, they got raises, cuz they completed their goal.

They did the dirty deed.

JB: They did the dirty deed, and they completed their goal.

They were rewarded.

JB: A lot of those guys left before it all went down there, but believe me, they went out with their little golden parachutes, too.

Yup. And the only thing that we got golden is the stuff that turns the snow yellow while we're laying face down in it.

JB: The old shower. That's it. But you know, I mean, I saw that back then, and they were trying to tell the plant, you know, I mean, if the corporation isn't going to be, home office isn't going to be in Bethlehem, do you believe for one minute they're gonna keep a plant in Bethlehem?

Yeah, I know what you're saying; I know what you're saying. If you ever had any authority to do anything different from what you saw going on walking through every area of that plant, what jumped out at you as being wasteful. Or is it just too many numerous things to repeat them all?

JB: Probably that, too numerous. I mean, the thing that really got me was they were cutting back, manpower, laying off the union workers. I mean, just like the labor gang for instance; you would have six guys out there doing a job, and you would have four supervisors out there watching them do it.

And you saw this regularly.

JB: Yes, and I thought, now wait a minute. Now those four guys that are out there doing that job, I thought, they had those guys out there because, you know, they had a certain job to do, they had union rules that they had to go by, but they were willing to pay, uh, if they had a grievance, they would take somebody who would have less seniority, they'd say, we're gonna put him out here. Well, we're gonna pay for it, but we know that guy can do the job, we know these four five people can do that job, and they would omit all the other people between and gladly pay out the grievances, because, I mean... That's, you know, I mean, I saw it, I mean, those guys...

Well, there was some strange stuff that went on, there's no doubt about it.

JB: There was a lot of strange stuff in there. Remember them rebuilding the blast furnace? I remember that, and there were certain guys that were gone from Bethlehem Steel, um, foremen that were laid off or retired, and they came back as consultants because they really realized at that point that they had absolutely nobody there that could lead a rebuild, because there was nobody there who knew how to do it.

They never went through it. They were all gone.

JB: Yeah, George, George, uh, from the riggers, I forget what his name. But they brought him back, and I mean, they got upset.

Well, there were a lot of guys that came back.

JB: They were telling him that, he was laughing one day to me, he said, "Yeah, they brought me back as a consultant, they were willing to pay me twenty dollars an hour, and I told 'em shove it; it's fifty dollars an hour, and they brought him back with no problem for about six months, till they got that job done. They got rid of all their knowledge at one point, so they were…

Yeah. The only guy they had left at the end that really knew his ass from a hole in the ground was Mike Dwelly.

JB: Blast Furnace, yes.

Mike Dwelly, the guys would walk through fire for Mike Dwelly. They really loved him.

JB: And Charlie Luthar. He was a good Coke Works man. Yeah, he was, he knew…

We had a lot of good bosses in the plant, a lot of good bosses.

JB: A lot of good bosses.

Unfortunately, you know, in the corporate structure, and I would imagine no matter where you work, you're gonna have, you know, you're gonna have a mix. And the mix isn't always, you know. Beauty's in the eyes of the beholder.

JB: Right. And it was, it was just a blame situation.

Yeah, I could imagine that. But I'll tell you what Jack, it was a real pleasure listening to your overview of the whole situation. You know, I'll tell you what, who would ever think in a million years that a mailman walking through the plant all those years probably knew more than most of the superintendents that were in there?

JB: Because I got it from both sides.

Yeah. You got it from both sides, but you know, I guess the real secret was ripping those teletypes off and circling them. But they told you, don't you dare read 'em.

JB: Don't you dare look at them. Don't read them.

Well, that's what the guys always said, here comes Jack, ask Jack that question. I can remember guys in the combo saws when we were going under, "Hey, here comes Jack, ask Jack that question." You know they looked forward to seeing ya. And I'll tell you what, I mean, let's face it, everybody that went into the plant, I haven't run into anyone yet that ever said I didn't enjoy going into the plant or going to work. And they said it for one reason, every day was different. Even if you did the same job, every day was different, and they loved that, and they spent time with all their buddies. And you know yourself from working there, look at how much time we spent among a certain group of people.

JB: It was fun.

Some guys ended up getting divorced. They spent more time in the plant than they did at home.

JB: It was a lot of fun, a lot of great guys.

Now if that plant was still back there and you were on a layoff right now when we're talking, would you go back?

JB: Yeah.

Okay. And what's the number one thing you miss from the plant, other than the paycheck?

JB: Paycheck? The camaraderie. There was a camaraderie.

That's number one, benefits are number two, pay's about four or five.

JB: The bennies, I mean, I figure right now I'd have about '41 years.

Yeah, you know, you and I would both be retiring like this year.

JB: With a good pension if it wouldn't have gone under.

Yes, that's true. I mean, we didn't do necessarily that bad, but you know, we could have done a little bit better.

JB: Could have done a little bit better.

Well Jack, I want to thank you for participating in this, and I wish all the best to you and your family.

JB: Alright, yeah.

JAMES J. BENNICK
31 years of service

Merchant Mills, EFM Maintenance, Basic Oxygen Furnace Maintenance, Coke Works

Jim was the most intense worker I ever encountered at BSCO. His troubleshooting skills were the best I ever saw for a man not holding a college degree in electrical engineering.

* * * * * * * * * *

It's June 10th, 2008; we're going on the record with James J. Bennick. Jim, is it okay if we call you Jim? Did you have a nickname in the plant? Everybody had one.

JB: Jim.

Okay, Jim, that's simple. You were a maintenance tech A; that means you had what, how many different rates?

JB: I was a welder A, electrician A, millwright A.

All right; starting in September of 1968. Was that after the service or what?

JB: Before the service.

Okay. In other words, you got drafted or you joined after you were in Bethlehem Steel.

JB: I got drafted after I was in Bethlehem Steel.

Yeah. Put in four years?

JB: Four years.

Okay, good enough. You came back here, and Bethlehem Steel said, Jim, we've been holding this job for ya. And you were in, at that time, up in the Merchants Mills, what, in the maintenance unit? And what was that, the 413 department?

JB: The 413.

And they did what?

JB: They took care of all the maintenance of rolling mills, and we took care of all mechanical repairs and electrical repairs.

And you became a, I'm gonna guess, a motor inspector while you were there?
JB: Motor inspector, yes.

Yeah, and do you remember when you got that rate?
JB: About a year after the service.

Yeah. In other words, you did not have it when you went in the service, but you got it as soon as you got back almost?
JB: I was only in there about two, three months, and I got the rate.

And what did you do in the Navy? Were you doing electrical related work?
JB: I strictly did avionics or electronic or electrical work on airplanes.

All right, so you had some background. So up there in the alloy division, you come back, in '72 from the service. You're back there, and the place was going pretty good then, wasn't it? I mean, like how would you put it, the best way to describe it?
JB: There were a hundred people out on the street looking for work, so everything was going quite well.

And the mill was running like 20 shifts a week, the 35-inch mill?
JB: Oh, I'd say even more than that.

And when repair shift came, you really found out what it was like to get a lot of work done in an 8-hour period, didn't you?
JB: That's affirmative.

Yes you did. Okay, and uh, how long were you in the 413?
JB: About fifteen years.

Fifteen years. And before you moved on, I see to the BOF, but let's talk about 413 and the alloy division. Describe what a typical motor inspector might do in a week's time.
JB: Well, you had mostly crane repairs on the overhead, everything electrical on the crane, everything mechanical on the crane.

Okay, so you know, you're up off the ground and you're working in all kinds of heat, cold, dirt.
JB: Yes. Plus we took care of all the electrical backgrounds, electrical stuff for the mills also, all the 10,000 horse powered motor.

Yup. And then we had some beauty motors there. And a lot of times you know the uh, millwrights had to do work before the motor inspectors could work and vice versa, so everybody more or less worked together.

JB: Yes.

It was a team. And you know, I remember we had a pile of guys there, I mean a real pile of guys, and we had some real, I thought we had some pretty good foremen up there. I remember the one guy that jumps out is Dick Wagner. I don't know how many times I went into Dick Wagner, and I said, Dick, "Here's what this crane's doing." He'd pull out the print and he says, "I want you to look right here." I'd go up there, right, and right where I'm supposed to have a signal, I didn't, and out comes the test light, and I'd find something broken, or I'd find contacts that weren't there. But when I looked at the board, I didn't see that they weren't there, they just fell off. You know, they wore out. And uh, it was just amazing you know how he could fix cranes from the ground. He ever do that for you?

JB: Very seldom because I mostly took care of it myself.

Yup, well you know what, some of us weren't that fortunate. You were always the guy that, you know, Dick knew; hey, if we send Jim up there, chances are real good it's gonna be fixed. Guys had reputations in the plant, and I don't want your head to swell up, but you had one of the better ones. But you know, what are you gonna do, if you're good, you're good. Now, you worked a lot of swing shifts too, I guess.

JB: Yes.

And how long before you were actually able to get onto something that was considered like steady? Did that ever happen?

JB: The last eight months of my employment at the Bethlehem Steel.

And that was it?

JB: That was it.

So while you were down there at the alloy division, you worked in other areas too, like the 12- and 14-inch mill.

JB: Everywhere that the alloy division covered, I worked.

You did it. The 3- and 9-inch mill? That was an old hand mill, wasn't that a sight?

JB: Yes it was. That was tool steel.

Remember they used to run that thing with bells and whistles. One bell meant go this way, two bells the other way; whistles, everything, you name it, and we had it.

JB: Yes, everything was strictly hand fed. The mills were hand fed. It looked like a long snake.

And they were making mostly drill collars. I mean high powered stuff; they were making real good steel.

JB: High quality steel.

Yeah this stuff was really, you know, top of the line. And uh, eventually you moved onto the BOF, the Basic Oxygen Furnace, about '80, '81? And stayed here until when?

JB: Till about, uh '97, then I had got laid off from the BOF, and after they shut down then I went to the coke works to finish up.

Yeah. So the BOF was a huge place, lots of noise, lots of dirt. And you were doing almost basically the same work, but more or less on bigger equipment.

JB: Well, the machine, the cranes were running faster, 200 ton capacity, solid state circuitry, and we took care of everything else too, internal communications there, all the tool systems and the pollution control systems, everything.

Yeah, and that was, compared to the alloy division, that was an even dirtier place.

JB: Plus it was more technical.

And, yeah, a lot more technical. Now, when you worked down there, how were your hours?

JB: I had regular swing shift. At least I could predict my swing shift.

Okay, in other words, you were on swing shift most of the time? All right, and do you think you spent more time down there at Bethlehem Steel than you did with your own family?

JB: Uh, yeah a lot times, yeah. You spent a lot of holidays and, uh, nights in there and middle shifts in there.

Well, I don't think the plant ever considered holidays anything special.

JB: There was no such thing.

No, but they always, all your buddies that didn't work at Bethlehem Steel, they always used to say, "Oh Jim, you're working the holiday making the big bucks," but they were sitting along the pool, right, drinking Budweiser and eating hamburgers?

JB: At the same time if they had to work in that environment, they wouldn't, or those hours. You froze yourself in the winter time; you roasted yourself in the summer time.

Remember when we used to get the 90-day wonders in the summer, and they would quick run to the schedule to see how they were working. They never believed what we told them, that you don't know from week to week how you're gonna work. They thought we were kiddin' 'em.

JB: How 'bout the salamanders? Man, did they they get warm. This was the real world; all of a sudden they couldn't find, they couldn't believe it.

And you walked into Bethlehem Steel the first time and you said, "Uh-oh, what did I do?" What was your first impression?

JB: I was in awe of the massive machinery.

Yeah, right out of high school and you said, "Wow, look at this."

JB: Well, I went to Lincoln electronic tech school before I went there. ETC in Allentown; that's years ago on Tilghman Street. Yeah, a good electronic school, but I couldn't afford to send myself anymore, so I got a job at Bethlehem Steel. And then I was there three months and Uncle Sam tapped me on the shoulder, and…

He said have I got a deal for you.

JB: Yes.

Yeah, I guess you only had to have 30 days in the plant to have your time continued to run, something like that. It wasn't a lot. I know if you got drafted or you joined, I think it was only 30 days you had to be in the plant. Because I know I got the love note, too; it said, "Greetings from the President of the United States of America." You remember that?

JB: Yes I do.

"You are hereby ordered to report no later than zero four four five hours at the Armed Forces Citadel at 10 N. Main Street," and then in parenthesis "(Salvation Army) for induction into the Armed Forces of the United States of America. Failure to do so will result in your immediate apprehension by federal authorities, and in the event you cannot serve for any one of the following: sickness, joined another branch of the service, report in person with this letter within 96 hours." Up I go to Minnie Brown, Well, I joined the Navy," she says, "Well, have a good time." Bang, that was it. I didn't hear no more from the draft board. But then I was in the service six years too. You know most guys are in four; I was in six. One guy says that's because you were so dumb it took you two years longer to get out." So Jim, you had some, probably had some real good taxing jobs in the plant. Is there any job you remember being on that really like drove nuts until you got to the bottom of it?

JB: Not really, no. Nah, troubleshooting just maintenance routine, that's all we did.

Yeah, so you just got used to it? It's just another day?
JB: It's just another day. That's all we did was troubleshoot.

Nothing but, and you're still troubleshooting, right?
JB: That's what I do for a living.

That's it. You're in heating and air conditioning right? So you know, you had a built-in ready source of work the day you left the plant almost.
JB: Yes.

Well you had been doing that right along anyway, hadn't you?
JB: You can see the cancer eating away at the plant years before this happened.

Yeah, when did you, when did you come to that realization that things were not right?
JB: When I was in Merchant Mills back in, uh, the '60s I guess.

Yeah, you knew it back then?
JB: When Trautlein come in there, he started chopping parts of the plant off; you remember that there? It was quite obvious what was gonna happen.

He was chopping heads off too.
JB: Yeah, chopping heads and chopping jobs just like a cancerous growth. And you could see it coming so.

Do you think that the plant could have been saved?
JB: I think so.

Yeah? If you would have had an opportunity, somewhere along the line, okay, to say, "We gotta stop doing this, it's costing us too much money and it's leading nowhere," what's the one thing you think you would have changed had you had the authority to change it?
JB: I would have changed the massive imports in this country. We would still be working there yet.

In other words, you think the government really never did a thing for us?
JB: No, there's too many people making money off imports.

Well, you know what, you're not alone with this, because I have almost everyone I talked to that I asked that question came up with the same thing. And you know that the sad part about it is you know how we would always talk about, well, we want to be a friend of labor, and this is both Democrats and Republicans, but in reality we had no friends.

More because of what you just said, there were too many people making money.
JB: However, not the right people were making money.

Yeah, there you go, the people in the know. Do you think the plant could have been saved?
JB: If it wasn't for mass amount of imports, yes, we'd be moving today yet.

In fact, I know if we would have probably stayed on another six months or a year, we'd probably all be working there yet. In fact, all of us, yeah. In fact, most of the people that worked there, they could have helped contribute their part too by not buying American cars. There you go.
JB: It's quite hypocritical isn't it?

Yup. Well, I'll tell you what, did you enjoy your time there?
JB: Uh most, it wasn't bad, it's a job, let's face it, but …

What do you miss the most?
JB: The health coverage.

Well, that's right, you're paying your own for right now, yeah, I guess so. And uh, a lot of that stuff we took for granted. You know, it was pretty good coverage, let's face it.
JB: Yes it was. You don't realize what you had until you lose it.

My wife's telling me that all the time. She says, be careful, she says it's never too late. I don't know what she means, but maybe I'll find out, I hope not. But anyway, you did a good job down there. I see you even spent some time as a subforeman.
JB: Little bit.

Yeah, was that down in the BOF?
JB: Both places. Merchant mills and the BOF.

And you worked at the Coke Works there at the end also.
JB: Yeah, I was a wireman there. They tried something new before we got out. They wanted to place motor inspectors in the wireman positions. And I was their guinea pig. The wiremen fought it because they didn't want a non-wireman in there because they thought they couldn't do the job, but unfortunately I did a lot on the outside; I had no problem bending pipe and running wires. The wiremen couldn't troubleshoot, so they kind of appreciated us after a while.

Yeah, okay. So uh, that was the last place that was running. Did you stay there right to the end?

JB: Almost to the end, but then, uh, I had to leave cuz because I started my own business, so I had to go. I had my 31 years, and that's all I needed for my pension.

Yeah, okay, that's good. Uh, would you go back if you had the chance?

JB: Yeah I would.

Yeah? Most of the guys I talked said the most things we missed is, it's not the pay, it's not the benefits, it's the people we worked with, because we spent so much time with them.

JB: Yeah, but I like working on the machinery.

Everything was, it was a challenge every day.

JB: Yeah, I liked it.

Well, okay Jim, I want to thank you for coming over here and being part of this, and this is the real story of what it was like working in the alloy division and the BOF as told by Jim Bennick, and I hope the best for you and your family. Thanks a lot.

JB: Thank you.

Bye.

ELSIE PRIBULA
37 years of service

Lehigh Dispensary

Called "Blondie" in the plant, Elsie was best known for her work at the Lehigh Dispensary. Elsie and her husband Joe, who worked in the saw shop, gave the company 81 years of service.

* * * * * * * * *

It's September 23rd 2008, and we're here with Elsie Spirk Pribula. Elsie how ya doin' today?

EP: I'm doin' fine.

That's great. Now Elsie, did you own a nickname in the plant or you just call you Elsie?

EP: No, they called me Blondie.

OK. They called you Blondie, so for this interview here we should just call you Elsie?

EP: I think so.

OK. We'll do that. Elsie, I see you started back in the early days of World War II. September of 1942. Tell me about your first day in the plant; how did you get the job, how did you even find out about it?

EP: Well, they were doin' lots of hiring at the time, and I went to the employment office, and I um, uh, filled out all the papers and stuff, and I was called immediately.

OK, uh. A lot of the women actually worked in the plant running cranes and things like that; did they ever offer you anything like that? What did they say when they hired you?

EP: No, I was strictly for clerical work.

OK you were for clerical work, all right. That clears that up. So what did you think when you got in there? You must've thought, boy, this is different.

177

EP: Well, it, uh, yes, it certainly was different, uh, and I really was kinda proud because to be able to get a job at the Steel company was quite an honor in those days.

I know, my uh, your next door neighbor, my grandmother, worked down at the Readington Test Center and they used to fire captured guns from the Germans and the Japanese at Bethlehem Steel Armor Plate. And she would go down and she would measure the damage that was caused by these captured guns and ammunition. Uh, so to make sure, yunno, that when they built something new, it would be adequately protected. And she loved her job, I mean she often said, "I coulda done that forever." But yunno, a lot of the women at the end of World War II, they gave all the jobs back to the guys that left the plant. It just, uh, it never caught on again for women till the '70s. And I've interviewed some of those women. So, what was your first job; which job were you in first?

EP: In my first job was in the Plate Shop, which was, um, as part of the safety shop and the trucking department, and it was directly across from the Lehigh Dispensary. So I started there, and then my, uh, career, I ended my career immediately across the street in the Lehigh Dispensary, so it was like, coming home.

You only moved like 200 feet, huh? Well yunno. The, the Plate Shop, now help me out, wasn't that somewhere around Number 4 Machine Shop?

EP: Yeah, it was um, right next to the carpenter shop.

All right. All right so.

EP: I think it, I think it was the old, maybe, they didn't call it Number 4 when I was there.

They didn't?

EP: No.

They didn't. Well, it's not, not that important. Uh, what exactly was your first job, what did you do?

EP: Uh, I did the clerical work. Um, it was an office that had all men, and I was the only girl, and I was the typist.

You were the typist. So you, you would probably ended up doin' more work in there than most of them guys.

EP: Well, they were busy, busy doing their own job.

Steady, steady. I mean they had their paperwork and everything to do. But as far as having something that was distinct. Typing. You were it.

EP: Oh that was it. Right.

You were it. How long were you in that shop?

EP: Well, I, whenever the merger was over at Number 6 Machine Shop. I don't really remember, uh, like years, uh, but uh, I would say probably about maybe, 5, 6 years.

OK. And then they had a merger with Number 6 Machine Shop?

EP: Number 6 Machine Shop. And I was there, maybe another 5 years.

Was it you'd stay in the same location the whole time, or did you move? After the merger?

EP: Uh, no, we moved over, we moved over to Number 6 machine shop.

OK you were in there. What floor were yous on?

EP: Well I was doin' a Flex-O-Writer, which was a typing machine. And uh, I also helped with shipping, and when the secretary to the superintendent was out, vacations, ill, whatever, I would do her job, and then also; um, I worked in the shipping department. So, there were about maybe six girls there, and um, I was like a filler-in.

Yeah. Now what year did you get married?

EP: I got married in 1948.

'48. So you musta been quite the celebrity in your time. Workin' with all those guys. Tell me a little bit about that.

EP: Well. Well, I'll tell you what, it certainly was an experience, because at one time there were like about 17 men coming, going all the time, and um, I learned a couple new words, let me tell you.

Yeah I bet, I bet you did. And I bet you heard some jokes you never thought you were gonna' hear.

EP: Yeah, you're right.

Cuz it was Bethlehem Steel.

EP: That's right, that's right. And in fact, yunno what, it was so unusual because, um, there was another girl that, because she was leaving, I guess that's why I was hired, and this man, it was my birthday, I don't even remember if it was the first year that I was there, but he wrote this little poem, and I lost track of that poem for 40 years, and this girl at our senior meeting gave me that poem.

You're kidding.

EP: Unbelievable. I have a copy of it at home.

Where did you go to High School?

EP: Liberty High School.

Liberty High School. You took the commercial courses? In typing and all that stuff?

EP: Yes I did. Shorthand. Um hmm.

That's something I wish, yunno I'll tell you what, one of the things I've really regretted in my lifetime is not being able to type well. And I had many opportunities to get into the typing classes. But you know back when I was goin' to school, you were sorta like, sorta like a sissy if you took typing.

EP: It wasn't a man's job.

But you know what. I had a couple buddies that took typing. And they were a lot smarter than I was, because they were in rooms full of girls, and I wasn't. And I often said, boy that was stupid, I shoulda taken that. But that's ...

EP: But you know what, I think in those days there were certain jobs that were for women, and certain jobs were for men. And if you crossed over, yunno, it was questionable for some, some people.

Yeah you're like, you like stood out in a crowd. OK. So uh, you're down Number 6 Machine Shop, uh, how long you were there before you moved on again?

EP: I'd say like maybe about 5 years or so.

Yeah and you went where?

EP: And then they merged with Number 2 Shop. So, didn't we realize that something's going on, that all these mergers we should've known that, we should've questioned, what is going on. But, we didn't.

Well. Did you get married before or after that merger with Number 2 shop?

EP: Oh Waaaay before. We were married in 1948.

'48. And the merger, the merger was after that. Yeah

EP: Yeah and I started in '42. Oh definitely, yeah.

OK. And where, where did you run into your husband?

EP: Uh, I met him at a dance because that was the popular thing to do in, in my day. And um, uh, every Saturday night you'd go to these different ethnic clubs and dance and he was a smooth dancer. And I loved dancing. And uh, I met him at this dance, and um, we went, a gang of girls, you, you didn't kinda' pair up so much like they do now. Uh, it was like a gang of girls went to the dance, a gang of boys went to the dance, and um, he asked to take me home, I said no, I came with the girls, I'm goin' home with the girls. And uh, he often tells the story that when ...

Did you all live in the area?

EP: Yeah, we all left, uh, lived in the area.

It sounded like you were walkin'.

EP: Yeah. Yes, definitely. Nobody had a car in those days. And um, when I left he said to his, uh, buddies; "Here's the girl I'm gonna marry." And, it came to pass.

You were married how many years?

EP: Before he passed away? 55 Years. 55 good wonderful years.

That's, that's amazing. And he worked in the Saw Shop, didn't he? He worked there the whole time?

EP: No he did not. He worked, when he first started.

His name was Joe, right?

EP: Yes. Uh, when he first started, he worked in, um, he worked in weldman; he worked at, uh, in the labor pool for a while, he worked at central tool, and then I guess the saw shop was a part of central tool.

Central tool, yeah, absolutely.

EP: So I think that's how he got transferred there. And he always said, "I found my home." He loved the saw shop; it was a very small shop, um, compared to central tool, and like weldman and stuff. And um, he, he was, he found his home at the saw shop.

I remember going down into the saw shop when I was workin' for the union. And it was just a great bunch ah guys there; it was only like, maybe 8, 9 or 10 guys workin' there; that was it.

EP: Right. I think at most it was about a dozen.

You work, you work steady day shift. The only time you ever worked Saturday or Sunday, is if they get steel in that was, blanks that were being cut the first time and it wasn't treated right. And uh, they'd have to keep up with the Combination Mill Saws, and the saws down at the Beam Yard, because without those saws down there that they made, and a lot of 'em right from the scratch, from blanks, uh, the steel mill wouldn't have operated; they would've never sent out a finished product. And there were a very few people that even know that steel would, was cut with a steel blade. Boy, I'll tell you what, when they cut there was some noise. There were noises, like, over a hundred decibels. And yunno, I always wore hearing protection myself. But still it, yunno, it still affected me.

EP: Yeah. Joe did, too. He always had ear protections.

Yeah you, you have to.

EP: And they would go periodically to the dispensaries, yunno, for the hearing for the hearing tests.

Yeah. Yeah. Yeah. I'll tell you what. So now you get down to the Number 2 Machine Shop. I guess it's right around 1950; what was that like?

EP: Oh no, it was longer than that. I would say it was in the '60s.

When you get down there Number 2 Machine Shop and …

EP: Cuz I, I left there, I left Number 2 Machine Shop to go to the dispensary. I think it was like maybe in 1969. So I was there several years at Number 2 shop.

OK. OK. And what did you do there?

EP: Well, again, being the merger, I was like the last girl that was sent down there with the result that, now that I think about it, I was too proud to say that I could not do a job, uh, if they, uh, wanted me to fill in anywhere. So, with the 7 girls that were there, whenever they went on vacation, I filled in. And uh, I don't know if that was a smart move or not, but, um, a lot of the other women that were asked to uh, do the job, they would say; "I don't know how to do it. I don't wanna' learn how to do it at this stage of the game." But I had too much pride. I didn't wanna admit that I could not do it. With the result that, I just moved from place to place.

OK. And uh, finally now you get up to your, how would you put it, your, your final area: the Lehigh Dispensary. That was like a miniature hospital, wasn't it?

EP: Definitely. They had like about maybe like about 6 beds or so. And uh, they uh …

And you always, you always prayed there was never anyone in it. That's true, that's one thing everybody knew. You didn't ever wanna be in a bed at the dispensary.

EP: Yeah. And I saw plenty there. There were some DOAs. And uh, we were very busy; we had, like, about maybe, uh, 6 lines, and then we also had a red hotline for the, uh, ambulance. And there were a lot of interesting cases down there. And they had quite a few doctors. I would say that maybe, when I came down there, there might've been like, at least 4 doctors. And then if they couldn't handle the case, if it was too severe or whatever, they would immediately send them up to St. Luke's.

OK So, so you were actually a record keeper down there for everyone that came through the door almost.

EP: A receptionist. Yeah. And the minute, yunno it was funny, but because the minute, um, anybody walked in the door, we already got used to their check numbers and all, and then, people would say, How do ya' do

182

that? How do you have their records out, yunno, before they're even sitting down in the chair.

Well, you remembered their names.

EP: Sure, sure. And uh, you know what uh, the people that came in there, they really had a lot of respect for you. Which, well most of the guys in that era were gentlemen.

Yeah. Now. What would you say the most prevalent accident you would run into in that dispensary? What was the big thing? Was it muscle strains and sprains, or, was it cuts and abrasions?

EP: I would say it probably was cuts and abrasions. Yeah.

I know I had a couple in my time. I'll never forget one time, I, I was putting a, a bearing race, in what they called the medart machine, and I put up a bar up against it, and I whacked it, and I thought I picked up a brass bar and I had not, I had picked up somethin' different, and this thing, piece chipped off it went right into my arm. I go down there and Doc Peters says, "Well." He says, "Here it is in the X-Ray. You see where it is?" He says; "Guess what?" He says; "It wouldn't be a good idea to take it out." He says; "Number 1" He says; "It's very slender. Less in diameter than a pin." He says; "Number 2, it's a high grade steel." He says; "It's not gonna' affect you too much and I don't think it's gonna' cause any damage." He said; "In fact I bet you if you came back here in a year, we won't even be able to find it." And that's exactly what happened, it sort of like dissolved or something.

EP: You mean did your body absorb it then?

Yeah, something like that. I, I was really surprised, because, yunno, I actually went back after 3 months and 6 months. To make sure, yunno, what was goin' on. And uh, he told me after 6 months he says, "This is breakin' apart." He says; "Look." He says; "It's in 3 pieces now."

EP: Yeah. Well, they follow ….

It was only like a half an inch long.

EP: Yeah they followed through.

Yeah. And then you know I had, uh, I had some crane accidents. I had a, a burn down there one time. I had a switch blow up in my face.

EP: You know another, um, injury.

And lemme' tell you what happened with that switch. They were treating me, OK, with uh, was it silverdine, it was for burns? It was a, it was a new type of a thing.

EP: Yeah. Right.

And a a friend of mine said look, he says, "You should be taking a whole bunch of vitamin E for this." I says; "I should?" He says; "Yeah." So, he says, "What will you do with it? He says; "Cut open these big pills, put 'em in a shot glass, "then take a Q-Tip, dip 'em in, and just brush 'em over the affected areas." So I started doin' this. I did it for a week and at that time I was coming back every 3 days to see the doctor in the dispensary. And Doc Peters looked at it and he says; "Boy, there's a remarkable improvement here; what's goin' on?" And I told him. He says; "Well!" He says; "I don't have any vitamin E here." He says; "But I'll have it here for you the next time you come in you won't have to buy anymore." I said, "Well, OK, yunno, that's what I'll do" and then, yunno, I recovered, but yunno if, if you look real close at my neck you'd still see the scar from it. Cuz it was a second degree burn. It melted my hard hat.

EP: Oh my gosh!

It melted my safety glasses onto my face. And I recovered from all that.

EP: Wow!

Yeah, it was just like a big flash ball goin' off. BOOM! That was it. And my buddy says, "Frank, are you OK?" And when he saw me, he says, "Whoa, we gotta' get you off this crane right away." Poor John Talbot.

EP: I remember John Talbot.

Took one look at, one look at me, he was the foreman, and he said; "Get in my car." He says, "We're not even callin' the ambulance." Took me right up to the dispensary. Yeah, that was really, that was really something. So you must've seen everything happen at the dispensary.

EP: Yeah. You know what? I think, uh, most of the cases were eye cases. Foreign, uh, objects in eyes.

Yeah, that was, that was tough. I had that too. I had that, I was workin' by the Beardsley Piper Grinder up in the alloy division and I got a, I got a piece come in underneath the side shield. The first thing they said, "Did you have them glasses on?" I said, "I did." I says, "And I got 3 or 4 witnesses." They said, "We're gonna' talk to 'em." I said, "Well, I expect you to." So, yunno, they were, they were careful about…

EP: And it had the side shields on?

Oh yeah, it still got underneath. It was just a freak accident.

EP: I'll be darned.

It was just like a one in a millionDid you ever work at that dispensary up there at the Lehigh Plant? I mean in the uh, alloy division?

EP: No. No.

OK. It was up in the end, back end of one bay. They had, uh, they used to have, like, 3 girls up there. Three women handling that. One, one did nothing but paperwork, the other 2 were nurses. But there was a lot a guys workin' there at the time. There was a lot of satellite dispensaries all over the plant.

EP: Yeah, they had the, the one down at Coke, Saucon, yeah.

So what's your fondest memory of Bethlehem Steel?

EP: Oh, my fondest, fondest memory is, I would say, I had a good life because of it. Uh, they uh, in those days, of course, the salaries were nothing compared to what they are today, but I think their friendships …

But they were usually, they were usually better than other places though.

EP: Oh definitely, definitely. Ah, but I would say probably all the friendships then that you made. Cuz I still, uh, see a lot of the women that I worked with. And we have a card club from the dispensary and, I see all those girls. And um, I, I think that was it, I think the friendships.

Yeah. Yeah that's, that's true. Uh, most of the people I talk to say. "Hey, I'd go back tomorrow. Yunno what I mean, if I needed a job."

EP: I would!

You think the plant coulda been saved?

EP: I certainly do.

Why do you say that?

WP: Well, I think that there were a lot of, uh, if the stories are true, uh, I think that there were too many what they called government jobs; yunno people, um, having things done, not paying for it, and um, I think they, maybe the salaries of the CEOs and all that other stuff, maybe were excessive. Certainly not what they are today. But, um, I would say that they could've been maybe like a little bit more conservative. And uh, definitely, a little more progressive. And I think if they would've been progressive, I think that, maybe the steel company could've been saved.

Well, the majority of people I talked to said, "When we came in there, an' started workin' in the '60s the place was like a junk yard, an' when we left it was still a junk yard. Because the, they never did anything with the equipment. There was no modernization.

EP: That's it.

The only areas that got modernization actually were the machine shops. That was about it; yunno, they didn't do too much in the other areas.

EP: How 'bout the BOF? That was about one of the newest things.

Well, that was one of the newest things, but we were also one of the last steel

companies in the United States to have one. Why? You gotta' ask yourself why.
EP: Why? Yeah.

But yunno, uh, like, most people are just tellin' me right out, they says, "Hey yunno what? We had a good time there; we liked going to work, because every day was a challenge, every day was different." You may have been a receptionist, OK, at the Lehigh Dispensary, but every day was different.
EP: Definitely.

And that is why people never got bored of their jobs. They never got bored of their jobs. Well, OK Elsie, I'd like to thank you for participating in this and, all the best to you.
EP: Thank you.

Thanks for showing up.
EP: Yeah. All right.

BOBBY ROBINSON
45 years of service

Central Labor Gang

Bobby Robinson, the father-in-law of heavy weight champion Larry Holmes, experienced everything that was bad about the Bethlehem plant as a man of color. Nonetheless, he prevailed in reaching the position of labor leader and finished with 45 years of service. Known throughout the plant for his jovial demeanor and exceptional memory.

* * * * * * * * * *

Today is February 29th, 2008, and we're here today with Robert Robinson. What did they call you in the plant? Did you have a nickname? Bobby?

BR: Bobby.

Ok, so we'll call you Bobby for this interview. Ok I see you started in 1951 back during the Korean War. How did you get to become a Bethlehem Steelworker?

BR: I was working with a contractor, tearing up trolley tracks, from the New Street gate into the plant. And we had got as far as the firehouse and putting a tunnel underneath where the fire trucks come in and out. And I got a call from my aunt that I had a letter from Bethlehem Steel. And I walked from there around to the main office and I put in an application.

How 'bout that? And at that time I would imagine that right in the middle of the Korean War, I mean how old were you at the time?

BR: 17, 18

Ok, all right, that explains everything. Did Uncle Sam grab you then?

BR: Right after I got married.

Ok, how 'bout that, what year was that?

BR: In 1952. I got married in 1951, and I went in the service in 1952.

Now your first day or your first week in the plant, tell me what it was like. A lot of people are saying that we were just amazed at all the accidents. What was it like for you?

BR: The first day of work in Bethlehem Steel was, I worked with a foreman, his name was George Wise, and I was at the Blast Furnace. I don't remember which one it was but I went over to the Blast Furnace.

That must have been like being in another planet?

BR: You better believe it.

I mean like coming from ripping up trolley tracks to working at the Blast Furnace.

BR: Working in the Blast Furnace

Like in a one week period, and what did you think of that?

BR: They took me up, I was afraid, because they took me up on the elevator and we had to go on a scaffold, to break the lining out of a furnace. Tearing the lining out of a furnace.

Yep. So you were up there with a crew then, huh?

BR: With a crew of about, I think. it was 8 or 10 men on a scaffold.

Was the furnace cooled down yet?

BR: Well, at that time it was cool around the top. But as we went down, it got hotter. And it was dirty.

That's almost like the same thing they tell you in church. Make sure you go up, don't go down (laugh), how 'bout that. How long were you on that job?

BR: I stayed there for three days, and George Wise took me off and put me on watching dynamite.

Watching dynamite? Where was that at?

BR: I had to sit around the Blast Furnace at the bottom and with the dynamite and another guy watched the caps.

Yeah, and this is what they were using at that time? To open the furnace?

BR: To open the furnace up.

That was before they had the mud gun and the drill I guess.

BR: Yeah, I guess that, ah, now that was, they were tearing the lining out, they were breaking the salamander and they had something else they were doing with dynamite. And all I had to do was sit there and watch the dynamite.

Sounds like a good job.

BR: It was the best job I had the whole time I was in Bethlehem Steel.

Now, you were in the labor gang, right? The plant labor gang? That was CSL?
BR: Right, CSL.

Okay, so you effectively worked everywhere in that plant?
BR: Everywhere.

Can you think of an area that you didn't work in?
BR: No.

That's really saying something, I have only a few people that I've interviewed so far that can say that. Now, scheduling, how was the scheduling when you started?
BR: We worked 5 and 6 days a week. It was first week day shift, next week middle shift, and then night shift. At that time, that's the way it went. But, as time went on, the scheduling changed. You worked two days one shift, and two days the next shift.

Yeah, and I would imagine that when you started in '51, '52, you were working with guys that had been there long before the union was in place. And I'm sure you must have heard some dandy stories about the organizing efforts.
BR: Well, not too many, but they did say that the union was no good; they didn't want the union in there. A lot of guys didn't want to belong to the union.

Well, I know there were still some provisions in the early '50s where you could actually get out. You remember that?
BR: No, I don't. I think I was in the washroom and somebody came in and signed me up for the union and they told me I had to belong to the union in order to work there.

Yeah, that was probably right after they had the provision for the closed shops. But I know there was a contract provision in the early '50s that actually allowed you to get out of the union.
BR: Somebody did tell me, I think, along around that time that I was going to get in trouble for signing up to be in the union. I don't remember who it was or how it was said. I know a lot of guys didn't want to sign it.

Now I was gonna say this, after 44 years there, seriously, do you think you wanted to work there without the union?
BR: No.

That's, well, that's, I'm glad to hear you say that, because I haven't had anyone say yes yet. And that would have really, now where would I have gone from that one? I don't want to, I don't like to edit any of these things. I like to put down everything people are talking about. So working in schedules like that and things like that, would you say the schedule was like pretty steady? Or, was it steady for a period of time and then it got a little rocky, because I'm sure you had a young family?

BR: It was a little rocky at times, the night shift I didn't want to work and sometimes I had to work night shift.

And those jobs were usually jobs that had to be done or they wouldn't schedule them night shift, right? Give me some examples of what they were.

BR: Like furnaces, hot furnaces. And sometimes they would call you out if they had a furnace go down in the middle of a shift and they didn't have enough men to work, they would call you to come in on a different shift then you were on. You were scheduled on night shift, they would call you to come in middle shift instead. They had to get this furnace done.

So they'd be calling on you for a double shift, is what they'd be doing.

BR: A double shift, you could be working a double shift, whatever you wanted to work.

Now the '50s we're still talking open hearth days here. Ah, give me the procedure for knocking them bricks out of that open hearth. How did that go? Cuz I know that was a hot job. And there were very few people that, I haven't talked to anybody about doing this. You're the first guy. So describe that to me.

BR: It was a scary job. You had to walk on top of the furnace sometimes while the heat was in there, before they tapped the last heat. You walked on top of the furnace, on the beams, with a long bar, and knock a hole in the top of the furnace. So as soon as the heat was tapped, and they'd load with scrap, you could run a cable up through there, and the crane would catch it and pull the roof and drop it right down on all the scrap. That was the way they did a quick roof job. They had these heavy cables.

In other words, the bricklayers were then coming in after that and they were bricking that back up?

BR: Well, yeah, the bricklayers come in after that.

What exactly did you guys do when you removed the brick, how did that go?

BR: We had to go in there with wooden shoes.

Wooden shoes? People told me they actually caught on fire.

BR: They caught on fire.

So you had to be quick.

BR: You had to jump in there and stay 5 or 10 minutes, whatever it was, and throw as many brick out as you could, and run out and put water on your shoes, wooden shoes, to put them out, they would be burning.

And how many guys did they have like in, did they do this like a relay? So many guys at a time, the other guys are outside?
BR: They had three gangs, about five or six men on each gang. Six men go in and throw brick out, and for 10 minutes or 15 they come out, six more go in. They come out, then six more would go in.

So in an hour's time if you were doing a job like that, what would you say, you'd be in the furnace for like 20 minutes out of the hour?
BR: About 20 minutes out of an hour, something like that.

You must have seen people get overcome in those situations.
BR: Yes, I've seen people pass out from the heat. In fact, it happened to me a couple of times.

In fact the number one priority then was to get them out of the furnace. What about water and salt tablets and things like that, how did you guys do that?
BR: You had to take salt tablets, you didn't have to but they provided them for you. They had salt tablets there and they would make some people sick. Yeah, guys would be throwing up all over the place from those salt tablets.

Yeah, I started in the alloy division in '65 and the old timers told me right out "We don't know if these salt tablets work, but we do know that half the people that take them get sick." The best thing you could do, and I was working on the bunk furnaces up in the, above the 35-inch mill, and that was a hot job, but that was sort of like what you had. You only went up there, you know, once or twice in an hour. You usually weren't up there for more than 5 to 10 minutes. You had a big book, you had sometimes a silver suit on, you had the face mask, the shield, to take the heat off you, and you had these long hooks, and you'd be maneuvering chains and loading red hot steel in or taking hot steel out. It was a really something. It was an experience for a young guy like me right out of high school. It was the same thing for you.
BR: I wanted to quit many a times.

Yeah, but every time you came home you saw the wife and the kids, right, you said, "Hey, wait a minute, nobody's going to put this food on the table." All right, how long did it take before you got yourself into a position where you didn't have to do work like that?
BR: Oh, it took quite some time.

Had to be in the late '60s for sure because that was the end of the...

BR: Well, I went in service and when I come out it was just about different. It was different foremen, leaders, there then. They had leaders at that time and they were different. With George Wise it was, you had to go, he was old, he was one of the older foremen there, and with the other guys, they had cold jobs then, like breaking concrete and stuff like that. You got with one of those leaders that didn't have to work the hot furnaces, you were much better off. They had special crews to work in hot furnaces, they were used to hot work, they could stand it.

And, did they or how would you put that? Give those guys preferential treatment or anything like that? Did they give them a better schedule or how did they do that?
BR: heh, heh, heh…

Or was that just a matter of whom you knew?
BR: It was a matter of who you knew at that time.

Ok, that doesn't surprise me, I mean I went through that myself.
BR: Being me, I got the dirt jobs, whatever come along. If it was dirtier, I got that.

Well, let's put it to you this way. As a man of color, you feel as though they sorta like "Well, we'll give it to Bobby." Right? "Bobby'll do it."
BR: It was a lot of prejudice in the Steel.

Well, I have to ask these questions, you understand that? I mean people don't know.
BR: They were prejudice, yes.

How long would you say it was until you got yourself into a position where you could do just about anything you wanted in the department?
BR: When I got, it was during the time that we moved from Lehigh Plant to Saucon, and that was in the '70s or '80s. And I got with bricklayers and laborers were combined, with Ron Merkle and that's when, or wasn't it with the Coke Works? I believe it was the Coke Works when I got a janitor's job. I'll never forget the day. We were putting in the new car tip. We had just started working down there and we come up to Saucon dispensary for x-rays, chest x-rays. And I was kidding with the guys, "I'll be the only one going back; everyone else will stay." And everybody else went back but me. They found something, a spot on my lungs. And when they found the spot, they told me I had TB, and they treated me for two years, 19 pills a day. And one night I swallowed a fish bone at home and went to the hospital and the doctor told me, he says "Did you know you had this problem?" I said "what problem?" He said "you have a tumor." I said they

told me I had TB. He said "You don't have TB, you have a tumor, I can take it out." And Dr. Herman took that tumor out of my back.

And Bethlehem Steel told you you had TB?
BR: Bethlehem Steel told me I had TB.

Were you working at the time?
BR: Yeah

And you remained at work?
BR: I remained at work, until I went in the hospital and had this tumor taken out. And when I went back, I got a janitor's job. And, I cleaned at the rigger building and then they put me in the washroom right across from the rigger building and then they brought me up right behind the dispensary, they put me up there. For the last 15 years Ron Merkle put me in the office as a working leader and I would go out on jobs sometime and then most of the time I was in the office answering telephone and doing whatever I had to do in the office.

So effectively you reached a point working for Bethlehem Steel where you became like the elder statesmen.
BR: Right.

Well, there's nothing wrong with that, believe me. You know everybody always used to say "Well one day I'm going to be an old timer and I'll have it good." And you know, I got cut off at the knees, because, you know, I started in '65, you started in '51 so you actually had a chance to put in your time and get out where I, ah, they gave me the boot. I went out on the end of their foot. But you know what, it still wasn't a bad place to work?
BR: No, it was a nice place to work.

Then most guys that I talked to said the same thing, we really miss the guys. And one of the things we liked about coming in there was there was something different going on every day. You couldn't get bored.
BR: I'll tell you one thing I'll never forget, I put in for transfers to get out of the labor gang and I looked back one day as I walked out of the office, I passed the transfer to the A.T. Roberts, he was my superintendent, he was general foreman. And I passed it to him and he looked at it and I walked out of the office, and something said look back, and I looked back and (laughs) he ripped it up (laughs).

Where were you trying to transfer to?
BR: I wanted to go to the trucking department.

Oh, okay. What year we talking about here?

BR: Oh, I don't remember the year but A.T. Roberts was the general foreman.

Was it back before the Consent Decree?

BR: I really don't, I don't remember.

Cuz you know before the Consent Decree you actually needed permission from your superintendent to transfer.

BR: Well he was the superintendent; no Bill Moore was the superintendent.

All I'm saying is at one time you needed permission from your superintendent to transfer. When the Consent Decree came along, ok, that went out the window. They couldn't stop you from moving then.

BR: Well they stopped me. During that time if you were black you didn't get out of anything that you wanted to get out of. If you wanted to move, they wouldn't let you move. And somewhere along the line I do remember they even paid us, all the blacks in Bethlehem Steel, they gave 'em, I think I got $2,000 for being held back from going to a different place.

Yeah, that was…that was the Consent Decree at that time. That was, uh, I hate to say this to you because you know what you went through but, believe it or not, the Bethlehem plant was probably one of the better plants, as far as, you know, blacks.

BR: Maybe.

I know I probably couldn't convince you of that because of what you went through but I talked to guys from Sparrows Point, I talked to guys from Lackawanna, you know, black guys, and they told me "Boy you don't want to be around here." I mean down at Sparrows Point it was really bad, it was really bad. And, they actually came in there, in fact the guy that was very instrumental with that was Marvin Miller, who became the head of the baseball union. And, Marvin Miller was actually running that case. It was gonna go up in front of the Supreme Court, and the company said, "Wait a minute, there's no way in the world we can win this. We have to reach an agreement." And that's what they called it; it was the Consent Decree, which was an agreement they said, "Here's what we're going to do from this day on, and here's what we're going to do for the people whether or not they had problems or not, we're going to pay them." And that was like a negotiated settlement. Of course, you never get enough, for the crap you had to go through.

BR: No (laughs).

Well, let me ask you something then Bobby. When did you actually realize the plant was in trouble? When did you first know that things weren't going right?

BR: I never knew the plant was in trouble.

No?

BR: No.

You were sort of like insulated from that?

BR: Right. Right, I thought everything was going smooth.

Yeah, and you left in '95, right? Or was it '96?

BR: '96.

That's a lot of time, 44 and a half years. But you know if, when you think about it, if the plant was still going, right now I would have 42 years myself. But you know what the queen said "Balls if I had them, I could be king." If you had a chance in your time there at Bethlehem Steel to do something, to make that a better place to work, what would it have been?

BR: Oh Lord, that's a question, I....

Well, some people told me they thought there were too many foremen. Some people I talked to said "Hey they always played favorites."

BR: It was too many foremen who didn't know what they were doing. I have had foremen to come to me and ask me "How would you do this job? What do we have to do to get this out?" See I worked with quite a few of the old foremen down there. Benny Silvetz. In fact we were just talking about him a few minutes ago from Consilium. He showed me how to take a jackhammer and run underneath steel in a furnace in order to get it out. He took the jackhammer and ran it and some guys filed grievance against him for working. You know, a lot of guys filed grievance against a foremen when he would take a tool in his hand. And Benny Silvetz said, "Let him file." And he ran it down and showed me how to do it. And it was one time there when Benny Silvetz left the job. He said he had to go to a meeting and he said, "You are the oldest man here on the job. I don't care who you are but the oldest man takes over the job until I come back. I'll be gone for two or three hours and you're the boss until I come back." And that didn't go over so good with the guys that had maybe six months less than me.

Well, thank God we have seniority. It may not have been the best thing we ever had but I don't know if we could have operated in that plant without it. I think it would have really, really goofed things up. Well, I'll tell you what, it's been a real pleasure talking to you.

BR: Sometimes even with seniority, it didn't help you; you still got the dirtiest jobs.

Yeah. So, in your opinion, what's the number one thing you miss about the plant?

BR: I just miss the faces.

Yeah, the guys.

BR: The faces, being with the guys.

Yep. I guess you know when you're working in the conditions that you worked under, especially in the early years and stuff like that, you really get to know people. And when you're working all those extra shifts, you people talk. You probably knew more about some families than their own relatives knew, because you were with them every day. Well, I'll tell you what, these stories that you tell put a face on what it was like being a laborer at Bethlehem Steel, because I told you earlier, I said I'm writing this book to dispel the beliefs that all we ever did was cook on middle shift and sleep on night shift.

BR: Oh, I did some cooking (laughs).

Well, there's nothing wrong, there's nothing wrong with feeding yourself. But then again, you know, middle shift isn't a normal shift nor is night shift. And I talked to many guys down at the beam yard that said, "When we had steel to pile, when we had steel to pile, we piled steel." We were glad there was a pot of sauerkraut and hot dogs on the stove because we didn't know when we were going to get in there to eat. Lot of times when we came in if somebody wouldn't have brought that in we never touched our lunch because that's how much work there was.

BR: Right, and some of the leaders would come in, you know, I would stay in the, I'd take care of the tool room sometimes and the office, have a pot of sauerkraut, as you say, and hot dogs on when they'd come in, on for lunch time, everybody had a roll and a hot dog and sauerkraut, they had something hot to eat. And they enjoyed it, and I'd take care of the time sheets for 'em and straighten things out and it was nice.

Yep, that's good, I'm glad you had good memories of it. You know, I think all of us have good memories, it was just a lot of us we feel that maybe got a little shortchanged like we should still be there working. But you know what, the best laid plans of mice and men. Well, thanks a lot Bobby, I'm glad to have interviewed you and I wish you the best for you and your family.

BR: Thank you.

You got it.

PAULA SCHNAUFFER
8 years of service

Central Labor Gang, Plant Patrol

Known as "the Keeper," as a plant patrolman she carried enough keys to sink a battleship. She looked like a jail guard with all these keys weighing her down. In addition, she was not hard to look at, hence, in steelworker language, "a real keeper."

* * * * * * * * * *

Today is March 10ᵗʰ, 2008; we're talking to Paula Schnauffer; Paula how ya doing today?

PS: Good, Frank, how 'bout you?

I'm doing real well. Uh, I see here we have you listed here as having no nickname. Was that common with the women, no nickname?

PS: I can't recall really nicknames on the girls that were said to our face. Except for bad mouth, of course, bad mouth Barbara.

Well, she was a legend, and we'll be talking to her later on. Now, I'm looking here and I see that you were hired in 1975; a lot of our women came in that time. In fact it was more than the 20-year period we had no women in the plant at all. And you came in here as a laborer. Tell me what it was like your first day on the job? How did you get hired at Bethlehem Steel?

PS: I think I just put in a general application hoping I would be called into the main office, and they had jobs, such as escorts that would help out, kind of like a receptionist and tour guide and, I just thought it would be a neat, glamorous job and make good money, but at that time they were hiring women for the first time as you stated, and when I got called back down to Human Relations I was offered CSL or the Coke Works. I didn't know which either one of these jobs were, but I had a lot friends that worked at the Steel. My fiance worked there, and he explained to me CSL is something they would call company slave labor, and the Coke Works, he just said don't go there, cuz just the fumes will turn ya, you know make you sick, but go for it. You know, you can make new money and it's something new, and that's what you want to do, so I was up for it.

So what happened when you finally told him I'm gonna go with CSL?

PS: Well, he knew that they would come into his plant at the 12-and 18-inch mill, and when the mill was down they would do the maintenance that their own labor crew wouldn't do, um, cleaning out the sluiceways underneath the rolling mills, um, just general gooky dirty labor.

And uh, you got, I guess, a real rude awakening when they took ya for your safety down the Hajoca building. I mean, what'd ya think of those shoes when you first saw em?

PS: I felt like Frankenstein. I chose the ones with the metal tarsels on the outside, and uh, the safety glasses were really cute too with the sides and my helmet, and you know you could wear what you wanted, and everybody wore t-shirts and jeans, unless you worked at the blast furnace. We would clean out the worm screws on the top, and the iron oxide would get jammed up, and we'd have to wear a special jumpsuit, special boots, special cream on our face so your skin wouldn't turn that red color. And it was still funny; there'd be a group of us girls working there, and we'd have the boots and the jump suits, and even the size small I think was made for a large man, and our helmets and the cream all over us and gloves, and we'd go for our break, and the guys would come by and still whistle at us, and I'd go, how do you know? As long as I kept a sense of humor, it was all right.

Well, steelworkers are steelworkers, let's face it, you know.

PS: Right, right.

Like most men, you know, they're pigs at heart, they can't help it. They see a fireplug and they lift their leg. But that's the way it was at the Bethlehem Steel. But everybody always formed close relationships with everyone else. It's been my experience for the very simple reason is everybody was in it together. And the name of the game was to get in there on your shift and get out the same way ya come in. You don't want to have missing fingers, missing toes, broken ribs, burns, or anything like that. So I guess safety played a big part in whatever you did there in the labor gang.

PS: Right. We were taught, we went to gas school, because a lot of our jobs would be going into the soaking pits, and we would reline the furnaces there, and they would do a gas check ahead of time, and it would be so hot, you were only allowed 20 minutes in, so uh, they would give you wooden shoes to wear over your safety shoes, so your shoes wouldn't start on fire. And heaven forbid you had studs on your jeans, cuz you'd get branded, or a lighter would ignite, and we would just do the job, 20 minutes in 20 minutes out, before you knew it, you had your eight hours in, and once in awhile we'd get a chance for an extra shift, and it was, I think you got paid what was called hot time or something, extra pay for that job?

Well, I'm not aware of that, but you know, that wouldn't surprise me at all. It might have been a different incentive for that job. You know, that they paid on that particular job. So I guess that was a real treat working in that heat. But then again, you worked in the cold too, what about that?

PS: Right, um, I just remembered the winds. I would go in the Bessemer Street gate to go to my, that was the lady's welfare room for the labor girls, and it was a re, it used to be a men's change room, and what they did was they painted the windows, blackened them out on the outside, and um, that long walk past the Blast Furnaces and the bridge there, you just get terrible winds, terrible. It was just so cold, and you just hurry out. There was a bus running, a shuttle bus, but at that time the steel was so busy, that you were lucky to get a parking place, and you would never get a ride on the bus.

So you ended up walking from the main gate, is that what you're saying?

PS: I would walk from the Bessemer Street gate.

Okay, I know what you're talking about now, down alongside the machine shop. And then your washroom was where?

PS: Uh, it was across the bridge off to the left, I think Number 2 Machine Shop.

Okay, I know abut where you mean. It might have been over in the Press Forge area.

PS: And then we'd follow that little, there was a little walkway down the bridge, and then we'd cross over that to go to our tool room. That's where we'd meet then in the morning. So you had quite a walk, quick get change and run down there, and you were supposed to be there 15 minutes before your shift started, so you'd race, and then at night when you come back the shower's felt so good, and then of course you could never catch the shuttle bus to go out, and if it was a night shift, you'd walk across that bridge and your hair would freeze. I had long hair, always had long hair, and your hair would freeze til you made it to your car, and…

Now, because you're a woman, I understand there were some incidents in those shower areas that weren't quite right. You wanna tell me a little bit about that?

PS: Well, as you said boys will be boys and pigs at heart. I guess um, some of 'em figured out where the welfare room was for us women, and they got a pile of pallets and scratched off the paint, cause it was painted from the outside, and we heard later on through the grapevine that there was a secret rating system that we were being spied on. But, uh, you know, we just reported it, nothing was done, um, a few weeks later they did paint the windows on the inside this time to insure our privacy, but the damage was already done.

How did they even find out about this?
PS: I believe it was probably Barbara that found out. She knew. You know, and they would tell her, and she had it in with the guys, and then she told us, and it didn't bother her one bit, but like I said I was very naïve, and it was just a shock to me and just didn't know who was doing the peeking and all, but oh well.

Well, that's just a part of being part of the plant, that's all it was. I guess, what else can we say about it, you know. There's nothing else to say. So what were some of the jobs you did in the plant?
PS: We would do a lot of shoveling; we would begin, if they'd have construction, we would be on the demolition crew to start the foundations for various pier buildings, so it was shoveling and a lot of times blasting, dynamite blasting, uh, we would run jack hammers, hand tools.

So you were a 21 or 22 year old woman at the time running a jackhammer? That must have been a treat.
PS: That job I liked, because that's your typical picture of a construction worker running the jackhammer, you know there'd be a big hearty strong person, but I found out that the jackhammer does the job, you just hold it. You don't hold onto the handles, or you'll bounce around. You lightly hold it and let the jack hammer do its job, and you would change the bits to the different lengths until you got to the desired lengths. But I remember one time working in front; we were working with the riggers, construction, doing a building; you would go in the Emery Street gate. I don't recall exactly which building, but it was a pier building we were putting up, and I was happily doing the jack hammer and minding my own business, and before I knew it, I stopped and looked up, and my friend the rigger was taking up a collection with his helmet, and there was a group of guys standing around, and I'm there, I was used to sometimes getting looked at, but this time it was a whole gang, and I was exacerbated, and I said what are you looking at, aren't you used to us by now? I forgot I wore a Mickey Mouse t-shirt, and they just said we're watching Mickey Mouse's ears wiggle and we're gonna take up a collection, which I just laughed; it was just harmless boy, you know, boys club fun.

So they literally thought you were putting on a show for 'em right? All right, that's really something. So, actually then jackhammer was one of the better jobs you did, because you actually enjoyed it.

PS: Right and you could accomplish something. You could see from the start to the end of a building. Now there were other jobs, like I said, the slush ways where you would go down when the mills were closed down and we'd clean out the grease, and you'd be shoveling grease all day, and the more you shoveled, the more grease would ooze in, and you could never get it off your boots, your clothes, your shovel, and it was just a whole day, and I don't know if we accomplished much, but the next day the mill would be back and running, and thank you very much.

So that fell under the category of some one of the worse jobs you did, huh? And you worked hand and hand with the guys on that gang. I mean how did that work out? I mean, did everybody like treat each other equally, or? Because that was a period of time you know in the country when women were basically saying, hey, uh, we can do that, too. You know, if you want to pay us the same, we can do the same kind of work. How did the guys treat ya?

PS: Well, I learned from the example of Barbara, who worked very hard and earned the respect of the men, that I was gonna do the same thing. If I was gonna put up with them saying hey hey, you know, what are you doin' here? You can't do this job. Equal job, equal pay, and that's what I tried to do. Now there were some girls that were hired that would last a day, and they were the princesses, and you know, they just wouldn't last.

Yeah, they just weren't cut out for the real life that involved being a steelworker. Okay, so a, that gives us a pretty good feel. I mean, you were actually treated just equally.

PS: I think they were hiring a lot of young minorities also at the time. I worked with a lot of maybe men that wouldn't get a chance for advancement, sub foreman, a lot of minorities, and I think they felt like they were in the same place that some of us women were, that this was their time to you know get equal pay for equal work, and uh, as long as they were in our age group, I would say like from 19 to 30, we had no problems. Maybe the older guys, some of them would want to take us under their wing and bring us like something their wife made for lunch, and, you know then they would get teased if they treated us like almost like a daughter or a granddaughter or something. Others just stayed away.

Yeah, but you must have had some guys in there that were real jerks though, or would you say that the incidence was pretty low compared to how the other people treated ya?

PS: I really can't recall any jerks, but I think that's because I was, after I started the Steel, about a year later I married a steelworker, and I was friends with a lot of people in the Steel, and they knew me, and uh, we socialized together, because steelworkers had to socialize together. If you're working all three shifts, you know, you didn't have much time with people that were on regular shifts. So we played softball I can remember down in, I think it was off Auburn Street in Allentown; there was a softball league, and there were a lot of picnics, and we'd get together with the other men and their wives that understood, you know, how it was to work at the Steel. You really. A Tuesday could be like a weekend if you were off a Tuesday and Wednesday, would be like somebody's Saturday and Sunday. So you know Tuesday, sometimes after a night shift everybody would go to Stahley's or…

Well, there was a lot of camaraderie there, and from doing these interviews, I'm finding out that number one thing people missed were their friends at the Steel. I mean they, they're devastated by that, that the people that they worked side by side with for 20/30 years, they haven't seen 'em in 10 or 12 years now. How about your bosses, how'd they treat ya?

PS: I didn't really have a problem with the bosses. Um, like I said we get down to our tool room, and they'd separate us, and we'd go off in the blue trucks with the benches and go to the work site, and as long as we did the job, we didn't have a problem. And safety was number one, um, like I said in something else, uh, one of the shifts I was working at, I was working on plant patrol at the time, but the soaking pits I was talking about, the retaining wall fell down and killed two of the sub foreman that were on that job, and you know, it was always, you know, you couldn't be mad, you had to look out for your buddy, and you had to be aware of safety. And we'd have a chart up. I think every building had a safety chart, how many days they'd gone without an accident? And that was very important. And I remember the only time that I had, like, I would never miss work because they would watch you twice as hard, you know make sure you didn't miss anything, and I was on a job, and I believe one of the couplings from hydraulic hose came off and banged my finger, and it split the fingernail, not broke my fingernail, it split the fingernail right down, and it was very painful, I went to the dispensary, and I was off the next day, when I came back to my tool room they were mad at me because this was a day of an incident, an accident, and they wrote down Paula broke her fingernail, which sounds like a woman, oh my God I broke my fingernail that it would be something petty like this, but this was, you know, the finger was smashed and it took awhile for the nail to grow back.

So you lasted there on CFL roughly three years, and now I see you became a member of the plant patrol. How did that happen?

PS: I was always checking the postings, and I saw that they had an opening on plant patrol, and I applied, and I took the test, and that was very interesting; you had to see if you could see any differences, and they would show you pictures, what's missing, what's different, just your powers of observation, and they said it would mostly be loss prevention, you would be stationed at the gates, and uh, you would patrol the gates and the grounds with a walkie talkie and a clock to / certain keys. Um, you had to be trained, you would go along with the ambulance, you were trained in gas school, any kind of emergency that would come up at the Steel; you would go along with the fire department, because they were self-contained. We had our own fire department, our own hospital that was almost like a state-of-the-art dispensary hospital. Ours was a police force, even if the police wanted to come in to talk to somebody, they had to come through our office first. So I thought this would be something I would be interested in.

And were you assigned to a particular location? What was your first assignment with the plant patrol? What gate were you at?

PS: I never had a regular gate. I always worked all three shifts, all holidays, all weekends; that's just the way it was, but I was used to that because that's the same way CSL was, you know the seniority, if you didn't have the seniority you would work those schedules.

And your husband was working basically the same as you, right, every shift there was?

PS: Right, but we weren't on the same shift ever, it was a swing shift.

It was back and forth.

PS: Right, right.

I see. Now, the plant patrol was mostly involved like in theft prevention and things like that. So give me a classic, a shift, what would you be doing on one particular day? Let's say you're out Saturday middle shift, what would happen?

PS: Um, Saturday middle shift, I could be stationed at any of the gates; um, you would be there at shift change.

Would you be an add-on, or would you be the only person there?

PS: Um, some of the gates were two person gates, um a lot of'em were one person gates, some of them were only open during the shift change, and then you would go on patrol or do something else.

Yeah. When you were on patrol, what did that mean? Were you driving around?

PS: No, um, the men with seniority drove around. The only time I would drive the vehicle is on my break, they would come relieve me, and I could take the vehicle to go to a lady's room or a welfare room, because there wasn't, there weren't many places for women to take a break at that time, or I'd get back to the office and I'd bring the blue Suburban back.

So that must have been interesting work though? Because you were everywhere.
PS: Everywhere. I mean everywhere from the beginning, was that Second Street gate, or Taylor Street gate was the…

The gate furthest west was Second and Adams, that was up at the merchant mill, and then the furthest one out would have been down at East Lehigh.
PS: Right; there was the East End gate, there was a gate that was called the North gate, and that was, there was a lot of deer and wildlife, that was a very open area.

That was East Lehigh.
PS: That was beautiful. We would call that the North gate though, that was beautiful.

Yeah, we often got down in that area; in fact I worked in that area for a while. So you actually worked everywhere then when you were on the plant patrol?
PS: Everywhere, and the keys were all over. Some of the keys were in buildings that were even, um, at that time vacated. I think it was Number 2 High House? I'd go in with this little clock and a walkie talkie and my little flashlight on night shift, and I'd have to open up the freight elevator to get upstairs. There was a key upstairs, and they were worried about fires, so there was a key way at the end, and the electricity you'd have to turn on like that, and of course at night all the cats would be sleeping and there'd be pigeons up there, so the minute you came up everything went jumping, you'd jump. I can't remember, ya know, so many times things would just frighten me; it'd be a cat or a pigeon, but I never for some reason when I think back, I never had any fear, and I think now today with, I don't know if it's just cuz I was young and, I'm not gonna say dumb, but I was trusting. I never had any fear. Now today if I think about doing that or having my daughter do that, I would say, ah, this is a different world, you know, you can't do that.

Now during your time on the plant patrol, uh, did you ever get the feeling that all of this was going to come to an end? Were people talking about the plant, it doesn't look good for the plant or anything like that? Did you ever have an inkling that one day you wouldn't have a job there?
PS: There were always rumors. There were always rumors of like a

black Friday or black Monday and layoffs. And I know working on CSL there was a lot of times I would get laid off; um, we'd always get called back. So the layoffs were part of the jobs, but you would always get called back, and what I found out when I went on plant patrol, I was still eligible to go back to the union job, which was plant patrol, or CSL, but on plant patrol I was union non-exempt, I think? So I was, if I got laid off on plant patrol, I went back and worked on CSL, and I think later on they found out that I wasn't allowed to do that; you weren't allowed to jump from union non-exempt, or I don't know.

Yeah, well, I don't recall anyone from the plant patrol coming back into the plant once they were on.
PS: I did.

I'm not gonna say that it never happened, but uh …
PS: I did though.

So how did all this come to an end, your time at Bethlehem Steel?
PS: Well, you could see the parking lots empty, and um …

You could see it coming gradually you mean?
PS: Gradually, the gates at shift change, the crowd, the offices that would empty out at 5 o'clock at the main gate where you'd have so much traffic. I used to do the, direct the traffic; it'd be like doing traffic in the middle of New York City in Times Square, and eventually it was just you know a few people working there, so you could see it coming, and um, there were rumors, but I know when the time finally came, we were offered a severance package, and since I was used to being laid off and back and forth, and you know I saw other guys laid off and they be called back, I didn't take the severance package, I thought well, this is just a slump, the economy's slow, this will get rolling again, but it never did.

So you had recall rights for what a period of time?
PS: Right, I didn't want to sign off. That scared me when they said if you take severance, you'll never have recall rights, and I thought why would I do that? You know, this, you can't close Bethlehem Steel.

Well, you know, the company had a long history of only telling you what they wanted you to know, so you know, you don't ever have to feel bad about that decision, because they didn't tell anybody when they were, you know, losing their job what was going on, very seldom. The only time we would ever hear anything like that is if there was gonna be a shut down for a specific repair, and then, you know, we would have an actual date when we were gonna come back. So finally it did come to an end, when was that? About?

PS: Maybe for me it was in '78, nope.

No, it would have been in...
PS: '82.

Yeah. Okay, so you actually got laid off in '82, did not take the severance.
PS: No, but they offered us job retraining. If you didn't take severance, they would pay for you to go back to school to be retrained in another skill.

And did you take advantage of that?
PS: Yes I did.

And you went for what?
PS: Computer programming.

Good for you.
PS: That was the up and coming career path, and I know a few of the men I worked with took the computer programming course, and um, I finished top in my class, and I didn't even get out of school when a head hunter came from Pentela Data, now Pencorp, they hired me as their first woman programmerMy son was one and a half at the time, and um ...

Was your husband still working?
PS: No, he was laid off before I was. For a short time he stayed home with my son, because I worked up until I had my son, because I felt safe at the Steel; that was on plant patrol; we had an ambulance, we had access.

Yeah, you didn't have to worry about anything radically happening.
PS: No, no, I was in a good place. And a lot of times on middle shift I wouldn't have to do a lot of the patrolling, they allowed me and there was one other girl on middle shift that would be the radio desk relief. And that was the first time I think that they let women work the radio desk, which I found really exciting. You were in charge of all the hits, each plant patrol would call in; they had a certain time that they would make hits. You would be in charge of all the communication with fire, ambulance, and I remember on middle shift every now and then Dick Adams would come in.

He was actually your boss right?
PS: Dick Adams, I think, was the CEO or something like that.

Well, he was the head of Human Resources was what he was. And I know he was in charge of the plant patrol.
PS: We wouldn't see him very often, but every now and then he would come in, and I think he kind of got a kick out of seeing me on the radio

desk, because that was something he hadn't seen.

Ever.

PS: Right, right.

I guess Dick's selling real estate now. I'm hoping I can get a hold of him to interview him. Now you really did a really good of explaining what you did here, and uh, you finally got laid off some time you know in '82, it's not important when. Have you ever told this story to anybody?

PS: Um, after you knew that the Steel was never gonna start up again, there seemed to be a lot of interest in putting out books, and there was a documentary on PBS, the Bethlehem Steel, and I saw an article in the "Morning Call" if anybody has any steel memories, and I wrote basically just a brief outline, and gave them my address and phone number, email, get in touch with me I can tell you more. No one ever contacted me, and I don't think I've ever read anything about a woman's experience at the steel until you asked me, Frank.

I'd like to thank you for your time today Paula, it was a real treat.

PS: Thank you Frank.

KAROL KEGLOVITZ
20 years of service

East Lehigh Roll Foundry

Karol was hired at Bethlehem Steel on a dare from her girlfriend. Known for her ability to adapt to any situation, Karol was one of the best crane operators ever in the Roll Foundry. She took great pride in doing jobs others passed over.

* * * * * * * * * *

Today is October 28, 2008. We're here with Karol Keglovitz. Karol, how you doin' today?

KK: I'm fine thank you.

Karol, did you have a nickname in the plant?

KK: Karol.

Karol, that's okay, that's okay. Most people had nicknames. Some nicknames were good, some weren't so good.

KK: I'm sure I got called a few names, but not to my face.

Okay, Karol, now I see here you started in the plant back in April of 1979. Tell me how you got to become a Bethlehem Steel worker?

KK: Well, I was just out of high school maybe a year and half, and my girlfriend saw in the newspaper where Bethlehem Steel was hiring, so she actually dared me to go apply for a job there.

She dared ya?

KK: Uh-huh. She said look, Bethlehem Steel's hiring, and she started giggling, and she says Karol I dare you go apply.

Wow, and you did?

KK: Yes I did.

And what was that procedure like?

KK: Well, I had to go down to the unemployment office, submit my name and all the information, and then they called me for an interview a couple of weeks later, which I was sort of surprised that they did. And at the time, I think I was working for a food services place, so I thought, I'll go down for the interview. So I went down for the interview wearing, it was sort of like still cool yet in April, so I had on sort of like a light wool suit with a blazer and a vest; back then vests were in style, and a skirt and black boots. I was all dressed up.

Well, people must have taken notice to you immediately then, right?
KK: Probably, because obviously I had no idea what I was getting into.

Did they give you the standard line; you really scored well on your test? That was the standard Bethlehem Steel line: you really scored well on your test; here's what we have available for you. How did that happen?
KK: Well, they probably said that to me. I don't recall, cuz I wouldn't have been surprised, I was, you know. Everything we got tested on I understood and knew. It was English and Algebra, and different types of mathematics, which I was always pretty good at, so if they did say that to me, I don't remember, because I wouldn't have been too surprised.

Now, I'm looking down here on your interview profile, and it says that your base unit was the Centec roll foundry, 581 Department. Is that where you originally went?
KK: Yes, because he told me there were openings, and he told me about a couple of places that were available, and he said where do you want to work?

Well, you didn't know anything.
KK: No, I didn't. So I said, just put me wherever you think would do well. But first before he did that though, he asked me where I was working, and I told him I was working for the food services; it was the cafeteria inside what was Western Electric at the time. So you know what he did? He goes, when I told him, he looked at me and goes, I heard the food sucks there, and I think he was waiting to see what my reaction would be to see if I would get offended or not, and I looked at him and I smiled and I said, I only make the salads, I'm not responsible for …

Let me ask you this, in your time at Bethlehem Steel, did you ever get a chance to eat in the Bethlehem Steel cafeteria? It was in the sales office, third floor I think.
KK: I think so.

Well, I'll tell you what, the food was great in there, you know, and anybody could go in there. I mean, I used to go in there when I worked at the union hall. I used to go in there, I used to meet people there prior to going to grievance meetings, you know, and we'd talk about that stuff and try to get most of it straightened out so there'd be no shouting matches when we had the actual grievances, because they were counter-productive; you got nothing done when that happened. So now you go into the roll foundry. Now, seriously the first day there, did you think you made a mistake?

KK: I thought I was in another planet. I remember going to the gates, and I was following Honi at the time. She met us down on Fourth Street at the, I think; ,no she took me from the Bethlehem Steel offices on Third Street and I had to follow her, and I didn't really know where, I wasn't familiar with that area at all. So I was just following her being careful not to lose her. So when we went inside, she took me in through the office, and I got to see a little bit a piece at a time, but it was overwhelming. I just remember being totally overwhelmed.

Now how long was it before you found out that the East Lehigh area you were working was called the Cabbage Patch?

KK: I never heard of that still.

No, I'll tell you what, how about that? Everyone that ever went down there or that I'd ever run into, would always say I worked down at the Cabbage Patch, where was that? Number 10 treatment, uh, 735 roll shop, right, 581. They considered 12- and 14-inch mill, that was the Cabbage Patch to them.

KK: What is, he's talking cabbage like money?

No, no, no, no, I'm talking about the guys used to plant gardens down there in the summer time.

KK: Oh sure, now I remember that, okay.

Yeah, so they called it the Cabbage Patch. So now you're here, you're down, you're in the department, and are you the first girl there?

KK: I started the same day another girl started, and she was older than I by about I think ten years.

So you were like, sort of like novelties.

KK: Oh yes. I was 20.

Almost celebrities, close to it.

KK: Well, probably, because it was something different for them, and my dad said to me, just remember something Karol, you're one of the first women working in that place and you're gonna set a precedent for Bethlehem Steel whether or not they're gonna hire anymore. He says so take that very seriously.

Your dad came from a union background, too, didn't he, so he knew what he was talking about.

KK: Oh absolutely, absolutely.

Okay, that's a great thing. So describe your first week there. What did you do?

KK: Well, I was doing sweeping and shoveling, and it was so large and so loud and so noisy which I wasn't used to at all. I'm used to quiet, a quiet neighborhood, quiet street, and this was so loud and dirty, and I just, everything was going on and furnaces were, all these sparks were flying out of the furnace and cranes were running, and my dad said always to keep my eyes and ears open at all times, and he said just be very careful; it's dangerous down there; always look, keep watching what you're doing.

And you found out he knew what he was talking about.

KK: Well, when I got home, when I left that day, I got lost on the way home because like I said, I wasn't watching where I was going, I was trying not to lose the car in front of me, so I got so lost, I pulled over and I was upset, because I had no idea where I was, and I pulled the car over to think about it for a minute, and then all of a sudden this train came by and blew its horn and just …

Where exactly were you, Freemansburg?

KK: I think I was in Freemansburg. And this train came by and it was just the last piece of noise I needed for the day, and I literally started to cry because it just startled me that bad.

Wow, I'll tell you what. So, how long was it until they actually put you on a job other than laborer, do you remember?

KK: Probably within two weeks.

And what kind of a job, wait before we go any further. You were in the roll shop, right?

KK: Yes.

What exactly did they do there?

KK: Well, they melted down furnaces, poured hot metal to make rolls.

Okay, rolls were for the steel industry. These are the actual rolls that roll the steel.

KK: They flatten out other steel.

And these rolls were for Bethlehem Steel and other companies. And was, would you say business was good when you started?

KK: Oh yes. We made the best rolls ever, from anywhere.

Okay, and uh, okay, let's now get down into your first job, what was it outside of laborer?

KK: Well I was chain man. They asked me if I thought I could do it; they told me it was dangerous, and I said, if you show me what to do I'm sure I'll do it well, and I'll do it right, and I won't have to worry about, just show me what I need to know to keep safe, and they did, and I didn't have any problems. And then the next one was, there was an opening for forklift operator learner. And I saw it on the schedule to sign up, so I told Jimmy Segesdy at the time, I want to sign up for forklift operator learner, and he said, " No, you don't, you don't want that job." I said, Yes I do," and he says, "No you don't." I said, "Yes I do." And he said, No you don't," and I said, "Yes I do, and you have to put me on it as long as my seniority allows it."

Can't deny you signing up for it.
KK: Right.

Go ahead, now what happened then?
KK: So he put me on forklift operator, which he really didn't want me to do, I don't know why, but I ended up running the forklift, and I did that well. See I was raised around boys, and that makes a big difference. I have two sisters, which is where I learned how to be a lady, and then I have three brothers that I grew up around, so I understood, and my dad used to have me help him do things, cuz he was good around the house, so I learned, and I, it just came natural for me to run the forklift.

So you were like a natural around pop, and pop showed you what was going on; you picked it up right away.
KK: Yeah, and plus my brothers too, and they used to dare me to do stuff growing up as a little girl. Betch ya can't do this, betch ya can't do that.

Yeah, and then you showed 'em right?
KK: Uh-huh.

Well, okay, that's a good thing, that's a good thing, that's really getting ya ready for the rest of the, how would you put it, the rest of your life.
KK: Well yeah.

Now, you get into this, now you're running forklift. When did you run into your first, how would you put it, controversy with the company? Everybody runs into a point where things aren't going right for 'em in the plant; when did it happen for you? We all have to overcome this. Was it just being a girl, was it a job, or did everything seem to go right for you all the time?
KK: They did, because they respected. I respected my supervisors and I would hear the way some of the guys would talk to them, and I used to think, how do they get away with this, and why do they even do it. We all have a job to do. You're not gonna like some of the jobs you get, but you do

it anyway.

So your attitude was we're gonna do the job and then if things didn't go right, we'll talk about it.

KK: Yeah, if I saw something could be done better, I would say something to the supervisor.

Okay, that's what I was getting at, yeah.

KK: If I saw, you know, and believe me, they, I, they really, I think they respected me for that. I wouldn't say, that's a stupid idea, I'd say, well, you know what, I understand what you're gonna do here but wouldn't this be a better way, and if not why not, cuz I was still trying to learn too.

All right. And now, you moved on from that forklift job. What other jobs did you move into?

KK: Well, I'm trying to think of the order. Then after the forklift operator, let's see, I think I worked on the pits next.

Yeah. Okay, and the pits is where they were setting up the molds in order to pour the actual ingots and get ready you know, and I understand you did some crane work also?

KK: Well, yes that was next. Then I said, I saw crane operator opened up on the schedule, learner, so I said to Jimmy once again, oh there's an opening for crane operator learner, I said I want to sign up for that.

Now what did Jimmy say?

KK: "No you don't."

No, you're kiddin'.

KK: I'm not kiddin'. He says, "You don't want that job." I said. "Yes, I do" and he goes, "No you don't. You don't want that job." I said, "Yes I do"; he said, "No, you don't"; I said, "Yes, I do, and you have to put me on it so long as my, as long as there's nobody above me in seniority."

So lo and behold again you become the successful bidder.

KK: He put me on it.

So now you're in training.

KK: I was in training.

How long a period was that?

KK: Well, I guess you get two weeks, I think it is. Two weeks and then you're on your own, and of course the guys said, you can't run a crane, blah blah blah blah. And they get nasty down there, they want things there right now, you know, they don't really give you a lot of time to learn, because there was incentive and…

So was that, were you gonna be just a fill in person? Was there an actual opening at the time?

KK: Initially there wasn't an opening, they just trained me. So it was probably two years after training, maybe a year and a half that I actually got a position as a crane operator.

Okay, a full time position?

KK: Yeah, I think I used to fill in once in a while.

And you found out as a crane operator more about the people working on the floor than you thought you'd ever want to know probably, because everything has to be done just so, so it goes nice and smooth, so everybody could make money. Because it was an incentive position.

KK: Right, so you, you know, there's no room for swings.

How did you make out there? Do you think you weathered that storm pretty good?

KK: Well, just like any other crane operator, we got stuck over in the molding bay where this one particular guy was so mean to new crane operators that they just threw away, they just went in the office and tossed their crane check and said they're not gonna run it anymore, cuz he used to bully 'em. So he tried to bully me, and I said, "Knock it off," and he said, blah blah blah "you gotta be here." I said, "I'm just starting," I said, "and I'm not gonna give up safety to be there in a second.

In other words, he wanted you to take short cuts.

KK: Well, he wanted me to run the crane faster and more accurately than I was quite able to at that point. So he, I said, he did it again, about fifteen minutes later he swore at me, you know, and I told him he was ugly, you know and I would start giving it back, and then I said you do this one more time and I'm gonna park the crane. He goes you better not, I said I'm telling ya, and he did it again, about half an hour later he started hollering at me again. I said, That's it John, I'm going." "Get back here." I said, "Sorry, I'm parking the crane until you can calm down and start behaving the way you should. " And I went down the steps, and he was so, he come running in the office, and you know what the foreman said.

What?

KK: Cuz I told him, I said, "I'm not running this." I said, "I'm all upset now, he has me upset and I'm not going back up there until I can calm down." So he understood that. When John came screaming in there, he says, "You upset her, now you're gonna have to wait."

Well, at least he recognized that anyway. Because the last thing in the world you would want is someone up there that isn't focused on what they're doing.

KK: Or nervous, right. You're nervous to begin with when you're just starting, because you don't want anybody to get hurt, and you don't want to knock things over.

But then again you also are recognizant of the fact this is an important job, it's gotta get done, and it's better to err on the side of safety than to err on speed, okay? Because safety won't get you hurt; the other side will, or somebody hurt. So okay, now, what was the scheduling like in the roll shop? How did you work?

KK: Swing shift. One week days, one week middles, one week nights.

Yeah, did you do that most of the time you were there?

KK: Well, unless you had a job that was strictly day shift, like you know, some people did.

Were you ever laid off?

KK: Oh yes, several times.

Okay, but the times you were laid off, you didn't work in any other shops?

KK: No, well, yes I did the very first year. I worked in the labor gang.

Okay, all right. And so you got to see some other areas of the plant?

KK: Well, I only lasted two days there. Cuz I went into the, I didn't mind the work, although it was, it was bad work, it was with, I was using a jackhammer.

Yeah. Karol, I hate to say this, but I just can't picture you running the jackhammer. Although I would have loved to have seen you do it.

KK: It was big. I loved it, I loved the challenge.

It was probably, you weren't much bigger than it was.

KK: I wasn't, I wasn't, and then when I first was gonna go turn it on, I thought this might just throw me instead of the other way around. But I was strong, I was tiny but I was strong.

Then you found out that if you handled it right, the machine did most the work, the tool did the work.

KK: Oh yes.

Okay, now your washroom facilities, when you started there? What did they have for the girls?

KK: Well, let me go back to that one story why I only worked there two days in that labor gang, because there was, I went in at the end of the day to clean up in the trailer that they had for that particular group.

Oh, they had a trailer there down at East Lehigh?

KK: No, when I was on the labor gang, for that lay off, they had their own trailer there. That's the first time I was ever in there, and some girl was telling me this story how the other day the mirror was broken, I said what happened to the mirror? Oh, these girls got into a fight, and the one woman smashed the other girl's face in the mirror, and she says they're really brutal around here, they took my towels out and used it on the floor and walked all over it with their boots, that's the way they are down here, and I said…

What area was that?

KK: I was so new, I don't know where I was.,, I didn't know where I was; that place was so big and so noisy and it was just so overwhelming, you know, I just knew I had to go through the gates on Fourth Street there right across from, I knew where I had to report, the bus took me to where I was going.

Yeah, you were down at the Saucon labor gang.

KK: So I told the supervisor there, I said, "I'm not gonna be a part of this," I said, "I only wanted to work to see what else was going on at the steel company, but I'm not gonna be around girls that are gonna behave that way."

So you actually asked to be returned to the employment office?

KK: Right, I said I'm not gonna do this.

Well, you weren't the only person that ever did that, I hope you don't think you were. A lot of people did that.

KK: Did what?

Well, when they went onto other jobs. They went back, hey I'm not gonna do this for whatever reason. That wasn't that unusual.

KK: I wanted to see what the rest of the plant was like, but I'm not gonna get into a fight with a bunch of women, and if somebody starts something with me and they hit me, I'm gonna hit em back. I don't even want to get involved in that.

So that was the end of your excursion outside. So now let's get back to when you first started there. What was the women's facilities like down at East Lehigh?

KK: We had a brand-new, it was a mobile home type thing; it was just tile on the floor and benches and lockers and those little shower things, four of those and then four bathroom stalls, that's all.

How long did it, did you wear a hair net while you were at work or anything like that?

KK:　　I always put a bandana on my head.

And that took care of the majority of the dirt?

KK:　　Well, I wore that bandana for two reasons.

It must have been a war, it must have been a war there taking care of your hair while you're working at Bethlehem Steel.

KK:　　Well, the dirt really damages hair, and I used to put, and plus it would get in my way, if I had a hard hat on, cuz my hair was halfway down, well, almost halfway down my back, so I don't want to have to deal with my hair getting caught in machinery or, and plus I liked the idea of the bandana because I didn't look real feminine, and I didn't look masculine. So I didn't want the focus of me being a girl; I wanted to be a co-worker.

Okay, so you just wanted to be like normal, literally one of the guys. You knew you weren't one of the guys, but you wanted to look like one of the guys.

KK:　　Yeah, but I didn't want to be one of guys either, you know. I just wanted to go in and do my job.

How would you say the foremen were as far as the women working down there? Did they more or less didn't give you too much grief or?

KK:　　Oh yeah, Porky did.

You had one guy that was on ya all the time?

KK:　　Oh he was. He didn't want me down there. He stuck me in the dirtiest holes and the worse things, and then I didn't make a face. I would just go ahead and do it, and when I was done, I'd come up; I'd say I'm done what's next, and then he'd find me a dirtier place, and I would go ahead, and I would do it, and I'd come back, I'm done what's next.

Now after awhile, after awhile, I'm sure some of the guys are taking notice to this, and they're coming over to your side aren't they? They realize you're like a normal person?

KK:　　No, I wasn't really. I didn't talk a whole lot to the guys at first. I just wanted to get to know my surroundings and how things ran and, I didn't ignore them, but I really…

I said that more because it was always my experience, new people came in, as soon as the people there realized, hey this guy or this girl can handle that stuff, they were like, you know, part of the crew, they fit in. So, I know that the girls had a tough time, because, you know, when I was up at the alloy division when the first girls came in '72 and '73, most of 'em were crane men, and they did a real good job, and the reason why is they wouldn't cave in to, how would you put it?

Susceptible speed practices. They did everything by the book. And after the guys come to the realization this is the way they work, there was no trouble at all. And I'm sure you probably had the same type of thing down where you worked?

KK: Oh sure, absolutely.

They knew after awhile that hey, Karol can run that crane, we have nothing to worry about.

KK: Oh no, and after awhile they, they, you know, they always, until one day, they used to put me down for being a crane operator for the longest time, until one time when we had, they were building this centrifugal caster. We had an outside contractor in there who was digging a hole for the, and he needed to get this big piece of machinery in, it was big. And it was, to dig more. I guess, first they dynamite or something, but he had the railing set, and it was night shift, and you ran the crane for, until it was time, and then there was a point where there's no work you can do until a little later on to get ready for day shift. So I would come down from my crane after I thought everything was done and go into my own private sort of a quiet room, and then one of the guys came in, I just came down, I don't think I was down on the floor ten minutes, and one of the guys who was actually in charge of taking care of the night shift, he says, "The guy down at the end needs a lift." I said, "I just came down; why didn't he tell me?" He says, "What does he want?" and he said, "I don't know," and I said, "Well, I'll go talk to him," so I went down, cuz I'd rather talk to somebody on the floor when it comes to a lift, because not that you're thirty feet up in the air and he's trying to tell me what he wants, and so I thought I'll go down and see cuz this lift was a different lift; obviously it was going to be out of the ordinary. So I walked down to this man, he's standing there looking around, and I walked up to him and I said, "I heard you're looking for a crane operator." No. I said to him, I said, "I heard you need a lift." He goes Yeah I'm waiting for the crane operator." I said, "I'm it." And he started laughing and he goes, "No, you're not." I said, "Oh yes I am." He goes, "No you're not," and I said, "Yes I am," and then his face turned white as a sheet. He says, "You're kidding me." I said "No," I said, "I'm your crane operator." He said, "No you're not." I said, "Look buddy, you either want a lift or you don't, cuz you know I said I already came down the crane; you want a lift or you don't? " I said, "I want to have my, I don't know, I want to eat something soon." So he goes, "Well," he goes, "Yes," and he goes, "and I know it can be done." Don't say it can't." He goes, "They wouldn't do it for me on day shift, and they wouldn't do it for me on middle shift because they said it can't be done."

Well, this guy's spending a lot of time there, huh?

KK: Yeah, he ran the company that was digging the hole.

Oh, he was like the foreman?

KK: No, he was the owner of the company. So he goes "And don't say it can't be done." I said, "Tell me what it is you want, you know." I said, "If you say it can be done, then I'm sure it can be done." So he goes, "I want to put this big tractor in between these beams." He had beams supporting the walls of the pit, the pit that was being built. And he goes, "I want to put the tractor inside these beams." He goes, and he goes, "I know it can be done." I said, "Did you measure the beams and you measured the piece that you want in there," and he said, Yes, I know it will fit," and I said "Well, then we'll do it." And he looked at me…

And he couldn't quite believe you.

KK: No, he goes, "Well," he goes, "You didn't see what the tractor looks like." He goes, "Let's go out and see it." I said, "I don't need to see it; you told me it fits, it does fit doesn't it?" He says, "Absolutely." I said, "I don't need to see it." But it's really big, and it was, cuz when I stood, if I stood next to the tires, the tires were actually taller than I, or maybe I was at the same height. So I went up, and we put it in. It just fit, didn't touch anything. I got it in, and after that the guys respected me as a crane operator, because I did what nobody else thought could be done I guess, or they were afraid to.

I guess they were a little nervous.

KK: Well, it was a brand new piece of machinery, he said it was brand-new.

What was it like, a pneumatic digger or something; do you remember what it was? It was something to move dirt.

KK: It was a big yellow truck that moves dirt and it had the tractor tires on it. It was huge.

Yeah, okay. It doesn't matter, you did it. Well in your time there, is, give me something humorous that happened on the job.

KK: Oh, there was a lot of those.

Pick one out. Remember, now the whole idea behind this book is to let people know down the road, okay, here's what Karol Keglovitz did at Bethlehem Steel in the Centec Department, because right now all people think about steelworkers is they cooked on middle shift and slept on night shift and they never did any work.

KK: Well, that's definitely not true. That is their perception.

A rendition of perception in the Lehigh Valley, and this book, the name, Thirty Years under the Beam, stands for the employees in the plant along with management. Held this company together the last thirty years. Okay, they did everything that was asked of them, and you know we still ended up behind the eight ball. So tell me about something funny that happened to ya down in the roll foundry.

KK: Oh geez. Every day something, and you know what, it was probably a good thing to keep your sense of humor down there and have funny things happening, because it was dangerous every day. Every day I used to wear a different t-shirt every day to signify, it was maybe a friend's t-shirt. Somebody was waiting for me to come home. So you had to have humor and there was always humor. I used to think they should make a movie out of it, because, but every, every, there was just little nuances of funny things that, there's…

But there's nothing jumping out. In other words, you had a good time in between work.

KK: Yeah most of the time it was because I was female and especially the outsiders…

Yeah.

KK: Like they wouldn't expect to see me, cuz I am so tiny. And I, like a truck driver would come in and need a forklift; he'd go in the office and say I need a forklift operator, and Jimmy Segesky says I'll send you our best guy, and zoom I come out on the forklift, and they'd say, "Don't wreck my truck. No, you're not gonna ruin my truck; please don't wreck my truck," and then they'll see that I go right in there and pick it up. He goes, "I gotta tell you, you did a better job than most; some people dig up my truck," and I think that's where I got the biggest kick out of surprising people.

Yeah. When did you actually come to the realization Bethlehem Steel was in trouble?

KK: I think that's always been a threat. I mean, that's always been. I think that was a threat you learned to live with, and I lived my life accordingly. I mean I used to keep a low mortgage, and if I could stretch it out for thirty years, if rates went down, I would take advantage of that and stretch if for another thirty, you know if I only owed another six, I would stretch it for the next thirty again, just keep my expenses low in the event that that would happen. You lived in a way that you never knew really how long your job was gonna last, but…

Okay, but, like I said about what year did you realize the company…

KK: That there was no turning around?

Yeah, that it was on the way down? And what set you off? I mean, what brought you to that conclusion?

KK: Well, I always had hope for that place honestly, because it was so big and so massive and there was so much potential, there really was, and I don't think I ever realized it was gonna be closed forever until, it was later on; it had to be probably in the mid '90's when I thought that threat was very, very...

Yeah, how was that perceived by the people in your shop?

KK: I think it depressed them.

It did? Yeah, I always got the feeling that that was one of the most dangerous times in the plant because there were just a lot of people that didn't have their mind on their work, and I've heard this time and time again from people, I'm really glad I got through the last couple years, it wasn't easy. Now, what do you miss most about the place?

KK: I think it was the challenge of doing those jobs and doing 'em well. And I do miss the guys. They were a lot, you know they teased me, but they were respectable about it. You know, it was, and it was a two way street. I used to tease them, you know.

Now did your particular shop have like a watering hole, a place they went to after work or anything?

KK: Yes they did.

And where was that?

KK: I think they used to go to the Freeman House and sometimes there was one down the road further than that, just...

The Washington Hotel, the Willow Grove?

KK: The Willow Grove.

Yeah, okay, they were close right in Freemansburg. You went every now and then or?

KK: Every once in awhile. Not too often, once in awhile.

These guys get invited to weddings and stuff like that or?

KK: I don't know, I was never invited, really only to one wedding, which I understand, because some of the guys they told me that they told their wives I was fat and ugly and if they ever see me at the store I should keep moving.

Get out, you serious?

KK: I'm serious. He says, don't say hello to me, 'cuz I told my wife, she knows there's women down here, and I told her you were big, fat and very ugly, and if she sees you walking over and say hi I'm dead.

What did you say when you hear that?

KK: I laughed, I said okay, I can respect that. And then I had another, some people said my wife doesn't even know there's a woman in our shop.

You know, like, it would make any difference.

KK: Well, I treated 'em like brothers, too, Frank.

Well, I'll tell you what Karol, you gave me a real good interview here. I'm really glad, and uh, the part I like most about this interview is the part when you said we made the best rolls there.

KK: We did.

And you know how many people bragged about the quality of Bethlehem Steel work?" Damn near everybody. If the company and Martin Tower ever would have known the pride that the employees took in what they did down there, I don't think they would have been able to close this place. And you know, everyone knows now, it's hindsight, had it stayed open another six months or a year, we'd still be down there; we would absolutely still be down there. Well, okay Karol, it was a pleasure talking to ya and I wish the best for you and your husband Bill and thanks a lot.

KK: Okay, thank you.

DOLORES BOYKO
25 years of service

Iron Foundry

Delores was a mild-mannered employee who never hesitated to speak her mind. Was always interested in bettering the lot of the female employees. An avid union maid, hardly ever missing a union meeting. Progressed through the ranks to the position of welder A.

* * * * * * * * *

Today is September the 4th, 2008, and we're here with Dolores B. Boyko. Dolores, how you doin' today?

DB: Good.

Good. I see you started here in the plant back in March of 1975. Could you tell me how you got to become a Bethlehem steelworker?

DB: Well, I was basically looking for a better wage, better benefits, and the Steel at that time was doing a big hiring, so I went on my own and applied and was accepted and started working.

Sounds real simple. Did you get it like from an ad in the paper, or just, you just knew they were hiring?

DB: I just kind of knew they were hiring.

Yeah, you heard, heard it from people

DB: Different, yeah, different people had told me that so.

When you were in the hiring area down there, did they offer you a selection of jobs, or did they just say that we got a job for you in the iron foundry?

DB: Uh, no, I didn't get a selection of jobs. I got put with CSL when I first started. Construction and Labor Department. That's where they told me I was goin'.

So, you're there for the first week. What was that first week like?

DB: It was hell.

223

And why was that?

DB: Well, basically, I don't believe that a lot of the people wanted women in the plant at that time. And that was part of it. And the other part of it was really you had no idea what the jobs were gonna be like and what the inside of the steel plant was like until you actually got in there, and it was quite an eye-opener.

Yeah I guess it was. What struck you the most, the noise, the heat, the constant movement?

DB: All of it. All of it. The size of it, the size of equipment we were around, and the heat, the noise, uh, you had to be dressed in all your safety gear in the dead of winter, the dead of summer it was, you know…

Well, I see you started the end of March, at least the weather was getting a little bit better. And uh, describe some of the early jobs you had with the central labor gang.

DB: Well, one of the things that always bugged me when I went into construction and labor there was how they used to schedule you first off, because back then I believe they had 200/300/400 people in that department, and your schedule weekly used to be three different shifts in a week, and my thinking on that was, well, they had so many people, why couldn't they just give you a week of days, a week of middles, or a week of nights instead of three shifts in one week, which used to really screw up your system.

Oh yeah, it takes, your body never gets used to that.

DB: That's right. I mean, I could never figure that out. There were enough people there. I didn't mind working any of the shifts, but I could just never figure that out why they didn't give you one week of a basic shift.

Well, if it's any consolation to you, when I worked in the electric furnace, I worked that way for years.

DB: I know the whole place did. I know the whole place did.

And a lot of people felt the same way that you did, but still the people on the outside, they thought all you did was go in there and sleep on night shift and you didn't do very much work, and this is the reason for the book to get to quell all these virulent rumors that are so untrue. Because, you know, unless you lived it, you know, and told your story, which is your story, outsiders would have no clue. So tell me some of these jobs that you had the first couple months you were there.

DB: Well, the very first job that I remember was I was assigned with a, I believe it was down somewhere around the soaking pits, somewhere in between the soaking pit and another department there outside with a big drill, a concrete drill to drill holes in so they could blast this wall away. And it was a pneumatic tool with this big drill on the end of it, and of course I had never done anything like that, and they sent me with this big guy, and I believe our boss was Nick Glovas down there, the first one that I remember. And we go over to this wall, and they basically didn't show me too much, and I guess they were waiting to see what was gonna happen. So I guess, uh, I don't remember the gentleman's name I was working with, but he started the hole, and then of course it's my turn to do some of it, and I have no qualms with trying anything actually. I, my whole steel experience was whatever they wanted to teach me I learned or signed up for to learn.

Okay. You definitely had a good attitude about it.
DB: That's what my thing was. And in the end, knowing a lot of different things, getting a forklift license along the way, that kind of saved me from some layoff time along my, my uh steel experience, it did. So anyway …

Did you ever get a crane check?
DB: No. I don't have a crane check. I had a forklift license and uh, well laborer, and then welder. And that was pretty much it. But, uh, back to drilling the hole in the wall, it was a vertical, so we had to hold it, you know, the drill up in the air. And of course I got it stuck. I got it stuck every time I tried it, and until you get the knack of actually how much pressure and that, and the gentleman and I worked very good together actually.

Yeah, in other words he wasn't a deterrent right off the bat? He more or less helped you through it.
DB: He saw that, he saw that I wanted to get in there, and he more or less told me what I gotta do, so…

And you found out when you're working with pneumatic tools like that, you really gotta let the tool do the work.
DB: That's right.

And that's where most people goof up with them tools, they're forcing 'em.
DB: That's right. Then another time we got sent down to Ingot Mould before when they were building Ingot Mould, and they were putting up Ingot Mould. And a lot of the foremen in that department gave the girls a hard time. Actually some words, I tend to think some of the jobs they gave us, maybe that, I basically feel like they wanted us to quit; that was my feeling on that. But, uh, we got sent down Ingot Mould, and there was a friend of mine, her name's Joanne, I can't even remember her maiden name.

Uh, her married name now, she's out in Pittsburgh, uh, she worked with me. Nick Glovas sent us underneath some railroad tracks, we had to dig out underneath some railroad tracks down there for some pipe and other things that were going through for what was gonna be Ingot Mould. And then uh, he was on us all the time, all the time on us, but we were doing what we had to do, and believe it or not, at the end of that job, he actually pulled us aside and told us, apologized to us about how he treated us, and basically told us that we did a good job and we could actually outwork or outperform some of the men he had under him. Because we basically did what he told us to do.

You basically knew at that time that you were accepted.

DB: That's right. That changed everything after that.

And that must have been a good feeling.

DB: Everything after that changed. Everything after that changed.

Cuz you had confidence then.

DB: He was totally different towards us, yes, yes.

Well, that's good. I'm glad to see something like that actually took place, but you know from talking to a lot of the women, you know, they all went through similar things like you did, and some of them way, a lot worse. I hate to bring it up but…

DB: I know.

In fact there's some things here that took place in this plant that we're not even gonna talk about because it serves no purpose. But, so you're in CSL for how long?

DB: Four years.

Four years, and then what happened?

DB: Well, four years, and basically the first four years I was pretty much in and out, laid off, uh, maybe worked six months, out six months, back in, back out, back in. And my last time I believe I was laid off for like 21 months, and back then we had pretty much two years of recall rights, and we had benefits for quite a long time.

One year

DB: Yes, so I was kind of getting worried at the 21 month mark, but then I did get called back.

Yeah, and when was that lay off, do you remember, the end of the '70s or?

DB: Yeah, because I believe in '78, somewhere around there, I bid on a job and went to the Coke Works. Because in '79 I bid on the iron foundry job. So, 78, pretty close to a year, I might have been down at the Coke Works, and that's where I got a forklift check, forklift license. So. And then with Coke Works, down at the Coke Works, that was, everything was an eye-opener actually until when you went there and saw it and worked there, lived half your life there maybe. Um, you know all the dirt and the dust and back actually then I don't believe we were wearing respirators back then in the Coke Works. I think that came a few years later.

Yeah, they put a big push on it in the '80s. About how long were you at the Coke Works that initial time?
DB: Almost a year.

Almost a year. It was probably right after you left they started doing that. Because they had some sort of a, some sort of like a consent decree with the union that had to do with coke emissions and stuff like that, and all the rules became specific. You had to wear the clothes, you had to do all of that stuff, you had to wear respirators, everything has to be provided, etc., etc.
DB: Because as I recall, I don't think we had the clothes to wear then either. I think I was wearing regular, my own clothes.

So how was the scheduling during these early years, other than what you described, you know the shifts in CSL? Was it basically the same at the Coke Works?
DB: No, at the Coke Works it was different. It wasn't three shifts in a week.

How was it?
DB: It was a week of this, a week of that, a week of nights, or whatever. You basically had more of a set, you know, schedule where your body isn't going haywire. Or sometimes maybe you'd be on middles for two or three weeks and then you'd be on nights for two or three weeks. It just depended. I think the schedule went around the work that they had to do down there for the laborers.

Okay, do you ever go back to any of the Coke Work reunions or anything?
DB: No, I haven't been.

All right, just wondering; they have one coming up. I guess in a week or two.
DB: Yeah. Most of the time I've been doing something else when people contact me.

Well, it's, when you think about something like that, working in an area like the Coke Works, you know, a lot of people in the plant say if the plant was gonna get an enema where the hose would go. There's an ongoing argument would it be at the Coke Works, would it be at the sintering plant, would it be at the iron foundry, or would it be at the blast furnace? And everyone argues about that. Believe it or not, the people that work in these areas they always argue the hardest for their own area. But you know, until you're there to experience it, there's no way to describe it. So now you actually get up into the iron foundry in '79. Tell me about the iron foundry. What did they do in the iron foundry?

DB: Well, the iron foundry made, uh, iron castings from, uh, they poured metal, uh, the uh, it was set up by a no-bake system. The no-bake system was a dry sand, they'd have a machine that went along the track, and I can't remember the name of that for the life of me, I was thinking about that, I can't remember that. Well it was basically a mixer machine is what it was. So the sand would come into the machine, there would be oil in the machine and a binder, like an acid type material, and heat, and then it would mix in there, and it would come out like a sticky bindy kind of sand, and they'd pour it into a flask which was a big metal, uh, what do you want to call it, a big uh…

A form?

DB: Well, like a form, yes. And then, uh, they would put a pattern in it. They'd put the pattern into the metal form, and then they would put the no-bake around the pattern, the machine head would like go around the pattern, and then the guys would scrape it off to make it flat, and then after the no-bake would harden.

And the no-bake was actually sand, right?

DB: Yeah, a mixture of sand, oil and acid, yes. And then after it hardened up, the crane would come, there would be hooks on the wooden patterns, and they would pull the pattern out. So then the thing was hard like basically cement, if you want to call it that. And, uh, that would be the…

How long would that take to set up?

DB: Uh, maybe and hour, two hours, depending on how big the casting was that they were pouring, okay. We had castings, we had a small area in the iron foundry which was called the dog house where they made little castings, maybe 5, 10, 15, 50 pound castings, 100 pound castings, then another area made flat castings called stools, where they would put a, an ingot on top of the stool, an ingot is an iron casting, maybe about a little bigger than a refrigerator with a hole inside. And uh, they would pour hot metal into that, and then they'd get their casting.

Their ingots to roll.

DB: Their ingots to roll down at the mills.

Yup, so the plant didn't operate without the iron foundry, the Ingot Mould foundry. You had to have this in order to get your ingots together?

DB: Yup, that's where they got their ingots from. And…

Plus we sold to other outside concerns besides.

DB: Yeah, yeah, the stools also went to our other plants, like Sparrows Point, or some of them went out to Indiana, some of them went elsewhere, and some of them also were sold to outside companies.

Okay, so you're in the iron foundry for a time. Uh, how did you advance in there?

DB: When I came in there, I came in one, as one of three welders. And I was kind of looking for job security. So as a welder you really can't get bumped out if you had, I think it was if you had a job position higher than, wasn't it like a laborer you could get bumped out if somebody…

Yeah pool job.

DB: Yeah pool job or something like that?

You wanted to get into a job that was not a pool job.

DB: That's right. So I figured, well, sooner or later the other two guys that were welders, the one had thirty some years, the other one was pretty close to forty also, forty or forty-two maybe. So I figured sooner or later if things happened there, that they're laying off or downsizing, maybe one or two of these gentlemen would retire, and then I would move into a secure position where nobody could really bump me.

What they called an incumbent position.

DB: Yeah, yeah, incumbent. I went into the iron foundry as a mechanical welder with, basically stationed with the millwrights, the maintenance crew, and the other two gentlemen worked on castings, repairing castings, welding castings, wearing welding sand pockets, like when they pour sometimes you get a pocket in there, like a void, it's called like a void, it's sand maybe that didn't set up right inside there, somewhere at the top and then you have to weld it to, basically for cosmetic to make it look, you know, presentable. Or weld numbers on the molds or, you know that type of thing, those two other guys were doing, and I basically worked with the millwrights, which was anywhere and anything that needed fixing in that whole place, equipment, roof, cellar wherever, that's where we went and that's where we repaired. I did a lot of stuff up on the roofs. Our foundry was a system of pipes that took the sand, the sand would run along there, and sand is very abrasive, so a lot of times it would wear holes in the pipes, that you know, the pipes that were transporting it. And that's how it got from the, the sand was loaded into a big silo and then it came out of the silo through a system of pipes, and went basically wherever they used it, like at the mixer machine or over, you know, another mixer machine in a low run where they did the molds, the bigger molds. We also had an area in our shop that was, they actually had to take plates out of the ground to make these big 150, we had 150 ton crane, and that casting in there was huge. And when they took these plates off the floor, they generally had to pump water out of there, because that pit was below, like they'd get river water in there somehow. So every time we made one of those, they had to pump that place out, that pit out, to get the water out, and then, you know, set it up to make the big mold.

Yeah, so how long were you in that area of the iron foundry? Right up until when it closed? That would have been what, '95?
DB: Yes. 95, the hot end. Well, along the way, too, uh, one of the welders retired, so then at that point somewhere in the '80s like the bottom dropped out, we were, didn't we have big layoff there or …?I don't remember what year or whatever that was, but anyway, um, I was gonna get laid off. We had no work, and they downsized big time, and I had a forklift check which I got at the Coke Works, so my forklift check put me on middle shift driving the forklift, and there were people, like five six people there that didn't have a forklift check, so my forklift check saved me from getting laid off. So that was one area where wanting to learn and …

Yeah, paid off.
DB: You know, the forklift check paid off.

And when did you actually leave the Bethlehem plant?
DB: 19… I believe it was '97.

Okay, and you were working at the Coke Works at the time?
DB: House, when the hot end went down in '95, and this is a little ironic too, because um, we had heard that they were gonna close down, and my general foreman, Clair Maury come out to me, and he says, 'I think they're going to send you somewhere to weld?" And I said, "Really?" He goes, "Yeah." And I said, "Look if you have anything to do with it, don't send me to the Coke Works." And he said, "I don't think I have anything to do with it." Because it was so dirty and dusty and hot, and, uh, I can't even describe some of the conditions down in that coke plant, and stinky. That was another thing, the coke plant smell, the smell. Um, so anyway, the next day he comes back, he had a paper from Dick D'Augustino, and he said, "I told you, I don't have anything to do with it, but you're going to the Coke Works." So in the end that was kind of a blessing because it extended my work life. Most people got let out at '95, and I went down the Coke Works

as a temporary welder.

Okay, you stayed there to '97.

DB: Stayed there till '97. In that process, I went into the little weld, I guess it was a mechanical shop, like a weld millwright shop there. And then the orders came down that they were going to keep A battery going, which was one of the newer batteries, uh, that was built, uh. I don't know what the year; I don't remember the year that was built.

No, I'm not that familiar with it.

DB: But A battery was a new battery that was built recently, all kind of German technology, so they decided the federal government came down with these standards where they had to eliminate a lot of this emissions and smoke, and they pretty well had it nailed down, but there was still a lot of seepage coming out of the oven doors as they would wear, so the welders, being that I and this other fellow, John Morani, were temporaries, we got the job over on the batteries, cuz nobody wanted to do it. They had us, uh, building up the front of the oven. They'd take off the door. When they put the door on the oven, it kind of went down, and it made like a concave area in the door. So the bottom of the door wasn't sealed right. So that had to be built out; parts are, you know, built out, so we horizontal welded and all that, and they put some kind of jig on, and then the millwrights would come out later after we got down and grind it, flush. And then if it needed any more repairs, we'd go back over and you know...

Keep working on it until you got it as good as you could get it.

DB: Keep working on it. So we kind of figured that the Coke Works would never go down since they spent tons of money getting the place up to specs, and what happened? It went down anyway.

Well, one of the reasons the book is here is that I believe that the people in the plant, including the management people in the plant, did everything they could the last thirty years to keep the place going for obvious reasons. You now, you gotta feed your family, you gotta take care of yourself, whatever it may be. I think they kept that plant going the last thirty years in spite of what maybe people on the other side of the river weren't really that concerned with. And I wanted to get this out, because I feel that these people actually literally held up the plant. Because the plant was known, okay, as a structural plant more than anything else, hence the name Thirty Years under the Beam. We carried the plant the last thirty years. But in order to solidify that, I can't just make that statement and call the book this. I have to talk to people from all over the plant to see what they did in there and ask them. Do you think the company did a good job of taking care of you as an employee? What did you like about the company's benefits and that?

DB: The company's benefits were actually very good. They were excellent. I don't have any bad feelings about the Steel. I'm kind of a person that feels what is meant to be will be, what happens happens. There was so little that you or I could control. We were just part of the whole process.

Just players.

DB: Part of the whole process, that's all. Other people made the decisions. Um, the steel company gave me a good life, it gave me a good wage, it gave me good benefits all the years that I worked there. I have no regrets whatsoever, and I really, it was sad that it went down. Whoever expected it to go down? My feeling is it should have never went down. Look at today, there's one big major steel company, now it's called Arcelor, and who's supplying all the beams around the area now?

The mini mills.

DB: The mini mills, the foreign companies, um, we could have had all of that, and we should have had all of that. I mean, there's still a need for beams. I went on a vacation down in New Orleans, and all I saw were those Z pylons, the ones that locked together. They probably sold the patent on that and somebody else has it now. That would have been a tremendous thing, like for the levees right now and all of that stuff. I don't know. And then when somebody tried to come in and buy those rolling mills, one or two of the rolling mills, they never would sell 'em. They never would sell 'em, and they should have, they should have.

I interviewed some gentlemen that they were actually involved with that, and the consensus was that the people who were gonna buy the soaking pits, the combination mill, the beam yard, and all the auxiliary services that went with it, uh, we're gonna make money almost immediately, and we're gonna make the people across the river really look bad. And that's why they didn't sell it.

DB: I know that.

And then another guy said to me, did you also consider that in that time period, between 1994 and when they actually took care of and sent the company into bankruptcy, there were people over there that were more or less looking out more for themselves, for their own pensions, then they were for the Bethlehem plant. Now who knows what the truth is. I mean, maybe we'll never know. It will be like Kennedy's assassination. But the bottom line is it would have provided jobs and probably would still be operating today. When did you first get the feeling that the plant was really in trouble, when your operation shut down? Or was it before that?

DB: Yeah. Well, I think you could see a little bit of the writing on the wall a little bit before that, because the orders started dwindling off.

Early '90s then.

DB: Yup. The order started dwindling off, and then they were kind of getting rid of their own people, foremen, they were talking foremen out of there and bringing foremen from other departments, and half of these people they brought from other departments didn't know their…

Ass from a hole in the ground, yeah.

DB: From a hole in the ground, excuse my language, but they didn't, and they basically depended on us to tell them what needs to be done or what was happening.

Well, see we were only the crew. We weren't the captain, the first mate or anything like that, you know, so we did what we could. But those guys were looking to save their own jobs also. But consequently, you know, there were some people there that did everything they could to save it to.

DB: And you know what, looking back at it, to like in the old days, people were put in management, a lot of them because of who they knew not what they know.

Well, they actually applied relative ability in the true sense of the word.

DB: Yeah, it wasn't based on what they knew. And that, I think, was a big part of the whole steel operation, because I think if they would have had more people in supervisory positions that knew a little bit more about what the operation was, I think things may have gone a little bit better.

So you ended up going up to the Lackawanna plant; you were actually forced up there?

DB: I went up there for my medical, for the physical and all of that, and I took an MRI my doctor gave me, and I got flunked, and I got sent back. And on the way up actually I was thinking about would I go there or would I not go there, and I based my decision on my drive up there. Some people took their wife, their husband up, whatever, spent, the Steel gave them money to stay in a hotel. I kinda thought, I'm going on my own, and I'm gonna make my decision based on that, and that's pretty much what I did. If he would have passed me, I would've probably said no. I don't think I would have stayed there.

So you ended up then in a position where you were able to get a pension?

DB: Yes.

Well, you were one of the lucky ones. You know that was one of the major discrepancies of that provision in the contract. You know. That was something that was put in by the company to appease the union to get 'em to sign that contract back in the '70s. They never thought they were ever going to use that. But when it came into effect, nobody knew how it operated, and there were lots and lots of mistakes. Depending on the luck of the draw, like the flip of the coin, junior people got pensions, and senior people won't get 'em until age 60, and it's really sad to see it.

DB: I know.

But you know, and then there were some people that ended up didn't have to go at all, etc., etc. Yours is a clear-cut case because it was a physical limit involved with you. So you know that's, there's no dispute there.

DB: I had some problems in my lower back like a year before all this happened, and I went to the doctor and I got my MRI, so my problem was definitely stated on the MRI. There was no denying.

Yeah, so they weren't gonna take any chances with a worker's comp claim.

DB: I suppose so, I suppose so. I mean, you know, I don't know.

Well, okay Dolores, it was a real pleasure having you here today, and I wish the best, you know, for you and the rest of your life, and what do you do right now?

DB: Right now I'm a Bethlehem Area school bus driver, and I love it.

Good for you. A lower stress job, huh?

DB: Yeah, right, right. I had a couple of welding jobs on the outside after my steel carrier, and I just, I could be in that field. I could still be making a whole lot of money, and I just wanted to get out of the, uh …

Rat race

DB: Yeah, yeah, yeah. And there was actually a point, too, in my jobs at the Steel when I got laid off, I took off a whole year and did nothing, because we had benefits. And that was one of the best things I ever did because I basically worked since I've been 16, and you don't really get a chance to do that.

Okay. You live in this area your whole life?

DB: Yeah, Bethlehem area born and raised.

Okay. All right. Good luck to you Dolores, thank you.

DB: Okay.

ANDREW F. PINGYAR
30 years of service

Reconditioning Welder, Ingot Mould Foundry

"Honest Andy" was one of the highest paid employees of BSCO. If you were putting a roof on your house at 5 a.m., he would be there.

* * * * * * * * * *

It's June 8th, 2008. We're here with Andy F. Pingyar. Uh, Andrew F. Pingyar. Now Andrew, what did the guys call you at work?

AP: Honest Andy.

Honest Andy. How about for the purposes for this interview, we just call you Andy? Andy, do you want to tell us how you became a Bethlehem Steel worker?

AP: I put an application in back in early February of '66, and I got called and the rest is history.

In you went. First place you worked Ingot Mould?

AP: In I went. Ingot Mould, yes.

It must be like going back in time. Do you want to tell us what it was like? What was your first impression? Were you ready to run right out again?

AP: Yeah I was ready to run right out. To me, I walked into 1930; I got a job with a wheelbarrow and a shovel shoveling sand. I did that for a good six to eight months on different shifts, and then I got a job as a chainman at the door, which was a nickel an hour more, big deal. And then from there, I kept my eyes open, my mouth shut, and my ears open and I looked for postings, and then they posted for welder learner in Ingot Mould. I applied for it, nobody else wanted it. I got it. And then I got on that as a learner and six months down the road, they posted for a craft welder; I took that test and I passed it, made me Welder C. Six months later I took another test, I went to Welder B. Six months later I took another test, and I went to Welder A and I stayed there in Welder A until I retired 30 years later.

Did you ever go to the company's welding school?

AP: No.

No. Everything you did was on-the-job training right there?

AP: I took some at night school in Liberty High School's Vo-Tech. And then from there I went into Ingot Mould, I had some basic knowledge of what was going on, and I got involved with a guy there who became my personal friend, Paul Cressman, and he taught me a lot that the school couldn't teach me, because he had it for three years in Vo-Tech and Dieruff. And between him and what I knew, I progressed into Welder A to a point where I could teach others.

Okay, that's really something. Now from interviewing people from all over the plant and other people from Ingot Mould, they actually came out and they said to me, "My first impression after being there about a month was that if the plant somehow, the world would give all the steel mills an enema the hose would go in Ingot Mould." What would you say to that? Was it that dirty a place?

AP: It was more than that dirty of a place.

Tell us how dirty it was.

AP: No matter what you touched, where you sat down, you got dirty. It was just black pitch dust all over the foundry and graphite unbelievable thick all over; and if one crane would bump into another one, the stuff would come down so bad that the people couldn't see where they were working or where they were going. It was that bad in there. We had an explosion one time on the hot side where water got into a ladle and the gasses compressed with hydrogen and oxygen, and it blew so bad that it shook all the overhead cranes and beams loose and took almost three hours before that stuff settled and cleared, and a couple guys got hurt trying to find a way out. One guy fell in a pit, broke his ribs. And I was lucky; I was at the door at that time, so I just quick ran out of there. Me and a guy named Pete Svanda. He was a millwright. And we got out of there real quick. It looked just like an explosion in there, really bad, and it looked like a bomb went off or something in there, and well like I said, took about three hours to clear. And that's something you never forget, everybody that came in or came out of there blacker than the Ace of Spades.

Now, on the safety sense, were there a lot of people who were wearing respirators?

AP: At that time, nobody was wearing them. They didn't issue them yet.

Nobody. No, in the '60s we're talking about. When did they first start showing up on the job?

AP: I really can't remember, to be honest with you, I'd say somewhere in the mid '70s or early '80s, in that time frame. They gave us them paper respirators which weren't worth the space they took up.

I remember coming back from the Navy in 1972, and I was in a maintenance crew. And we used to go to school every now and then. We would run into guys from the plant and we'd run into Ingot Mould guys. We'd ask them, "What's it like down there?" Because you never knew when there was going to be a job posting or something like that, and they started talking to us. They said, "Well, you know blah, blah, blah. You know," he says, "we have a couple guys right now that are being monitored for silicosis." I says, "What's that?" I didn't even know what they were talking about. Well I guess that was one of the first places in the plant where they actually confirmed workers comp cases of employees with silicosis. Do you remember that? Okay, and I'm sure that must have gone a long way to get people to wear respirators. I know some of the guys that were working as chippers and things like that, where they're in a nasty environment, they told me, "We wore them as often as we could." There were a couple of jobs where you just couldn't use them because of tight confined areas but he said, "We always wore them." How about with your welding there? Was that an issue with your welding? The dirt, breathing that in?

AP: Yeah, it was but I had air suckers that would take the fumes away from me, and if you had a black light and you went through the area, you could see all these microscopic particles of dust graphite floating in the air. And we had a foreman in, Ted Lipsky, he's the one that came in one day with this little black light that he rigged up at home to show me and the other guys the dust on the portion of the area which is in the Sand House in the annex. They had some chippers out there chipping stools, and he showed us the dust that was flying around that you couldn't see with the naked eye. And as far as welding, we had metal fume respirators that we could wear. You had to have a special hood on your face called a bubble hood to support the respirator. With all that on, it gets hot, it's hard to breathe, and most of the guys that welded there didn't wear them, because they were a nuisance more than an advantage to the fumes. The air suckers would take the fumes away and shoot them right out the door.

And this foreman that rigged up this black light, do you feel that he was doing that just so people would be aware of their environment?
AP: Absolutely, yeah.

I guess there were a few more people wearing respirators after that.
AP: Just some.

Well, if it was one person, I guess it was worth it. Good.

AP: He passed away then several years ago.

Now, a lot of the guys that were in the plant in the old environment like that, a lot of them were tested by the law firm. How did the guys at Ingot Mould make out with that? You got around to see them that often. How did they fare?

AP: Well, the people you're talking about is Peter Angelos Law Firm. They send flyers out, paper out, to certain individuals that they can get contact with including myself, and they are trying to get compensation from anybody that made asbestos or asbestos-related products that were used in Ingot Mould. They give you a certain amount of compensation, but out of 100 percent they get 33-1/3 off the top. Then if you had to go for medical tests, that has to come out of that, and by the time the smoke cleared, you're lucky if you got 10 or 20 percent out of 100.

Okay. I mean I don't know if this is for sure, but I heard more or less through the grapevine that like 68 percent of the people tested in the Bethlehem plant, tested positive for asbestos. That's really a high amount. In fact, I've often been amazed that something like this was never on "60 Minutes."

AP: I can't make a statement on that because I don't know the percentages there.

Well, no you can't talk about what you don't know but you were there during the, how would you put it, the "hey day" of Ingot Mould when they were making money and everybody was making money. In fact you guys I believe at the time probably were the highest paid people in the plant.

AP: Well, it's possible.

Yeah, well, I'll tell you what, how long was it before you encountered a layoff in this position?

AP: The first time, I'd say maybe 12 or 13 months.

Yeah, it wasn't very long. Where did you end up at?

AP: Outside, looking in, collecting unemployment.

Yeah. In other words, they didn't have a job for you.

AP: Didn't have a job then, no. Didn't have no time.

Okay, so, would you say that was like a real part of your job over the 30 years, working different areas and being on lay off?

AP: Yeah. I know we got a total in the beginning 60 dollars per week unemployment when I first started there on unemployment compensation.

Yeah. I can remember some of that myself. Okay, I see here one of the places you went to on lay off was the Beam Yard. I guess you thought you were working in some kind of a clean room after that.

AP: I had never worked in the Beam Yard. Until I worked down there, I couldn't believe what I saw. People, they're on top of each other, they don't follow safety rules there, lot of wise guys down there, and I worked swing shifts over there. I got my first encounter with a guy, I was chaining up beams, and these two chains that come down—one in the front, one in the back—I put the front one on and went around to the back one, he lifted the beam just enough for all the water to run down my shirt and down my pants. And I went like this to him, I says, "Come on down here." I said, "I'm gonna take your teeth out of your face." And he wouldn't come off of the crane. He had me hot under the collar. Well, that was my christening down at the Beam Yard. After that I knew better. I don't remember who the guy was, but he thought it was really funny. This was like when it was cold outside, and there's ice and snow on the beam, and the water's cold, and I was not amused when this cold water went down my pants.

Well, you know what, did you get the feeling that you weren't the only guy he ever did that to?
AP: I'm sure I wasn't.

It's not funny, but you have to laugh about it.
AP: Yeah, after the day was over I laughed it off, and me and the craneman, we shook hands, and he said, "That was your christening." I said, "I let it go in one ear and out the other and the hell with it."

You probably ended up at Binney's after work having a beer or something, shooting a game of darts.
AP: Could be.

Okay, I see Number Two Machine Shop, what did you do in there?
AP: Labor, sweeping up chips. I was there for like three months, four months.

Yep. Blast Furnace.
AP: Labor, braise man, car dumper, and basically chainman.

Did you ever get promoted to maintenance and do any welding up there?
AP: No, not in the Blast Furnace.

And I'm looking here and I see you also worked with the bricklayers.
AP: Yeah, that was a hard job. I think I did everything but lay the bricks.

Yeah, that's a labor-intensive job. Now, how about your scheduling? Were you married when you first started at the plant?
AP: Yes.

Did you have children?

AP: Yes I did.

Did you get to see them a lot or was it always swing shift?

AP: I was always swing shift and so I'd seen them but not that often, I mean not too much in the time frame of a day. I worked days; by the time I came home, supper was on the table, I was with them for a couple hours, then they had to go to sleep, and the next thing you know I had to get up for work the next morning, so I hit the sack on account of I had to get up at five o'clock and go to work.

You know I've had men tell me in these interviews that in a one-month period, all four weeks of the month, every one of those weeks they worked days, middles, and nights. Did that ever happen to you?

AP: Yes, swing shifts.

I bet that was enough for you to pull your hair out.

AP: Yes, it was.

Wow! That must have been something in the winter and the summer, the hottest part. And then on top of it, you're going into an environment that is just nasty dirty, nasty hot. Unreal, but you know there's a lot of people that think that all this product that we did down there making molds in Ingot Mould Foundry, the molds were made specifically so that they could pour hot iron and hot steel and make something easier for the manufacturing process, either to roll it out or, you know, make some sort of a cast product. But the bottom line was you were in there for most of the holidays, most of the weekends, because the place never shut down.

AP: You went seven days a week, 24 hours a day, every day.

Did you feel like you were getting paid right?

AP: For what I was doing and for the conditions, I felt that I should have gotten a little more in the beginning. But you had to go with union scale.

Yeah. Do you think you could have worked there without the union?

AP: I honestly don't know.

Well, that's a good answer. When did it come to you to realization that that plant was really in trouble?

AP: I'd say about three or four years, maybe five years, before they shut it down.

In the early '90s.

AP: Things were breaking and they don't want to fix nothing. They just shut that portion of the operation down trying to work around it. And there were just continuously things breaking, and you couldn't get parts for the machinery, you had to make your own, and you can't machine a part without an engineer doing it perfectly like on a blueprint or something. You try to do it by what you know and if it don't fit right then you got vibration and everything else and it screws up the rest of the machine that's functioning at the time.

Yeah. I was told by people that the main reason Ingot Mould did so well was not only did they make molds for the other Bethlehem plants, but they made them for other steel companies in that we probably had the best molds in the industry for a long period of time.

AP: That's very possible and I can't comment on that either but I know we did our best to make a good mold over there.

Okay, and they actually had guys that would go out onto the job, quality control people, and that would actually find out where there were problems, come back to the shop, make sure they were corrected, and all of that was going on. So now we come down and somewhere around '93 or '94 and we've had all kinds of programs—Partners for Progress, Juran—all designed to get the working man to work with the company. Do you think that was too little, too late?

AP: Yes. It was too little, too late.

You would have liked to see that from like the day you started. Everyone's telling me the same thing. What do you miss most about that plant?

AP: The benefits. I lost all my benefits—medical, dental benefits. I miss the money that I made there. The money was good for me, especially towards the end there. We were making big money down there, because a lot of the older welders retired, and it gave us more overtime, and I was very content with the pay. But what can I say; the benefits were the most important factor. Without the benefits, I don't think a lot of the guys would have stayed there.

You always slept better at night knowing that umbrella was over your head, how about it? And it's not there anymore.

AP: Nope, I'm on my own.

Well, if you had ever been given a chance at any time during the 30 years you had in the plant to do things better down in that shop, things that you'd see on a daily basis, you know that were just like wasting money, wasting time, and things like that, is there anything that you could put a finger on that if you were the boss you would have changed immediately?

AP: A lot of waste. People wasted a lot of good materials there. They just didn't care. They would make something, if you needed 50 foot of an angle and you only used 35, they'd throw the rest of the scrap out. I'd seen this done a lot of times down there. "Don't worry about it," they'd tell me. Foreman said, "Don't worry about it. You're getting paid to do what you're doing. Don't worry about nothing." So, a lot of waste; a lot of materials were wasted.

It would have been just easy to save that stuff at a location somewhere.
AP: Sure. When they ran to the pits, sand that they processed to run, a lot of it was left over from another day for another day, throw it away. There were so many pieces of metal and material that could have been saved. But everything was scrap piled, loaded up in a scrap car, taken down to the furnace, to the BOF, and melted down. That keeps production going.

Yeah. Now you were also more or less classified as a reconditioning welder also, weren't you?
AP: Yes. I did that, too.

What exactly did the reconditioning welder do? We know what regular welders do, but what did the reconditioning welders do?
AP: Well, if a mold needed a lug or a trunnion done or a break in a mold.

And a lug is a lifting device built right onto the mold, so that something can pick it up.
AP: If there was a piece of it missing we would brick it up and put a lot of sand around it, put the preheaters on it, which generated a tremendous amount of heat with oil and compressed air for at least two or three hours sometimes, depending how big the break was. And that portion of the mold got cherry red. When they got cherry red, we put on these silver suits, like asbestos protective suits, and special gloves. They gave us a bucket of flux, cast-iron rods, welded two rods together, and used the third rod as a handle. And took a torch in one hand, a big heating torch, and the amount of degrees had to be over three thousand degrees to melt the rods. And you work and you build this thing up out of nothing, out of molten cast iron going into the hard cast iron. But because of the cherry red, it's huge. And then you would wash down the excess, let it cool, crane men would come down later on, hook the chains on the lug that you just welded, lift it up, or sometimes they picked them up with magnets, loaded them right in the car for shipping. And that was the reconditioned welder's job.

So that was the job that was saving the company a lot of money.

242

AP: Yes, thousands of dollars it saved.

On each piece that was repaired, yeah.

AP: On each piece. But if you couldn't repair them you'd have to scrap them, because the customer wouldn't take them. And they had to be done right the first time, too.

Yeah. And all molds had the same sort of warranty on them, correct? In other words, you didn't send something out that was considered inferior. Everything was up to the same safety standards, the same specifications.

AP: Absolutely. And that job is a hot job, let me tell you. You sit over something like that with all that heat in your face, for 45 minutes and you do the job for an hour. When you get done, you walk away from and you take off the silver suit, and your clothes including your shoes, your socks, and your underwear, you're soaking wet. You sweat.

How about that. You know, let's say it was 20 years ago and the plant was doing well and you were on layoff and they called you back. Would there be any hesitation?

AP: No.

You'd go right back in there.

AP: There was no place in the Lehigh Valley that paid better than Bethlehem Steel Corporation.

And actually when you went in there, you probably spent more time in there, with your buddies, than you probably did with your own family.

AP: Yeah. We were like a second family inside the plant. We all depended on each other.

Let me ask you something. I'm going to ask you this. Now don't laugh when I ask you this. How on Earth did all that work get done if all you did was cook on middle shift and sleep on night shift?

AP: We didn't do that. Maybe some guys did. I didn't do that.

I asked that to everybody, because I want to see how people answered that. And you know the funny thing a guy in the Beam Yard told me. "There's five guys in this crew." He said, "If we're making the 300 or 400 percent gain on the shift, and I don't do my job," he says, "they'd firebomb my house." He says, "They'd total out my car." He says, "There's no telling what they'd do." He says, "That's a myth." He says, "I'm not telling you no one ever cooked on middle shift, but I'll tell you what. If we were making money on middle shift, and somebody had a pot of hot dogs and sauerkraut, and we got a five-minute break, we really appreciated that.

Because sometimes that's the only thing we were going to eat. We didn't touch a lunch."

AP: Well, when you work in direct incentive, you work. You don't think about eating. You think about that almighty dollar that you're making. So in between if there was, like you said, a five-minute break, ten-minute break, you ate and you were hungry. If there was something available, all the better. And soon that break was over, you're right back on the job if you want to make your money.

All the better, and if you were lucky enough to be in a shop that had a lot of people and a lot of, how would you put it, non-incentive jobs, a lot of those people did get a chance to cook. And that was an opportunity and everybody came. If a guy had a pot of sausage with onions and peppers and stuff like that, and fresh rolls, man that was a treat. I can remember buying many of them for two bucks a piece, back in the '70s and early '80s. And, I'll tell you what, it was a great thing. So, Andy, I want to thank you for coming over here today and participating in this. And I hope all the best for you and your family.

AP: Thank you.

THOMAS J. WILEY
31 years of service

Ingot Mould Foundry

TJ was involved in the customer service end of Ingot Mould Foundry. When the integrity of the product was questioned, he went to the customer to investigate. This is an aspect of sales that was not used enough at BSCO. This interview shows just how dedicated our men were. BSCO never realized that their most important asset was their quality workforce within the plant.

* * * * * * * * *

Today is June 4th, 2008. We're sitting here with Thomas J. Wiley. Tom worked basically in the Ingot Mould Foundry. How are you doing today, Tom? Tom, did you have a nickname or did they just call you "Tom?"

TW: Ah, "TJ."

TJ? Okay, is it okay if we just call you "Tom" for the purposes of this interview? Do you want to tell us how you became a Bethlehem Steel worker?

TW: Sure, Tom...Well, I actually worked at another steel place, the Bethlehem Fabricators, and got laid off.

Where were they located, up in Fountain Hill then or what?

TW: Yeah, along the river in Bethlehem, down there along where the Perkins is now; or, no, on the other side of the river, on Lehigh Street. And I got laid off there on December the 7th, 1964, and the next day went to Bethlehem Steel. Put my name in, and they started me on December 11, 1964.

How old were you at the time, remember?

TW: I think I was 21, around 21.

Okay so you had a little bit of life's experiences under your belt by then. When you got hired, did you first go into Ingot Mould?

TW: I went right into Ingot Mould, yes I did.

Did you wonder if you were ever going to make it through the week? Let me ask you about that.

TW: It was an eye-opening situation. I'll never forget the day the assistant general foreman at that time was Al Hokenson, and he gave me a tour of the foundry; and, at that time in the early '60s, I mean you didn't have the pollution equipment as they did in later years, so it was so black and so dirty, and I have to admit, I was just afraid to walk around in the place. But I'll never forget him saying, he said, "Listen, young fella, we're gonna give you a job, but we don't want you quitting after a week." And I'll tell you, it was pretty hard that first couple months to stay there, but I stuck it out.

Do you think that that was a part of a repertoire that he used? I'm sure he probably had a lot of people that didn't go beyond a week.

TW: Oh sure, there were people that walked through there, and at the end of the tour, turned around and said thanks and walked right out.

Yeah, I wonder how many of those actually became steelworkers after that. I guess they probably took some of them.

TW: I don't know, maybe they got jobs in other departments, but I know of a—not personally—but I can remember fellows walking through there and getting a tour and then you say, "What happened to that guy?" "Well, he didn't want to work here." It was too dirty, filthy dirty.

And you know this guy, Bill Potter?

TW: Oh yeah, I know Bill Potter.

This is an amazing story. His dad was a craneman there: Stanley Novak. And, Stanley Novak said to Bill who was going to graduate on a Friday, "Hey," he says, "You don't have school Thursday." He says, "No." "Go down to Bethlehem Steel." He says, "Go see this guy. Tell him I sent you. Tell him you need a job." Graduating from high school, so Bill went down, he gets a hold of this guy, I don't remember who he was, and says, "Ya know I'd like to have a job. My stepfather works in Ingot Mould; he said this is the place to go." He said they were like, he says sort of like foaming at the mouth when they heard this, because whoa boy we got one on the line now. And the guy says to him, "Ah, let me ask you something. Is there any chance that you can come out Friday night for Saturday?" He's graduating at 7 o'clock Friday night. That night he went to work. Guess what? He got seniority over 40-some guys that started on Monday. And that was because his dad told him, "Hey, you better call that guy up and tell him you will come in." He says, "This is the way it works." And it's just an amazing story. So what was some of the first things you did down there?

TW: Well, when I first started, I was a laborer and just cleaned up, shoveled sand, and did almost anything they told you to do.

And there was no shortage of sand in the Steel foundry, was there?
TW: No, it was loaded, loaded with sand. Well that was one of our main ingredients to make the molds.

Yeah. Now these molds were the actual heart and soul of the ingot production that were used in the rolling mills. How exactly did they make these molds?
TW: That's correct. Well, they took sand, and they mixed it with bentonite, and, of course, some water. It was just like having a recipe for a cake. You made a recipe of that mixture of sand, bentonite, water. I can't recall if we put anything else in there. And it got all mixed up with a big mixer, and the crane would put a bucket of this in, a bucket of that, and it would go into a swinger where it would mix up, and then they'd swing it into the core boxes and the flask. And that's what made your mold. And after that, it was sprayed with a coating, a blackening they called it, and from there it went into an oven and baked at a couple hundred degrees, just like you'd bake a cake. And it might be in there, depending on the size, some molds had to be in there eight hours, some molds had to be in there eighteen hours. The bigger the mold, the longer the baking time. And from there it came out the other side into pouring area, and they would put along the platform, and that's where they'd pour the hot metal into it.

Okay, and I want to get this straight so everybody understands these. These molds were necessary to pour the molten steel or iron into these molds so that they had a way to reheat the temperature so that they could put them into a rolling mill or actually forge them into some other shape.
TW: That's correct. They would, after they'd pour them, if I'm correct, I don't know, maybe it's 2100 degrees, and they would set so many hours and then from there they would go to the knock-out floor; and there, in the early part of my career, they would just bang them against another old mold to knock them out. And then as the years went by, and the government wanted the pollution control, they had what they called a shaker deck with a lot of suction in it, and they'd set these molds on the deck and shake the heck out of them, and the dust would, of course, go into the holes in the screening, and it helped a lot. Bethlehem, I think, was one of the few companies, as far as I know, that was sort of ahead of their time on pollution control. And then these molds would come out on the deck, they'd take them off, and then they would just set them on buggies to cool off. And that would take sometimes days.

Yeah, now those molds actually were used over and over again?
TW: Not in our shop. Once we shipped them to the customer, it

depends on how they treated them. Some molds they could get a hundred heats out; some molds they would get ten heats out of them. It depends how the molds were treated. If you bang them around, now you've got to remember, they were cast iron. You could crack them. If you put cold water on them, as I saw when I was in quality control. We used to sell molds to U.S. Steel down there in Fairless, and I would travel to Fairless and to Burns Harbor. I traveled pretty much when I was in that part of my job, and Fairless was complaining Bethlehem Steel's molds were cracking early compared to some of their other people that they were getting molds from. Well, when I went down there, I found out why they were cracking. They were using fire hoses, because they wanted to use the molds, turn it over so fast, they would put ice cold water on it to strip the ingot out. Make it strip easier. You can't do that. By them putting cold water on the mold that was a couple hundred degrees, they would crack. So we had some negotiations with them, and they finally listened to us and stopped that procedure.

Do you think there was any truth to that other customers' molds were better that they could use water? Or do you think that was just something they told you?
TW: That's just something they said. It was just something. We saw it with our own eyes.

You really couldn't get any molds better than ours, could you?
TW: Ours were the best, although later on I saw some that were made—I can't think of the company, but they were really, really good-looking molds. And, of course, at the time we did improve somewhat. We had people up at the Homer Research Labs. The mold walls used to be real thick. And here we found out like over in Japan and stuff they were using thin-wall molds and were getting more heats out of their thin-wall. Kawasaki was one of them. And, uh, I can say it now, we actually bought some, and we drilled into them, and send them up to the research and analyzed what they put into them. And the engineers up there at the research center, all of a sudden we were making thin-wall molds.

In other words, they'd seen something?
TW: And they saw and they learned something, I think, from the Japanese. Now if that's stealing I don't know, but I know we did it. I was right there when they drilled them.

Well, I would imagine if you bought molds on the open market, I don't know why you couldn't do anything with them you wanted to do.
TW: Yeah, but that made a difference once they went to the thin-wall molds. It was cheaper for us; we used less metal, less of everything. And they developed a good mold.

Do you remember about what year that was?
TW: Uh, that was probably in the '70s sometime.

You went to the thin-walls?
TW: Yeah, I'd say in the late, sometime in the '70s. In fact, the fella still working up there at the, for this new company, Mittal, or whatever it was, up until a couple months ago I used to see him. He was an Indian fella. Neustoffa, I think his name was. And, uh, yeah he was the guy who developed them.

Yeah. You know, uh, would you say that that's a classic example of what Bethlehem needed to get their costs in line? Going to those thin-walls?
TW: Yeah, well, that was one of the things, yeah. I mean there were so many variables, not just, it wasn't just that. I mean it was a lot of variables.

Well, okay, we'll get to that, but you know as you were mostly a shop foreman down there, basically in Ingot Mould, give me like an example of what a day's job would entail for you.
TW: Yeah, well, when I was in charge of the railroad, we had our own engine that we bought, because we felt that the PBNE gave us such poor service as far as bringing in gondola cars to load our molds, we'd have to wait for hours, therefore losing shipments, on-time deliveries. So at that time our superintendent, who was Rudy Ashman, and assistant was Hokenson, they decided to buy an engine. A remote control was just like something you'd have under your Christmas tree, but it was the real thing, a broad gauge. And they sent us to school, the company that built this thing, I forget where we went.

So it was a new one then?
TW: It was an old engine they rebuilt and remodeled. Retrofitted. You could run by remote control or manually, and you had to know how to do it both ways in case the remote control gave out, you could actually get in that cab and run the engine. But it was a really neat thing, fairly new. I mean we were amazed that you could sit there. It was a box of about 10 inches wide and about 6 inches high and it had the horn with sanders on it; anything you could do inside, you could do outside with that box. Hook up subs to move the hot metal cars, put air into the subs, into the gondolas. And once we got that I actually started as a brakeman and then an engineer before I was put in charge of it. But we went to school, and what they did, once we got that engine, that PBNE would drop the cars off down below; they didn't have to come up into our yards. According with the union, with the railroad, we couldn't go out of our jurisdiction, but they would drop them off, and it made all the difference in the world. And our

guys, they would work, it was just amazing. We got so much more product out the door, we could move the subs when we wanted to, we didn't have to depend "Oh we can't start pouring because the PBNE isn't here." We could move the sub. We poured at two places at one time. We poured in the annex and we poured in the old shop, which is two different tracks. And when we set the subs up, then the hot metal crew would take over from there, and then our crew, the engine crew would actually go and move sand cars, they would move the cars that were loaded with Ingot Moulds, put them out on the freight line to be picked up by Conrail or the DNH or whoever it was. And thinking back, after that we were short a railroad car so Rudy Ashman, he was a little ahead of his time, he was a Lehigh grad, he was a pretty good guy, he went out and bought a hundred railroad cars. And we had just, no one else could use them, we had them stamped "Ingot Mould only." We put 12 by 12 timbers in there, maybe 50. I forget how long the cars were that could handle these big molds. But if we sent a mold to Burns Harbor or Sparrows Point, those cars in the beginning came back empty, and there was a quick turnaround, so that we never had to wait for cars. We had a hundred cars constantly flowing back and forth between Steelton, Lackawanna, Burns Harbor, Sparrows Point... er, that's about it.

Now we had a little bit of an advantage, because we were able to buy these cars from Bethlehem Steel, correct?

TW: We actually bought them from; I think the cars were made out in Johnstown. That's another plant I forgot. Yeah, we shipped to that plant too, and they were one of our biggest customers, Johnstown. And I think the cars were made out there, and I'm not sure, I think we bought them or we leased them. Maybe the Lehigh Valley Railroad or one of them at that time and we leased them.

You know I was fortunate enough in my time at Bethlehem Steel to actually see that car shop in full production, out in Johnstown. I want to tell you it was a sight to behold. Listen to this. They made, are you ready for this, 18 cars an hour. An hour. You should have seen the operation that was. That was unbelievable. They had their own shop for painting, everything was done automatically, it went into a drying bin. These babies come out the other end. Boy, you'd swear, just like when you were a kid, "All I want to do is be a railroad man." They really looked good.

TW: The cars we ordered were special made for us, because our product was so heavy. I think the load limit on most of them was over 200 thousand pounds. So if we were loading smaller loads, we could really load them up. And what was neat about the process, the bigger molds with that permanent blocking in, we used oak 12 by 12 blocking, you just pick the mold up with the magnet, and set it on the block, and just eventually let it roll down onto the blocking to keep what they call the lugs or the ears so they wouldn't get damaged. But, yeah, that was one part of the operation I was in charge of. For me, I think I was in that business for about 9 years if I remember correctly, and then after that is when I went to quality control, when I got to travel and make sure Bethlehem was doing everything they could possibly do to keep the customers happy.

Tell us some of the lengths you'd go to, to keep the customers happy. People want to know about things like this. You know, they always heard about Bethlehem Quality, et cetera, et cetera. In fact, they'd hear that from their own employees. Let's hear it from an insider's view.

TW: Well, what we had to do once we cleaned the mold, that was a chipper's job, and we actually machined it according to their specifications, we had one big planer in the annex, 84-inch for the big molds, and two planers in the old shop, which was the 60-inch and a 72-inch planer. And we'd plane the bottoms to make them perfect, so that when they set them on the stool to be poured, they didn't have any leakage. We had our guys actually clean them out with a broom, which wasn't done all the time; and, in fact, that's when I happened to be put on this job to check on stuff like that. So, nothing was supposed to get by as far as quality. And, of course...

What would we be talking about, like shortcuts? You wanted to make sure that shortcuts could cost you too much money.

TW: Right, there was shortcuts taken, and I'm sorry to say, some people didn't always do their job, and I'm not just talking about a union worker; there were salaried people, my own people that I worked with that would try to cheat, and it was a bad situation at times. I mean I worked with these guys, some of them were my friends; and when things got tough, sometimes I had to do stuff that I didn't like to do, but that's what I was getting paid for, and I did it. I didn't make many friends but the quality of the product got better, and eventually some of the fellas that didn't want to adhere to what Bethlehem wanted to do, were transferred out Ingot Mould foundry and put in other departments. There's no names going to be involved here. But, yeah, I'm sorry to say that there were times that people took for granted. They just thought they had a paycheck coming and anything could go. But as things got tougher, as the rest of the world was making a better product with a continuous cast machine, although we did have one out in Burns Harbor, other companies throughout the United States and overseas had these casters where they completely eliminated Ingot Mould's, and we were trying to stop that elimination from happening here in Bethlehem for as long as we could.

Now I see here that, in addition to Ingot Mould, you also worked in the iron foundry. Was that like later in your career? And the brass foundry. Let's hear about those two places.

TW: Yes. That was later in my career. Well, what happened was as things got slow, starting in '82 when Bethlehem started to leave people go, let people go, they also let foremen go. And I always used to come home and say to my wife, it's like playing for a professional team. One day we had 62 foremen for I don't know how many couple hundred men, and the next day you had 10 less. And Bethlehem would just work like this, and you never knew. Times were tough, you had a family, you didn't know if you were going to make the cut. And as things got worse, it got up in the '90s; in '92 they got rid of a bunch of foremen throughout the foundry division. We actually had 60-some foremen, and in 1992, between Ingot Mould and the iron foundry, I think we had 8 guys. And what I did was, I'd run back and forth from—I had the cleaning section and shipping, I was in charge of both things at the same time. That's how bad things got when we were trying to save the plant and they were trying to save money. So I had a terrific crew at the iron foundry. The first thing I did when I went there, the very first day had a meeting with all the employees, invited all the shop stewards, because the guy in front of me actually lost his job for not doing it, and that wasn't going to happen to me.

And you wanted them to know that. You wanted to know you weren't the bad guy; you were the guy trying to save their jobs.

TW: Right. And so I had a meeting, and I said, "I'll work with you; anything, anything you want." In fact, I stepped on some toes in upper management. I felt—and this is no bull—they did basically the same job at the iron foundry, cleaning molds, as they did at the Ingot Mould foundry. But yet the chippers at the Ingot Mould foundry were making thousands of dollars more than the people at the iron foundry, because of the way the incentive system was set up. And I made up my mind after I was there a month or two and saw how these people worked, and I could trust anybody, because half the time, I must say, I wasn't there all the time. I had too many things to do. And yet, everything got done. So I took it upon myself to try and get them more money; and believe it or not, I did. But I had a good boss that happened to work down there, and I will mention his name: Trevor Shelhammer. And he went along with anything I had to say. The piece-rate department, I blew their mind. They were pulling their hair out, and they weren't happy with me; but I figured I didn't care.

Well, you know the bone skinners are never happy. I was in a meeting one time in Central Tool where the shop steward came in and showed them two similar jobs just like you're talking about. One paid one rate; one paid substantially less. And he said, "These are the same jobs. The procedures are exactly the same. These guys, you're not getting this production out, you're getting in trouble, because you're not paying these guys properly, and the men that should be on this job won't take that job. What are you going to do about it?" He looked at it and he said, "I agree." He says, "Figure out how much you owe these guys." Well these guys went crazy. From the rate setters, you know, well they were nuts. They said, "We're not sure you can do this." And he says, "You're not sure?" He says, "Well I'm positive I can't, because it's right in the contract book." And he took it out and showed it to him. In the opinion of the superintendent, in order to facilitate operations, blah, blah, blah, blah, and like the color drained out of their faces. But you know what, the guys were happy after that. Everything got done right. And you know what, it didn't cost them more money, because they made it up in increased production.

TW: Well, that's what happened in the iron foundry. I can't tell you what the percentage of on-time deliveries were with the other person that I replaced, I really can't; but when I got down there, I'll be honest I never did 100 percent, but I did 97 percent, which they were very happy. They never told me what their percentage was before, but I thought it must have been pretty damn good, getting 97 out of 100. And the workers were thrilled and they just couldn't believe it that I could get them more money, because they tried for years. But you got to remember, times were tough at that time; '92 they were talking about closing this, closing that.

And you're talking about substantially less people, too.

TW: Right. There was, like I said, at that time we were down to maybe six foremen at the time. So, out of 62, I'm down to 6. They left all those people go. We closed it up; actually the last 6 of us closed the place up.

What was your handle from going from 62 to 6? I mean, do you think that was the direct result of the loss of business, or do you think that was people coming to their senses about cost? You know I'm talking to you because you were a foreman. And you know the company's not there any more, and you know what the union said about the foremen. There was always too many. What do you think?

TW: It was a combination of both. At times it did seem like we had more people than we needed; but as the hourly man got laid off, they couldn't keep foremen on. I mean, there were too damn many. So for every so many guys they laid off, they did the same with the foremen. Now some were laid off completely; some went right out the gate. I was lucky I was in the union for, I think, nine years. So, according to union contract…

Your beginning, the beginning of your time at Ingot Mould?

TW: Right, I could go back. But, actually I never got to the point where I lost my job. I actually left on purpose. I saw what was going on. Well, there were four of us. We all had union time, and we went into our super and said, "As of Friday we are no longer gonna work for you. We want to go back into the union." And he said, "What, are you crazy?" And he said, "Do you realize you'll be going, you're not gonna bump anybody. You're going to go in to be a laborer." And I said, "I don't care," I said, "I shoveled sand in the first couple months as a laborer when I started." And that's what we did. The four of us, we all left. And we went back and we were laborers. This was about eight months before the plant closed in '95. And it was the funniest thing, because we were laborers for about four days, and they found out you can't run a shop with a superintendent and a couple general foremen. You have to have some type of supervision. So they offered us a… what was it called? Working leaders or something?

Yeah, you had the seniority to get those jobs.

TW: Yeah, so we went back on. They paid us a certain class. But the funniest part of it, everybody thought a foreman made a lot of money, my first check as a working leader was $250 a week more than when I was a foreman.

I bet you were ready to pull your hair out of your head.

TW: I said, "Why didn't I do that years ago?" And if they said we wouldn't make it, but it was so smart on our part, because in the end when we got better benefits, we got $400 a week on our pension, and in the beginning…

And no offset for years of service.

TW: Right, so it worked out because after a while when they tell you, "We're gonna save the plant, we're gonna do this." I finally realized, "You're lying to us." I could tell you a story.

You can tell any story you want here. There's nobody from Bethlehem Steel going to come and strangle you.

TW: This is the honest-to-God's truth, I'm a skier. My wife and I went up to Shawnee one day and I'm skiing up there. Now this was—I'm gonna say 1990; I'm just guessing at the year. I'm skiing. So it's break time. I was tired, so I go in. I ordered some food. I had no place to sit--my wife and I; and there's two fellows sitting at a table who said, "Hey buddy, c'mon sit with us. You need a seat." So we're sitting with them and we're talking. He says, "What do you do for a living?" I says, "Aw, I work at Bethlehem Steel." He said, "You do?" He said, "By God, we're going there tomorrow." I said, "Oh yeah, what for?" He said, "Well, we're brokers. We're going to look at your mills." Now get this. This was around 1990. I said, "What do you mean?" He said, "Well we're going to see what the equipment's worth down there, because when they start, you know, closing up." And, of course, I'm saying, "What in the hell are you talking…who're you…?" He said, "I'm not lying. Bethlehem called us and wanted us to come in there. They want to try and get everything they could with the salvageable equipment." I said, "Are you telling me?" And I actually told the guy, "You guys are full of crap." And then we had just a general conversation, and I said, "Goodbye. Thanks for letting me sit here." But that was two years before. That was about 1990. So what does that tell me? That tells me Bethlehem Steel knew what they were going to do. Of course they do say there are 10-year plans in most of your corporations and companies. But the average guy, we didn't know it. Who knew it? And I stumbled.

And you were with management at the time.

TW: I was with management. I stumbled across this. Stumbled across this.

Yeah. Well I stumbled across it the same way. You know I was working for the union, sort of like what you would call a business agent, a grievance committeeman, and we went to hear grievances one day and the boss wasn't there for the company, and here we found out the boss was at Harvard. This is in the summer. Did a little research, I found out they had one class up there for executives only on how to close major corporations. Well, I knew from that day on we were in trouble.

TW: And when was that?

That was like 1993. So I found out after you found out. But that was still long before the hot end went down, which was November of '95 and the rest of the plant in '98. So it's amazing. So now that we've gone through all that, what you did in the plant, have you ever been put in a position with Bethlehem Steel to make changes to benefit the plant and cut costs? And I know this is Monday-morning quarterbacking. Where did you see that the fat could have been trimmed and maybe we'd still be working there today? Where was the money seeping out the cracks?

TW: I don't know. I don't know if I could answer that off the cuff like that.

That's a mouthful, I know.

TW: Yeah, I mean, I have some theories where I feel they spent a lot of money where they shouldn't. Like, when you look at that Homer Research Center up there. All the money they spent and what they developed out of that research center I think wasn't enough. Well that Galvalume, maybe that carried it.

That carried the company for some time.

TW: It carried it. I said, I don't think I'm qualified to answer that. Maybe some basic stuff like we talked about earlier, have a better product. They cut back on both hourly and salaried workers to try and save it. But I think by that time it was too late. I don't think they invested enough money into the equipment we had. It was a joke. Down at the Iron Foundry, I used to get the electricians to meet me every morning before the shift started. We had one crane in the yard out there. If I'm not mistaken I think it was from the 1912 or 18 era. Can you believe that? And we had to jury rig this, not me but the electricians, to get this thing going. I mean, some of the stuff we worked with was so outdated it was pathetic.

You mean they were just milking and milking and not buying any new cows?

TW: Right. And when you looked at it and you looked at the stock report and the proxy statements and all this stuff and all the presidents they had and vice-presidents and this and that, and some of the salaries they were making, I actually this it was not just the company. I think it was both. At one time I think it was the union and the company. I think it was both their fault. I'm not against the union. I was a member. Way back those fellows that started this—my father, my grandfather, everybody worked there, our whole family. I don't know if your dad?

You came from a steelworker background, no doubt about it.

TW: Yeah, they had it rough. You did need improvement and wages and health benefits and everything else. But then it got to the point where I think the contracts got carried away. And the company, they agreed to it so it's really just as much their fault.

I'm glad you said that, because there seems to be a misconception that when you went to negotiations, the union stood over the chief negotiator from the company with a hammer and just started beating him on the head, but that's really not the way it was.

TW: It was both.

I was at national negotiations. I saw what went on. And it was a cat and mouse game is what it was.

TW: It was both, both their fault.

Some guy was trying to save a bigger piece of the pie, and the union was trying to get an extra slice of pie, and it just went back and forth.

TW: Yeah. But you know like I said that there were some things the company signed on like this four-hour deal, I can't remember the wording, but if a foreman was working or something. I can remember my guys, before we had I told you about the big blocking we used, he'd have to put that in my hand, but they were just six by six. And you'd have two guys lifting this and they'd be struggling because the cars, and you'd just go over and you'd help them. And then if another worker would see it, I'd wind up just for helping those guys I'd wind up and have to pay them.

Well, those were penalties that were assigned by arbitrators, and the only reason that those things ever got to arbitrators is because the two sides could never get together. Now, remember the Partners for Progress and the Juran? Now those were steps in the right direction, but I always felt that those are things we should have had in the '60s and early '70s. And the company had to come to the realization that the people actually doing the job were their best source of knowledge on how to do it better.

TW: Exactly, exactly.

And the foreman was only there to gauge, ok, the success or failure on any particular shift.

TW: Yeah, that's exactly right. I agree with you 100 percent, because at times I was transferred to—I couldn't believe the company would do this—they put me in the 48-inch mill. I had no idea what was going on there. I mean, although the job, I wasn't in direct production. I was in inventory control. But I didn't know what I was looking at. To answer a question that you said earlier about saving money. This is another one. Honest to God's truth. I'm on the job a month. I had to order Babbitt bearings for the mill. Okay? I follow the booklet. There were two different sets. You had a reconditioned set and a new set. By accident I used the wrong control number. I ordered a new set: $21,000. I catch it a day later. Just goes to show you what, now I'm talking from supervision. The superintendent down there, I can't remember his name. I go in there. That's the type of person I am. I say, "Listen. I want to tell you something. I made a big mistake yesterday. I'm new here. I ordered new bearings at $21,000 each when I should have ordered rebuilt ones." I said, "What can we do, we got to change this?" The man looked at me and said, "Don't worry about it." Twenty-one thousand versus seven thousand. And I said, "No, no, there must be something." He said, "I'm telling you young fella, just go back in your room back there and do what you gotta do." Well I wasn't satisfied with this. And I had just remembered I had a friend working in purchasing. His name was Frank Gerencher. He lives here in Hellertown. He goes to St. Theresa's church. I call him up. I says, "Frank, I made a mistake." He said, "That thing is setting on my desk."

Right now?

Tom: Right now. He said, "Tom, I'll take care of it. I'll cross that number off and I'll put the rebuilt bearing number in its place. Don't worry about a thing." Right there I saved $28,000. I went back in thinking, "Oh I'm a good guy." You know. "I'm going go tell the superintendent I saved him." I went in there and told him, and he looked at me and he said, "Okay. Oh, alright." That's it. Not a thank you or you did good by following up, nothing. Couple months, was there like three months, there was a couple of us there. I go in to work on a Monday morning. That same superintendent comes up to me. This is no bullshit. "What are you doing here?" I says, "What do you mean? I come to work." He says, "You don't work here any more. I laid you off. You and those other two guys from the Ingot Mould foundry, Eddie Wright and Harry Musgnung. If they're coming in you go out there and tell them, 'Put your street clothes on and leave.'" I said, "Is that the way we run things? We're not even notified? You didn't even have enough balls to tell me ahead of time or what, someone to let me know? I come in to work Monday." He said, "Someone should have told you. I notified somebody and they didn't tell you." But, yeah, that was a big disappointment. I was out on the street for 16 weeks, from being a salaried foreman. (laughing) yeah, yeah. But that was an experience I had as a steelworker.

And that was just prior to you actually taking your pension?
TW: No, no, that was way back, that was in 1982.

Actually that was like your only period of layoff while you were in the plant?
TW: Yeah, yeah.

Well I'll tell you what, it was a real pleasure talking to you about this today. I'm sure you know that this is the type of thing we are looking for. You know people want to have knowledge. They have a thirst for knowledge. What went on in Bethlehem Steel? You know anything that they can read about it. I mean, it's a good thing, because let's face it, everything was controlled. If the company didn't release it to the press, you didn't hear about it, and the press was very particular about what they put in.

TW: Oh sure, the press was, I think, controlled by some of the Steel, I really do.

Well, you've taken the words right out of my mouth, and this is the main reason for the book. And I want to thank you for your cooperation and I wish the best for you and your family.
Tom: Well, thank you.

FRANK ZELENA
34 years of service

Ingot Mould Foundry

Stringy or Stringbean was a quiet genius. Until you talked to him you would never expect his grasp of current events pertaining to his job and conditions in the plant. Officer and grievance committeeman for Local 2599, he served the United Steelworkers with distinction.

* * * * * * * *

Today's date is July the 7th, 2008; we're here with Frank Zelena. Frank, uh, did you have a nickname down the plant?

FZ: Yeah, they called me Frank, they called me String Bean, Stringy.

String Bean and Stringy, so for purposes of this interview what should we call you?

FZ: Frank.

Frank, okay, that sounds good to me. Frank, how did you get to become a Bethlehem Steel worker?

FZ: Well, I was working in a body shop, and, uh, I was planning to get married, so I started looking for a job, so I put some applications in; one was down at Bethlehem Steel, one was down at Western Electric, when it was Western Electric, so I could make more money and support a wife and that type of thing, so that's what I did. And I took the test, and I got hired at Bethlehem Steel on September the 29th, it was, I think it was the 29th, '64.

You know, now when you, when they hired you, did they give you a choice of where you're gonna work?

FZ: No, they, after I took the test and stuff like that, they said well where do you want to work, and I says I want to work in some place where I can make a lot of money.

Well, they sure sent you to the right place.

FZ: So they sent me, yup, to the right place. They said it's not dirty, it's all sand.

They actually told you it wasn't dirty?
FZ: They said it wasn't dirty, it's all sand, they said, uh, nice place to work. You can make a lot of money.

And before long you were down there at Ingot Mould, and what did you think, like your first week there?
FZ: Well, the first week there was sort of a learning experience where everybody was; whatcha gonna do, your arms and legs ached, and but that was about it. It was hot, not so much, didn't do much.

And were you, like, taken under the wing by the old timers; how did they do that?
FZ: Yup, yup, they assigned me with an old guy, and the old guy showed me what to do, and how to do it, and he said just take it easy and learn how to do it, and that's exactly what I did.

Did you think that those old timers were trying to always impress on the young guys what not to do so they didn't get hurt?
FZ: I don't think they knew any better.

Everybody was there wanted to go out the same way they came in, with all the body parts still intact.
FZ: Yeah, basically yes.

And what was your impression of the place when you first got down there?
FZ: Well, I was astonished by it, because everything was big and humongous and heavy, and I think it was a different place, a different world.

And then you had the dirt, you had the noise, you had the heat.
FZ: Well, that I didn't pick up until maybe once I started getting into uh, three, four months of service, because it was the end of September already, it was Fall, going into Fall. There wasn't much heat, you know; it was nice and cool, I was working by an open door, it wasn't dusty, dirty, nice breeze blowing at your back.

And what your first jobs down there were, you were doing what?
FZ: I was a chipper, started as a chipper.

That was right, right in the mix of the people that could make a good buck. So you must have been almost astounded when you saw some of your first pay checks?
FZ: As a matter of fact, when I went to the bank to get a mortgage

to build a house, they didn't believe the amount of money I made per week, and I had to bring in pay stubs and everything like that. They said nobody makes that kind of money, and I showed it to them, and they were astounded.

Wow. You must have started right down there just a few months after, like, Bill Potter?
FZ: He started a little bit before me.

Yeah, you know, he was telling me basically the same thing that you just said. I mean that, that's really something, you know, because when I started, I started up in the Alloy Division as a chain man, a laborer and a chain man. You know we made when I started $2.28 in a half an hour, and we were happy, but we didn't have an incentive like you guys had. You guys were actually in the driver's seat as far as if you give 'em a good day's work, they paid you for it.
FZ: Well, you had to sort of fight for it because you had rate setters that were company-oriented, and uh, what you had to do was a lot of intimidation and that kind of thing and getting what you wanted and what you thought you deserved.

And you think the best helper you had down there was probably the union then?
FZ: Oh, absolutely.

Could you have worked there without the union? You personally?
FZ: No, I don't think so. I don't think anybody could have.

No. Is it more because of the danger, or is it just because you just never knew what they were going to throw at you?
FZ: Well, it was, the union gave you, the union gave you, after you learned them, the union gave you a self-confidence that you had. You weren't just another number, you had rights and that type of thing. I mean the benefits were nice and you know safety was always preached to you, but they didn't tell you everything in the safety meetings, they didn't tell you everything. Never did they tell you everything.

And Ingot Mould wasn't really known as the safest place in the world to be working either.
FZ: Not at all. Some of the old guys had their sides all burned up and everything, and that was from experiencing explosions in the hot metal and stuff like that.

Yeah. Did you ever go through anything like that?
FZ: Later on, I believe it was in the, uh, I don't know if it was in the late '70s or early '80s, I was down on a repair shift. They had just had an

explosion on a night shift where for the first time they put metal into water, which you don't do, you put water into metal, but you can't put the metal in the water. And it blew the roof off the place, so they finally got it fixed. So I went in for a repair shift, I was working a repair shift running crane, and they were going to light this mixer up, and what you do is they turn on air valves and mix it with fuel oil, and they light it, and it gets up to temperature. Well, lo and behold they put this mixture on, and we waited and waited and waited, and then the foreman threw like a torch into it to start it, and all of a sudden there was so much of a build up instead of lighting up it blew up.

And you're above all of this taking it in right?

FZ: Right in front of it. As a matter of fact, there were carpenters working down below in the pit, and I was giving them a lift, and I see nothing but black for must have been a half hour. I didn't know if I was dead or what happened. And uh, finally it cleared and they had the fire company came up, the Bethlehem Steel fire company came up, so I was still in shock, and a guy waved to me come on down, so I got down off the crane and just shook my head and couldn't believe it, because it was an open cage crane. I could have flew right out. It blew me up against the back, but it could have threw me right out, that's how much of a concussion it was.

That's what people don't understand that never worked there. Uh, they can't comprehend that, that any day you went in there, and one of the nice things about going in the company is every day was different. You couldn't really get bored, because maybe if you were a chipper, okay, you'd run into something chipping you never ran into before. So it wasn't a problem getting in there, but the real knack was getting yourself back out in one piece, and you can't explain this to someone that was never there. This is the reason for these interviews, and you know this is the reason for the book to let people know, hey.

FZ: Like I said, they didn't tell you everything in the safety meetings. They didn't tell you about silicosis, they didn't tell you about COPD, they didn't tell you about the hazards of smoking with silicosis, they didn't tell you the hazards of being around the chemicals they put into the hot metals, acids and stuff like that, what it does to ya. They never told you that stuff. You found that out later on.

And some guys found it out the hard way.

FZ: They're still finding out the hard way.

Yeah, they're still finding out too. It's really something; in fact I remember the Coke Works is probably one of the first places in the plant where the company actually admitted on a worker's compensation case that guys had silicosis from

262

their operation.

FZ: Well, we had groups, maybe the first group that ever went out of there was about 11 people with silicosis, black lung. Some of'em they put down into maybe Number 2 Machine Shop, into the Combo Mill, some of them took pensions, some of them took disability here and there. Most of those people are all dead by now.

Yeah. So the job you started out as a chipper. How long did you stay on that?

FZ: Well, I worked that intermittently through the 33 years I was working there, but what happened is that as you became proficient in what you were doing, it became boring to you, you want to do something else, so you started learning another job, and another job, and another job.

And what were some of those other jobs you did there?

FZ: Oh, I worked as an expeditor, I worked as a rammer, I worked as a flask fitter, I worked as a chain man, laborer.

Let's have, what did the expeditor do?

FZ: He got all the equipment that you would need to make an Ingot Mould together, and that was his job. And you did that for eight hours because of the levels of production.

Because you had the 24/7 operation, and so you always had to have somebody there getting everything ready.

FZ: Well, different phases, yeah, different phases. One shift had to get ready to set up the next shift and the next shift set up the other shift, and that's how it went.

Flask maker I heard, what did the flask maker do?

FZ: That was a hard job. You put like horseshoe clamps on the flange, and then you clamp it together with a steel wedge and the clamp, and you drive the steel wedge, and you have to jack up to make sure the tops are leveled, and you're talking about moving a piece of equipment 200/300 pounds.

Yeah, you're actually putting a jacket together so that you can form the mold, correct? And that is the main thing that you guys did down there was make molds, and I've been told…

FZ: That was the main thing.

I've been told from people that were involved with the quality control that I've already interviewed that the Bethlehem Ingot Moulds were among the best in the industry.

FZ: That's true.

And people were always trying to get the Bethlehem molds.

FZ: They were the number one mold producer in the country before they shut down.

And they were actually producing molds for other steel mills all the time.

FZ: Absolutely, yup, yup. US Steel, couple places in Mexico, Robling, out on the west coast, Jones and Laughlin was out there, I guess. Yeah, they were nationwide, they were producing up in Canada, they took 'em up to Canada; Gary, Indiana. But then in 1967 an interesting thing happened is that when Bethlehem Steel built Burns Harbor, they needed mold. So the question was do they make their own foundry or do they have a foundry in Bethlehem where they can get 'em from? So they decided, well, they're gonna get them from Bethlehem, so in '67 they put up a big addition onto Ingot Mould, and they made the molds for Burns Harbor.

Was that called the annex?

FZ: Yes. And then you made everything big. But they never realized the mistake they made. The mistake was they put all their apples into one basket, and we had control of that basket. If we wanted something, all we had to do was slow down or stop working; Burns Harbor didn't get the molds, Burns Harbor couldn't roll steel.

So you say that this was like a double-edged sword, it was good and it was bad at the same time?

FZ: Absolutely, yup.

And you had some legendary bosses down there at Ingot Mould. I mean, I was told, correct me if I'm wrong, these guys were the absolute highest paid superintendents the plant ever had.

FZ: They were good super, I want to say we never had a bad superintendent once you got to know 'em. We had…

In other words, they knew the business, they knew the business.

FZ: Yup, they knew the business, they knew their business. And they had, they had a feeling for the men. We never had, until the last guy that we had, we never had a superintendent that didn't care about the people, and we had guys like Rudy Ashman who was legendary, because when I started, the first thing he told me, he says, Frank, he says, "This place is gonna close down," and I thought he was kidding me.

And this was when you started?

FZ: When I first started. Thirty-three years later it happened, what a visionary. And we had a guy named Al Hokenson who was, he was an engineer and he was really a, really an intelligent person. He became superintendent of the foundries. His picture hangs today down at Silver Creek Country Club as the president of the Silver Creek Country Club; when it first started, he started that. Uh, we had a guy named Ron Morello, he became superintendent of the foundries, and he was really a good engineer and a smart person, and he was a smart labor negotiator. We had a guy named Warren Kunsman. Warren Kunsman was like a father to me. He took pension. I begged him not to go; that's how good he was to the guys.

What year are we talking about there?
FZ: Oh, we're talking in the late '80s, '90s yup.

And uh, I'll tell you what, I guess there toward the end, you know, anybody that you had had working for you wasn't under such a microscope that you could never really put a handle down on were they good or were they bad.
FZ: Yeah. Most of the bad decisions came from the main offices. That's where most of the bad decisions came. The superintendents had no choice but to follow 'em.

Well, we know that, we know that, and you know, it's water over the dam. But, you know, when did you first suspect that the company was in trouble, your own opinion?
FZ: Well, I would say around 1973.

And what tipped you off there?
FZ: Well, we had big massive layoffs at that time. We had a big hiring, so it must have been maybe in '70, '71, '72 where they had big layoffs, and uh, it was all about cost cutting and working together and all that other nonsense propaganda, and uh, they worked through it, and in '73 they hired big time because the industry picked back up and uh, I guess the fears that they had at that time were gone, but, uh, so were some of the customers that we had.

Yeah, uh, did you ever work in the railroad, the Ingot Mould railroad?
FZ: Never on the railroad, nope.

I understand that was one of the biggest cost reducers that you guys had. You had initial outlay, and because of having your own railroad, you weren't waiting for the PBNE, you were able to do what you wanted, when you wanted to schedule it, and that was a big thing, I was told.
FZ: Yup, it was hot metal and everything else. It was really …

Yeah, I guess it made a big difference?

FZ: Yup, saved a lot of time, yup.

So, somewhere around the late '80s or early '90s when everything is getting goofy in the plant; we start out with this Juran School, we have the Partners for Progress. Do you think that those programs were just too little too late?

FZ: I don't think any of those programs hit the nail on the head. They didn't, they taught you stupid stuff like what colors are hostile colors, what colors are friendly colors; um some of the problem solving things that they taught you really weren't applicable to what was going on in the plant. Some of it was good, but most of it really here today gone tomorrow.

Well, you know I haven't asked too many people this question, but do you think that those programs were just smoke screens to soften people up for the big ax?

FZ: I don't know. I couldn't honestly say, I don't know. I know the people that were participating in it were conscious, very conscious about what they were doing. What the motive behind it was I don't know. Maybe they were preparing everybody for the elimination of the middle management and the working force taking it over.

Well, you know I asked that to one guy; you know what he said to me, he says "You know, their problem would have went away," he says, " if they would have removed a pile of foremen and put working leaders in their place." He says they would have had the same control, they probably would increase production because of fewer layers of management, because the guys instinctively knew the job. But you know, when you talk to the foreman about it, they say, well, you know, a lot of the guys were out for themselves. I says hey look, this is a tough world, I mean, whether what side of the fence you're on doesn't make a difference. There's a lot of guys out for themselves.

FZ: Well, while we were negotiating, one of the big, we had six foremen, he said come up with a, you know … what are you guys looking for during the negotiations or restructuring? So one of the items was…

You played a part in that then?

FZ: Yes I did. One of the items was we want you to replace the foremen with working leaders, and we talked about the number 6.

You guys actually went that far as to bring that right out on the table?

FZ: Yes, yes, we brought that right out.

Beautiful.

FZ: And the superintendent says, no I can't work without my foremen. So with that, the negotiations ended, and we left for, I think it was, two or three days, we left. We didn't talk. So he came back, and he finally agreed to eliminate four of them. And as they introduced simplification for incentive plans and stuff like that, the foremen gradually came off.

Yeah, and the place did just as well as before.

FZ: Just as well or better.

Well, I'll tell you what it was quite the place, and Ingot Mould, you know there's been some talk there were probably three places in the plant if the plant was gonna get an enema the hose would go, Ingot Mould, the Coke Works, or the Sintering Plant. What do you think? You probably worked in all of them?

FZ: Yeah, I was down the Coke Works for about six weeks, and I didn't enjoy working down there at all. I was never in the Sinter Plant, although I visited. I visited both of the areas when I was doing job study, job equity they called it. And I visited both areas, and I really didn't care for both areas, because it wasn't what I was brought up on. It was a different type of operation.

Yeah. So you were active with the union also, weren't ya?

FZ: Yes I was.

And what exactly did you do at the union? I see you were a trustee for a while.

FZ: Yes, I trusteed for a while, and then uh…

You were on the wage and equity?

FZ: Wage and equity, yup. Uh, I was on the grievance committee, and it's something I enjoyed. I remember going into the union hall the first time to complain, and I complained to somebody that was there, and he just brushed me off, and it just so happened a guy named John Tagyi was sitting there. And John, who was a staff representative, John Tagyi says wait a minute, he says, You come back here and talk to me; what's the problem?" And I sat down and talked with John, and I told John it was an incentive problem like most of the problems that were going through, we want more money, want more money, want more money. And John told me what to do and how to go about doing it, and I listened to some of John's words, and then later on I ran into guys like Tony Buffo and Owen McFadden, and uh, Hector Nemes, and a bunch of guys that were really …

These guys were in the incentives too, weren't they?

FZ: Yes they were, all of them, yup.

Yeah, they all came from shops.

FZ: And they all knew the short cuts. And I used to go in there at nights after work until the union hall closed at 5 o'clock. I used to go in there on my own two, three days a week. I just used to go in there and sit down and read arbitrator's decisions and everything else like that, and as a steward in a department, a shop steward in a department, when I first started filing grievances I used to lose a lot. After awhile, it was the opposite. I won everything I touched. And it got boring.

Eventually got boring.
FZ: Yup. I was ready to move up to higher places.

That's when you decided to do what?
FZ: Then I moved up the wage and equity, and I wanted to go higher than that, because that was really intricate.

Wage and equity was all about rating jobs, correct? How much a particular job would pay.
FZ: Yup. And then one of the grievance committee men got an appointment to the staff, and I filled his position for two to three years, I think it was.

Yup, yes sir. And what did you think of the grievance committee? Was that where the action was, or you thought it was more back with the incentives?
FZ: There was some head knocking moments, but, uh, they, we used to go out at night even, and you go out at night and instead of just talk about any old thing, the only thing you talked about was union. And they taught me about unions, they taught me about contracts, they taught me about arbitrator's decisions, and we used to sit for hours at a time just talking.

Yeah. I remember them days.
FZ: I was, I used to, Butch Engler, I remember sitting with Butch Engler.

Oh boy, you were, like sitting with a legend then.
FZ: I don't know how many times, sitting at one of the hotels here in Bethlehem just talking about 'em. Or with Tony Buffo or with Owen McFadden, or with Steve Nemes. And we, and they did it at lunch time, they did it after work, they did on the weekends. The more you heard the more you liked it.

Well, you know, you're talking to the guy that almost wrote the bible over here across from you, because, you know, I did all that stuff too, and I did it before you and I did it after you, and a guy said to me one time, "Bamie," he says," how the hell could you get elected as an officer in the grievance committee and two locals?" I said, "Listen, I had hundred percent approval rating; 50 percent loved when I showed up, the other 50 percent when I left." I says, "I couldn't lose." Well, it was only a joke, but you know I got the point across. But I'll tell you what, we had some great times, and we had some spectacular failures. But you know what, it's not how many times you get knocked down; it's how many times you get back up. And we kept onto the grindstone; that's all we could do.

FZ: There was a time when I was, uh, chairman of the home association for the local union.

Okay. The home association paid all the bills, correct?

FZ: Paid all the bills for the union hall. And it just so happened that on this particular couple months period, the chairman of the, um, the tri-local…

Finance committee.

FZ: Was off or on vacation or something like that, so being chairman of the home association, I took over his spot. And when I took over his spot, I couldn't believe the motivation that came forward from guys like Marvin Peters and Steve Nemes, and Owen McFadden, and you wouldn't believe how they motivated the officers that were there. They were ready to go down into the plant because the staff people apparently had a meeting with them and seen what was coming, to go down into the plant, and they want to go down and tear it apart. And the meeting went on for hours and hours, and I then, I kept yelling, no we ain't gonna go down and tear the plant apart, no we ain't going to go down and tear the plant apart. Really frustrating.

Do you remember what year that was?

FZ: I don't remember what year that was.

Must have been in the '90s the early '90s.

FZ: It was close to the end, yup.

Well, what do you miss most about the plant?

FZ: What do I miss most? I don't miss the plant so much, I just miss, I miss the guys, and I sort of, and I shouldn't be this way because, I don't know, people that were involved with the people feel this way, a lot of 'em. You miss the people.

Oh there's no doubt about it.

FZ: You miss the people, because…

Because of the amount of time you spent with them.

FZ: Because, yes, you became a family. You became a close knit family.

Yeah, there's no doubt about it.

FZ: Once they accepted you and you shown that you could cut the mustard and do what you were supposed to do and go above and beyond that, you became part of the family, and there was nothing like being part of the family, both at work and over at the union hall.

Were you there the last day the Ingot Mould was open?

FZ: Yes, I was there the last day.

What was it like?

FZ: Well, the last day they had like a hot dog roast and things like that. I just, I went in, the guys were sitting around eating hot dogs and stuff like that, and I just couldn't, I just couldn't look 'em in the eye because I felt guilty that the place was closing, that I didn't do enough to keep it open.

Well, you should be looking at that along the lines of what you did do might have kept it open longer.

FZ: That's true.

And that's the only way you can really look at that, because you remember what the queen said, "Balls if I had 'em I could be king." And the bottom line, the bottom line is, uh, people knew in the early '90s what was happening with the Bethlehem plant. You know our union people were basically told your job is to go back there and keep that place going as long as you can. And you know on the day it closed, I remember on the day it closed down at the beam yard, I was down there, the maintenance crew, and this is a hard thing to say, but we had guys that didn't believe on that day that it was really closing. It was just a disgusting thing to see. I mean guys were just losing it. I mean it was a sad spectacle.

FZ: It was very sad.

The first thing you would say is how could anyone be that dumb, but then the more you thought about it, the more you realized these people aren't dumb, they just haven't come to grip with their emotions.

FZ: The last day I could remember this. We normally worked till about 2:30 in the afternoon. By about 1:00 there were no bosses around anymore or nothing, so we said, ah, the hell with it, we're going. So when I clocked, we went up, we showered, and stuff like that. So the guy next to me came from up the line, and he as a young guy, wild guy, and he was changing next to me, took a shower, changed came back. He says, "Frank," he says, "I don't think I'm gonna make it." I says, "What do you mean you don't think you're gonna make it?" He says, "I don't think I'm gonna make it with this place closing; something's gonna happen to me." I says, "Stop talking foolish." I says, "You go someplace else, you get another job." You know, I felt it inside, too, but I had to tell him, make it positive for him. You go someplace else, you get a job, you got your whole life, you're young yet. Two months later he was dead.

Wow.

FZ: Lo and behold, didn't I get a job at Martin Towers.

You?

FZ: Yes.

How about that?

FZ: How about that is right. And I got it through, it was a Manpower job, and I got it through Manpower, I was working at Martin Tower. And I would see all these people that worked at the main office and now were working at Martin Tower. Mickley and, uh, what's his name?

People from the employment office and stuff, you mean?

FZ: Yeah, oh yeah, industrial relations, they were all working at the main office, down at Martin Tower. And I seen the abuses that were going on there up to the 21st floor, the chairman, you had to scrub the carpet, not get it dirty and blah blah blah and all that nonsense, and you used to watch who was it, Floyd, Troy? Whatever his name was. We used to be vacuuming the halls, and Floyd used to park his car in the garage and come walking up, didn't even say hello to ya, you know, and stuff like that. And that really, it really, uh, it made you realize what people, those people thought of you. But the people that were working in the main office that got transferred over there as well, they opened up to you; they welcomed you with open arms because they knew what they were going through.

Yup, they knew they were next, too. That's what they knew more than anything. Is there ever a time that you sat down and you thought about this and you said, you know, had I'd been able to do anything, this is what I would've done to save the plant. What would it have been?

FZ: Well, I think you hit the nail on the head. I think you would have gave more opportunity to the working force to lead the direction of where the plant was going, how some of the money was spent. We had one negotiation where they said, well, they're gonna have somebody on the board of the company or something like that, when they put the president on the board or something like that. What a bunch of shit that was. He didn't have no idea what was happening in Bethlehem, and didn't care what was happening in Bethlehem, they cared about US Steel and that was it.

Well, you wanna know something? Years ago, and you might remember this name, Ed Sadlowski, campaigned on that issue. Why don't we have representation on the board of directors for the companies which we work for, we labor for, and he was right on the money, but I guess he was a little bit too smart for his time.

FZ: We had a meeting about that one time with the company, and it got, it got, it got nasty, that's using a nice word, and after that, we didn't have any more meetings like that.

Oh yeah. Well, Frank, I want to thank you for coming over here and participating here, and I wish the best to you and your family.
FZ: Well, it was a pleasure you know thinking back a little bit, but, you know, uh, you still get that feeling you did something that, did you make it too tough for the company or something like that, yeah, you still have that riding with you, you know, even after ten years. It's a shame but …

You think you'd still be there if the place wouldn't have went under, you'd be retiring right about now?
FZ: I would've retired awhile ago.

Yeah, you would've got out.
FZ: I thought I had it made. So did everybody else.

But you know, life goes on.
FZ: Yes, life goes on.

Okay, thanks a lot.
FZ: Okay.

ROBERT GORAL
37 years of service

Metallurgical, Central Tool, Treatment, Drop Forge, Press Forge

Without a doubt, one of the most interesting men that I interviewed. The nature of his work was critical to our finished product. One of the few people in the country certified in critical testing procedures.

* * * * * * * * * *

It's August 24th, 2008; we're here with Robert Goral. Robert, how you doing today?

RG: Okay.

For the purpose of this interview, should we call you Bob?

RG: Yeah, that's fine.

Okay, Bob. I see here you have some college education. Where did you go to school?

RG: Penn State.

Penn State, how about that! "WE ARE!" You got it. And I'm looking here at job title, NDT Engineer (Non-destructive testing). What exactly is that?

RG: Well, I was responsible for training and qualifying all of the NDT people, that is the people that did ultrasonic inspection, magnetic particle inspection, uh, and uh, liquid penetrant inspection. That included all of the inspectors in the plant.

That's uh, I'm really glad I ran into a guy like you. I mean you must have really seen a little bit about almost most of the plant, you probably worked in one time or another.

RG: At one time or another I did.

Yep, okay. Started back in July of 1960. How did you find out that Bethlehem Steel was hiring, or did you get a break, did somebody tell you come on down, we'll look at ya?

RG: Well, when I was graduating from school, and they had people come out to school to interview college graduates.

So, non-destructive testing, they came out to Penn State and they said, Robert Goral, would you be interested in working at Bethlehem Steel, here's what we may have available for you.

RG: Well, they didn't say what they had available. They were just looking for people at the time.

Was it the Loop program?

RG: It was the Loop program. I also, uh, had a job through Sam Christine, who was head of the Employment Department at the time in 1960. A friend of my family used to, well, he worked for Bethlehem Steel, and he knew Sam Christine very well, they went hunting together, and he sold Sam Christine dogs, so he had me talk to Sam Christine, and Sam Christine said that I had a job with Bethlehem Steel. When I then got the offer to come into the Loop course, I talked to Sam Christine, and he says, go into the Loop course that's a better program, so I joined going into the Loop course. I didn't know whether I was going to be in Bethlehem or where, but at the time there were almost 200 loopers that they hired.

That many?

RG: Back in 1960.

Wow, that's across the country though?

RG: Uh, yeah, that's in all their plants. And ten of them, the people came into the Bethlehem plant. There were ten of us come into the Bethlehem plant, three of us come into the metallurgical department. We started in the laboratory in the metallurgical department.

And what was your degree at Penn State?

RG: Chemical engineering.

Oh, okay, all right. Now, uh, I'm thinking, uh, were you working under a guy by the name of Brugger at the time? Was he running the Loop program at the time?

RG: Uh, no, Rusch was the, well he was a recruiter at the time that we came in. And then as soon as we came into the plant, we were assigned to different departments, and we just worked in those departments.

Okay, all right. And where was the first place, you know, explain a little bit about the Loop program first. Let's hear how exactly that worked.

RG: Well, it started. The Loop program really went on for, you were supposed to be in the Loop program for about two years, and uh, you were supposed to get training in various departments. Uh, when you first came in, you have two weeks in which you visited almost every, every uh, department in the Bethlehem plant. Uh, you would go there for maybe a day or two days and learn what that department did, so you had an overall picture of what was done in the plant. So that was, that was really about two weeks. And then you got assigned to a department, uh, and three of us were assigned to the metallurgical division, and all three of us went into the laboratory, because they felt that the laboratory was a good learning experience, uh, and we all worked on steel failures to learn. I guess I was at a little bit of a disadvantage to the other two guys that went in there, because they were metallurgical engineers. I was a chemical engineer, so I knew very little about metallurgy, and I learned all my metallurgy just being in the laboratory, and you had to learn it, because when a customer sent in a piece of steel that failed, you had to investigate why it failed and what happened to it, and many times it was maybe bad heat treatment or something like that, so you had to really research all this stuff to try to find out, you know what the proper heat treatment was and everything else, and I learned most of my metallurgy just doing that work.

So effectively you were a forensic scientist in the Steel.
RG: Right.

And it was all directly involved with customer service, and for all intents and purposes you never want to send anything out the door unless it's the best you can make. Because your job depends on it.
RG: Well, we, see what had happened, the company, the plant would sell tool steel and alloy steel, and this is what most of it was. We did some work for the brass foundry when they had trouble with some of their tuyeres or something like that to try to find out why they would fail, but most of our work came in from companies that bought our tool steel or alloy steels, and they would make parts out of it. They would make dyes and everything else, and they would have them heat treated by maybe a commercial heat treater, and then while they were using them, maybe they would fail. Well, we had a customer service that we would help that customer out and tell them what was wrong with that steel so it wouldn't happen. We still wanted to sell them more steel. So if we would help them out, they would buy more steel from us. So this is what we did. I did that for two years in the laboratory, before I then went into raw materials control, and then we followed all of the coke that was done in the plant, the loads that went into the blast furnace, the material that came out of the blast furnace, the iron that came out. When it went into the, uh, when it was sent down to the Ingot Mould foundry, when it was sent to the iron foundry, when some of the molds would crack that we had in the steel foundry, we investigated

that and try to find out why, why the steel would, or the iron would fail, and I worked in there for one year. So then I went into the plant office in the experimental department, and I followed all of the experimental work on cast rolls and steel castings.

Did you spend, I imagine you spent some time up at Homer Research then also?
RG: I would go up to Homer Research to get material done, uh, investigate it, try to find out why various things are failing. Uh, I followed all the cast rolls, steel castings. Uh, got down into Saucon plant because they used all the cast rolls from the steel foundry. So I know at the one time the B36 sections were developing a galling effect, and the New York Highway Department wouldn't use them, because there was nothing wrong with them, it's just that when they painted them, they looked funny, there were little marks on them. So I ran a big experiment on that to try to find out how we could eliminate that. Uh, and uh, in a round about way I did eliminate it. I wrote a paper on it, it was published in Foundry magazine, and, uh, then we were able to sell that material to the New York Highway Department.

Yeah, that was mostly for bridges and stuff. That was some big stuff wasn't it?
RG: Yeah, yeah.

And there was, where was that actual testing done, in the main lab or was it done at central tool or a combination?
RG: Well, it was done in the main lab. I had sections of the steel cut out in the test house, down in the Saucon test house, and I used to come in weekends and nights and everything else to get those pieces and get them up to the main lab, and then we looked at them in the main lab to try to find out, you know, how the material was looking. You know, I'd photograph them up there and everything. We tried a number of different things. We tried using duct-iron rolls, uh, they worked fine, but they didn't hold up. They wore out very quickly.

They weren't cost effective at all.
RG: We tried using a, uh, a buttering, a weld over top of our rolls, and that turned out to be too expensive, so then we changed our rolls, and we changed the analysis of them a little bit, and we were able to normalize 'em and make 'em a little bit harder, and when I made, when we made them harder, it eliminated the galling effect, you know. And it accomplished two things. When we did that, one of the things that they always had with the section rolls is they used to shatter. They would break right in two, and many times, even before they were put into service. Well, we used ultrasonic tests to make sure that they didn't put that roll into service

because it would cause damage to the mill, and, uh, the analysis that we put in eliminated that shattering. So we eliminated that. So I worked there for five years doing that, and then, uh, I was offered the job in Central Tool.

About what year did you get up to Central Tool, do you remember?
RG: 1968. '68 to '78. I was in there for ten years.

'68 to '78. I was interviewing one of the guys that you would know, Frank Reinhardt. He was telling me he taught Carter Wolfe how to inspect chains and what to look for, how to put them together.
RG: Yeah, Frank used to work over in the annex.

Were you involved with that also?
RG: He was the chain inspector. No, not at the time. I was, I was responsible for the heat treatment, the heat treatment department, and we used to do all of the carborizing of rolls, nitrating of parts, tools, we did all kinds of heat treatment, induction hardening, uh, and everything, you know, so.

You guys were still doing gun barrels at that time, weren't ya, for the Navy in the '60s?
RG: Well, gun barrels were done down at Number 10. They were done down at Number 10 treatment.

Yeah, down at the cabbage patch.
RG: I got involved in that when I was in Number 8 treatment.

Now Central Tool is like, how would you put it? Would you call that the machine shop of Bethlehem Steel Corporation? They made stuff for all the other plants plus this one.
RG: Well, they were a repair shop. They made all kind of repair parts for the whole corporation, you know. They made gears, they made sheer blades, track wheels, and I treated all of those. I treated all the gears, I treated all the track wheels, uh, depending on how that gear had to be used. Some of the gears were nitrited, some of the gears were carborized, some of the gears were inducted hardened. All the track wheels had to be carborized.

You know I think just prior to you getting down there to Central Tool, my grandfather worked there 48 years, Willie Wiley. You probably heard of him. I don't know if you ever ran into him.
RG: Oh, I knew Will very well, I bowled with Willie.

Did you really?
RG: Yeah.

Well, I'll tell you what, he often used to tell me these stories about treating and stuff like that and problems they had.

RG: He worked in the treatment department.

Yeah, I know that, I know that. And he had several patents down there for treating of tool steel bits, you know, actual stuff used on the lathes and things like that, and I said, "Did that ever do you any good." He said, "Well, you know," he says," your name really never goes down on there. The only thing that happens is you get a pat on the back and a raise." He said, "Well, I took every one of them raises, never had a problem accepting one." I said, "Good for you." But, uh, he would get in there, and he'd tell me all that stuff. Now we interviewed another guy from right in that area, Mike, remember Mike Matlock?

RG: Oh, Mike Matlock. He worked for me. He was one of the heat treaters.

Mike gave me a great interview so that the end of the treatment part of it we have covered really good. You know, now we're getting into, you know, the testing part of it, and luckily we got here today. You know we got you, the guy that actually showed these guys the process. And it was a process, correct? You didn't want to deviate from it.

RG: Oh no, no.

That was the name of the game, to make sure it was practiced the same way all the time.

RG: Yeah. Well that was just like, see, when I got in there, the guy that left before me didn't want to start up the rotary hearth furnaces again, and they were starting up and he retired. And I started up the rotary hearth furnaces, which he treated all the drop forgings, so what was happening is before that all they were treating was central tool products, and then all of a sudden then we start treating drop forgings again, and that was crusher hammers and shell bodies and, uh, cylinder barrels for airplanes and stuff like this, and I treated thousands of those, and nose cones and everything else, all different types of treatment. I would have to specify what treatment that had to, by the specification the customer wanted, and I would specify that, and then I would tell the guys how many pieces per hour to pull out and everything so that they were able to meet the properties.

Yeah, it's really interesting. So years in Central Tool, '68 to '78, were working on specific projects more or less, in addition to everything else that you did. Because you know there's a lot of people they have no comprehension. When you say to a guy, here's what I did at Bethlehem Steel, a lot of people have the misconception you did one thing. Well that's, you and I both know that's nowhere near the truth. I mean everybody down there, even a laborer, had multiple things to do every day. And I'm hoping you know that down the road somebody can pick this up and they're going to take a look and they're going to say, "Hey, here's a guy that was a engineer, a Bob Goral from Penn State, and here's what he did." And this is what we're trying to get from you guys just by picking your brains, and you know it's, let's face it, it's been awhile since any of us have been there, so you know, just bear with me. You know, maybe I won't ask all the questions, but if you want to add anything extra, feel free to add it in. I see then after Central Tool back to treatment again.

RG: Yeah I went into Number 8 treatment.

Okay, what did they do?

RG: Well, Number 8 treatment took all of the forgings from the press forge, and they, uh, preliminary heat treated them most of the time. We did some final heat treatment there, but most of the time it was all preliminary treatment for all these big forgings to go into the machine shops for machining so that they could machine em. They wouldn't be hard anymore, anything else. Uh, so then they would go into Number 2 machine shop, Number 8 machine shop, and they would do the machining on all these parts, and, uh, maybe down the Number 10 treatment, the gun barrels and everything, we would do those, harden steel rolls. We preliminary treated those. They went down to forge specially, uh, they were treated down there, and then our machine down there, and then, and then treated, uh, for properties.

So the, the forgings yeah, did you guys do anything down at Centec, you know with that stuff that they were doing down there?

RG: Uh, well, I had inspectors down there ultimately when I got to be NDT engineer, and I went down there. And I did some work for them down there when, because when I was NDT engineer I was allowed to go to an NDT conference, the fall conference, once a year, and I got to know a lot of people from other companies, and, uh, it sort of helped us a little bit, because I got to know some of the Navy nuclear people, uh, that went to the conference. I got to know some of the people that I, I got on a lot the committees that were there. I was on the penetrant committee. I was on the ultrasonic inspection committee, the mini-particle committee. I was on the steel group, turned out to be the metals group. So I got to know some people from the aluminum industry, and the one time they had trouble with one of the plates from their furnaces down there, and, uh, it bent on 'em and everything, and they didn't know how to straighten it, and, uh, we weren't that familiar with aluminum at the time, so I was able to call up some of the people that I had known from these, this other group from Alcoa and, uh, talk to them on how to straighten this and how to treat this, and they told us how to do it, you know, so. So it sort of benefited us a little bit.

Yeah, I would guess so, I would guess so.
RG: But that was later on. Uh, when I was in Number 8 treatment, I was in there for five years, no seven years, from 1978 to '85. I was in Number 8 treatment, and, uh, there we did, we were doing, they were doing a four pole generator shaft at the time, the big 700 and some thousand pound rotors that were being made, uh, they uh,

Were those GE or Westinghouse contracts, do you remember?
RG: They were GE.

GE, yeah. I remember, I was in the electric furnace; we poured some of them.
RG: They were, they were, they would come into the press forge over a million, about a million and a half pounds, and, uh, when they shipped them out, they were about 740,000 pounds when they shipped, and I couldn't even lift those with my cranes, the press forge had to put that. I only had one furnace that would do that, uh, Number 32 furnace, and uh, that, that uh, furnace, it took about a month to treat each of those, and as soon as I got in there we had treated one of those every month. We had treated one of those every month for twelve months, and then they stopped the nuclear program in this country, so then we stopped making 'em. We had shells all over the place for the nuclear industry. Now they're going to be going back to the nuclear, and if they go back to commercial nuclear the plant that's in there right now can't even make 'em, because the new things that they did, the new equipment and the shells are much bigger, and they can't make 'em in there. The press isn't big enough.

Wow. Who'd ever think we'd ever hear that?
RG: Well, I thought that they made a mistake when they rebuilt the press. Uh, to me it was a mistake, but, I was only a general foreman, they didn't ask me.

Well, we all know how the company operated. You know, if you weren't at a certain level, no matter what you said, sometimes it was never heard at the top. I mean, we know that from working there. I mean it was the same for just about everybody.
RG: They rebuilt the press in about 1982, and uh, the rebuild of the press cost, it was supposed to cost 17 million dollars, it actually cost about 21 million, and they built the whole rebuild around a 50-year-old base.

Well, the way that plant was laid out and the way they, if they ever spent money on anything, spending money on anything was more or less like a blessing, and we all, we're both smart enough to know that the place would still be there had they ever modernized anything. I mean, they could have instantly decided we're going to make a mini mill out of it. They could have done it right to the end, but they never did, and it was actually at the point that when we had people to buy that operation, hardly anyone would have lost their job, you know, hardly anyone even knows about this. I mean, I talked to Dick Adams. Dick Adams just laid that all out on the table. There's gonna be some jaw dropping when this book comes out when they read what he had to say. Everyone's gonna say, you gotta be kidding me. But that's neither here or there right now. When did you actually get a feeling yourself that the plant was in trouble, about what year?

RG: Oh, about 1985, somewhere around there when they really started cutting, well, before that even when they shut the alloy tool steel department down, in '81, when they shut that down, uh, that to me was somewhat ridiculous, because the steel, the people that we sold the alloy steel to came to Bethlehem Steel and said to Bethlehem Steel, stay open, raise your prices, because if you shut down the other companies aren't going to raise the price anyway. We'll help you, we'll pay for it and everything. And when Trautlein was in and everything, and I think it was an accounting error, they thought they were losing money down there, and when they actually shut down and looked at it, they found out that they weren't losing the money that they thought they were.

I was told by people up there, office people, that they never lost money up there. The only difference was that in the early '50s or at the end of World War II, on a certain grade of steel they would make x amount of money. Now they were only making half of that, but it was still like a 50 percent return on investment, which really was nothing, you know, to sneeze at. It was still a good buck.

RG: Yeah, and when they shut that down, you know, everything just, you know, they kept cutting, cutting each appendage off, particularly of the Bethlehem plant. They shut that down, then they shut the steel foundry down, then they, you know, they kept shutting different pieces down, and then they kept saying the plant isn't economical. Well, you know, you had so much overhead in the plant, and you're eliminating everything to pay for the overhead.

Yeah, yeah it was a shame the way it happened, because it's something that didn't have to happen. So now we're up to with you 1985, you're back over at the drop forge, what happened? How long a period were you there?

RG: I went in the drop forge, I was in there for three years. I became chief inspector in there of drop forge and central tool, and I was in there for three years, uh, overseeing all the products that went out of drop forge and central tool, and then all of sudden they decided that, hey they're shutting the drop forge down. Now, you know, we thought at one time that something is radically wrong here, and apparently corporate sales knew, must have known beforehand that they're going to shut down, because they weren't getting any forgings.

Yeah, I remember when a guy would be working for a month and then off for two, three weeks. Work for two weeks, off again.
RG: Well, they, they, drop forge for years had, they got orders for certain customers, like Reliant Electric. It was a steady customer of theirs, and all of a sudden they didn't get an order from Reliant Electric for three years. And all the people in the Drop Forge were asking sales, how come we're not getting any orders from, and they could never give us an answer. I think they just weren't going in. I think they were told that they're going to shut down and not to even go and try to get orders. So they just let the place go without; now what started happening is when you start getting fewer orders, you know, you're operating costs go way up because you don't have enough product going through. You know, and all of a sudden they come down and say...

That always made their figures look good.
RG: We're shutting drop forge down, and they told me at that time, go and get my pension figures.

That was what '88?
RG: Uh, yeah that was in '88. And uh, at that time, uh, a friend of mine who was in the laboratory, because that's where I started out, uh, said to me, he said don't worry about it. You have a job. So I didn't know what was going on, but he knew that the metallurgist that was in the laboratory had gotten a job elsewhere and was leaving, so when he left, I was offered the job to go into the laboratory as metallurgist. So then I went back in the laboratory for a little over a year, and we were trying to go commercial, so we were doing a lot of work for PP&L, and uh, uh, a company down at Colmar that made off-market automobile parts, you know, and we were, what they would do, is they would design a part, and they would send us in the original equipment part and their part, and we would test both of them to make sure that they were both the same, and I had designed a lot of equipment to be able to test this stuff. Like they would send in lug nuts, and I had to find some way to test them. They would send in parts. I had to find some way to test those, uh, shock mounts, I would find some way to test those. You know, so we were doing all this testing, and we would give them reports. In the nuclear plants, everything that they used in the plant,

little tiny screws and everything, had to be verified when they bought it from the customer, so they would send maybe a half a dozen into us, and we would have to test them to make sure that they met their specifications. So we were doing an awful lot of work for the outside beside what we were doing for the plant, we were doing work for the outside. And then all of a sudden the company came to us and said, "We're shutting the laboratory down."

What year we talking about now?
RG: 1989.

Okay. Where'd you end up after that?
RG: Well, the NDT engineer that was there for about 17 years was retiring, and then they asked me if I wanted to take the NDT engineer job. Apparently nobody else wanted it. It wasn't an easy job. You had to, they sent me through a crash course, they sent me out to be qualified, or to be trained for ultrasonic inspection out to Kramer in Louistown, and I went out there, and I went out to the school, and I went for the Level 2 school. The guy said, "Well, did you take the Level 1 course,"and I said, "No." He says, "Well, you have to take the Level 1 course." I said, "I'm only doing what the company told me to do. I'm out here for the Level 2 course. You know, I'll take that and I'll see if I pass it." Well, I took that and I passed it. I passed the Level 2 course with flying colors. So then from there I had to go out and be qualified for the Navy nuclear. So then I had to go out to Pittsburgh, and I had to take three solid days of testing out there, and, uh, I passed the Navy nuclear test, so now I got to be a test examiner. So now when I passed all of that, now I had to come back, and I had to qualify, every three years, I had to qualify all the people in the plant. And every five years I had to go back out there for requalification out to the Navy nuclear people.

And the whole name of the game there is when you bid on contracts, you had to certify that you had people that were capable of testing all these things.
RG: Oh, definitely. They used to come in and check. We had to be audited by them every now and then, and they checked all my records. They checked my records to try to find out that yes I did qualify these people. They took the exams, and everything. I had to have all those records. You had to have eye examinations once a year.

Now were you doing this all by yourself, or did you have office help?
RG: No, I did it all by myself.

You must have been one hell of a record keeper then. Because I know how many people are involved with testing in the plant, there was a pile of them. Okay, so that takes you right out to the end there, huh, November 1997, the roof caved in.

RG: Yeah, that's when they shut down, yeah, when they shut down then, then I was rehired by Lehigh Heavy Forge, because they needed, again, they were doing Navy nuclear work, and you have to have a full-time employee, a test examiner

And you were him.

RG: And I was him. So they hired me there. I was there for seven years.

Well, you did real good. I understand from talking to people at the heavy forge, they're doing great down there.

RG: Oh they are.

They're buried in work.

RG: Yeah. And the men are making a lot of money.

Yeah, that's what I heard, everybody's happy.

RG: Profit sharing, the profit sharing, it's amazing Bethlehem Steel couldn't make it, and now these guys, they're not making the money hourly wage-wise, I think about the highest salary in there is about $17 an hour, but they're getting almost $8,000 a year profit sharing.

Yeah, that's another $2/$2.50 an hour.

RG: Yeah, they're getting almost $2,000 a quarter profit sharing.

Well, okay Bob, it was a real pleasure. I'm really glad I came over here. You know, you, a guy told me right out, you know the guy you really want to talk to is Bob Goral. You know that was Mike Matlock, and he said you better be talking to him if you want to get the fine details of all of this. So it was my pleasure. Congratulations. Good health for you and your family.

DAVID GOLDSTEIN
26 years of service

Press Operator

Very dedicated individual with a powerful work ethic. Dave told me "We did all we could to save the plant." Did we ever have a choice? You readers decide.

* * * * * * * * *

And now we are on the record with Dave Goldstein. Today is June 26, 2008. Dave, what did they call you at work?

DG: Goldie.

Goldie. Should we call you Goldie for purposes of this interview?

DG: Sure.

Okay. I see here you're a press operator. You started May 14th of '73. And what was your first impression of the plant?

DG: Well, it was like nothing I ever saw before. I was 18 years old. Um, I knew people that worked there, but I had no idea what I was getting into.

Did you have anyone from your family work there before?

DG: My mother's brother. And I had a cousin that worked there over the summers when he was in college.

And, describe the hiring process. How did you get to become a steel worker?

DG: Well, actually there was an ad in the paper for people, and that was in January '72 and it was during my mid-term break of my first year in college, and I thought I'd get a job there for the summer. And what happened was, I applied, and about three weeks later, our friend Dick D'Augustino, who hired everybody at that time, gave me a call and said I could start whenever I wanted to, and I explained to him that I couldn't start before May because I still had classes, and he said fine, call me as soon as you're out of school. So the last class, the last exam I took, I called him that afternoon, that was a Thursday, Monday morning I started at the Steel.

And did you start in the Press Forge?
DG: No, I actually started in Saucon Roll Shop.

Saucon Roll Shop. What did they do there?
DG: What they did there is they redressed the rolls for the mill. After the mill, the rolls would be used in the mill for the beams. They had to get re-trimmed down and dressed up a little bit, and my very first job was when these rolls came back from the mill, they were all greasy and full of all kinds of gunk, and my job was to get the gunk off and the grease before they went in the machine, because the machine would be turning them down, the metal chips would catch the grease on fire, and the shop would get too smoky, so it was my job to clean the rolls before they were machined again, or re-machined.

So you were cleaning them with what?
DG: Probably mineral spirits and God knows what else at that point. Mineral spirits and cotton moist.

Yeah, did you have rubber gloves, or how did that go?
DG: I think, yeah we did have rubber gloves.

You know there's a long history with using solvents and cleaners in the plant, and it's not a good history. It's not a good history, and that's why I asked you that question.
DG: Well, they told me it was mineral spirits, but who really knows what it was at this point. My hands and fingers never fell off, so I guess …

I know down at East Lehigh there was a lot of problems with cleaning material and guys getting sick. I mean, when I say this, I mean deathly sick.
DG: Well, I never had that problem.

Well, they did. Anyway, so now you're down there, and, uh, how long were you in that shop?
DG: Actually I worked there from May until actually the beginning of September where I went in, I was gonna go in and tell them, you know, I was giving my two weeks. I wanted to come back the following summer, and there was a foreman, a general foreman there, and he said let me talk to you. He said listen, you're going to school. How about this, we really would like you to stay. How about if we work you middle shift and you go to school during the day, and you know what you have to do during middle shift, and bring your books with you on your lunch hour or free time you can study here. I thought about it, I thought okay, I'm gonna try, I'll see what I can do, and 26 years later they finally said to me game's over.

Wow, did you ever finish school?
DG: Yes. I did.

What'd you take?
DG: Business management.

And you were with, what school was it?
DG: Community college and then Penn State extension. I ended with a BS in Business Management.

No kidding, that's an amazing story. I mean, there's been a couple of guys I talked to, but believe it or not they were not bargaining unit guys. They were foremen that went to school. And they told some amazing stories. You know, they really had a nice working relationship with the company, treated 'em good. So, how long did you stay with that shop Dave?
DG: By the end of October I was laid off from that shop. And then I went up to the Treatment Department. And I was a janitor for about four or five weeks, and then they made me a laborer, and then I progressed up the ladder from there.

So you were in treatment for how long?
DG: Seven years, eight years.

That's where they used to put all the stuff in for the press.
DG: The Press Forge was first, then came the Treatment Department, there was a machine shop in back of it, it was like straight…

Number 9 wasn't it?
DG: Yeah, that's it.

Number 9, famous Naz Medei territory.
DG: Yes.

A man whom I told was a legend in the plant. Anyway, uh, so what was it like, the scheduling?
DG: Well, I did, I continued to work steady middle shifts, which was never a problem. Nobody wanted middle shift. They either wanted nights or days.

And you're still in school then.
DG: Yeah, still in school.

Boy, that was, that was really a nice deal, though, the way that worked out. Now, were you married at the time?
DG: No.

Okay, so you weren't married; that was even better yet. Okay, now the Treatment Department, what exactly, describe a week working in the Treatment Department. You're there and you're working around these furnaces; tell me a little bit about it.

DG: Well, it wasn't long after I got there, we went through this process. I got on the repair gang. So we'd do repairing the drag outs for the furnaces, general repair.

And they were like sort of like small railroad cars that would, the material would sit on there that was gonna be heated up. It was going to be brought up to a certain temperature and kept there so long, and then they would pull it out and get it over to the press right away.

DG: Well, they would either quench it in oil or quench it in… Depending on what the treatment called for.

It was any one of them processes, it could be. It could be the press process, it could be the treatment process, the heating up process, and you did that, and were you on that gang the whole time, like the maintenance gang or…

DG: No, I ran the maintenance there, I ran the furnaces there, I ran crane there. There was a lot of guys running crane just about everywhere everybody ran a crane, so everybody had a…

Yeah, describe to me the size of these furnaces.

DG: The furnaces were about the size I'd say of maybe two box cars put in then, and the bottom part is the part that would pull out that the material would be put on for the treating.

It was on railroad tracks, and that whole thing would heat up. And what did they use to heat?

DG: Gas and oil. Depending on what the treatment called for.

Yeah, and what was the difference between the gas and the oil?

DG: The gas actually got them hotter. The higher temperature

Now were they using gas, waste gas from the plant?

DG: No, some waste gas, yup from the BOF and the Blast Furnace just came up there, but they also, when we needed a higher temperature, they could call for natural gas to be added to the line. Then it would really get hot.

In other words, they'd enrich it. And what kind of temperatures would we be talking about?

DG: Anywhere from 1600 degrees to 1800/1900 degrees.

Wow, I know those things were cherry red, yellow. They were really up there.

And if you put in a piece, let's say you put in an ingot that was the result of maybe four furnaces being poured into one ingot at the electric furnace, how long would it take to bring something like that up to temperature?
DG: Couple days.

Couple days. That's round the clock, round the clock. Okay, now I see you eventually moved on and you became a press operator.
DG: Well, there's a couple steps in between there.

Okay, let's hear about the in-between steps.
DG: Well, being young at the time, I did get a little wild at one point and got myself in a little bit of trouble. Coming into work late, oversleeping, you know the four-day off, like everybody else, and I was strongly advised by…

And you weren't married then?
DG: No, absolutely not.

Well, you were just trying to get that out of your system right?
DG: I was strongly advised by a general foreman, who just passed away last week as a matter of fact, that it might be better if perhaps I went to another department cuz the senior supervisor, the supervisor of the department really was out to try to weed out in making examples of people that were not falling in line, shall we say. So at that point I actually bid out to the Trucking Department.

What are we talking about? Are we talking about the early '80s now?
DG: Yeah. Late '70s early '80s.

Well, that must have been like a revelation going to a shop like that.
DG: Well, that's where I ran into the famous Burkey.

Bob Burkey? The legend, the Sneakin Deacon himself.
DG: Yeah, the day I took my test, before I took my driving test, he pulled me aside, he said, Don't forget to check the oil in the truck or the air brakes before you get in the truck or they'll flunk you," and they gave him a hard time about telling me that. And I passed the test. I stayed there for a while, then I went back to Treatment for a while; then I went to the Beam Yard for about a year and a half.

The Beam Yard for a year and a half, the beam world. Now that was a different place, wasn't it? Because you know, what was the only thing that they made at the Beam Yard? I know you know this answer.
DG: Beams.

No, money. They didn't make nothing there but money.

DG: I didn't have enough seniority at one of those good money jobs. I had a decent job piling, but, uh, piling in the snow in the middle of the night just wasn't my...

Well, now wait minute, now hold it, Dave. I was told that it never rains or snows in the beam yard. That's not true?

DG: Well, it did for me. And, uh, I was not real happy out there, I figured three o'clock in the morning I should be home in bed instead of standing out here in the snow.

Now I think I told you several times already the reason for this book was to dispel these rumors that all we did at Bethlehem Steel was cook on middle shift and sleep on night shift. Who was piling them beams on night shift, that's what I want to know, while everyone was sleeping?

DG: Must have been me.

Little guys, little guys crawl up from the river up the riverbanks and do it?

DG: I heard that. Steel gremlins

Yeah, steel gremlins. Okay, I just wanted to hear it from somebody that was actually right there. Now all this time, right, how were you doing as far as scheduling and working holidays and getting vacations? Give me a little inside into that. You were still a pretty young guy as far as seniority line.

DG: I was doing pretty good. Most of my friends who went to schools were making half of what I was making, which was one of the big motivators for me staying there at the time. I had job offers, I just didn't take 'em. I was just happy where I was. Which didn't make my parents any happier, but uh, that's how that was.

Did they expect you to be over at Martin Tower, or what did they expect?

DG: I don't know what they really expected, to tell you the truth. They never thought I'd be a steelworker.

Yeah, well okay. Were you the first one in your family to go to college?

DG: No. I have two older sisters, and they both went to college. One's a teacher and one's a nurse practitioner.

Well, I guess you know, when you think about it, you really didn't make any bad moves. You just made the moves you made.

DG: I think there was somebody watching out for me, because I seemed to stumble along through it the right way.

So now after the Beam Yard, is there a posting or something for the Press Forge? How'd you end up back there?

DG: Well, a good friend of mine, I met him in Treatment, his name is Jay Hallaman. He kept telling me, come to the Press Forge, you'd like the Press Forge. You'll like it there, make good money, and be out of the elements. So a posting came up, and I bid on it. The next thing you know, I was in the Press.

How about that? So about what year was this we're talking?
DG: Uh, '80, '81 maybe.

'80/'81. Okay now, I'm going to ask you something straight out, and you can elaborate on this a little bit. These areas that you're in, there's a lot of activity, you're in the heat, you're in the cold, you're around flames, you're around gases. Do you think you could have worked down there without the union?
DG: No.

Why is that? See there's a lot of people that don't understand that.
DG: I heard stories from the old timers that worked there before there was a union, and the conditions, they were dangerous enough when we were there. Before that, without the union, there was really very little safety precaution, very little concern for the men, I think. You were more like a, it was like having a mule in a mine. If you dropped, they just got another one.

And then as you got a little seniority under your belt and you were down there as a press operator, you actually did become active with the safety program, didn't you?
DG: Well, even before I was an operator, Frank, I worked on the press crew. Which worked outside of the pulpit as they called the press operator. So I burned the ends off things, I had to scrape the scale off as the pieces were being forged.

So when you talk about burning, you're talking about lancing with an oxygen line? That's some big time burning. How bout telling us a little bit about that?
DG: I have some scars.

And how big were these ingots you were working on?
DG: Uh, some of these ingots were maybe, I would say 120, 140 inches round and maybe 40/50 feet long.

Wow, that's almost hard to comprehend something like that. So you would burn off the one end; okay, how big of a piece would that be size-wise like?
DG: Size-wise? Maybe four, five foot long, and maybe, depending off which end it was, anywhere from 60 inches down to maybe 10 or 12 inches, depending on what the machine, the rough piece had to be sent into the machine shop.

So you were getting this thing sized up so it could be sent to the machine shop? And the press would more or less finish it off?

DG: Well, first the treatment and then the machine shop and then back to treatment.

Yeah. During this time, we're in the '80s now, did you have any inkling that the plant was in trouble?

DG: The day I started some old timer said to me, kid don't get comfortable, you're not gonna be here that long. An old machine operator from Saucon Roll Shop.

Well, you know, I had some guys when I was in the Alloy Division in the '60s before I was even in the service told me if they don't change the way they do things around here and get some new equipment, you may not get a pension out of here, and you know, I didn't know what to think, I really didn't know what to think.

DG: Well, at the time I really didn't care because I thought it was just gonna be a summer job. I never thought I'd be here 26 years.

Yeah, yeah, it never sunk in with you. And then when you get about 20 years in the place, you start thinking, boy it's gonna be nice to get a pension out of here one day, I hope I make it.

DG: Well, we all fell a little short of that about four years.

And what happened with you? About what time did your time end at the Press Forge?

DG: I believe it was September of '89 or '90, I think it was.

Yeah, and what transpired then?

DG: They just told us, well, at that time they'd already closed the hot end of the plant; that was long gone. We started getting steel blocks in from Steelton on railroad cars. So we knew sooner or later that was gonna be a problem, the supply of the ingots just so we could forge it. And they had told us that it was sold to somebody else. We all would be offered jobs if we wanted to come back. And I made a decision at that time that I wasn't gonna come back. I thought that they were just trying to get work out of us, try to get out what they could, and they'd leave us hanging high and dry, and, uh, in short order. That was, I think it was the right decision for me, but a lot of people feel it was the wrong decision because that operation was still going on.

Well, yeah, it's still going on.

DG: But I had had enough.

You know they really have a captive market there, you know, with those nuclear vessels.

DG: They do now. And I'm glad for the guys that stayed. They made the right decision for them. I made the right one for me. I just had enough burns and scrapes and cuts and scars to last me the rest of my life. I was glad to get out of there.

And you had, not only did you have life experiences, you still had that Penn State degree to fall back on, and you figured what better time to see what I can do.

DG: Except the problem with that being they see steelworker for 26 years, and you know the resume went out the…

Ah, yeah, you know what, you're right. Because after I became the first four-year graduate at the same school you went to, okay, the first four-year graduate they had without going to the main campus, they came to me and they said, go out here with this and you should be able to get a good job, and guess what I found out? They didn't want to hire 53-year- old ex-steelworkers. But I didn't lose any sleep over it. Here I am, you know, at least I'm working on this book. I had a whole bunch of jobs in between, but you know what? What's the number one thing you missed about working down there in the Press Forge?

DG: Working with the guys. Being a part of a crew.

That is the number one answer followed by benefits right after that.

DG: Well now yeah.

And actually wages were number three. And a guy said to me, "Every day I'd go in there," he says, "I might be a press operator," he says, " you know what every day was different. There were no two days the same." Different challenge, same people, and you know you really got close with those people because technically you probably spent more time with them than you did with your own family.

DG: True, absolutely true.

Did the Press Forge guys, do they have anything going on the outside now where they meet every month or anything like that?

DG: A couple of times.

Well, I guess the reason why is most of them are still working.

DG: Most of them are still working. A couple of times we got together and did breakfast and things like that, and what I have going once in awhile too now, uh, since a lot of guys when I was on the safety committee, they're still working, we try to get together on holidays because three or four of us work for the state at this time, so we have off the same day, we know that, so we try to get together for lunch once in awhile.

Well that's good. Let's say at the time you knew things were getting bad, you know, like the mid-'80s and stuff like that. If someone had come to you and said, "Dave, you got a free reign to do the things that have to be done to save this place. What would you have done?

DG: Went over to Martin Tower and cleaned house.

Well, I'll tell you what, you're not alone in your feelings. In fact you know, one of the things about Martin Tower that always amazed me, and this is a terrible thing to say, I'm gonna say it anyway, nobody ever walked in there with a shotgun and started shooting, and that is an amazing thing. Because on the day the plant shut down, like I was at the beam yard. I got the picture of the last beam coming out of the combination mill going onto the cooling bay. I mean I have the only picture. Let me tell you what, we had guys that day that still didn't believe it was over. It was a sad thing to see, a sad thing to see.

DG: What finally convinced me was the day we watched them pull the ore bridge down from the Fahy Bridge. We saw that come off the rollers and crash down there. They pulled it off to destroy it. I knew it was over then for absolutely sure.

Yeah, I guess you guys were right there; it was right at the end of your shop. You had a bird's eye view.

DG: I have a video of that.

Yeah, how about that. So what would you tell people if that plant was open now and they asked you, Dave, are you going back if they call you, what would you do?

DG: I wouldn't go back. I have worked all my life, I have a better position now, I have a cleaner position now than I ever had down there.

Yeah, what are you doing now?

DG: I'm a manager of a liquor store.

Pennsylvania Liquor Control Board huh?

DG: Which was one of the few employers that were glad to take us on.

Yeah, well, that's because they knew you were gonna be coming to work every day.

DG: I guess so.

Well, sure. You were dependable, they knew that, they knew that. And they knew after the conditions you worked in, you could work in any condition.

DG: But at the time we were in nobody knew it was that bad Frank, not really. Not really, I don't. We knew how bad it was.

Oh no, no. Guys look forward to going into work. I mean it was never something like, oh God, I gotta go into work. It was never...

DG: There were some days like that, but not many.

Well, yeah it was snowing or it was raining, or it was you know really bitterly cold, but you know, we didn't have a lot of that. But we had a lot of happy people working there. And you know, like any other business, you know, we had what we call our office voice. And you know, their main job in life they figured was to go and squeal to the boss. But as long as we knew who they were, we could live through it.

DG: Work around it.

That's right. Okay Dave. It was a pleasure interviewing ya. I wish the best for you and your wife, Candy, and happy trails. Thank you.

DG: Thanks for the interview.

RON KESCHL
33 years of service

Sinter Plant, Blast Furnace, Coke Works

Known for his ability to lead his men. A dynamic boss with a "can do" attitude. His close friends called him "the streaker."

* * * * * * * * * *

We're on the record with Ron Keschl; today's date is June 25th, 2008, and Ron did you have a nickname or everyone just call you Ron?

RK: No, no, I had a nickname; they used to call me Fin: F-i-n

Okay, now for the purposes of this interview what should we call you?

RK: Ah, just call me Ron.

Okay, we'll call you Ron. Ron, I see you spent most of your time as a foreman in the plant. But tell me how you started in the plant. What was it like your first week?

RK: First week I remember starting in June and I remember a labor foreman showing us around the plant. His name is Mike McKitga It just so happened Mike took us for a tour of the place and he had to take us at the hottest place ever. We walked up the pan conveyor, which was nothing but red hot sinter coming up. And he was standing there as cool as could be trying to talk to us and explain; we wanted to get the hell out of there.

And you thought you'd walk right into hell, huh?

RK: Oh, I thought I was in hell for sure. I thought, "Oh my. Medic!" I forget the guy who was with me but he was telling me, "What the hell's the matter with this guy standing around here like that? And what are we doing here?" Well, finally we moved out of the place and we started going around back to this labor shanty and then he starts to explain some of the different jobs that we were gonna do. And I'm thinking about this freaking heat all of the time, so was my buddies thinking about it too. Well, we kind of learned some kind of stuff. We wound up going to a place called the second floor, and I'll never forget that. You want to see something hot, you had to see this. This stuff kept falling off these machines on the bottom; we kept picking it up with shovels from one of the end to the other. We'd get done at the one place, go back to the other from the front end again, start picking it up with wheelbarrows, wheeling it down, throwing it away. Labor foreman would come down, get a little pissed off at you once in awhile, say, "Hey, guy, you're not moving this" or whatever, you know.

Now, let me get this right; you're on the second floor of the sintering plant, and the process of making sinter, right, these various ores and mixtures are being heated to drive the impurities out of them but some of them spill over the side. They're still hot? Red hot and you're shoveling them up?

RK: Oh yeah, fell right off the bottom. Oh, red hot. And some of them are little pieces and some are big clinkers; they weighed like 40, 50, maybe even 100 pounds some of them.

Now, what shifts did you work doing that?

RK: Well, that was strictly a day shift job, but once in a while it would fall off into like the nights and the middles. If things were running pretty bad there for some reason they would adhere to the bottom of these pan conveyors, which were really, really big. They were actually called pallets. And they'd hang onto those things, and sometimes you really had a bad time with them. We had some really bad incidents with them, like at the other end where the crusher used to be; it would crush the pieces up. And for some reason they were warped, the plates at the bottom, and we had to get these bars that were at least 15-20 foot long, some of them, maybe ¾ inch wide, inch thick, and you had to break these down to little pieces so it wouldn't build up in there. Let me tell you something, we had some really bad times there. You just wanted to get the hell out of the damn place. But we were working there, so this is what we had to do. And I kept thinking all the time, "You know what, I ain't going to do this shit the rest of my life." Well, pretty soon a few guys retired, and then some jobs opened up, and we started to learn different parts of that plant. Then the next guys come in, they were the laborers, so … But all the time I said we just worked, we worked feeder tender, which was right above us. Middle of the night sometimes, you'd come down, you had to do the same God damn thing over again, just help everything out. It was hard, hot, filthy, hot and dirty.

And the old timers always told ya, "Kid, just be glad you got a job here. You're working at Bethlehem Steel, you'll be here forever."

RK: Yep, that's what they told us.

Oh, there's no doubt about it, that's what they told me. I started, ya know, just a couple months after you and that's what they told me. "You come to work, they don't like part-timers, you keep your mouth shut." He says, "They don't like bull shitters either." I says, "What else, Joe?" He says, "You come to union meeting tonight." Ha ha, I only went over because I could drink for nothing, ya know, and I was only 19 at the time. Oh, what a time we had.

RK: A lot of those old timers, though, they were afraid to tell you stuff, too, ya know.

Oh no, they were really worried that you were going to take their jobs.

RK: That's exactly right; they were afraid of that.

They, they had worked so long actually without a union, there were no holds barred, that they had a hard time comprehending that they were protected by the seniority.

RK: Oh yeah, they couldn't understand that.

But you know what, if they liked you, they'd do anything for you.

RK: They would, these guys would, they worked hard and they'll tell you, like you said, they'd do anything for you.

And I always thought their best asset was they always looked out for the younger guys. Cuz they were smart enough to know what happened to them when they were young guys and they wanted to make sure it wasn't going to happen to you. So now you're in the sintering plant and you worked all three shifts, I'd imagine.

RK: Oh yeah, right around the clock there, 7, 7 and 6, that's how we used to work.

And Ron, were you on a regular schedule then?

RK: Oh yeah.

That was one of the few places that had an ongoing schedule like that, ya know, from the beginning of time, but I guess they almost had to do that. What was it like, 19 guys on a shift?

RK: Well, I'm trying to think of that. I thought of that before, I think it was about close to 19 guys on a shift at least. It was like an ongoing operation, something you couldn't stop. One period of time on a Thursday we had a shut down, that we shut the place down for like an 8-hour day for maintenance operation and stuff like that. But that place went 24 hours around the clock.

Yeah, every Thursday they'd be down there, they'd be working. Hard facing, you know, what was that at the end, the crushers? They'd be hard facing that, the riggers would be there. Our guys would be working on the pans. It was really something. They went round the clock, ya know, as long as those furnaces were going. And you know, all the blast furnace people would rather use sinter than pellets. And the reason why is that it was a better product, more impurities were out of it and the air circulated through it and it actually created a heat faster on sinter than it would ever do on pellets.

RK: Absolutely. Yeah, if you ever saw a piece of sinter you could see the reason why.

Tell me exactly what sinter is Ron.

RK: All right, sinter was, they tried to put this into a very palatable form. They took iron ore that was raw, like a furnace would basically like to use something that was big, like hard like a rock, with voids in it.

Now when you say furnace we're talking about a blast furnace?

RK: Yeah, about a blast furnace. They would like to get something that had like voids in it, like bigger pieces, that would be ideal but all of that rich material that was iron ore material had to be put into a sort of like palatable form that you could use. So as they would mine iron ore, it was like ground. Now you put this in a form, you mixed it with different ingredients and you put it under heat, you had your fluxes in it, which was sand, you had reverts around the Bethlehem Steel. Nothing got thrown away there; they reclaimed everything.

You'd have metal filings from the machine shops.

RK: Yeah, metal filings and it would be called "scale." Then you had flue dirt that came out of the stacks of the furnaces, and that had carbon value in it, that's what you use a lot of that stuff up. You re-burned it again, and when the product came out of there, it looked like miniature pieces of sponge; you picked it up there were voids all over it. And that blast furnace would take that much better than they would the pellets.

Yeah, because you could get more hot air on a piece than And, uh, there were actually four lines there, right?

RK: Yeah, we had four furnaces—one, two, three, and four actually. And sometime if we had trouble with like the one side of the place we could shut down or run two machines, but it didn't quite come out as good. It was a lot harder working that way; the product had changed a little bit, you know, because of the mix level and stuff like that. You had to really be careful with that. Ideally, four machines ran the right way.

Yeah, yeah. Do you remember a period, correct me if I'm wrong, I'm thinking the early '80s, they were running one and two, and three and four in alternate weeks and stuff like that.

RK: Yeah, there was some kind of repair thing. No, it wasn't. It was actually, there was a shutdown value in there. They couldn't take it. They couldn't take as much for some reason. We had a slowdown, I think, something happened down at the furnaces where they couldn't take all of it at one time.

Which might have been a rebuild?

RK: Or something like that but they couldn't consume as much. Now, when we had the stock sinter out in the yard for some, we also stocked sinter when they couldn't take as much, but that had a breakdown factor in it. They didn't want to take too much of that stock sinter down there because already you had to reheat it again. It was a little bit on the colder side and start to break down a little bit. They'd rather have it coming right out of the sintering plant into the furnace.

Right out of the car and into right down to the furnace. Do you remember when you started how many furnaces were going down at the blast furnace? 1964?

RK: I'm gonna say, we weren't too sharp on that down when we worked at the sintering plant but I'm gonna think there was three of them going; I'm not quite sure, but I think there was three of them going.

I know for a period of time in the '70s they actually had four of them going for a while. I don't remember when it was, but I can remember being at the union hall and someone bringing it up at the union meeting that the schedule was in chaos because they added a furnace. And the one guy got up and he said, "Listen," he says, "this is the kind of chaos we want as long as possible." He says, "When four furnaces are running," he says, "we're doing real good here." He says, "We don't ever want to go below three furnaces." Well, we know what happened there over time, ya know. Four, three, two, one. And then we went "off into history."

RK: Yep that's what happened. That's exactly right.

So, during the time that you were at the sintering plant, ah, were you ever laid off?

RK: Only one time, and this is ironic, I was laid off as a foreman. And that was weird.

Well, then let's talk about when you became foreman.

RK: Okay, I'm trying to think now… it was about early '80s. I think I went on in the early '80s. In fact I turned the job down a couple times. And the only reason I…

And what were you doing at the time you turned it down, what was your job in the sintering plant?

RK: I worked up as a machine operator up on the third floor and if you got kicked back a little bit I wound up back down in the Pug mill. Pug mill was mostly the place I did work at. But I ran the machines upstairs on the third floor and ah…

And what did you do in the Pug mill?

RK: Pug mill was a return place. What happened was when the product got done off the third floor and the crusher would crush it, these small fines that could not go back into the system right then and they would go back into the Pug mill, which was down below. It was like a big vibrating tube on both sides. It would pick up that fine material and now would mix it in with the material that was already coming out of the bin house. It added a little bit of heat factor and it worked out pretty damn good coming up that way; you got rid of it; you never threw it away. Nothing got thrown away.

Ah, that's good. And for the benefit of the people who are listening to this and wondering—sintering plant, four-line operation, four blast furnaces running— we're talking about the area right in the middle of the Minsi Trail Bridge. And every time you drove over it you used to say to yourself, "Boy I'm glad I don't work there." But you know there was a lot of arguments and you'll hear it from Coke Works guys and you'll hear it from Ingot Mould guys, if they're ever gonna give the plant an enema, where the hoses are gonna go? The sintering guys said, "Well, it's got to go here." And the coke guys said, "No, no. It'll go here." And the Ingot Mould guys said, "No, it'll go here. But ya know what, those were three dirty places, but you know what, they fed a lot of families for a lot of years.

RK: Oh yeah, exactly, a lot of families put some kids through schools and college and turned out to be leaders of this country.

That's right, so tell me then how you became foreman. Early '80s?

RK: Yeah, early '80s, the guy I used to work for my shift foreman, one of the greatest guys there, Donnie Schier, his name was. And I worked for a guy named Charlie Fritz, another super great guy. Donnie was looking for a guy; he needed a guy to put on as an extra foreman. Well, he couldn't really pick on anybody too much, so he ran the gamut with a lot of people, and I didn't want to take it.

In other words, he was trying guys out?

RK: Yeah, he asked me a few times, I filled in a few times, and I wasn't that crazy about it. The responsibility drove me nuts for a while, ya know. It was kind of nuts, and I thought, "Oh the hell with it." The reason I changed my mind was really weird. I'm coming in one day in a snowstorm. Now, foremen could drive in. Okay? I'm walking up the goddamn hill from the Army-Navy gate, and I must have fell about four or five times and I said, "The hell with this shit, Next time he asks me, boom, I'm taking this job, so I could drive my goddamn car in here." And that's how I turned out to be a foreman.

And I'll tell you what, that was really nice when you could drive in there; that was a walk in and out. That was about, what was that, at least 10 or 12 minutes?

RK: At least that.

10 or 12 minutes to get to the Army-Navy gate, and then if you couldn't park in the lot, you were parking across the railroad track, then if the train was coming, you had to either wait for the train or go up around the Fourth Street Bridge, I mean it was ... it was really something. And then you worked all three shifts, and you drove by the neighborhood swimming pool on July 4th, everyone was sitting there having their cookouts and lifting their Budweiser, and you were going to work. Then your buddies would say, "But Ron, look at all the money you're making." But you know what, that was the nature of the beast. And that's what the people who never worked there know nothing about. How did you do as far as accidents over the time you were there? Did you ever get injured?

RK: Yeah, I had a few injuries and stuff there. In fact, one of the worst injuries I had was actually walking across the Minsi Trail Bridge one time. I got hit by a car. I was coming into work. It was just before Christmas, and I can't think of the year right now, but I was coming across, and I hit the "push light" to come across the bridge. At the north end, and it was a bitter cold rain coming down, it was early December. And the cars on the north side, they stopped. And I looked up at the light, and it turned, it was red. But coming from the South side, they were cranking pretty good yet. And I figured they'd stop. Well, this guy came with a round Beetle, VW Beetle, and I saw him, and I had my collar turned up a little bit, and I swung myself into it. He threw me. I hit and went right over on top of the car. That's how hard he hit me. I actually thought I was dead, and behind him was a nurse coming back from St. Luke's. Part of my hand went through the windshield, and I went over the top of the car behind him. And I actually thought I was dead. I like saw flashbacks to when I was a little kid. And I just laid there, and all of a sudden my eyes kind of flittered open a little bit, you know, and here this woman was there, she was a nurse coming back, and she wrapped something around my hand. Right here, the blood was coming out, I have a scar here. Well, anyway, by that time a cop showed up. He turned around from Minsi Trail and he came down there. And it was still raining pretty hard. And there I was laying there all screwed up. But I knew one thing, I could not feel my legs, any part of my legs. The cop called up, he even had an accident coming around. He hit a guard rail up there. And, ah, he said, the cop called the ambulance, the ambulance people said, "Now where do you want to go?" I first said, "St. Luke's." Then I got in the ambulance, I said, "No, no, make it Muhlenberg, because it will be closer for my wife to come down; I know she'll wind up coming down." So I wound up going to Muhlenberg. And they wanted to call my wife, she worked at Cross Country Clothes in Egypt at the time. Worked there many years. I said, "Don't call her, I'll call her when she gets out of work. I don't want her to get shook up." So I waited until she got home and they gave me the phone. I called her up. I say, "Had a little trouble down here. I'm down at Muhlenberg." "Oh what happened, what happened" she was all worked up. I said, "Bring some extra clothes down here, they had to cut my pants off me." So she came down there. Well now, I could hear the doctor and her talking, "Blah, blah, blah." You know. "Well, this guy can't get the hell out, he can't even walk." She came over and she soothed me down a little. "Well, you're going to have to stay here, like overnight maybe until they figure out what's wrong with you." Well, it turned out to be a little bit longer than overnight. I did myself, I walked myself out of that thing, though. I did it myself, I think I got a lot of, did a lot of exercise and I did some weird stuff at the time, so I did get out of there. I got lucky. I had no broken bones on me, which was ironic.

Yeah, that is ironic. That is ironic.

RK: Yeah, so that was the worst time I got ill.

We actually had a fatality over there once in the '70s. I remember the guys. When I came down there, I came down there in 1978 as a motor inspector with ore handling. And I remember them talking about that, a guy had been killed a couple of years earlier. Yeah, I'll tell you what, that was really a treat going across that bridge in nasty weather. Oh my God! You know that had grating. It'd go right up your pants leg. I'm not going to tell you what it froze, but it almost froze them right off! But we still showed up for work.

RK: Oh yeah, we were there, we were there, oh yeah.

We were there. So now you'd become foreman and was that like something that took a little getting used to?

RK: I'll tell you what it was like a big, it was like, culture shock all over again. Now, you start to feel guys out, how they, the reaction of everybody. You know you don't want to be a prick to anybody, but you know?

And you know everybody, you know everybody already, cuz you've been one of the gang.

RK: And I grew up with them, I knew them all and I knew a lot of their traits. I knew what made them work and I knew what didn't make them work.

You were already there 15 or 16 years.

RK: Yeah, I talked to those guys just as though I was working with them all the time. I didn't put any airs on like I was someone special or anything like that. I never did that all the years I was a foreman. I never did that to anybody.

Did you ever feel as though that was a good way to connect?

RK: I did. I could actually connect a little bit better than when I used to work with the guys, alongside them, because I could spend a little bit more time with them. You know, if they had any kind of bullshit problems or anything like that, even home problems, they would bring some baggage in or something like that, I'd lend an ear to them. You know?

Well yeah, you wanted to make sure they were there for the next shift. You did what you could.

RK: You know, well yeah, you got that right.

I remember talking to Dave Scurry, he used to tell me, "You know" he says, and you're never going to believe this, and this is up at St. Bernard's, he says, "I never had to discipline a guy." I said, "What?" He says, "Yeah" he says "I've been on this crew now" he says "14 years; I've never had to discipline a guy." "How on earth did you do that?" He says, "Well" he says, "we're a team here." He says, "You know" he says "at the end of every middle shift" he says "we go up the club" he says "we have a little party. Every month we do that." I says, "Yeah?" And he says and he says, "Guess what?" He says, "If a guy had to have off a day, we gave him off a day." He says, "If we have to do this, but we made it very plain to him, 'if you step over the line or I can't help you any more, that's exactly what it means, I can't help you any more; you got to help yourself. So come in here and tell me what the hell's wrong.'" He says, "Now I had a couple guys" he said "had problems, you know, drinking or whatever. Whatever it was" he says "and we lost those guys." They weren't on the gang anymore. They didn't necessarily leave the sintering plant or anything like that, they just weren't on the gang. We had a tight bunch of guys. You experienced basically the same thing I think.

RK: Same thing. I never, ever, 22 years I think I was a foreman I never, ever disciplined one guy. Never.

Now, you're at the sintering plant and you're moving around. Where did you go from there? When the plant started tapering off. I know you spent time at the blast furnace.

RK: Yeah, what happened was the sintering plant shut down for a short period of time one time in '83 and they laid me off. That was the first time I ever got laid off. Ever, as a foreman, they laid me off for six months. Now what was really weird about this thing was they laid me off, they shut the plant down, and they never shut the plant down before for any period of time. I came back off the layoff. I wound up starting the damn plant up after being laid off for six months. And trying to remember a lot of things was kind of tough to get that place going again. And we'd start putting furnaces on one at a time and, I'll tell you what, there was a lot of people, like big people, that went off the floor. They were afraid something was gonna go, ya know.

They weren't quite sure.

RK: Yeah, so we just lit 'em up and what the hell is what it went it went, ya know.

Well, ya know, you remember probably when you were up the Blast Furnace during the rebuilds all the guys that came back as consultants? They were only back there for one reason. They didn't have anybody that remembered how to do the job.

RK: That's exactly right. You start losing skills down there. And you know what, the jobs down there, I tried to explain to somebody before, you know, when you picked up a job down there, you learned a job you worked at a place for a while. It took you years to learn that job. You didn't learn that right, you learned something every day. It was not just like an ordinary off-the-wall job outside some place. You had to watch yourself down there, because you know the equipment you worked with was so huge and so dangerous, you know, you didn't want to screw nothing up. You worked with gas all the time, you worked with heat.

And Ron Keschel came in every day, did the same job. Every day when he was getting in there, the first thing on his mind was, "What's gonna transpire on this shift?" So even though you were the same designation every shift, every shift was different. And this is what a lot of guys said they liked about the company. I might have been a machine operator for 25 years but every day was different. And I always looked forward to it.

RK: Yep, every day was different, it was.

And most of the guys tell me and I'm going to ask you: what do you miss most about the plant?

RK: I'll tell you what, I miss working with the people I worked with. I'll tell you what, I worked with some terrific people. To this day yet, we remember. You know what, we got reunions going on today yet, and that plant's been down over ten years; the sintering plant's been down longer than that. And you know, we get together, we talk about stuff as though it happened yesterday.

And you know I was talking to a guy who took his pension two days before from another company, a ten- year pension. He had to work ten years to vest his pension rights and his 401k. And he said in that entire ten years he was there, he says in this other job, he says hardly anybody talked to each other. He said, "I couldn't wait to get out of there. I just couldn't wait to get out of there."

RK: Yeah, you get on the outside, and I'm talking about getting on the outside of Bethlehem Steel falling down, and I've worked in places where that's exactly what you got. You got people that don't even talk to each other. You could work along side somebody and they won't even talk to you. They're afraid somebody's watching you and they're going to, ya know, jump on you or whatever the hell it is.

So Ron, when did you reach the point where you actually knew for sure the plant was in trouble? About what year do you figure that was?

RK: Well, the first time we got laid off, in '83, you could feel that they could survive without us. They told us there before that nothing, that the sintering plant will run forever. But in '83 when we were shut down for six months, that was a sign right there. Hey, down the road here something different is gonna happen. That's when I knew we were in trouble.

Yeah. And during that six-month period what were they using, all pellets?

RK: They started to go into pellets, yeah, they started to go into that new type of pellet that was designed, that flux pellet. They used a small portion of them, but then they started to kind of like them, they worked out for them. And the sinter would kind of like drop off a little bit. I remember going down like the two machines for a part of time, ya know, because they tried to incorporate more of those flux pellets into the system. And eventually when the sintering plant went down, it was all flux pellets. And it worked out.. For years they ran on those flux pellets, that put the sintering plant out of business. And that machinery wound up going to another place. They didn't throw it away; it ended up going to someplace out in the Midwest somewhere to another sintering plant.

Wow. Now, during the time that you were there in the sintering plant, in the Blast Furnace, and I see the Coke Works, ore handling, you must have seen a lot of things that you figured that you thought were kind of dumb? What was like the dumbest thing you ever saw that was costing the company money? I got a lot of different answers for some of this. What's the one thing that pissed you off the most?

RK: Aw, jeez. I got to reach back into something with that. I ran into a lot of that shit, but I can't put my finger on nothing right now, but I'll tell you what, there was a lot of things that were dumb. And if you told like maybe one of your supervisors about the damn thing, he actually didn't want to hear it. But he knew that you were right, but he didn't want to hear nothing about that, you know. That was like, ah how would you call it, like a status quo or something. It had to run that way, that's the way we ran it before and we're going to keep running it that way kind of thing, you know. We knew a lot of stuff. The younger foremen that we grew up in that system with, we knew there were different ways to do it, and better ways to do it. But the older people didn't want to hear that shit, ya know? They didn't want to it because they didn't want to feel like they did something wrong. Ya know? But we could do that on a daily basis almost.

Yeah, so what it really comes down to is there was no other place quite like that. And you know when the guys left and they went to other employment and stuff like that, when I say to them, "If you were just like on layoff for a year or two and they called you back, would you go back?" One hundred percent said, "Yes."
RK: Oh, I'll go right along with that. I'll go back now, I'll 66 to start.

It wasn't necessarily so much the money as it was the camaraderie, the money, the benefits, everybody knew each other's buddy. Most guys knew their buddies' wives and kids from going to, you know, outings. Softball games, things like that, it was like one big happy family. And you know, think about it once, the company never really lied to us. They always told us, "Don't worry about a thing, you'll get it in the end." But we were only steelworkers and we didn't know what they meant when they said "in the end." But I think we know now. Well, I'll tell you what, Ron, this is really a pleasure talking to you. The whole idea here of the book, you know, is to let people know that Thirty Years under the Beam, had it not been for both management and the union people in the plant…in the plant…the place would have gone under a lot sooner than 1998. And I think everybody knows that. That just about everything we were asked to do, the union guys took cuts; the salary guys took cuts. Everybody suffered trying to make an impression, trying to have some sort of effect, but you know the writing was on the wall. I think it was just bigger than any of us. Okay, Ron, thanks a lot. I wish the best to you and your family.
RK: You too Frank.

RAYMOND McFADDEN
38 years of service

General Foreman, EFM Maintenance

Beyond a doubt, one of the smartest foremen I ever came across in the plant. His knowledge of the Electric Furnace prevented him from advancing within his own department. Refused to kiss-up, and paid the penalty for it.

* * * * * * * * * *

Today's May 9th, and we're on the record with Ray McFadden. Ray, everybody at the plant had a nickname. What did they call you?

RM: Mac, but not for everybody.

Mac, that's what I thought it was. Well, ya know, some of us had several nicknames, some of 'em weren't good, but we'll go with Mac. Mac, how did you get a job at Bethlehem Steel.

RM: I went down when I was 18 and I applied at the office, and they hired me as a chain man in the cold draw.

Chain man in the cold draw, wow.

RM: Yeah, that was 1948. So I worked there for, oh, I'd say about three, four months, and I could see that all I was doing was labor work, and I decided well, I'm gonna go get some better employment, so I went and joined the Navy. I was in the Navy for four years, and I got out in 1952, and I went to the employment department after working as an electrician in the Navy, a 2nd class electrician, and I gave 'em all my papers, because I had recommendations from the Navy, and they offered me a job as hot slide man on the blast furnace, and I told 'em, "Well, give me my papers I'm leaving." So then they sent me to the electrical department, and I saw Charlie Boyle. Charlie Boyle, I told 'em I worked winding motors and everything else, and he should put me in the shop. He didn't put me in the shop; he put me in Press Forge out in the field, and that's where I worked until, I went to college, when I got through college I went in the Loop course.

In other words, you started college while working in the plant? How did that work out for ya? How did the company help you out there?

RM: Well, Dave Washstetter helped me out. He let me have my, watcha call it, days off and on so that I could attend class, and during the summer he let me work during the day so I could be home, and he helped me out a lot, he did.

Did you have, you had a family by then, didn't ya? Were you already married?

RM: Yes, I was already married. I had a boy. So anyhow, they let me go into the Loop course, and when I went into the Loop course I wound up in the electrical department.

Now, the Loop course, what was the Loop course, Ray?

RM: Well, they took you throughout the whole plant and gave you an introduction how the plant operated, how it functioned and so forth and so on.

So if I said the Loop course was a training position for foremen, that would be right?

RM: That's right. That lasted for about maybe two or three years, and uh, I used to go out and check cranes, and test 'em, and wherever they had electrical problems, they'd send me out on a job, and I ran into problems with the man in charge; they sent me to EFM of all things, crane 78, and I wrote a report, and he didn't like the report, so as a result I wound up in the Alloy Division as experimental engineer for Pete Petrocko.

Now, when you say they didn't like the report, are you saying that they were having a hard time living with reality?

RM: That's about it.

Cuz I know you pretty good, and if you wrote up the report, I mean you were sure what you put in it. Well, tell me a little bit about that.

RM: They were tearing N section companies out, and what happened was they didn't realize that the one had caved in in certain parts, and when the crane went down, it was trying to spread the tracks apart, and as a result they had an old Clark controller, which wasn't current timed, it was varied timed and it was accelerating too fast and went to the last step when it was in the bind position, and the current went over the chart, and as a result it was such a torque force it tore the coupling bolts right off. So what we did is we changed the timing on it so that it had more time to work its way out of that spot, and a result was they didn't tear any more coupling bolts, and he didn't believe that, so as a result, he went on vacation and I wrote the report, and when he come back he was furious; so he sent me, he asked me did I like my job. I said, "Yeah I like my job," and I says "The only reason I come here is because they pay me," and with that he sent me to the Alloy Division.

And you worked for Pete Petrocko, and you say he sent you to the Alloy Division. Where were you working then, what physical area of the plant?
RM: I was all over the plant.

Okay. You were talking like around the 35-inch mill and areas like that. And you were mostly doing the same thing you did before?
RM: Yes. Troubleshooting where they had problems, like the cranes were dropping blocks in the annex and stuff like that. I fixed the controls so that wouldn't happen, and I did other work like that, or if they had something that they increased the machinery they put in, I rewrote the synopsis of how it worked, how it functioned, to help the repairmen.

You must have been up there right around the time Dick Wagner started then. I was just talking to him the other day. So now as you, you're doing this trouble shooting thing, you must have advanced at some time or another, into a position where you were in charge of men. How did that come about?
RM: Well, Johnny Rice, he was foreman at number 3 Open Hearth, and he got, he was in an accident, and he was in pretty bad shape, so they put me up at number 3 Open Hearth to fill in for the foreman, so I worked up there as a supervisor, substitute supervisor. Then what they did was after that when everybody go on vacation, I had to fill in for everybody, and it wound up I was down at EFM when Pete Petrocko got out of there and they put Len Elly in, and then I left Len Elly know what was going on, and he told me, he got rid of the two general foreman we had, and he made me general foreman after so many years of taking everybody else's leavings.

Yeah, well Len Elly was actually considered the master mechanic for the plant, wasn't he?
RM: Yeah, he was.

Yeah, I remember Len Elly. He was a guy that if you could explain to him why, he'd listen to ya. You know, in later years, you know it's true in the plant, we got a bunch of guys that really didn't know north from south but they somehow became our bosses. And we had troubles.
RM: They were the fair-haired boys I called 'em.

Well, yeah I guess. I heard a lot of different descriptions, but that's a real gentlemanly way of saying it, the fair-haired boys, yeah. We used to call 'em office boys.
RM: Well, when John Freeh, Pete Petrocko retired and John Freeh came

in there, uh, and I told him what was going on, he gave me a 10 percent raise in bonus and in pay, and then when he left to go to Saucon, then they came back again and I was in the same place, put me under their thumb again until Len Elly got there. And then when I got to Len Elly and told him what was going, he realized, and he made me general foreman.

How, about that, that's some story. So now a general foreman. What did you do as a general foreman in the Alloy Division?

RM: Well, I didn't do what our other general foreman did; he just used to pass notes. I went out into the field with the guys and found out what their problems were and helped them and gave them assistance, and that's what I did.

So you would call yourself a hands-on general foreman.

RM: That's right.

Okay, you didn't sit at the desk?

RM: No. I sat at the desk, but only during certain periods; the rest of the time I was out in the field to see what was going on and what had to be done to correct things.

Well, ya know, when I worked for you, and I can tell you the general feeling in the shop is when you came out onto the job we were gonna get something done, because you know, we just knew. You and Dick Wagner were the two guys we knew, if it had to do with cranes the problem was gonna be fixed. But I have to be honest with you, you had to set off an explosion to get Dick Wagner up on the crane. But I'm not gonna say that he tried to get away from it; he would only go up as a last resort. But that was really interesting working with you guys, because as the years went on we never really got a chance to work with a lot of people that knew what was going on.

RM: Well, I used to get the guys to tell me what their problems were, and then I'd try to solve those problems, and what I did was I tried to make improvements to the vacuum system at EFM, to the furnaces, to the hydraulics, you know, all of that, I made improvements to the thing. And why they didn't let me do things the way we should have done, but they had to hire people from outside concerns, and they'd give 'em a bill like say $20,000 or $30,000. If they'd of given us the money, the job would have been done already and we would have fixed the place up, but they didn't want to do it. They wanted to go through engineering. And then you lay the engineering department off in 1980, and then who did the upgrading for EFM? I did. I did all the upgrading to vacuum degaussing system and the whole nine yards.

So as time went on from when you started at Bethlehem Steel in 1948, things got early on progressively better, and then you reached a point where they got progressively worse. Where was that mid point where things just weren't running as smooth as they could have been? Was it in the late '70s? Was it the early '80s, or…

RM: It was the early '80s when everything went to pot. And I blamed it on, I blamed it on greed. Because what happened was when everything was going fine, they'd operate 21 shifts, and on 21 shifts you couldn't do any maintenance, and then they'd always say it was poor maintenance, because we didn't do very much, and at the end they were trying to skip on maintenance, and as a result things went to hell. And when it keeps getting worse, then they want to say, well, why are we operating here? They used bean counters. They counted what the profits were. They shut down, did you know that they shut down the 35-inch mill, and when they shut down the 35-inch mill they didn't get the hot butts to the electric furnace melt, and as a result they didn't have enough steel; they had to use steel, but they were making it, what's his name at the BOF, and they were losing $100 a ton. Believe that or not, they were losing $100, but they had to keep the furnace conditioned, in order to condition the furnace for stainless heats, they had to make heats in that furnace to condition the lining, and as a result they lost $100 a ton. So the people that did the work didn't know how the steel functioned; steel operations functioned that's all.

So you'd say the further you got into your steel career the more you had to work with people that didn't know what they were doing? That's a sad thing, because you know everywhere I've gone and everyone I've talked to has basically said the same thing, but they all said something else. They said that plant could have been saved.

RM: Oh yeah.

When did you first come to realize that the plant was in trouble, in your own opinion?

RM: In my own opinion. I went to England, and I went up to Maryport, and they had a steel mill up there, and I found out that they shut down the sintering plant, they shut down the hot end of the plant, and they were getting stuff from a mother plant, and they were rolling rails, and uh, so when they happened over there, I figured, hey I went to see the general manager, and I asked him, are they gonna shut down the hot end of this plant? And he said he didn't know, but I think they did, because they had Sparrow's Point had the biggest blast furnace in the world.

About what year you think that was? '82 sounds about right. You know, '82 that sounds like that might even have been Jack Roberts. Do you remember if it was Jack Roberts?

RM: I don't remember, I don't think his name...

Well, you know it's a funny thing, you know, and I'll interject this here, the operation at the Bethlehem plant after the hot end was shut down, Jack Roberts, who used to be the general manager at the plant, he got out of there when the getting was good; he went to the company and said, "Hey, I want to buy the soaking pits, the combination mill, the beam yard," he says, "and I wanna keep an ongoing operation," I expect to keep like 700 people. They wouldn't sell it to him. You know, I saw him, like, two years after that in town; you know his kid is now the Chief Justice of the Supreme Court? And I said to him, I says, "Jack, what on earth happened?" He says, "Frank, they couldn't bear the thought of us making money immediately while running that combination mill. They would have been so embarrassed, and that's the only reason they didn't sell it. I know it sounds far fetched but that's just the way it was."

RM: Well, when they laid the engineering department off in 1980, they laid off a lot of good people that knew what was going on. There were people that had hands-on in the field. And another thing too, when they put the stripper crane in down at the Saucon plant, now I worked up in number 3 Open Hearth when they had the continuous caster, and the Japanese told 'em not to put a stripper crane in, because with ingots, you know, when you have an ingot, you had a certain part of the ingot that has the hollow point and you can roll pipe and the rest, and they were rolling more scrap than they were rolling good stuff down at the mills. That's what the hell the problem was. And they wanted the caster so that with the casters they wouldn't have the problems that they had with foreign ingots, but they didn't listen, so...

Well, we had the caster plans; they actually did all the engineering work to get ready for it, and just never started it.

RM: We had it at number 3 Open Hearth.

Oh yeah, I know you guys worked on it over there, an experimental one.

RM: We had a five-stage ejector, and where you vacuumed the gassed and ladled and they poured it into the caster. You vacuumed, you gassed it and poured it into the thing.

That was in operation from like between 1960 and '65?

RM: Yeah, something like that, '60s, because I was over there, and they put me over there in charge too.

Did they ever have that to the point where it was operating where they knew it worked?

RM: Yeah. Andy Slabakosky was in charge, you know he ran that.

Yeah, and what torpedoed that, what happened?

RM: I don't know; there was four, five different people that were involved. Research was involved and other people were interested in the casters, and uh, I don't know what really happened. I wasn't involved with it, but I know they used to pour two heats at a time. They used to pour, like, uh, use two cranes to lift the heat, and uh, cuz I remember one time they, whatcha call it, the repairman came down and said to me, they can't adjust the brake, and here they had a feathered key inside the brake hub and they used the chisel to hit the shafting and it hit the hub and then told 'em to stop with a heavy load and shift it. So they wanted to pour this heat, and I told 'em no way. And then of all things they tried to blame maintenance, and here I had written an order for the shaft that it was in question, which we could have changed. And they tried to put it on me, and I said, "Oh no." I got the old folder out, with, it's a CYO letter and it said the one foreman said to the other well, at this time we don't have $1,500 for the shaft, so one walked one way, and one walked the other way, and I walked back to my office and we got the thing changed. But see that's what happened. They didn't want to spend money to keep it going.

So technically, you know from going from that point forward the people with the expertise that knew what was going on were being ignored.

RM: Well, they were all, they got paid on bonus, and anything they could save would increase their bonus, so I figured out from what I thought when the things were running great they put, instead of putting any money aside, they just boggled it up, so it was pure unadulterated greed that shut that place down, because when it had the money to spare, they didn't do it because they were getting 100 percent bonus; the superintendents were getting a hundred percent so they were worried about themselves. And that's when I think the plant shut down because of pure unadulterated ... and you know another thing, Frank? They was gonna retire a guy from the Blast Furnace, all right. They poured more hot metal in that furnace and it spit out more times and wrecked more equipment, just so, like the roller he had a, he put all the stuff in and soaking pits and had everything ready, and then he'd roll it up in a heap. He wound up with a special accomplishment, you know. He did this, he did that, but how much did he wreck a room? You know.

Yeah, well you know, when I first started interviewing people for the book they said, Well, who else are you gonna interview?" I says, "Well, have a lot of foreman in there." "What are you gonna interview foreman for?" I says, "Because you may not realize the things we're talking about they're gonna verify 'em, because they're not stupid. They were right in this mess with us, and they were subjected to the same things we were subjected to." I says, "How many times did the foreman come and said this is what they want us to do, and we would say well, that's not right, that's gonna cost more money, or it's gonna take that much more time," and we always used to get the answer, "Well, that's what they want, that's what we'll give 'em." And a lot of guys could not understand that.

RM: What I didn't like about it was when they shut the Alloy Division down, okay? And all that machinery was there. I had all the information and all the telex and filed on some of the machinery, and the rest of it, and as a result they put me in charge of letting these people take this machinery out. They even had people come in that I had marked the machines up and they were so thankful, they wanted to give me money, and I wouldn't take it, you know, and uh, but the thing is this, when they had all of this stuff, they, like I'll give you a typical example, like the treatment; treatment had all those big furnaces in there. They were low voltage furnaces, they had enough copper cable in there to supply a copper mine and all the nichrome wire, and the rest of it, and I used my people when they were slow to supplement these people for work so that we could salvage the machines and take the machines out. And I told em what they should have done instead of letting this Brandenburg, they made millions, must have made millions with all that equipment. I had tubes coming from that furnace over there that were $5,000, they were stainless tubes and the rest of it. And you wouldn't believe the number of equipment and chain. There must have been enough drag off chain in one car to fill a car full and just scrap. Like I thought man, I couldn't see all the waste that was thrown away, and I watched it. But if they'd of left the people in the plant get ready, the company would have saved money, but no, they didn't. And they took all the spare parts that were down at East Lehigh, and I was in charge of that, too, you know, the 413. They sold it for 6 cents a pound, and then, now when they needed something they had to go to Brandenburg and buy it back.

Amazing.

RM: Yes it is.

So Mac, I'm gonna ask you a question now and you can go off any way you want. Let's say you had been in charge in 1980, you were the man, you're the guy that said here's what we're gonna do. What would you have done? I know it's in hindsight, but what would you have done? What were the moves to make to make the plant as viable as possible?

RM: What I would have done is this. When we were operating good I'd have put so much money aside so that when things were slow we could improve and fix the plant. What they did was, they ran the plant down, just like some people run a taxicab. They run it to a rubber spare and they're not changing oil and they're just getting the profits. Like some people all go in and they take a plant and then they run it down. So what they should've done is they should have provided for improvements to the plant, and if they'd of done that, they'd improve the plant and they'd of been making money, but no they didn't; they ran it till it stopped and that's what happened, and then when you take the figures, and you figure don't lie but lies figure, you know. And when they saw they were losing money, then they decided they were gonna shut it down because they're not making so much. They were supposed to make 15, percent but they were only making 10 percent, but the reason they weren't making the 15 percent was because they never made improvements; they just kept running it and running it, you can't run a car and not give it any maintenance and improvement.

Now in your own opinion, do you think that the Alloy and Tool Steel Division that was shut down in, like,1980, do you think they actually ever lost money or they just weren't making enough?

RM: They weren't making enough.

They weren't making enough. Because I heard several people say that. I know in the next three years after we shut down, Allegheny Ludlum out in Pittsburgh was making money hand over fist with tool steel, they, like, turned their company from almost ready to go bankrupt into making millions.

RM: Well, they made 803 grade, they made all stainless grades, and look what they had in their cold drawn, especially steel, they made special steel, and uh, I don't understand how the hell they did it, but they screwed up real bad, that's all.

Well, Mac, what was the high point of your career with Bethlehem Steel? What gave you the most satisfaction?

RM: When I was at EFM I changed the design of the electric holders for the furnaces, they held the electrodes. I changed the design of the mass rollers and redesigning how to fit the holder, you know with the clamps, get the right pressure and everything else, and even, they even screwed up, they bought the springs from the wrong place. They didn't have the right springs in the thing, and then the electrodes would slip and they'd burn the holder and the holder was worth $16,000 so the guys had to go up there with a chain jack and jack it in the heat and the rest of it, so I straightened that out. And then they decided, we used to have preventative maintenance on this thing. We knew what had to be done. They decided that they didn't want to put a foreman out and four or five people to keep this up so that the furnaces weren't right, and guess what, they burnt six holders up, that's $90,000 for $1,200 a month they were. You know who did that, don't ya?

No, we don't want to go into that many details. Well, you know that was your high point, getting that situation so that it worked right. What was your low point? Just watching everything go to hell?

RM: Yeah, everything I accomplished started to go to hell. And then that killed me, because I had, you remember, how we had that office, we had everything in book form and we had everything going the way it should be and the inventory was set up, we could have anything picked out in about two or three minutes, and uh, then all of a sudden they decided that it wasn't necessary; they didn't do this, they didn't do that no more. They figured they were gonna fold so they...

There were no more Alex Fartels, huh?

RM: They just gave up. They gave up. They decided they were gonna take it and throw the plant away, and that's what they did, they threw it away. Then I wrote a letter and told 'em that I saw it. First of all they took our benefits away, then they were gonna take this away and that away, and they saw no room for improvement to yourself or advancement, and supposedly I was supposed to be going over to the blast furnace and got the job over there, but then that changed when they shut everything down, so. You could see it eventually eroding to the point where you had no interest to try to better yourself because they decided that they didn't want you anyhow. Then I wrote a letter and told 'em that if that's all I had, I might as well take my retirement, and they told me within minutes to take your retirement, that was it.

Well, how about that. It's just like the horse that plowed ten acres every day for years. All of a sudden he plowed nine acres and they didn't want him anymore.

RM: That's right.

Well, that doesn't surprise me. Well, Mac I want to thank you for your candor in this interview. I'm sure it's gonna be one of the high points of the book because people don't really get a chance when they talk about Bethlehem Steel to hear the inside operation from a perspective of a general foreman, so I want to thank you for that, and good luck for you and good health for your family. Thank you.

NATALI VIVIAN
36 years of service

Superintendent, Saucon, Electric Furnace Maintenance

Nate was the best at solving common sense problems. As a Superintendent with hundreds of men under him, his ability to relate to the working man made him a pleasure to know and work with. The plant needed more like him.

* * * * * * * * * *

Today is October 22nd, 2008, and we're here with Natali Vivian. And can we call you Nate for purposes of this interview?

NV: Sure.

Okay Nate, uh, I see you started with the company back in 1960. Were you from this area?

NV: No.

What area were you from?

NV: I'm from Jersey, Trenton.

Trenton, New Jersey. Did you go to college here?

NV: No, I went to college at Lafayette.

No, kiddin', Lafayette, isn't that something. And here I am working for Lehigh. All right, fine, but that's neither here nor there. I drive a van at night.

NV: Oh I thought you worked for an undertaker.

I do both, I have two part-time jobs, because nobody wants to hire an old guy like me, you know what I mean, full-time.

NV: How old are you now?

'62 next month.

NV: Uh, you're young.

Some people say a baby, but ya know I wish I had the smarts I have at 62 at 22. Boy, would I have been a terror then, huh? Okay, so you're a Lafayette major.

318

What was your major?
NV:　　Electrical engineering.

Electrical engineering. When you got hired at the program was it through the Loop Program?
NV:　　Yes.

Okay, what did you think of the Loop Program?
NV:　　I was awed; it was really something, a good program.

It was a lot for a young guy, right?
NV:　　Uh, it was just an awful lot to grasp.

What would you say was the longest period in that Loop Program you were in any one shop?
NV:　　I don't know, three days maybe four days at the most.

You were just in one shop to another. You went through the whole plant almost.
NV:　　Yup, we went through every operation. They took us through steel making, coke, steel making, the rolling of the steel, and like in the fabricating shops. I don't know if you remember the merchant mills?

Oh yeah, I started there.
NV:　　Uh, we went through human resources, uh, and we went through the corporate, what the corporate people were doing, too; that's how I met, at that time Grace was still alive but he was very ill. In fact the week I started in the Loop course the week or the second week he passed away. And we had Edmund Martin of Martin Tower fame.

You met Ed Martin and …
NV:　　Yes.

How about that. And there's a lot of people, you know, they've heard these names, and they've never met any of these people.
NV:　　We never, I never met Eugene Grace, but he was still alive at the time, I guess he was still active, but he must have passed away, I think it was the first or second week of the Loop course. I was a young kid coming into Bethlehem. That was a big organization. You found out what big was. Very well, lot of protocol, lot of …

Well, it was like John Strohmeyer said in the book, like the sales office, the halls were lined in gold. You got a sales job at Bethlehem Steel in the '60s, you were in pretty good shape.
NV:　　I wasn't in the sales end.

Well, I'm just saying, that's what he alluded to.

NV: All's I know is that when I came there I started in the Electrical Department, as a young electrical engineer, I majored in college, and I got an awful lot, I got more experience there than I would have gotten any place else, putting substations in, converting the plant from 25 cycle to 60 cycle. Went down to the 12- and 14-inch rolling mill putting that in, and started to work with plant engineering and with all the conduit, and you didn't lose one. And uh, we wired it, tested it out, and uh from there went back up to the electrical office. I was still in the Electrical Department, and uh, got assigned as an electrical engineer following up the installation.

And they started on the BOF what around '66, started working on it?

NV: I don't know remember the exact year, Frank. I remember I started there was working following the outside contractor and we would field testing the equipment as it was finished, and at that time I got transferred over to Saucon maintenance, which was a new experience for me, because up to that time I'd been doing engineering. And I got transferred over to Saucon maintenance to help the maintenance people at the BOF. Next thing you know I find myself as assistant general foreman of maintenance at the BOF. And then they united the basic oxygen furnace and electric furnaces into one unit, and the superintendent of the operation, steelmaking operation wanted his own maintenance department, so I ended up being superintendent of steelmaking maintenance. And I did that for quite a few years, and then when the company started to change and reorganize

In the '80s.

NV: Yeah, they started up a maintenance department using the Juran principles the Japanese had instituted. And I found myself being superintendent of maintenance in the plant. I had all the assigned maintenance departments, and I had the labor construction group. I did that about six years. Then like everything, you know, tried something like maintenance department's back, and I still had the engineers that went around and backed him up, and we did special projects if they had troubles, and I had the labor construction group at that same time. We had big jobs, and that time it was the 48-inch building, and that job was handled by basically plant forces. You had a lot of outside contractors in there, but when it came down to making the thing go Charlie was the lead engineer from my department. They did a wonderful job, they had a tight schedule and they did it. We always did it.

And you were involved in putting the electric motor in the forty number one also?

NV: No, that was done strictly by the Electrical Department.

Okay, all right, because I used to work on that motor all the time at the 35-inch mill. I used to go down there every Friday day shift you know and work on that motor.

NV: Well, I didn't have the Electrical Department at that time.

You didn't get that I guess until the late '70s.

NV: No, I never got the Electrical Department, that went to control division, they split up into the control division, which included the combustion department and the Electrical Department. My job was to keep the, that the foundation work, but the electrical part was done by the electric department, you know, thank God.

I'm getting the impression from you that you're alluding to the fact that in the early years when you started there, that the plant was doing just about everything on its own.

NV: We did everything on our own.

When did they, when did you see the transition over to outside contractors and things like that? When did that start, late '70s?

NV: You know, I'm trying to think. I guess, I noticed when the BOF was built, they brought an outside contractor, Buffalo Electric. That job was so big that we just, we didn't have the people to run that much combo and that kind of wire that had to be there. Plus we had, they were the contractor that built BOF's before, so you know, it wasn't like something new. The superintendent Bob, what the heck was his name, Petsky, Bob Petsky, he was a pretty sharp fella; he could see when things weren't the way they should be from the get go. So he saved us a lot of money and grief. But, you know, that was my first encounter with outside contractors, was the BOF. But then once the BOF came in I didn't have that association anymore to tell you about outside contractors because then I became assigned maintenance. I was in the mill and of course we didn't need any outside contractors. I'm sorry, we did, we brought a guy in to splice the conveyor belt. And that's all those people did, but you had to have somebody like that because that was a specialized job. I'm trying to think what else we had that in, and I'm trying to think what outside contractor. Somebody came in, nah.

Well, you know that's ironic you're telling me about splicing that conveyor belt, because when I worked at the sintering plant in ore handling that's all our people did was splice the conveyor belts.

NV: No, this was a special belt. Uh, I'm trying to remember what was peculiar about the belt, otherwise we would have done it. And I'm trying to think. I think that guy would come in and we were using our people, he was showing us how to do it, but we'd bring him in to show us how to do it. Well, now that you bring it up, yeah that's right. The first time they came in, after we saw them, we started to do it.

Now for purposes of this interview, explain to us what you mean by assigned maintenance?

NV: Assigned maintenance is a group of people, a person who works in a particular area. It could be Saucon Mills, BOF shop, the Electric Furnace Melt Department, and you worked just in that area okay?

Okay. In other words, the best way to describe it is assigned to a particular area. So the 48-inch mill had x number of millwrights, x number of motor inspectors, couple welders, some, you know helpers.

NV: And they worked, they worked almost exclusively in that area. If you had work that was over and above what you can do, you would call up the service division, and you would bring in riggers and carpenters, and pipe cleaners to help supplement the crew on bigger jobs, like when we had a furnace reline, we used to bring the riggers in cuz maintenance could never handle all the work that had to be done in that given period, we only had a small window.

Okay, now one thing that we know here is you started in 1960 right after the '59 strike, left in 1996. When did you come to the realization that that plant was in trouble? When did it really drive home and you knew the days were numbered?

NV: I was surprised that they shut it down. I thought we could limp by.

Well, there were a lot of people surprised at that considering that they had a buyer and they didn't …

NV: Well, the thing is that I, as we had talked before, when I looked at the people that I had or the people that worked there, I'm going to talk about a specific group, the gentlemen that worked for me, under me, the BOF maintenance, the steel group. I wouldn't trade them. I would not trade one of 'em.

Yeah. You had good guys.

NV: We had, we had real good guys to work with, nothing was too much for them to do, you know, and …

I interviewed one of those guys, Jim Bennick. I'm sure you knew Jim, he was a real go-getter, a motor inspector.

NV: I'll look back and I think about not just the maintenance people, but the combustion department people, you know. And we had a good mix. The BOF started up, because the open hearth was falling behind, we couldn't compete. I was told that the goals that they have for that shop to take place in a year, year and a half were met before a year one time, so many talented people.

That's good, good to hear. Is there anything that you saw on a day-to-day basis in that plant that you wish you could have changed yourself personally, that would have made that plant more viable? I mean everybody has something that sticks out in his mind what he didn't like.

NV: Yeah. Well, I would have to question why the mills rolled the way they did, why they rolled to orders.

Instead of rolling to stock.

NV: I always felt that you know when you start a new active order you rolled until it was completed.

They used to do that, you know?

NV: No, they didn't not in my time.

Well, they did it, the Beam Yard guys all told me that at one time they used to roll a certain section three, four, five days in a row, round the clock.

NV: And figure out what it cost you to roll it.

Well, it was really knocked down in price by doing that.

NV: Like I said I didn't know all the ins and outs of the business, but it just seemed to me that roll changes were used excessively, but you know it was a specialty plant.

Yeah, it was. We were the only ones that rolled them to size, cutting to size.

NV: And the thing is there were certain sizes that we were the only ones in the country that were making, the big foundation beams up to the World Trade Center. The only other person, the only other outfit was over in Europe. I'm trying to think of the name of the steel company, can't think of it now. You always heard that things weren't good, that they weren't making the profit. I guess that was a sign of the times.

How did you enjoy your time at Bethlehem Steel?

NV: I loved it. I loved the people.

Was it because of the people?

NV: Yeah.

You were working with a lot of good people. Yeah, that's, uh, I heard this from a lot of guys. I said, hey if they called you tomorrow would you go back, yeah I'd go back. And you know what, even though everyone has an ax to grind somewhere with the company, overall it wasn't a bad place to work.

NV: You know, I was in maintenance, so I didn't have a chance to be political. I was geared more reactive, okay?

Yeah. Putting out the fires.

NV: I was very, very fortunate; I had a lot of good people, lot of good line engineers, I think, but I had a real good work force. Oh God, when I stop and think about the talent.

Yup, and you were actually superintendent of several different operations in your time there?

NV: Uh yeah, steelmaking, maintenance, and then the "maintenance department" which was labor and construction, and uh, my special engineers, we used to go out and help solve problems when the maintenance people couldn't do it, that's working together.

Now I see you finished up in Human Resources, you were working directly with the safety and with the union, how was that?

NV: I loved it.

No kiddin', cuz you knew you were getting things done.

NV: Well you know, I worked with assistant grievance committee men on that safety committee, and every one of 'em, with the exception of one guy, and the union took care of that themselves. Why our safety record wasn't better, I'll never know, because we went to other plants to see what their safety program was like. You know what I think, I guess they fudged man hours per ton. I mean those guys they went out of their way to save that plant to make that plant a better place.

Well, if it makes you feel any better, you know, I want you to know up front that all the guys that ever mentioned your name never had anything bad to say about you, so you must have done one hell of a job while you were in there. I can remember going down and having grievance meetings/ with ya, and we never felt as though we were slighted, you know what I mean? Because you looked at people more than you looked at the contract book.

NV: Everybody with a grievance has a reason for it. Whether it would be overtime, discipline, etc.

Yeah that's right, it's the biggest thing in his life at that particular time.

NV: You know we handled all the grievances with the assistance grievance committee man, and we never had anything that we didn't solve.

Well, I was really, really glad that I got to sit down here and talk to ya. It was a process, you know, getting ya here. Go ahead.

NV: You know when I worked in Human Resource in the safety department there was one thing that really made me feel good. Danny Mills, you remember Danny Mills? One day Danny Mills, myself, and the plant manager were all together, and uh, the plant manager said, "Well, how we gonna resolve these things?" and Danny Mills said, if Nate's going to agree on it, I agree with it. And that was it.

Well, that's a good thing that you could have a relationship like that.
NV: And after that I never said anything that I wouldn't back up with facts.

*Yeah. Well, okay Nate I'm really glad that you came over here and … *
NV: Well, I hope you write a good book about…

Well, yeah, well, hey I, the name of the game here is to let people know that the people who worked in that plant felt; union and management did everything they could the last thirty years to save it, hence the name Thirty Years under the Beam.
NV: They worked, I tell you what, the hourly guys, I worked with, and my engineering staff you couldn't beat them. The men, they gave it their all; they never looked at the clock. They stayed until the job…

They did what they had to do.
NV: It's like I said, when I see people they ask, how could we have failed? But I guess, like I said, you don't see the big picture.

No, you don't. You don't see it, when you're inside the bottle; you can only see so far.
NV: And I imagine because of our location.

Yeah, there's a lot of things like that, landlocked and…
NV: Bringing stuff in cheaper would have been all right.

Sure, but you know that water is already down in the Atlantic Ocean. All right Nate, thanks a lot.

THOMAS COOPER
30 years of service

Ore Handling (350), Maintenance Gang (412), Coke Works Maintenance (411)

The company never knew what they had with Tom. His work habits were known by all to be of the highest quality. Working in either production or maintenance, his work was always done right the first time. If there was ever a man who should have been offered a foreman's job, it was Tom.

* * * * * * * * *

We're on the record with Thomas Cooper, Thomas J. Cooper. Uh, Coop, that's your nickname, isn't it?

TC: That's it.

Okay, we're gonna go by that, we're gonna, you know, call you Coop from here on out, and today is February 26th, 2008, and I see here Tom, that most of the time you worked at Bethlehem Steel you worked as a motor inspector, and you started on June 26, 1966. What was it like when you started? Give me like a break down of your first day.

TC: Well, at first I had to get directions on how to get there. Somebody told me you crossed the Minsi Trail Bridge, and in the middle of the bridge there was a gate. You go down a bunch of steps, go pass the guard, show 'em your brass badge or tag, whatever they called em, then you come to the railroad tracks. There's a coke train going into the Blast Furnace. I had to wait for that. Go another twenty feet and you almost get run over by the ore transfer cars that are going into the Blast Furnace. And at that time between the gate and the office where I had to sign in or meet somebody to assign me to a place of work, you ran into maybe a hundred people. The place was crowded.

In other words, there was a lot of people there and you're starting, you're describing, the ore handling/plant area that was located right underneath the

Minsi Trail Bridge. Actually roughly around the mid-pointthe south side of the river. So how did that first day work out?

TC: Being 18 years old and not doing anything else in your life except school, I mean it was another world. You go into the office, they introduce you to everybody, Mr. Liedich who was my schedule maker. He was a piece of work, let's put it that way. They had all the clerks in there. There must have been at least ten people in the office. There're clerks, and they had other assorted jobs. They took me upstairs, gave me one of these lockers.

And a locker really was what?

TC: A hanging basket. You had, over on the sides you had large tubes about six foot pipe holes grilled in them and chain ran inside of 'em. You pulled down, either the one catch, they had a big washer that would hold the basket in place, you pulled it out, unhook it, and let the chain up in the air, and this little basket comes down, I'd say it's like a large salad bowl with four hooks on it, and that's where you hung your clothes. Your work clothes and your street clothes.

And if you were lucky, you had two baskets, right?

TC: Yeah, after everybody got laid off years later, we got two baskets and three baskets

And then you were really living high then? And if you were really lucky, you go to sneak up to the alloy division when they went out and cut down one of the fancier baskets, right? Am I telling you the truth or what? There ya go. I remember many a field trip going up there to raid the old wash rooms, and that was really something. Sintering plant and ore handling. Sintering plant, what is sinter?

TC: Well, they take a mixture of all the different types of ore, coal, sand, uh, flue dirt from chimneys, any waste product they mix together, and then they super heat it and it turns into like a rock material, and then they crush that into a finer sinter or I guess the size of baseballs down to size of marbles. And they use that in the furnace for aeration.

And sinter actually worked way better in the furnace than pellets, didn't it? In the blast furnace. Because the air got to circulate around, and it covered more surfaces faster. So it was actually more efficient. Yes, I could remember the days in the sintering plant myself, you know, working alongside you, you did most of the work, I did most of the running back and forth. Uh, in fact a lot of people told me most of the running I did was my mouth. But you know, only your buddies tell you stuff like that. But, ore handling, okay. That was really your forte when you first started. What did you do in the ore handling department?

TC: Like I say, after you went up to the wash room they gave us about five, ten minutes to change around and go down to what they called a labor shack, uh, probably the size of a good lawn mower shed in the backyard. You had room enough in there for four people comfortably, so they packed about ten in there. And there was a little old guy, I still remember his name, George Bizara, he sat there with a pencil in his hand and he checked off the people that came in, and starting time was seven o'clock. You had to be there before seven, because at seven o'clock he's handing shovels and brooms out and sending you out to work.

And isn't really a fact that there was a little bit of preference shown to the people that came early?

TC: Yeah, pretty much so.

Yeah, usually the guys that were late, you know, if there was some conflict as to who was gonna do what, they ended up at the less preferable jobs, not that there were a lot of preferable jobs, they were jobs. Tell us a little bit about the dirt and the heat.

TC: Well, the funny thing about, it always seemed that the most work in the summertime had to be indoors where you have no cross drafts, no breezes, no air movement, and the winter time it was all outdoors, where that's all you had was the cold air, the drafts, the breezes, the winds, the snow, the freezing rain. That's how it just seemed to work out. The heat, there were some places that would hit 150, 200 degrees while you're working.

Well, that's different. I guess in your time when you first started there, a lot of people that started around your time, some of 'em didn't stick around, did they?

TC: Well, when I started it was, I would say 90 percent of the labor crew was college people. They needed summer jobs, they'd work for three months, and then they'd go back to college. That's when they hired what, between twenty and sixty people just for the regular gang for the summer time.

That's good. You know one of the reasons, and hardly anybody goes back into time and understands that, when you talk about steelworkers and the thirteen weeks, one of the main reasons the company, and the company asked to bring in summer help, because they wanted to bring their kids in for the summer, because they were going to college, and in order to entice the union into agreeing to this, they said not only will we take our kids, we'll take your kids, and we'll give you this thirteen weeks vacation every five years. So, contrary to popular belief that this was something the union beat the company over the head with, that's not really the way it was. You just heard the real story. So, Tom you spent some time there in ore handling, uh, and other than your broom work, you must have progressed.

328

What did you move onto?

TC: Took awhile. I stayed laborer until I went in the service in 1967. When I came out, because of the time accrued in the service, I ended up going up to car dumper. That's where they would empty out hopper cars that were filled with ore and other miscellaneous material like coal, sand.

And how did the car dumper work Tom?

TC: Well, they had something called a mule that would pull one car in at a time. A brake man would uncouple it, the mule would push it into the car dumper where they had brakes that would stop the car, then it would, two large cables would roll the dumper over, and where the car ended up was right above a hopper, this large screening over top, I guess you can call it screening, and it went on a belt and sent it either out to the ore yard or up to storage in the bin house.

So you're telling me that they had a device that would take a forty foot long railroad car, a shorter one, or you know usually not longer than forty feet, clamp down on it and actually turn it upside down and dump the contents out? Well, I'll tell you what, where that car dumper was located, if you were driving down Third or Fourth Street, you almost had to stop your car and take a look to see that thing operating because of the other equipment around it, you know the house that it held all the conveyors and stuff like that and the belts and the controls. But, uh, I remember the first time I saw it, I mean I had a little bit of an advantage when I went down, in that I went down there just as an electrical guy, so you know I spent some time working on that, you know along with you, and when we were on swing shift, we'd be over there working on that thing regularly, even if it was something as simple as changing the light bulbs. You know, it's something that had to be done. So, during that time that you were doing that you were a motor inspector, did you do anything? I mean, how was the scheduling at that time? What kind of schedule did you work?

TC: Well, we had a 28 day rotating schedule. We worked seven nights, and we had two days off, we worked seven middle shifts, had one or two days off, because our shut down was Thursday, so either we had to split like a Wednesday and a Friday off, then we worked our six day shifts, had one long weekend, and we'd start nights all over again. It worked out for 28 days. Did that for 25, 26 years, rotating schedule.

I remember that schedule. I remember that was always a bone of contention, especially right after I got in there, and I'll never forget, I said to a guy, "There's gotta be a way to set this thing up so that everybody can be happy, or as close to happy as possible," and the guy said to me, "The only way this will ever work, you're going to have to get the silver fox to agree to it." I said, "Who the hell is the silver fox?" *Tell me about the silver fox, and may he rest in peace, a good guy.*

TC: Silver fox, all I really knew is he went to church with our maintenance superintendent from the blast furnace, and anything he suggested or wanted done, it got done. Anybody else would bring it up, they wouldn't be listened to, but if the silver fox brought it up, it had to be gospel.

Well, I remember I did some serious listening because Roland Shively said to me, "Whatever you do kid, don't come in here as the new guy and rock the boat." He says, "Make sure you know who you're talking to and what you're talking about." And from talking to you guys, I found out the way to get things done was through the silver fox. So I said to the junior guys in the shop that never knew how they were gonna be working, what if we knew we had a set schedule and they wouldn't deviate from it? What should that schedule be? And we came up with that schedule. It was the seven night shifts, we would get off on the Thursday morning, wouldn't come back until Tuesday afternoon, work seven middle shifts, get off at the end of the seven middle shifts, come in and work Wednesday, Thursday, and Friday, off Saturday and Sunday, come in and work Monday, Tuesday and Wednesday, and then start the seven night shifts again. Well, it was like dying and going to heaven, because we knew how we were working, we picked our own gangs who we wanted to work with, but the big thing was all the guys that were the friends of the silver fox got to work day shift, and they thought this was the greatest thing since Charmin. In fact, the only question they asked was what happens when these guys go on vacation? And that was the one that really sold it. I says we'll start from the bottom of the list of the day shift guys and we'll just go from there on up. And if you know Tom Cooper's gonna be on vacation in two weeks and you're at the bottom of the list, you know you're gonna be working that week that Shaffer's on vacation, his schedule, and everybody was happy with that. Because when we, when I first got done there, those old guys were working a lot of swing shifts, and they didn't particularly care for it. This took care of it. Of course, I was probably one of the greatest cooks that ever worked down there in the ore handling maintenance crew, I mean we did real good; in fact we even did a little bit of baking. But, Tom, tell the people how we were able to do that. Like if a call came in at 4:30 and I'm cooking pork chops, how did that work?

TC: Well, we had three people on the crew, three mechanics and actually then three motor inspectors. Call came in, the other two, depending on the severity of the job, maybe one would go out and handle it all and leave the other one available for any other calls coming in, but most of the time we went out with pairs, and the third guy would stay behind and prepare our meal.

And if it got down to the point where it's something you needed three people, the meal got pulled off the stove, and we did it. And this is the same thing on night shift. Yeah, I'll tell you, we had some good times down there.

TC: But the thing you had to remember, we may have dozed off on night shift, we may have cooked a lot on middle shift, but what do normal people do at those times?

They're sleeping or watching TV.

TC: That's it. But when you weigh it for the years we spent on maintenance and the heavy equipment we worked on, it balanced itself out, because when we had the work, we had to work. There was no small task in any of the work that we did.

All you have to do is drive past Third Street today and take a look at the ore bridge where they're building the new casino, and you know you and I worked on those things regularly, you a lot more than me, but that was really something in the winter time on the top of that baby. I can remember too many shifts up there doing gear sets.

TC: Gear sets, changing resister banks, which weigh about seventy pounds and they're about one foot high by two foot wide by three foot long, and you had to carry those a thousand feet, and then you had to go up approximately 80 steps, go up over the top of the operator cab and then come back down and install it. I mean it was no easy task. Or changing cables.

Oh yeah, cables would tear pretty regular because of the amount of use. Those ore bridges were running usually at least five hours out of every shift, so in a 24 hour period, they were running between maybe 15 and 20 hours, depending on what the work load was. And if anything went, it really gummed up the works, you had to get them ore bridges going right away. The amazing thing about that was in the winter time that was like working at the end of a funnel, that wind come whistling alongside Number 2 Machine Shop, the Blast Furnace and the Power House, almost blew you off the top of the ore bridge, and in the summer time, I don't know what happened, the wind just disappeared, and you broiled up top there. I mean it was hot. Yes, it was hot. And those cabs were never air conditioned or anything. The best thing they ever had going for them was, you know, a good fan that was operating.

TC: Open the back door and keep the front window open.

There you go, that was as good as you could do. And that was, God, you know, a lot of people had the opinion you know that the sintering plant might have been the spot that if the plant was gonna get an enema, the hose was gonna go right there. Although, the people in the Coke Works would probably argue with you, because they were two hot, nasty, dirty places. You worked in both of them. Tell us how you got down to the Coke Works.

TC: Well, I came off a leave of absence in '91 and went back to the sintering plant because they needed motor inspectors there, and then all of a sudden they found that, well, we don't need as many motor inspectors at the sintering plant, but they need them at the Blast Furnace, so they shipped me down there for a year, and I really didn't care for it. The extremes there were more harsh than at the sintering plant as far as heat and then cold. So I transferred down to Coke Works, because it had a more of an appeal, let's put it that way.

Yeah, it was more defined as to what you were gonna do.

TC: Right, plus it was steady day shift that I would be putting in for instead of the shift work down the Blast Furnace.

Well, I guess that's a big thing, you know. When you talk about shift work, you know over time, I mean, how did that shift work affect your family, vacations and things like that?

TC: Vacations, I can't remember if I ever got vacation in the summer.

Until when?

TC: I don't think I ever had it, cuz I never had the time, never had the seniority. Because the older guys would take the summer months and hunting weeks, and what was left is what you got, January to March and September and October.

So if you didn't fish or ski, you were actually in trouble? Okay, did you do a lot of fishing and skiing Tom?

TC: No, I did none of that.

Well, I'll tell you what. You went to school while you were down at ore handling, didn't you? How did you pull that off?

TC: Well, I went up to the office and asked if I could have a special schedule. Of course the silver guy had to be contacted about that. And it was more to their benefit to allow me to work steady night shift to go to college full-time because all the old timers would have steady days, and only one of them had to work every other weekend night shift, because that's what I would have; I'd work ten in a row and have four off. And somebody had to fill in the other four that I wasn't there. So they would work shift work once every four months, it was more to their advantage, so they agreed to my schedule change. So I worked steady nights.

When I first came down there, you were on steady nights at that time. You were on steady nights, I remember that. And I said, "How on earth did this happen?

And the answer was simple, uh, "Coop asked for it." I said, "Oh well, that's a simple answer." I says, "You know fortunately sometimes at Bethlehem Steel whatever you ask for you might get," but it didn't happen often did it?

TC: No it didn't. Had to be to their benefit.

Okay, so you weren't really enthralled with your Blast Furnace position, you ended up at the Coke Works. So tell us a little bit about the Coke Works.

TC: Well, I had worked one time down there for a week, and um, because of the by-product odors and the dust flying around, I really went home with a headache every day, so I didn't know if I would last down there, but they had improved the area quite a bit. The first week wasn't bad. I've talked with Frank Trautman, he was in the middle of doing new projects with PLC control of the machinery, and him and I hit it off pretty good, so mostly I was in charge, not in charge, but engulfed in the projects down there for redevelopment.

Oh okay. So would you consider that as a result of your training, going to school?

TC: Yeah.

That's good, that's good. You know a lot of people think you know all we had was a bunch of dummies that went to work at Bethlehem Steel and didn't know nothing else. Well, that's not really true, that's not really the way it was. And you were there up until the time the place actually closed?

TC: No, I retired a year earlier because I was tired of working in the snow and the sleet in the wintertime and working in the hot places in the summertime. It just started to wear me down.

Do you remember what year that was, '97?

TC: In 1996 I made the decision I have a year to go, so the end of January '97 is when I retired. And Frank said, you can't go, I need you, and I told him, I said take a look around you at the other workers that work with you or work for you. I said, there were at least two of them here that are half interested in what I'm doing. I said train them the last year I'm here and then when I leave you won't even know I left. I said have some faith in the people you work with.

And how did that work out?

TC: Worked out great. Because I called him up three months after I retired, he says, you were right. These guys are great, they're interested, they're enthusiastic in learning something new and getting involved with it.

That's good. Were they younger employees or guys that were there the whole time or…

TC: They were down in Coke Works the whole time. They were younger, they were in their early 40s, late 30s.

Okay, that's good. Now, when you left there, is their life after Bethlehem Steel? Tell us about life after Bethlehem Steel?
TC: There isn't any.

Well, then it's time to ask you the big question, could the company have been saved?
TC: I honestly believe it could've been.

Okay, what did you see as the defining factor as to why it wasn't, why it's not there today? Take your time, because you may have a lot to say.
TC: I mean you look back at the history of it; the first thing they blamed was the imports. Yes, there were imports coming into the country, more than should have been, but that's our government's problem, and then you had the continuous casting company Nucor, they were competitive. That was part of the problem. I actually believe it was our own people that were running the company that were blind to what could have been. At that moment in the '80s construction contractors were starting to build bridges with concrete. Bethlehem Steel could have expanded and gone into construction shapes, and they could've gotten the concrete business instead of just the plain old steel industry business. They were headstrong, producing steel and steel only, where they could've expanded and gone into concrete. And then got the upper percentage of bridge building, but they didn't do that. And then you had the, the point that I think really broke the camel's back, other than their spending, was when they wanted to put a continuous caster in to compete with Nucor. I understand that they had the surveyors out, ground was breaking for it and all of a sudden it just stopped. That was the end of their, that was actually their downfall.

Then the caster ended up down in Harrisburg at the other plant.
TC: Yeah, Steelton I think it was.

Steelton, yeah, right on the outskirts of Harrisburg along the river. A lot of our people who didn't have enough time for pensions ended up down there working because they needed it to get their Rule of 65 pension. So okay Tom, I'm not gonna say anything yet, but down the road I'm gonna ask you like for a final synopsis of what you thought of your time at Bethlehem Steel and stuff like that. But at this time, after you left there, what did you get into? I know you're not the type of guy that would've just taken your pension and sat back in a rocking chair.
TC: No, I couldn't do that. I started out, I went over to the community college, I mean I've been teaching basic electricity and motor controls and

sensors. And been doing that now for 11 years. I still do it. I figure, you know I'm not the smartest cube on the block, but what I've learned over 30 years just from the steel company, I can pass onto somebody that really wants to learn, and that's what I want to do.

That's interesting. I see here you also worked at a place called US Intech; what did they do?
TC: Yeah, that's part of GAF Organization. They make roofing. Under roofing is what they make there mostly and flat roof rubberoid products. But uh, it's a good company to work for. As all companies go, they do have their problems, but most of all they utilize what skills I've learned, and it made me feel that I, 30 years at the steel wasn't wasted. I transferred from there, because that was an hour, hour and ten minute drive into New Jersey, so I transferred to the Quakertown plant.

I see. And that, that come to an end. And you ended up at Davis Beverage. Okay, so you're still there at Davis Beverage. All right now I see here you were also a shop steward during your time there. Do you want to talk a little bit about that, but before you even start, I'm gonna ask you, do you think the union did a pretty good job, or do you think they were in a no-win situation?
TC: Personally, I think they were in a no-win situation, but I think they could've done things a lot differently to avoid some of the problems that were in the steelmaking process. I mean, I understand what unions are supposed to do, protect positions, protect benefits, but when you're looking at, you have to look into the future and see, what will my decision make an impact on? And I don't think they ever did that. I mean, as an assistant grievance committeeman I made a suggestion when they had their convention one year for contract talks, get better benefits for pension instead of raises, because if you have more people going out on pension, more people would get advanced in the higher paying positions, but they ignored that.

Well, you know what, it's ironic that you brought that up, because you know, I was the guy that presented that, you know to the negotiating committee. I remember you had to come over to union hall and actually fill out a form, and it had to go in front of the local union, and they voted on 'em, yours passed. Everyone thought that was a good idea, but it never really went anywhere out in Pittsburgh. And you know yourself, because you know you were a shop steward, assistant grievance committeeman, I was on the grievance committee, and we both know that we spent 99 percent of our time on 1 percent of the people.
TC: That's true.

It was unfortunate, but by the same token if you didn't take care of these people,

I mean we'd really have trouble. You'd probably remember the gentleman we had fired on the ore bridge and everyone said well, good, he deserves it. Okay, on the day it happened, the following day people were calling me at home and saying, you better get him back, that's not right what happened to him, and within four days that guy was back to work, and I'll never forget when he came back to work the thing just flipped around 180 degrees again, and people were cursing me, saying why did you do that?

TC: Can't win, can ya?

But by the same token, you know, under the conditions that that occurred with that guy, we would have done the same thing. I mean, it wouldn't have been any different. It's just that, would you want it to work in the Bethlehem plant without a union is really what I'm saying?

TC: No

Because of the safety.

TC: Safety wasn't really the issue with me. I started work at I guess you could call it a good time, because most of the supervisory force and a lot of the workers were there in the generation gap. They started when the first people that worked there were working. So I bridged the generation gap from the beginning people to the time I started, and a lot of them treated people with respect. I mean, there were two bosses I worked with on night shift, and some of the old timers, and they treated you with dignity, with respect, but I don't believe that without the union that it would've been like that. I mean, human-wise those two bosses and the older workers that I worked with, that was their upbringing, but there was some people that looked down on people because of their position in the labor force, and knowing if you didn't have regulations guiding them or telling them what to do, they would've been a lot worse than they were.

Well, I can remember two people, Bela Hoffert and Dave Scurry. Dave Scurry from the sintering plant and Bela from the ore handling, these guys really had the respect of the men. And I often said to Dave Scurry, I said Dave, "I heard a rumor that in the 40 some years that you're here you never had to discipline one of your employees." He says, "Nno, everything we did, we did in-house, we took care of it right on the spot. It never got into that office." He says," because I told these guys if we don't handle it right here, I can't help you. Once it goes in the office, you're throwing caution to the wind." And that was really something. In fact you know later on when I got there, you know, of all the people that were in the office, we had some real characters. I'll never forgot Ron Emge. We were having a grievance meeting one day and a particular guy came in and the superintendent came down from the Blast Furnace, Carl, and this particular individual handed him a receipt for four tires, and he says, "What's this?" He says, "The last grievance meeting you were here you paid me; when you forgot to call me out I got four tires for my truck." He says, "Now I have some other grievances in," he says, "and my wife's car needs tires." And this guy got up and left. And about 10 minutes later the phone rang, Ron Emge said that was Carl Weber, I'm supposed to finish this meeting here, he's authorizing me to be his agent, and Carl Weber never came down to a grievance meeting from that point on. And you know the ironic thing about this, this guy won that grievance. He got another set of tires. And all he said is, "I didn't do nothing wrong. They were supposed to call me." He says, "They called the junior guy. And you now that's just some of the funny things that happened down at the plant. I mean sometimes it was a three ring circus. But Tom at this time I'm gonna give you your free reign and I want you to just get everything off your chest you want to say about working at Bethlehem Steel. Just let if fly.

TC: All right, that's a license to kill. I guess I could say I never regretted starting there. To me it was family, and it's something I haven't seen in the places that I worked afterwards where you had pension parties, you have retirement parties with people you work with. I mean there's no such thing outside of Bethlehem Steel that takes place like that anymore. So it's one family, that's why we didn't take advantage, but we had cookouts and we celebrated while we were there, I guess you can call it celebrate, some people wouldn't understand that. But it was a home away from home. And do I regret going there? No. My dad worked there, my two grandfathers worked there, the first one passed away, and the other one was still working there. And it was a family event. My brother worked there. So if you go to high school, if you don't have plans for college, there's always Bethlehem Steel. And we got a bad rap, we were overpaid, you enjoyed great benefits, but if people would've really dug into the pile of manure that the newspaper was spreading at the time, you'd find out teachers were getting better benefits and pay, Mack was getting better benefits and pay, but it seemed like the Bethlehem Steel was the target. And my family lived good, decently, let's put it that way, than most. But everyone had a choice. They could've gone to Bethlehem Steel back in the '60s and worked there. You work in the snow, you work in the sleet, freezing rain, you work on hot floors, near the furnaces when they tap 'em. In the Sintering Plant you worked near the hot beds in the summer time. It never seemed to work the other way around when it was cold you'd work in the hot areas, it was opposite. And of course there was always the big thing with the holidays or a family function, you could never get off. Well, Christmas dinner is at four o'clock, well I gotta be to work at three. How about Thanksgiving, nope I'm working night shift, I'll be sleeping during the day. Hey, we have a picnic Memorial Day, how about the Fourth of July? No, I'm working both of those. I had to give up a lot of family time. Of course the rest of the family went and they told you about it afterwards, but it's just like not being there is more harmful as you get older. But we put up with it, that's why we got the higher wages, we got the benefits, because we sacrificed more than most people do.

Well that's good Tom. I mean that's what people want to hear. They want to hear what it was really like. They want to hear it from the people that actually worked there. They don't want to know the "Morning Call" story. They don't want to know the "Express Times" story. They don't want to know the Bethlehem Steel story. They want to know the Thomas J. Cooper story, and you did a good job telling it, and I'd like to thank you.

TC: Thank you.

THOMAS GODUSKY
32 years

Combustion, Instrument Repairman

You could search far and wide to find another person as nice as Tom. Active in the community of Emmaus, PA he currently runs the combustion department reunion party yearly.

* * * * * * * * *

Okay, we're on the record with Tom Godusky; it's May 9th, 2008. Tom, did you have a nickname at Bethlehem Steel?

TG: Uh, for awhile at the Saucon plant they called me Mr. Clean because I was in the military and I wore military type clothes and I tried to be neat at all times.

Yeah, now how were you hired? How did you become a steelworker?

TG: Back in 1964, May, I was laid off, I had no job, I had a wife and two children, lived in an apartment, and I heard Bethlehem Steel was hiring. So I went over there and took the aptitude test, and I was hired not knowing what the Bethlehem Steel was all about. They asked me what I wanted to do there, and I said I just want a job, I'll do anything. They recommended the combustion department because of the scores on my aptitude test and my mechanical ability, and I was hired in combustion as a repairman helper.

And they did what?

TG: Repairman helpers carried tools, they were gophers, hold the ladder, get tools, stick close by because at a big plant with all the hazards, uh, I wasn't allowed to roam by myself.

So you were just like the baby duck following the big duck?

TG: That's about it.

Yeah, and you moved on then to other jobs from there?

TG: From uh, combustion repairman helper to instrument, to meter man helper, same department, was a jump of two classes from four to six, pay grades. More money, and that was basically the same type of job helping instrument repairman rather than repairman working more on the automatic systems rather than repairing the systems when they're down. That uh position I held for a matter of months until I find out that the test man position was opening, and here again that would have been a progression of six, eight, and ten classes for more money, so I immediately applied for that, and was given that job of a test man.

Now, getting up to test man position was that in your first year. First year, now during that first year, did you make any dramatic moves in your home life?

TG: In 1964 when I lived in an apartment with nothing to do, no place to go, and got hired, I immediately wanted to look for a permanent place to live, and uh, I had a house built October of 64, broke ground right here in Emmaus, Pennsylvania, corner of Second and North streets where I live right now and we're conducting this interview. I've come a long way since then with adding features to the house, but we had a third child, I was active in military reserve program, voluntary fireman, and many other community activities while I was working at Bethlehem Steel.

And you just went to the bank and they just gave you the money? How'd that work?

TG: Basically that's about it. I was known in the Borough. I was born and raised here. I knew a lot of people. I knew the bank, and uh, they knew me, although I was just a young fellow out of the military only since 1961, graduated from high school 1959, uh, I got a loan. I insisted there would be no co-signer. If they wanted to build me a house, they had to get me a loan at my percentage, which they agreed to, and I've been living in this house actually since January of 1965.

Yeah, okay. Now that sounds like a real good start. And you progressed further down the line in your second year at the company. Where did you finally eventually end up as? What particular job?

TG: After the test man position which I held for several years, openings were for instrument repairman class C. This was years later. I remember I applied for that. I made that with no problem, and for a matter of a couple years I had to be Class C, then I could be tested for Class B.

Class C had an established rate of pay?

TG: Uh, yes, I don't remember exactly what the rate of pay was Class C. I think it was somewhere around a twelve. Yeah it was a twelve, because a test man was ten, I went to twelve, and then the B rate was fourteen, if I remember correctly, sixteen was A rate, or maybe it was even eighteen.

Now, here's a question that a lot of people can't remember, and some of 'em spit it right out. Do you remember your first rate of pay at the company, pay per hour?
TG: My first rate of pay, uh, it was a little over, I seem to think it was a little over $2, but that sounds pretty high. I don't remember exactly.

No, not really, because when I started as a chainman up in the Billet Yard, I started at $2.18 an hour.
TG: It was about $2 an hour.

Yeah, okay. Now, your job as an instrument repairman; what exactly did they do?
TG: Instrument repairman installed, maintained and serviced control systems for pressures, flows, temperatures, water, air, gas, oil, any kind of liquid or gas that would flow, and they were controlled by originally by hydraulic systems, an old ancient type of dinosaur control system. Then it went into pneumatics, and eventually as everything else went into electronics, electronic controls four to 20-milli amp services.

So you actually, like, just moved right on into that as it became available.
TG: Absolutely. Uh, taking advantage of any schools through the Bethlehem program to advance in the particular job categories.

So now we're talking, we're basically talking here about maybe the first seven years that you work at Bethlehem Steel until you actually get up to be an instrument repairman, is that about right?
TG: Uh, by that time I was probably an A instrument repairman.

What was your first impression when you, like, the first week you were in the plant?
TG: It was very hectic. Downtown, getting there in the first place with the traffic from Emmaus to Bethlehem, uh, places to park. In bad weather especially. I parked in South Bethlehem, that would be in the Lehigh section. And then, uh, down the Saucon wasn't too bad, but we're talking about the time when they were tearing down the Heights to build a basic oxygen furnace. So there was a lot of construction and hectic traffic going on down in that area then. And then my last twenty years was spent at the Coke Works mainly as an instant repairman down at the Coke Plant.

So then you were more localized then, just basically in the Coke Plant?
TG: Yeah, one of the better parts about that was you could drive right in and park on the parking lot in the Coke Plant, although naturally as everybody realizes the environment was very stinky let's say; the cars took

a beating from the vapors in the atmosphere down there, but uh, eventually as the years went by things were cleaned up, the air was cleaned up and things like that. It became a much cleaner place to work.

How was your scheduling in your early years? How did it affect your family, I mean vacations and stuff like that?

TG: Prior to being hired at Bethlehem Steel I worked mostly day shift, although there was a period of time where I worked steady night shift from 10:30 at night till 7 in the morning, and I said if I ever had to stay on the job like that all my life I probably would quit. Now, when I was hired at Bethlehem Steel naturally everybody said you're not gonna work long, you're gonna be laid off every summer, you're gonna work swing shift, and you're gonna hate it. Fortunately, the combustion department had some shift work, although it was basically day shift. In all my years at Bethlehem Steel I believe I was only laid off once for a period of about two weeks and that was because the main oxygen line ruptured coming across the river for the oxygen furnace, and uh the plant, that part of the plant was basically shut down for about two weeks until they repaired the oxygen line.

So it looks like you walked in the right day to get hired when they said how about going to combustion?
TG: Yeah, it was not a big money department, but I had a steady job, and uh, I guess in the long run it paid off.

So you know the last 20 years at the Coke Works, you must have got to know a lot of people being in one area like that.

TG: Well, in the whole 30 almost 32 years being all over the plant from East Lehigh to Lehigh, Saucon, Coke Works I got to know a lot of people.

How did the people, like, co-mingle within the combustion department? Did you guys, I understand ya's played, you played a lot of softball? You had pension parties and things like that. Tell me a little bit about that?
TG: In my department I got involved with running a family picnic. We started out playing softball, and at the end of the summer with the co-workers we decided to have a little picnic and invite the wives, which we did, and it went over so well the first year or two that everybody said let's open it up to the whole department, now the department meaning the Saucon area where I was in, the Saucon meter room, and it got to the point where we'd have a couple hundred people at Emmaus Community Park.

Wow.
TG: One group was in charge of getting the corn on the cob, the other

group with getting the soft drinks, the other group in charge of meats, the other group, and uh, we started out charging $10 a family, and at the end of the first season we had so much money left over that the next year we didn't charge at all, and this thing went on for years and years as a summer family picnic. We had to move it to different areas, rather than just Emmaus Park. Uh, in the meantime, we had, occasionally we had some older fellows retiring, and if someone liked the fellow, they'd have a retirement party for him. If it was somebody that nobody cared for, they didn't have a party. I figured it wasn't right, and I got a couple of the other workers to say, "Listen, we're gonna have a retirement party every year, and whoever retires is gonna get a free dinner and a $50 savings bond," and that started, I can't remember, probably 25 years ago I'd say. And I'm retired since 1995, and I still run this party; however, it's now called a reunion rather than a retirement party. Like, no one's retiring from the department; we're either dying off or the younger fellows have jobs.

Well, that's really nice, you know. I know that every area of the plant did not do that, and you know, it's just really good to know that because of the time you spent with each other, okay, that you could still find time to get together in your off time.

TG: Right, I never joined a bowling league as a lot of the guys did, or a golf league. I wasn't a golfer or bowler; however, like I say, softball, we had our softball game, and then uh, a lot of my spare time was spent with the reserve program and the Naval reserve, going for two weeks every year, going to weekend drills, that kind of thing, and the Bethlehem Steel cooperated in working my working schedule along with my military schedule.

Where did you end up in the military when you retired?

TG: I stayed for 20-plus years, and I was an E6 gunner's mate; that's a first class gunner's mate, in the CB's construction. My first couple years before I started at the Bethlehem Steel company was actually more destroyers, active duty Navy, destroyers.

And what was your best memory of Bethlehem Steel.

TG: I guess some of the best memories would have been the fellows I got to know and spend a lot of off time with, like the retirement parties, the family picnics we had, because it involved a lot of people, not just closer friends in the smaller shops. Our shops were throughout the plant, and even though each shop had its own little clique we got together as a big clique.

What was your worse part?

TG: Well, my worse part I guess was working at the Coke Works on certain jobs when it was extremely hazardous with the gases, the temperature and the gases because of the danger of them, and maybe people don't realize it, but there was a time I believe we lost five steelworkers in one week. I remember one day there were three killed. The Coke Works, we had several killed over the years. I came to work on Easter morning one day, Easter morning, and there was an unusual amount of cars and people at the Coke Works for Easter morning, and I found out that during the night a fellow was killed, and the people were there Easter morning to investigate it.

Yeah. Now here's one, here's one Tom, how do you think the company looked at you, as an asset or a liability?
TG: The company overall probably didn't realize I existed as an individual, although my immediate department thought, I feel like my immediate department and supervisors thought, it was well worth my being there.

Yeah, well, you know, that's just something I've asked a lot of people. Now, when did you actually realize that the company was in trouble? When did it first dawn on you, say, "Hey, this isn't lookin' good."
TG: Well, I'd have to think back on that naturally, uh, things were going strong when they built the BOF, and then it was going strong at the Coke Works in '75 when they put the brand new A battery in, so things really looked good through the '70s, and I guess maybe into the '80s; at times there were lay offs and cut backs, but then things got better. I can remember being at Saucon when the New Jersey battleship was gonna be put back into commission, and we were gonna make shells. I don't think any ever got completed to reach the ship, but there were times when things were up and down, and I guess into the later '80s probably is when I more realized that things were not progressing anymore like they were.

You were like at the top of the hill and you were starting to go down the slide.
TG: And then later on actually as the BOF shut down and the place started shutting down. I actually could have stayed, with my seniority I probably could have stayed till they turned the lights out in the plant, but in '95 when there were 20 instrument repairmen and they wanted to get rid of four, I volunteered to be one of those to get out, and the senior man who already 65 years old and 45 years of service elected to stay, and the number two man had me by one day seniority elected to stay; this was November now of '95, and I was number three man on the list, and I said yes, I am interested, I would take it, and when they said when do you

wanna leave, I said when can I leave, and the answer was from the shop steward and my interviewer, next Friday. So from one week to the next Friday I was no longer employed at Bethlehem Steel. I was on temporary layoff until my pension went into effect in February of '96.

Yeah, I know about that. Now, do you think the company did all it could to save itself?

TG: Uh, no, I don't think they did all they could, no.

Now, if you had been a position where you could have called the shots, from the beginning, let's say from 1985 on, what would you have done that you think would have made a dramatic improvement in the way things were?

TG: Well, that's hard to say because of what the company was being more or less forced to do through politics and cleaning up, like at the Coke Works. So much money had to be spent on cleaning up the atmosphere, and throughout the plant where a lot of foreign companies weren't doing that, and their products were cheaper, and a lot of the sale went overseas. In the Bethlehem area probably because mini mills were coming along and being progressive, uh, Bethlehem Steel maybe should have invested more into mini mills, although we were making the biggest beams and so forth for high rise construction and bridges, and nowadays there's a lot of plastics being used, where restressed concrete is being used, where a lot of times big beams were used before, the way I see it.

How big of an issue was safety in the plant when you were there?

TG: Well, safety was preached to be a very big issue. Naturally they provided hats, glasses, gloves, at the Coke Works especially, but a lot of it was forced on by the government and OSHA to provide men with safety equipment.

Do you think the company would have provided that without the union?

TG: Not unless they had to or there was proof that it had to be used. I mean, if no one got hurt, you probably didn't need a certain part of equipment.

Now, if anyone, like today, you went up to Lehigh Valley Mall and you ran into someone from high school, and they said, "Do you know, Tom, you'd still be working if you wouldn't have slept on night shift and cooked on middle shift. What would you say to a person like that?

TG: If I wouldn't have slept on night shift and cooked on middle shift? Well, we worked out of shops, and it's like the fire department nowadays; everybody knows the fire department goes in there, they have a schedule, they cook their meals, they stay there, they sleep there, and even though it might be a 48-hour job of tour, whatever you might call, a shift, a 48-hour shift, Bethlehem Steel, our shift were eight hours. However, I for example would get in early in the morning put coffee on, and sure I'd have coffee there before I worked. At lunchtime if you could put something on the heater to heat it up and have something hot to eat at lunchtime, fine. Middle shift, nightshift, people at home don't usually eat a big meal during the nighttime, so if you had a chance to close your eyes for your lunchtime or whatever, so be it.

So you're saying overall even though this did happen, it didn't really play any role in the demise of the company?

TG: I wouldn't think so, because everyone I saw, if you had a production job, I don't believe anybody was sleeping on a production job, or how would you make your incentive?

Well, that's obvious, that's obvious from interviewing people from the Beam Yard.

TG: And there were a lot of repairman positions and jobs where if the equipment was running, you weren't working on the equipment, but maybe sweeping the floor or doing something else.

Yeah. Could you have worked there without a union, you think?

TG: Uh, I'm not sure how it was without the union. I've been a union member since day one; uh, I don't know how rough it was before, but I appreciated the union.

Well, that's good. Well that concludes our interview. I want to thank you, you know, for taking part of this, and I wish all the best for you and your family.

TG: Well, we're doing all right so far. Thank you for interviewing me, and I don't know, the more I think about it there's probably a lot more I could say if I thought.

Oh, I'm sure we could talk forever about all kinds of things. The main idea here is to get the message out of what it was really like working on the inside, and I think we did a real good job of that.

TG: That would be interesting to really talk to a group of people that would be interested in knowing from a steelworker, like, what did go on in the steel company, you know, and what's a worker's opinion?

Well, the good news, the good news is when this book is done, they're gonna have something to look at and they'll know for sure. Thank you.

JAMES J. McANDREW
27 years of service

411, 412, 413, 414 Maintenance Gangs

Known as "Irish Jim" or "the Leprechaun," Jim was known for the best fish fries in the Saucon Mills. One of the best troubleshooters ever employed by BSCO.

* * * * * * * * *

Okay, we're on the record with James M. McAndrew; it's February the 19th, 2008. I see here that you spent 27 years working for Bethlehem Steel. You were all over the place. I understand you started in the 413 department. What was it like there, the 413 department?

JM: Well, I started right off the bat, when I got hired. I started in maintenance, so I didn't have to work production, which was a good thing.

Why do you say that was a good thing?

JM: Because I think you're better off in maintenance, especially right in the beginning, than you are in a production job. Maintenance is more, uh, not so much "nose to the grindstone" like a production job.

I see. And uh, the 413 department, what area of the plant was that?

JM: Mostly the 35-inch mill. Alloy and Tool Steel.

What about the Electric Furnace?

JM: Electric Furnace and East Lehigh.

And East Lehigh?

JM: And Tool Steel.

Yup, East Lehigh, they had a nickname for East Lehigh, didn't they, the cabbage patch. Remember the guys down there.

JM: They had those gardens up in the top of the hill, and the deer loved 'em.

Yup, not only were they feeding everybody that came down there on the weekend, they were feeding all the deer in Lower Saucon Township.

You must have some memories of 413. What comes right out, right off the top? Foremen that you worked with, guys that you worked with, jobs?

JM: Oh, guys like Sterling Frable. He was quite the character, and some of the other guys were really funny, and very helpful. If you had a problem and you asked somebody, you could make a lot of connections. Like I got help from different guys down there for different reasons: they knew somebody, or they could hook you up with a phone number, things like that.

Yeah. Tell me a little bit about Sterling?

JM: He was a Dutchman, and he talked like a Dutchman, and he used to say in the morning, "Nah if ya's don't do nuthin' you won't get hurt." At the safety meeting.

I'll tell you what, those words truly are, you know, coming right from the heart. Especially, I knew Sterling too, so I know what you're talking about, and uh. 413 I see here down to the Coke Works. What'd you do down there?

JM: Electrical helper. Working on a new battery mostly, Ben Pinkey was my foreman, and he ran me around like a dog. I even said to him one day, "You know Ben, I'm getting paid helper." And he had me, he was treating me like I was the guy in charge, like I was the A man, you know, and he had me running around. He had long legs. I had a hard time keeping up with him. I imagine he's still down there at Number 1 Machine Shop.

Yes, he's still working down there in the plant, yeah, with West Homestead Engineering. Now, 413, Jim, how long, how many years were you actually there?

JM: About three.

And then you went down to the Coke Works?

JM: That was temporary, yeah, they sent me down, 7,000 number.

So your first actual base unit that you stuck around for a while was 414?

JM: That was January of '78; they called me at home and said, we have a job for you. Motor inspector in the Saucon bull gang. Bring your tools.

Well, that's right up front, isn't it?

JM: Right up front. I started on the middle shift, didn't even know where I was going. The guy on the phone was named Hilbert, and he told me, "Walk down the hill, follow the guys, the washroom's on the right, and we're on the left." Couldn't beat that. That's where I ran, in the washroom I ran into Chester Conrad, and he says, "You the new motor inspector?"

I says, Yup," and he said, "Well, I'm Chester; me and you are working together." I said, "Well this is good. You can show me the ropes here." He was quite the character, too. You meet a lot of characters down there. I think when Bethlehem Steel hired, they just threw out a big net and dragged in whatever they got.

Yeah, well, I know one thing, when I was hired the first thing they said to me after they told me I was hired is do you have any friends that are looking for a job. I mean it was amazing.

JM: Yeah, it's hard to believe in this day and age what it was like. They had big ads in the paper: no experience necessary; come on in; we'll train you.

Do you remember when the buses were still running from the coal regions? The guys would get on the buses. Okay. Now 414, that was the Saucon mills, the rolling mills and stuff.

JM: Upper mills maintenance. I also worked in lower mills maintenance.

Yeah, tell the people what, what was, what were you known for in the 414 department?

JM: Cooking.

Cooking?

JM: I was the head cook.

The head cook. Let's hear a little bit about that. Everybody heard about this, but nobody heard it right from the horse's mouth.

JM: Well, after I was in 414 awhile, they transferred me up to the soaking pits. Apparently, nobody wanted that job, and you had three-man gangs at the soaking pits, and you worked steady swing shift. So when we would go seven middles in a row, the two guys that I worked with would take turns cooking, so naturally I fell right into that. And when you work seven middles in a row, you don't get supper. You're working from well, you leave the house at two in the afternoon you get home at midnight, so there's no suppertime. Unless you just open a brown paper bag and eat a sandwich or something, but, so if you wanted any kind of meal it's up to you; do it yourselves.

Well, give me an example of the type of meals that you'd make on middle shift.

JM: Well, a lot of times we'd either make game, pheasants, turkeys, uh trout, fish, a lot of chicken, things like that, and we cooked a lot of one pot meals, where you could combine rice and onions and peppers and chicken and all these things, and you'd make a big pot full; everybody would contribute and everybody would eat.

Well, believe it or not, when I first went down into the Beam Yard maintenance area we had a guy that drove back road all the time, worked for the fire department. Wesley Beers. Wesley Beers always kept a sharp knife with him, he'd run into a lot of deer killed on the road. Off come the hindquarters. You know, we'd call that road kill special. We had the deer cubed up and ready to go in the freezer all the time. We'd bring in potatoes, carrots, onion, peas, corn into a plastic bag right into the oven. It took about a good fifteen minutes to get it ready, and the only thing we really had to bring in from that point was bread and butter. It was great. I'll tell ya. But when you said one-pot meals, I mean that's what I remember about it.

JM: Oh yeah, absolutely.

Now, you spent how much time in 414?

JM: From '78 till '87, about nine years.

About nine years. How'd the foremen treat you down there?

JM: Not bad. If you did your work, they pretty much left you alone.

How was your schedule? Did you have trouble with the schedule?

JM: I adapted very well to it, but I don't think a lot of people could, cuz you're working seven, seven, and six all the time, which is seven middles, six days, seven nights, so you're always rotating. You just get used to one shift, and bang …

Were the majority of the people working on the swing shift? Or how was that?

JM: Well, it depend. Nah, I'd say pretty many, maybe two-thirds were day shift, and maybe the other third were swing shift. They had to have coverage on middles and nights and weekend.

So depending on how the days would fall, you spend a lot of time working holidays …

JM: Holidays, night, weekends. Yeah, you didn't spend a whole lot of time on standard day shift like a lot of people in the country.

But that was the life of a steelworker.

JM: Well, yeah, the plant runs 24 hours a day seven days a week so, there has to be people there to do the work, and that's the way it is.

What did your daughters think of that when they were growing up? I guess when you were on swing shift, middles and nights, they didn't get to see much of you?

JM: No, they didn't, but they got used to it. My wife got used to it, which was even more surprising than my daughter.

Yeah, that's great. And one of the best stories you ever told me about your wife,

Dot, was the time the lawnmower wouldn't start, and you said, "Honey that'll never happen again"; you went out you brought her a brand new electric start one.

JM: The first time I remember about you is I was at the 35-inch mill, and I was sitting in the shanty, and I called my wife and said, "Did you mow the grass like I told you to" and she said yeah, and I said, "Well you know I'm gonna inspect it when I get home," and you were sitting there laughing and saying, "There ain't nobody on that phone," so I handed the phone to you, and that was the first time you talked to my wife, and you couldn't believe it, and you said to her, "Did you really mow the grass?" and she said, "Well yeah, he told me to." And then you said, "Does he really inspect it when he comes?" "Yes he does," and you were quite put out.

I think my exact words to her, "Them Marines are all the same." You did all your military time prior to coming to Bethlehem Steel, huh?

JM: That's correct.

What'd you do in the military?

JM: Electronics.

Electronics with the air group?

JM: Yup. Worked on the F4 Phantom.

F4 Phantom, how 'bout that? Okay now, I see you got yourself into the 412 department.

JM: I bid in.

Which was the sintering plant, ore handling,

JM: Ore handling with Cooper and Kresge; in fact it was your position. When you went to the union hall, it went up for bids, and I won the bid.I have a funny story about that too because I was working at the pits at the time with Glenn Allman, and we were both night shift, and every morning he'd say to me, "Oh, I gotta go down and bid on that job at the sinter plant, I keep forgetting to do that." Well, I had already bid on it, and I'd say, "You do what you want Glenn, I'm going to the washroom," and every day he would say, "Ah, the hell with it," and we'd go to the washroom, and him and I were sharing a locker. So he comes in Monday morning, opens the locker and my tools were gone, and he says to the guys, "Where's Jimmy?" "Oh he won the bid to the sintering plant; he's gone."

Oh boy, I can just picture all that now; I bet he still talks about that?

JM: He says, "I'm gonna squeeze his fat neck," cuz obviously he had more time than I did. If he would have bid on it, he would've got it.

Now, Jim almost every steelworker I've ever known had a nickname. What'd they call you?

JM: Pockets.

Pockets.

JM: That was my nickname, given to me by an old guy named Henry Straub.

Henry Straub. I remember Henry. I remember one thing about Henry Straub, I never saw a guy that could eat like him.

JM: How 'bout ingot?

Oh yeah, Frankie Andrecs in his hey day. You know what, I saw Henry Straub eat two whole chickens one time on middle shift.

JM: Well, there was a little skinny guy we worked with that could eat like crazy, too, I'm trying to remember his name. He went into where they had the gas detectors and all that stuff. You know he came around and serviced stuff. I'm trying to remember his name, but for his inch for inch and pound for pound, I never saw anybody pack food away like he could, unbelievable. I wish I could think of his name.

Well, we had some guys that excelled at various things down at that Bethlehem Steel. I think most guys excelled more at telling stories than anything else. And a lot of these guys created their own stories. I see you ended up at the Blast Furnace? How was that?

JM: How did I end up at the Blast Furnace? I was laid off, and uh, D'Augustino called me up and said, "Would you like to go maintenance at the Blast Furnace?" I said sure. So me and Gibby and Barry Stein, the three of us were sent to the Blast Furnace.

I'll be seeing Gibby and Barry Stein before too long for interviews.

JM: Well, I'm sure you had nicknames from our favorite boy Hawny. George Hahn.

When I was down at George Hahn's, at his funeral. We got up, and I told the story about the time he brought the watermelon in for Big Walt. Walt was 6 feet 10; he was black, he got laid off, and we told him get out of here, go up and bid on them jobs at the Allentown Police Department. In fact, Hawny told him, "You'd make a good cop." He says, "One thing for sure," he said," you'd stand out in a crowd. But that's the kind of guy Hawny was.

JM: Oh, Hawny was a character.

Stand, how could you not stand out in a crowd when you were 6 foot 10?

JM: I think he was actually 6 foot 11.

But you know, we told that story there, and I'll tell you, it brought the house down at the funeral.

JM: They called him Tree.

Yup, and there's Tree sitting there.

JM: From the Black Forest. Frankie Strauss. told him all kinds of crap, and Tree used to say, "Frank, one day I'm a cop and I'm gonna pull you over." And guess what happened. The Tilghman Street bridge, he put his siren on and pulled Frank Strauss over, and you could just hear the commotion when Frank realized who it was, carrying on, and he said, "I told you Uncle Frank"; he used to call him Uncle Frank.

Yeah. I'll tell you what, the stories go on and on, but the friendships that were created down there go on and on also.

JM: I can believe; that's the one thing I miss about the place, the camaraderie, being with the guys.

Yup, and at the Blast Furnace you were doing motor inspector work, but what exactly did that entail in the Blast Furnace area; that's where all the hot iron came from. What exactly were you doing?

JM: Anything electrical: lighting, heating, motors, uh, anything that ran on electricity.

How long were you out there at the Blast Furnace area?

JM: Oh boy, not long, maybe a year.

Were you up there under that special deal with the 7000 number?

JM: Yes. When they put the C furnace in.

Yeah, that was a contracting outfit, that Lester Clore had put in so that we could get guys back to work that were on layoff.

JM: Okay. That was the only time I worked at the plant that I wasn't in maintenance. An opening up for Number 1 Machine Shop, just entry level, just floor hand, and I bid on it, and I won the bid, because I knew that Number 1 Machine Shop in that area of the plant would still be open when everything else went down, and it's still open today; it's just not called Bethlehem Steel, and I could've been working there, I could be there right now with some of the same people I worked there with.

Well you know what, would've, could've, should've.

JM: But I really didn't want to do that work. When they called me up and asked me to come back, I said, "You mean as a motor inspector?" and they said, "Oh no, no, back to what you were doing, shoveling chips and …

Yeah, but that really meant nothing down there because over time you probably would've went right back on the maintenance gang.

JM: I had no way of knowing that at all.

Well, yeah, you would've known that.

JM: I never worked maintenance there. I was strictly a, well what they'd call it, a utility man, and then the next progression was chain man, which was the roughest job probably in the steel company, and then crane man. Well, I didn't like cranes. I never liked to run cranes. Never had a crane check, so I was not interested in progressing to crane man. So I was the utility man; they put me on chain man, and the guys told me if they ever knock you off chain man and you don't want to go back on chain man, you tell the schedule clerk, I'll stay utility now, don't put me back on chain, because they ran you ragged as a chain man. You had these big pieces you had to hook up, and you were by yourself. If you got lucky, somebody would give you a hand, but not necessarily, and it was the worse job probably I ever had at Bethlehem Steel as far as what you had to do, and how fast you had to do it, and how critical it was; it was a tough job.

How long were you in that job?

JM: Geez, I don't really know for sure, two or three years.

Two or three years. And you went down to Steelton?

JM: Well, in that two or three years they would close up and say the place was sold. Then you'd be home six months and the phone would ring, "Well, it's not sold; come on back." So two or three years went kind of quick. Then it came to the pension nonsense where if you didn't have enough time, the company had the right to call you a rule of 65 employee, and the rule of 65 employee was vulnerable, all the company had to do was say we have a job for you somewhere else, and if you said no, I'm not taking it, I'm not traveling all the way to that place, you didn't get any pension. So they weren't gonna do that to me. I told my wife I'm willing to go as far as Steelton, but I'm not going any further than that. So I went in and say to D'Augustino and told him, "Put my name on the list for Steelton." And at the time there were guys in it who were still working at the Coke Works trying to go to Steelton, and he told them, "You're still working, you can't put your name on the list." They wanted to have their name on ahead of time while they were still working down at the Coke Works.

They wanted to get a little head start.

JM: Yeah, yeah, because they didn't want to get shipped to Indiana or Baltimore. So I had to drive down the thruway; it took me exactly 80 minutes one way, straight down the highway; you didn't even have to make any turns. Right at the end you made a turn or two right into the plant. I drove my car right up to the trailer that I worked out of, didn't even go to the washroom. Went into the trailer, got my piece of equipment, did my job, and that was that.

What did you do down there?

JM: I was a sonic test man on rails. They sent me to school while I was down there for the week. It was pretty funny down there. I always laugh and say that the people down there had humps on their backs. Compared to the Bethlehem plant, they were backwards. Like, I'd be standing out there watching forklifts back up with no back up alarm, and you're standing there looking right at the buildings in Harrisburg, the Capital of Pennsylvania, and nobody even bats an eye; they didn't even have things like that. And I always think back to the Bethlehem plant, and think, "My God, they don't even have a safety program."

What did you think of the safety program at the Bethlehem plant?

JM: I thought it was excellent at the Bethlehem plant, despite the fact that people got hurt and killed. You worked in that kind of industry, and some things you just can't control.

Well, we all know about the guys that came into the plant and only lasted a couple days.

JM: I know guys that never paid for their safety shoes. They didn't last long enough to make enough money to pay for their safety shoes.

But when they heard the noise, they felt the heat, the cold, okay, found out that we were telling 'em the truth when we told 'em, "You won't know how you're working next week until Thursday," they thought that was a joke; they didn't really believe that.

JM: No, no, no, and you can get three shifts in one week.

Thursday would come, and they'd look and they'd say, "Oh my God, it's true," and you'd never see 'em again. They were gone. They were gone. But you know, I often said to people who say to me, "Frank, you'd still be working if you wouldn't have been cooking on middle shift and sleeping on night shift." You know what I say to those people? "How many of your buddies have you carried to the ambulance? How many holidays have you missed? Sure, they paid us double time and a half, but still, how many holidays have you missed with your family?" How many summer vacations couldn't you get for years and years and years?

JM: Oh, when you were a young guy in the plant, you couldn't get, I used to get my vacation in March. Everything else was filled up.

How about your wages Jim? What'd you think of your wages when you were at Bethlehem Steel?

JM: I liked 'em, I thought they were good. I thought they paid fair.

Okay, I get a lot of variance on that. You know, some will say well, you know laborers on the outside were making more than us, you know the union laborers and stuff like that, but by the same token a lot of guys had to admit, "I put two, three, four kids through college working at Bethlehem Steel"; it wasn't that bad.

JM: Yeah, well I was out there. I used to get laid off. I was laid off like twenty times. I used to get other jobs. So I could compare.

Now when you were down there, how were you perceived down there, as like an outsider at the Steelton plant? How did your union brothers treat ya?

JM: Well, I didn't really have that much to say with them, because the guys I got sent down with were the guys I worked with, so I didn't really have all that much contact with … some, I had some contact, but not really that much, but they were very, uh, backwards as far as knowing what their rights were, and, like they'd say to me, "Wait till next week when they lay off so and so and you're still here working," and I'd say, "Well, they can't lay off so and so because he's one of the oldest,." Oh yeah, but they do because he gets unemployment and he plays in a golf tournament"; they said they do it every year, I said well they're not doing it this year. So the Bethlehem boys kind of brought a little definition to the union rules and kind of straightened some of the stuff that used to go on down there. Cuz they would just look and say, "Ah, that's what the company does, so they're gonna do that to you, too," and I'd say, Oh no, I don't think, I'm the youngest guy in this department, and I need so many weeks of lay off to get my pension, so if there's one guy off next week, guess who it's gonna be, the youngest guy."

That's right. I don't blame you for thinking like that. Now, here's a good one Jim. Do you think the company did all it could to save itself?

JM: Never, no way. All you gotta do is look what's going on. The parts of the company that are still operating are making so much money they need a wheelbarrow. Why couldn't Bethlehem Steel? I had a boss at the Number 1 Machine Shop look right at me, he was a general foreman. He said, "This new guy's gonna take over and he says he's gonna make money, I don't understand it, we can't make money." I laughed at 'em. I said, "13 guys running around in here with green hats on day shift, we're paying three of 'em general foreman and ten of 'em foreman; how much money do you think it cost to pay those 13 guys and their benefits?" And then we have to take a guy off the machine on middles and nights for a straw foreman because you guys only work days. Just right there alone. How many pieces you gotta sell just to pay that? We had a guy come from Georgia to work on one of the machines; he carried his suitcases down the steps, got out of the taxi cab, hadn't even gone to his hotel yet, and Ben Pinkey lights right into him, "What are ya doin'? I've been waiting for you for." The guy picks his bags up says, "See ya" and Pinkey says, "What do ya mean?" He said, "I'm leavin', the hell with you." Ben Pinkey got down on his knees and kissed this guy's butt for 20 minutes before the guy decided, "Okay, I'll look at the machine for ya." Here was a guy that really went out of his way and he was hearing this crap. I mean, their supervision, if you took a batting average like a 300 in baseball, their decision, they had to be battin' like 0/50. I think the only time they made a correct decision was accidental. They were trying to make a wrong decision, but somehow they got it right.

You know, Jim, the three parts of seniority in the plant are length of continuous service, the knowledge to perform the job, and relative ability. Now when we talk about relative ability and foremen at Bethlehem Steel, what did that mean to you?

JM: Oh my God, a painter helper as general foreman, why? How could that be? Cuz his father was someone.

I remember. I remember many guys like that, but you know, did you ever take notice, particularly there at the end, you couldn't get a foreman to even hint at how much he was getting paid.

JM: Right, cuz they were overpaid.

From 1987 on I never heard a foreman at Bethlehem Steel ever complain about his pay.

JM: I never heard a word out of them.

And you know and to this day, they won't tell you. They won't tell you. It falls under the category of best kept secret. It's sort of like how did George Bush get elected. You know, well, that got a laugh out of ya. Now, Jim, we talked a little bit about everything; you are getting a pension right?

JM: Absolutely.

Well, I'm really glad to hear that. Some of the guys that went off into the other areas did not get pensions; they got buyouts and that was it.

JM: Well, the thing is if I would have been sent to Indiana, I probably wouldn't have got a pension, because I'd of probably just said no. That would have been it for me. But Steelton was doable; I could drive down and drive back. As bad as that sounds, it's better than the alternative.

Well you know, you and I have talked a lot about the plant, you know, over a long time. I know you from the first day you probably were in 413, and uh, and I remember somebody said to me, "Hey, go over and see the Marine over there and bust his ass a little bit." I says, "What Marine?" I'm looking for a big guy right, and the only guy there was you standing at the table talking to Tommy Petro; he said, "The little guy over here." I said, "Okay." I had a good time with that.

JM: They like little guys in the Marines. They said you make a small target.

There ya go. Now, one thing I always told you is that when we did this interview right at the very end I'm gonna give you time to say anything you want and like get it off your chest, sort of like a closing statement. Go ahead, it's all yours. About your time at Bethlehem Steel and working there.

JM: I had a good, what I considered a good job, because I liked working with the people that I worked with. We had fun, we did our work, and when our work was done, we could do what we wanted to do, and I thought it's better than any kind of job where you sit at a production at a machine, cuz I was in maintenance, and when you had to work, you had to work, you had to know what you were doin', but when you were done, you could go have a cup of coffee or shoot the shit, and the characters that we had down there, I could write a book just on that, just on the characters, from the crazy guys like Hawny onto guys like Big Ingot. It was just amazing what you met and experiences you got learning about these guys and the things they would say. It was incredible, and I actually enjoyed most of my time at Bethlehem Steel.

Well, I guess that says it all, and this is what people want to know. They want to know what the insiders thought about working there, and they never were able to find that out from the "Morning Call," the "Express Times," or from Bethlehem Steel themselves.

JM: Well, I would've stayed at the Bethlehem plant until I took my pension; I wasn't gonna leave or go anywhere. If it would've stayed opened, I would've stayed there.

From doing these interviews, the majority of the people think had the plant stayed opened another six months or a year, we would still be working there today.

JM: I can believe that.

And we, you and I would both be getting ready to take our pensions right about now.

JM: And there's no reason that Noble Venture couldn't run that mill and make money. The only mistake they made was telling Roger Penny that they were gonna make money from day one; that sealed the deal. That closed their fate. They said, "We're not selling."

Well, I remember in '95 when Jack Roberts was in there and was gonna run the combination mill; he told us, "We'll be making money within three months." He says, "And within a year we'll have our own electric furnace and our own caster," and when that deal went down, I often said the only reason it died was the Bethlehem Steel executives knew that Jack Roberts was gonna do all those things and they were all gonna look bad.

JM: Oh of course they'd look bad. Well, look at they're looking bad now at what we called Number1Machine Shop. What do they call it now?

West Homestead Engineering.

JM: The guy's making so much money he doesn't know what to do with it, trying to figure out how to hide it from … Did you ever have any body tell you any funny stories from Hawny before we conclude here? Do you wanna hear one?

Go ahead.

JM: My favorite, Hawny, George Hahn was a person that you would have to meet to believe it. He had nicknames for everything. He was a character, he had stories, and he did nothing but mess with people's brains, and he could really have a ball. And one of the guys we worked with was an oiler; he was a little short guy about 5 feet 2, and had big bushy eyebrows and a little stumpy pipe, and his name, I don't remember his name, we called him Buckets. Well, Buckets comes into the shanty one day and he happens to say that he's looking for a dog. Well, Hawny's ears of course perk right up. "What do ya say there Buckets? I can get you a puppy?" "Oh," he says, "Hawny, I want a small dog." "Yeah, it's a puppy." "No, no I want a, it's gotta be a small animal." "Oh yeah," Hawny says. Well, of course, these are monsters, these are Pyrnees or something, some huge animal. So he tells Buckets, "Don't worry. I'll bring one in for ya cuz," called everybody cuz. "Are you sure it's a small dog?" "Yeah, he's only this big. You know what I mean?" "Yeah, yeah, yeah." So he brings this dog in and it's free; that's an important thing to Buckets. So he gets this puppy and he takes it home, and he says to Hawny, "Boy, he has big feet, Hawny." Everybody in the place is just trying to hold it in. So he comes in the shanty about two weeks later. "Hawny," he says, "This dog, he's this high," about two foot with his hand. "Oh," he says, "Don't worry, cuz; that's full grown." "He better be full grown, he's got big, he's eatin a lot." Hawny says, "Don't worry; that's it; he's all over." Okay. So about a month goes by and Buckets comes in the shanty, "Hawny, this thing is four foot high. He's steppin over the coffee table." Hawny says, "Oh my God, what else?" "I hooked him to the dog house out back and he dragged it right into the house." He says, "Oh my God." He says, "Cuz, you got one of the rare ones; bring 'em back." "Oh no." Bucket says, "He's not for sale." And that was Hawny. I can go on and on with stories about him, but that's quite enough.

That's almost as good as Kenny Ziegenfuss and Joe Novak. Smiley Kollek in the Electric Furnace, gives 'em a beagle and they're going on three weeks vacation; this is back when there was still pheasants and rabbits. And like the first three times they took the dog, he ran down groundhog holes chasing, you know, game, and Joe would be out there with Ziggy, they'd be digging this dog out of the groundhog hole. One day, they said, "What happened here?" He says, "Well, the dog ran down the hole." He says, "We listened for him, we couldn't hear him so we left figuring he would come out and we'd wait at the car for him." He says, "We never saw him again." Okay, Jim I'd like to thank you for your insight into your personal observations in the plant, and like I said, it was a great place to work. You knew it was a great place to work, but the memories go on forever.

GLEN B. SNYDER
32 years of service

Alloy/Tool Steel Maintenance,
Field Millwright, Saucon Maintenance

Glenn only did things one way – the right way. There were no shortcuts. He remains today a wood craftsman of renown and a lifesaver for antique car buffs needing duplicate wooden steering wheels and other inlaid wood for classic autos.

* * * * * * * * * *

It's June 13th, 2008, and we're here with Glen B. Snyder. Now, Glen, did you have a nickname in the plant?

GS: No.

Okay, so we're going to call you Glen for this meeting here, is that okay? I see you started in October of 1964, and I'm guessing right now, looking at this, down at the Saucon mills?

GS: Yes.

What was that like, the first day you walked in there? Did you think you were going back in time? Into the bowels of hell or what?

GS: Well, we were in tabernacle; that's where we started, and we worked in there a couple days. There was a few of us that started on the same day, and I would walk out of there over toward the 42-inch mill area, and I would see the cranes bringing the whole complete mill down to change rolls, and kept thinking, what am I doing here? And, uh, people were good, the workers were good, and uh, you know, we just started working and doing whatever we had to do, you know, and following directions of the millwrights.

What caught your attention immediately, the noise, the constant movement?

GS: A lot of the crane movement.

Yeah, there's always something going on around ya.

GS: Yes, all the time.

And that's, I guess that took a little getting used to.
GS: Right, and also all the hot metal coming down the roller lines. You know, you're not used to seeing things like that, and you have to be aware of everything around you 100 percent.

Yeah, you're not used to standing ten foot from the roller line, the ingot comes by getting ready to enter the mill, and you look down at your clothes and they're smoking. And a lot of people got their baptism that way. And usually somebody would grab 'em by the arm and say, "Hey kid, don't stand there.". That happen to me at the 3- inch mill, one of the first shifts I ever worked, but you learn real quick, real quick.
GS: Yes you do.

And how long did you last down there at the 414?
GS: We were only down there about seven or eight weeks, six weeks, and then they laid us off, and we went up to the employment office, and at that point they sent us to the 413 department, which was alloy and tool steel division.

That was up by the New Street Bridge? And that encompassed how many different shops in the plant, do you remember? What were their areas?
GS: Their areas were treatment, cold draw, electric furnace shop, 39 312 mills, 8, 10, and 12, 35-inch mill, annex, saw shop.

22-inch mill.
GS: 22-inch mill, 18 inch mill, mold yard, soaking pits, East Lehigh.

Did you actually see the hand mills, the 8, 10, and the 12 in operation?
GS: I saw the 8.

Yup. Give us a little description of what that was like when you saw it, because a lot of people cannot even envision this.
GS: Well, we were, they were rolling a lot of file steel in the 8-inch mill, and I saw the other mills running very little; uh, they were really shut down and really quickly after I started in that department. But the 8-inch mill, they would, you know, have billets in the furnace, and they would pick 'em up with a pair, pick 'em out with a pair of tongs.

How big were they?
GS: Like four by four, I seem to remember. They weren't very long, maybe four feet, six feet, something like that. They would pick 'em up with a pair of tongs that were on a jib, on a trolley, and they would bring 'em over to the mill, and the mills had three rolls in 'em, and the steel would go

through one way and come back through on the bottom, and they would break the billet down, and they would keep moving from mill to mill. And an operator, once it got longer, the mill man, he could grab that when it's coming through the mill, and grab the end of it and just turn completely around in a U and feed it into the next mill and stand there, and that steel would just whip right around completely until…

You know, I told people about that, about guys standing in the loop of the actual piece of steel that was on the deck, and I couldn't, no matter what I did, I couldn't explain to them without pulling out a piece of paper, you know, what these guys were really doing. I know the first time I saw it, I'm thinking, these guys must be crazy, and I said to the boss, I says, "What are the chances that I would ever work there" and this was really funny, the answer: he says, ", the only people that work there are the sacred cows." I said, "the what?" He says, "The sacred cows." I said, "What's a sacred cow?" He says, "That's the guy that's got so much seniority that the superintendent comes and asks him questions when they get stuck on something." I says, "These guys, they're in the number one washroom right at the time clock, and you gotta have forty years to be in that washroom." And I always remember that sacred cow thing. I mean, I was like amazed. Most of these guys, the foreman told me, He says, "They didn't even speak English," and this was in the mid '60s. I only started right after you. So you probably saw, you know, a lot more of this than I did.

GS: I could never, I used to read the orders, and they were Nickelson file, and Nickelson file, and railroad cars full of this went out on a continuing basis, and I kept wondering who's using all these files? I mean, they're …

And actually if you wanted to know, all you had to do was go to your local hardware store, and they were all over the place, every size you could think of. Yeah, that was something else. And uh, you were up there as a mechanical helper? And what did a mechanical helper do?

GS: You just helped the millwrights, which was doing the same thing the millwright did no matter what.

And the equipment up there? Give us some sort of an example of what kind of equipment was up in that merchant mill area. And we're talking the area right around the New Street Bridge, the Fahey Bridge.

GS: Well, we had the saws. We had the marble saws. And we had all saws. Uh, in the annex we had the bicycle grinders.

Describe a bicycle grinder.

GS: It's got handlebars like a bicycle. And in front of that there's a stone running. They were five horse power motors, I believe. Because I rebuilt a lot of the grinders working up there, and they were five for sure, and they were running, eighteen inches in diameter of three inches wide. They ran that stone, and they ground defects out of billets, that's what they did.

Yeah, that was tool steel they were working on, so it was high-priced steel. These guys were very well paid, and it always helped to be a big guy on that job.
GS: Yeah, it was a hard job. It was a very hard job.

Yeah, I talked to guys that were crane men up there, and they said if you were a crane man up there, and they had a good run of steel and everybody was making money he says, you were lucky if you could take a sip of your coffee, he says, you were going all the time. I guess they had two cranes in there working that area? Yeah, and they were both scheduled all the time.
GS: They had billeteers up in the annex. I never worked on 'em. They weren't operating when I was up there.

I understand that was one of the nastiest jobs ever in that plant.
GS: I heard that, yes.

Because those were machines that had a wheel about two, two and a half feet in diameter and a cutting tool embedded in it, and they would just rotate, and they would bring these things down, and they would just like pack out pieces, defects in the steel. It was a little bit of a time, but the problem was you'd be breaking bits, then there'd be pieces flying, and the safety protection wasn't as best as it could be.
GS: Not at that point and time.

And a lot of those guys had back problems from lifting that stuff. It wasn't set up to the standards that we would have today, you know, because they would recognize immediately somebody would be wearing their back out. They're just lifting too much weight too far away from their body. You know, uh, if there was a way that you could've picked it up, you know and handle it without all that work. Yeah, that was something. So when did you progress up into the millwright level? How long did it take?

GS: Well, we had temporary C millwrights that they would put us on. Uh, that came pretty quick. You know that system worked where you had to work 1,040 hours as a temporary C before you could move up to a B, and to an A, and if you only were on temporarily, it took a long time to get to that point. But in the meantime before that happened they started the millwright school, and so I got into the millwright school, and when the millwright school was over, I took my test right away, and I passed my test.

How long did the millwright school run?
GS: Eight weeks, one week every eight weeks, until you had eight weeks

in. They had eight classes. And it was good, it was good. We had a couple good instructors that enjoyed doing what they were doing and weren't, you know, they really taught you a lot of things and brought you a lot of things, and we would, you know we had blueprints, blueprint reading, we had to do a lot of that, and uh, I didn't have trouble with blueprint reading. I did a lot of my own drawing and stuff with my hobby, so I could get through that pretty good.

You were always big into woodwork right?
GS: Yes I am. Picked up from my dad.

I'll tell you what, that's something, and it must have served you well over the years though?
GS: Taught me a lot of good things.

And it probably taught you that everything is done in a procedure, which helped you as a millwright.
GS: There are certain rules you don't deviate from. No matter where you go or what you do.

If you're gonna burn when you get that torch ready, you gotta get it ready the same way each time. You gotta purge the lines, you gotta set the cages. Everything is, you know, is designed so that you don't do anything dumb. And you know yourself in that steel mill, one wrong move, and then you might be going home in a box. A lot of people can't understand. You know, we talk about it as steelworkers as something that is just an every day occurrence, but it really wasn't. How many guys did we see come in there, and a couple days they were gone. They just could not get acclimated to it.
GS: I got burnt pretty bad down there one time at the EFM, probably in the '70s, '80s. I was burning a sticker, and I was the only person out, and the production people were supposed to be there to watch me, and evidently he must have went somewhere.

And you caught on fire.
GS: Came back I caught on fire, yeah. And you can't see because you got dark goggles on and everything else. You're working with an eight foot long torch, you know, and that stuff really flies, and it got inside my clothing, my coat and stuff, and I caught fire, burned my chest, my back, under my arm really bad. I had a good hole under my arm, and that's the only place I have a scar. The dispensary was, the nurses in the dispensary were terrific.

Well, you know at the height, you know, probably when that happened to you, you know, the dispensary had five or six doctors.

GS: The nurses were really good, because that's who really took care of me.

And the nurses on the middle of the night shift, I really, I don't believe they had very many doctors out. There might have been one for middle shift, one for night shift. Most of them were there on day shift, because there was always ongoing testing and ongoing therapy and things like that, and like a guy like you that got burned, you were probably coming in there for how long, getting your dressings treated and things like that?

GS: It took awhile, yeah about six weeks.

Yeah, I went through the whole procedure, you know. I don't know if you remember, but I had crane 78 blow up in my face, the switch. Burned the hair right off my head, melted my hard hat, it turned into like a piece of paper. My safety glasses were melted onto my face. And I'll never forget what the foreman said to me in the dispensary, "What do you think you did wrong?" I said, "You son of a bitch. I didn't do anything wrong, get the hell out of here, and the nurses pulled him away." They said, "You stay away from him, we're treating him, "and uh, that was a long process. And you know I sat in the office for weeks and got all the paper work in the office more or less straightened out. But, uh you know, it was just something that happened, and here they found out that those cranes had been wired wrong in World War Two. There were four or five other ones there in the area that were wired the same way, and uh this was just a first, first incident. But I was glad I got out of there alive, and I'll never forget the guy that was up there with me, Bobby Morgan; he didn't know whether I was dead or alive when the thing stopped, because I had the door open, and I went in with the tester, and I bumped the wire, I don't know exactly what happened, and this thing just like, it just like melted right off the wall in front of me, and the smoke was coming up, and Morgan said, "Frank, Frank, are you okay?" I said," I think so." And when I turned around, he says. "Oh," he says, "we gotta get you out of here," and I had no idea what I looked like. But uh, I'll tell you what, it definitely throws the fear of the Lord into ya. So, so now you become a millwright, now you start working on particular jobs. I mean, what kind of jobs did you do up there as a millwright?

GS: A millwright's job? In maintenance, is they break, we fix.

So you worked on everything?

GS: It makes no difference, we worked on all kinds of machinery, hydraulics, pneumatics, fabricating, uh replacing bearings, you know. No matter what, troubleshoot the machine and get it back online, that was the main thing.

Changing rolls on the roller line?

GS: In the mills changed rolls, uh, scarfing machine, we were continuously doing...

And then we had guys that did nothing but work on the rolls. And uh, you know, put new pinion gears on them and things like that. Everything was set to a certain distance. We had templates to work with and things like that. That was always a good job.

GS: Repair soak and pick covers.

And we had our own guy that was hard facing rolls, didn't we? Did we do that? I thought we had a guy there was hard facing rolls.

GS: We were hard facing rolls down East Lehigh. I was down, I was doing the grinding on 'em and stuff, yeah. That was a back breaking job. You were grinding below your body level. You were sitting on a roller line, and you were grinding below your feet. That was back breaking. I was on it for one week, and they put me on the second week, and I told 'em, put somebody else down for that week. I'll go back after that, but I'm not going to do two weeks in a row, I says, that's just so hard on ya.

Now, back in the '70s you had a two- or three-year run where you worked on the Beardsley Piper Grinder, we call it the BP Grinder. Tell us a little bit about that. Describe the machine to us.

GS: The grinder is a big grinder. It took, you know how big those stones were? They were three foot, weren't they?

No, they were two foot.

GS: Two foot, twenty-four inch, okay.

Two foot in diameter, and I believe they were five inches wide.

GS: No four. I think they were four inches wide.

Yeah, and uh, most of them were, what company was that?

GS: Beardsley Piper.

No, there was a company that, Norton Stones.

GS: Norton Stones, yeah.

Well, we used to get other stones, but the Nortons were always the best stones. They tried other ones, I guess, you know, for costs, but they didn't, couldn't cut the mustard. In fact the one guy, he says, "Listen," he says, "I can get more work done with these other stones, but I have to change two of 'em to get the same amount done. He says, "It isn't worth it."

GS: Well, we used to do, uh, you know, I was up there steady. I took care of the grinders, and I worked from six in the morning till two in the afternoon, because I came in and I was through the change of the shift, and I did a lot of just preventive maintenance.

You were able to get that thing gone over before the day shift guy got to it.

GS: And that really helps a lot, and uh, I remember when I went up there that they were having so much trouble with the hydraulics on it, and the reason was they just weren't changing oil enough, they weren't changing filters at all on it hardly, and uh, we ended up, we cleaned the tanks out, and we put all new filters in. I had to order 'em and wait for 'em, but we changed the filters.

But it was worth it in the end.

GS: And Billy Richards was the boss there, was my boss, and uh, we did that, and I changed all the valves out, and we started fresh, put a new valve block on, and after a certain period of time I changed filters. I ordered filters, and they were reluctant to change, to buy filters, and I would try to buy 'em by the case, and I'd say we're out of filters, we're out of filters, they would keep hoarding 'em, and I stockpiled 'em, because I made sure the filters were changed every week, because to me it was very important. Uh, after about six months, Billy Richards said to me, he says, "We're going to change oil in the grinder," and I says, "What for?" He says, "It gotta be dirty," and I says, "No." I says, "They're clean." He says, "No, we're going to change oil." He says, "Next week." I says, Okay." Next week come, I didn't change oil. He jumped on my case about it, and I said, "Well, we don't gotta change oil." So he said, "I'm gonna come up there, and we're gonna look in that tank." I says, "Okay, come up." I says, "Here's a light, go up and look in the tank." I says, "Take that cap off." I says, "Look straight down." He's up there, and I says to him, I says, "You see that quarter?" He says, What quarter?" I says, "Look down in that tank, straight down, take a flashlight; you see that quarter?" He says, "How'd that get in there?" I says, "I put it in there." He says, "What for?" I says, "That's how clean it is."

So you could come up and check to see how clean it is.

GS: I says, "That's how clean it is." I says, "You don't gotta change the oil." I says, "There's nothing wrong with the oil." I says, "The filter's doing the job, that's what we need to do. For the cost of the filters, to change filters every week for $30, it's a bargain." We had no down time, we had no hydraulic problems anymore, we had no sticking valves. And I went and rebuilt all the other valves and put 'em on the shelf, and as we needed 'em, we put 'em on, but we very seldom ever had trouble.

Yeah, I remember the two guys that worked up there; they were the two Horvath boys. In fact that one name was Joe, Joe Horvath, I think was the older of the two. And I can't remember the other guy's name. The one guy was a big guy, and the other guy was ...

GS: Small

But they were brothers. And I'll tell you what, those guys knew how to run that machine. Boy they'd make it sing. And a lot of people, you know, that are reading this book or listening to the audio part of it, that machine is situated exactly where you walk in to the Starters Riverport. That's exactly where it was, when you walk in that door, right at the main entrance to go into the bar and restaurant, that's exactly where that machine sat, and if you look up, those are the cranes that used to service the bicycle grinders and that Beardsley Piper Grinder.

GS: Correct. And then the Midwest after that.

Yeah, and we had another grinder put in there, you know, years later that was more state of the art, but uh, it worked well, it could do more, but we had a lot of problem with that one also.

GS: Oh yeah. We had a good problem one day.

That took a lot of tender loving care to keep that thing in operation.

GS: Well, I got a call on that one day, and I went up there, it was on night shift, and he said, he called up on the phone, and he says the head fell off the grinder, the Midwest. I says, heads don't fall off. So I went up with a forklift, and I looked at it, and I said what happened? He says, "The head fell off." And I'm looking at the collar where the, you know, how that rotated? You know how that head rotated? I said, "I'm looking at that big collar and all them bolts are going through, and all the bolts are all bent one way," and I looked at him and I says, You came down with the head too fast, and hit the end of the billet," and he just looks at me. He tore the head right off that machine.

Boy, I'll tell you what.

GS: I just laugh, you know. What are you gonna do, you know, go to work and put it back together for him.

I remember the guy that seemed to have a knack for running that machine was a guy by the name of Joe Gmitter. Remember Joe? Pretty big kid, I think he was from up around the Northampton area, and he could make that baby go.

GS: Well, they did a lot of work with that. That thing could grind, absolutely.

Yeah, that was a grind in full. You had to keep it running though. So Glen, you're down there, you worked on everything, and you spent some time down at the electric furnace? But that was in what, later years though, after like 1985, on?

GS: Later years, yup. We were down earlier than that, but not on a steady basis. I was down there, yeah; I did a lot of shift work down there when the bag house was put in. We were down for that. We did a lot of work in that bag house, on the dust collector.

That bag house made things dramatically different in South Bethlehem; that was for sure.

GS: It's amazing how much dirt that bag house took out a week.

Yeah, you could fill railroad cars full of it.

GS: Well, we had five ID fans on there, and they were 900 horsepower a piece.

I can remember going over there; uh, those fans used to trip off every now and then, you'd have to go over and check 'em out and restart 'em, and that was a, usually when they kicked out, you did not have a problem restarting 'em. It was very seldom that they didn't restart. I never really, one time McFadden tried to tell me what was going on. I couldn't figure out what he was telling me. All I know is I'd go over there to restart 'em, and they usually restarted. So when did you actually get an inkling that the plant was in trouble?

GS: Through the years you could just see so much where they didn't want to make the improvements to critical areas, and that should've been done. You know, they said they went out of the alloy and tool steel business because there was no profit and there was no work, and I keep wondering is how can you go out of a business when the technology and the demand for higher and better alloy steel is greater all the time? That's the time to get into it, but you can't get into it with, you know 1895 equipment that we were running like in our steam hammers; those blueprints are back from the 1800s, uh they were put in there. The forges, you know the equipment we were using, was just really that ancient. And alloy and tool steel business, you should jump in with the latest technology you can get. Right up to date and as far into the future into the future as you can see.

Well, you probably know most guys that worked in the alloy division knew that once that division was shut down I think around 1981? Our chief competitor, Allegheny Ludlum, their profits went through the roof. They were hiring people, I mean it was just amazing what happened. Somebody, I think, really dropped the ball on that one, and uh, everybody paid the price for it, because guys lost their jobs, and it's just something that probably should have never happened.

GS: The other thing is, you know, with uh, you could see things coming over … it slowly comes to you as you see it. When Nucor came in and they took away all the little structural steel sections that were very highly profitable to Bethlehem Steel. They took all that work away because it was easy for them to do, but they couldn't do what Bethlehem did. No way could any company. Hardly any companies could ever produce what

Bethlehem did. If you look through history and World War Two and what that plant did is unbelievable, and if you look at what they built and go look at the equipment they built it with, it's amazing that they got it out the door.

Well, you know, down when I worked down in the beam yard with maintenance there, we had, we used to make a lot of sheet piling, the stuff that's driven into the ground, you know, with big air hammers, and it's for cofferdams, retaining walls, uh, harbors, airports. This stuff was so good you could actually pull it out of the ground years later and use it over again. Nobody else had a product that good, but you know, what are gonna do? You know, they made decisions, and that was the end of it. So overall, how would you rate your standard of living in the Lehigh Valley when you worked at Bethlehem Steel?

GS: It was good.

What impressed you more than anything on the benefit package?

GS: Health benefits. And we, working man, you know the hourly man, gave up a lot of benefits and a lot of wages to have benefits for the rest of their life. That was one of the things that we paid for up until the end, and then they reneged on it, and they dropped them benefits, and I don't think that was ever right, because we ended up paying for it again.

Well, you know we had a labor agreement in place that should have taken precedent over any stockholder.

GS: Correct.

And the bankruptcy judge just slapped us in the face and said tough luck.

GS: That's right.

And uh, it just didn't work out. You know, the international union was there to argue that point, they did, and uh, we went down in flames. I don't know how to explain it.

GS: And if they say there's no money in steel through the bankruptcy ISG bought up Bethlehem Steel, and then through that Mittal Steel bought it up. Their profits are greater than anything in history today. And thankful for that that there was some agreement with some of that with the union that we did get some of our benefits back, and I really, to me it was a big godsend, because it was a struggle paying COBRA. It was a struggle, believe me. People in this world today do not realize what healthcare costs, and I tell 'em. I say if you got healthcare, decent healthcare with your company where you're working, start to look at it and see what it cost that company to give that to you, and maybe you'll be a little more receptive of the company.

Yeah, now in the time that you were there, uh, how about, you know, your vacations, getting days off, or otherwise planning your life? Did you have any trouble with that? You worked a lot of holidays I would imagine?

GS: Yeah, we worked a lot of holidays and stuff, but you know, I think we all have to sit there and try to realize in our life we can't have everything we want 100 percent of the time. Uh, I felt fairly fortunate that I got a good percentage of my time that I did want. That was important to me, and doing, and doing it in a way that I could go down and talk to them. And you know everything you have to reciprocate on to a certain degree, you know. You can't sit there and not work no overtime when they needed you. You can't just sit there and do that, then all of a sudden go down there and expect some favors. And Bethlehem paid me well. They came first for my time, and I gave it to 'em, but they also reciprocated when I needed to do things. I'm into antique cars, and I needed six days off to go look at a car across the country, and we were working four days a week, four and five days a week. So I went down and talked to my supervisors, and they arranged it for me that I got off Thursday, Friday, Saturday, Sunday, Monday, Tuesday, and I worked two four day weeks in a row, and I got my time off to do that, and many other things you know. And if it wasn't for the money from Bethlehem Steel, I wouldn't have my shop, I wouldn't have my hobby.

There were some times that you were on layoff and you ended up with the field millwrights. Tell me a little bit about that.

GS: Same thing.

Same thing, but all over the plant.

GS: They break, we fix. They're a good bunch of guys. They're a good bunch of guys there, and we had a good bunch of guys at 413 for the most part. We had a lot of good guys.

A lot of guys told me that the best part about working in the field millwright gang was being associated with a gentleman by the name of William Vosh. William Vosh, not only could he do anything in the shop.

GS;   He was good.

But he was sort of like a shop man, and the guys started thinking, hey this guy, you know, every now and then he puts together a nice meal on middle shift and something like that. But they got it down to the point where Bill had it figured out that you could put stuff on the stove, and these guys would be eating every day. I mean, and a lot of people say, hey look, you should have been working, not eating, but you know what, they don't understand that Bill probably took 15 or 20 minutes in preparation, left that stove area, was working around there, and was still producing the whole time.

GS: Bill was a good guy.

And on top of that, on top of that you know, not only did Bill eat, the foreman ate, everybody was happy. And every time I bring up field millwrights, people will always bring up Bill's name. They'd say, oh man, what a guy.

GS: Well, Bill and I had a lot of things going between us, you know outside of the Steel. He collected trains; he was into that kind of stuff, and toys. He's been in the shop many times, and uh, he used to set up in the flea markets, and we would go to the train show once in awhile together over in Allentown, and he was a talented person. He was a very talented person, and his death was a shock to me.

Well, it was a sad event. You know, I found about it long after the fact. I don't know how I ever missed it, because you know I would have been there. But he was the type of employee that the guys really could relate to. I mean, I don't think he ever had an enemy. And the nice thing about working at the plant is we had a lot of people like that. Most guys, when I say to them, what's the one thing you miss most about the plant?

GS: People.

There you go. Now that's the prevailing, that's the answer 90 percent of the time. Some people will say next would be benefits, and I've only had two or three people say the money, which is really strange.

GS;   Well, working in repairs and stuff like that, you get to talk to a lot of operators of the equipment, and you know, you learned which ones cared and which ones didn't, and the majority of the people cared about their jobs. They cared about doing a good job. They didn't want to do a bad job, and they were proud. You know, there was a lot of proud people in that place.

If you had an opportunity, knowing what you knew, going through that plant, is there anything in particular you would have done to insure that that job became more secure? You know, I say this to people, and somebody will say well, there were too many foreman. But you know what, the foremen didn't think there were too many foremen. You know what I'm getting at here?

GS;   We had more foremen on night shift sometimes than we had workers.

You wonder what was going on there.

GS: When things were slow, we had more foremen on middles and night shift than we had on day shift, and weekends, than we had people scheduled to do that work. Why was that done? I guess you can't see 'em;

why didn't they just give 'em different colored hats and nobody would know.

Yeah, I guess they more or less stuck out there. But then again, you know, like my friend Ray McFadden said, there was relative ability. There was a lot of people hiring their relatives. But that's neither here nor there. But, Glen, if you had a chance, if you were in the prime of your life and you'd been laid off from the plant for a while and they called you and said you wanna come back? What would you do?

GS: I'd go back.

Well, almost everybody, that's almost 100 percent; they said they loved it. They thing they loved about it the most was that every day was a challenge, whether you were in maintenance, whether you were in production, or what. Well, I want to thank you, Glen, for participating in this, and I want to wish you the best for you and your family.

GS: Thank you.

You're welcome.

NED FINK
31 years service

Saucon Mill Engine Gang

Known to close friends as "Fountain Hill Fats," current mayor of Fountain Hill, PA. Kept those 1906 model steam engines going.

* * * * * * * * *

Today we're talking to Ned Fink from the 414 Saucon Engine Gang. Today's date is the 4ᵗʰ of March. How ya doin' today Ned? Is it OK if I call you Ned?

NF: Well, I'm doin' OK. That's all right, Ned.

Ned, tell me how you came to become a Bethlehem Steel worker.

NF: Well, I went there in 1965 and I applied for the job. They wanted to put me in the cinder dump, and I told 'em, "No, I don't wanna' go there. I'm a mechanic." So they didn't hire me, but then about two weeks later they call me up an' they said they had a job for me workin' on large stationary steam engines as a mechanic and I said I'd take that job.

OK. You remember who the guy was that hired yah'?

NF: No. Was just somebody in room 28. He was a big guy. But I don't remember.

I remember the guy that hired me, uh, had a crew cut, I can't remember his name but he was a, really a big guy. And when I came back from the service, yunno, he, he was the guy that got me back in again. I came back, he says, "I have good news and bad news." I says; "Gimmie the bad news." He says; "You're still on layoff." I says, "What's the good news?" He says; "You're eligible for five weeks of vacation; do you want it?" I says; "Well no." I says, "Do I have to take it all?" He says, "You only have to take two weeks." I says, "Well, I'll take two weeks." I says, "I'm gonna hold that other three." And I did; at the end of the two weeks they called me back and said come back to work; it was amazing. So OK, Ted, now, when did you start in the company?

NF: It was, according to the schedule, because two of us started the same time so they hadda' go the, the, by the birthday, it was uh, February 15th 1965.

How about that; February 15th of '65. All right. Tell me what it was like your first day there. You must have been like in awe of what you were seeing.

NF: Well, I was, I walked around, they took me around, they had a pretty good safety program at that time where they showed ya what you hadda watch out for, like overhead cranes, and when they rollin' ingots the, uh, slag would splatter off the ingots and, being aware of gas, where there was gas, uh, fumes that could uh, make ya pass out if you were in the area too long. They showed us all stuff like that. For a couple weeks we did that; it just helped. And uh, the older, uh, millwrights would show you what to do. And they, you were trained by them, and one of the foremen, Bobby Bayer, was the one foreman that trained us a lot.

And would you say, would you say that the old guys more or less just, like, took you guys under their wing, like young bucks or what?

NF: Yeah, that's, that's the way it worked.

That's a good thing. I find out from talking to people all over the plant that it was basically the same everywhere. One thing I did find out, though, and tell me if this happened in your area, there was a lot of guys that started that never really got through the first or two, first or second week, they couldn't, they couldn't handle it.

NF: Yeah, there were one guy one time, he, he worked for us, and uh, he said, "That's it I'm quittin'." An' Bobby Bayer said, "You can't quit. You didn't work long enough to pay for your safety shoes." So he took his safety shoes off an' threw 'em at 'em. {laughing}

Wow. I guess that's one way of saying I, I'm leaving the job.

NF: There were a lot of guys left, they just couldn't take it.

Well you know, it was when I started up in the Billet Yard most of the guys quit when they come to the realization that we weren't kiddin' about the schedule. It would be posted every Thursday and that's how you knew you were gonna work the following week. They thought we were kiddin' them. When they found out it was true they said, "Oh no. I'm not gonna work like this."

NF: You, you have, you can't get people to work like that today. They don't care how much money you pay 'em; they don't wanna work middles or nights.

You got that. But uh, in your time down there at the mill, I would imagine you worked a lot of holidays?

NF: Almost all ah' the holidays. If you, if your shift fell on the schedule on the holiday you hadda work it and that's all there was to it. They paid yuh good but, you had to be there.

How long, how long would you say you worked down there at the Saucon Mills before you were able to get a vacation in the summer? Sorta' like a normal person.

NF: Well, I couldn't start to get a vacation in the summer till maybe I was there about twelve years. I could get, I could touch the end of spring, and early fall, but, in the summer I just couldn't get anything, cuz there were too many men with seniority ahead of me.

Yunno, that's something that a person that never set foot in the plant has a hard time understanding, yunno, and there were thousands of employees. And in your department alone, I would say probably in your gang, wha'd you have, about 50 guys?

NF: Originally, they tell me before I started there, there were 200 guys, but by getting a new barometric condenser and backing system, that eliminated a lot of the guys. There was about 80 in my department when I started.

OK. And, yunno, there were only so many allowed to go per week.

NF: Right. And I forget what our vacation bogie was; I think it was three.

Yeah, well, I remember goin' around many times with the company over vacation bogies. We should have more in the vacation week, cuz' after all the guys wanna' be home with their families. An' the company's attitude always was, you're not here.

NF: You don't have to work here.

Don't worry about your families. Worry about your job. The ordinary person that never set foot in the plant doesn't understand that. So, even though you had a dangerous job, and there was a lot going on around yah', you had the heat, you had the cold, you had the gas situation … Tell me what it was like, a typical job, when you first started. A typical, like a week maybe, what would you do?

NF: Well, I remember the first week we changed crank bearings, which are like connecting rod bearings on a car engine; the only thing is, they're huge compared to a car. Remember the crank shaft weighed a hundred an' ten tons. The bearings were 14 inches sometimes, the bearing bar, the babbit bar, 14 inches in diameter. You couldn't pick these bearings up, you hadda' use a crane to pick 'em up.

So, so when you talk actual physical size? I mean, give it to me like in feet. So much by so much; what would you say was a close match?

NF: I would say if a connecting rod bearing for the 48 was settin' on the ground it was, settin' there like a U, it would be 2 foot long and about 14 inches wide and about a foot high.

OK. And the actual crank shaft itself would be what?
NF: Well, on the, on the 46 and the, and the 40 Number One bloomer, the, the journal was roughly 14 inches.

Yah. OK. And the, the actual size of the crank shaft, gear and all attached, what would it be, like in length?
NF: Well, for the Number One, I would say that was, oh 20 feet by about, when that was settin' on the ground it was taller than me settin', 'bout ten foot high. You could see it here in the picture.

And it weighed, it weighs like a hundred and fifty ton.
NF: A hundred and ten ton.

A hundred an' ten tons. So yunno, these weren't tinker toys you were playin' with; this was big time stuff. Now, I understand that this mill here, the 40 Number One that you're showing me a picture of, this was like the main mill that was rolling for the Beam Yard and the Combination Mill, is that correct?
NF: It rolled, uh, it rolled ah, ingots for the 32-inch mill. Then the 32-inch mill, which was electric by the way, rolled certain sections to go the, uh, Combination Mill when the Combination Mill was built. Before the Combination Mill was built, the 32 would roll some ingots into sections of their own, and they'd also roll billets for the 28-inch mill.

OK. And all that stuff was moved around on transfer beds.
NF: And when they, when they would roll a billet, and it would go for the 28-inch mill, it would come up a roller line behind our pulpit, and you had hot steel behind yah' goin' to the furnace for the 28 to, to re-heat it, and you had hot steel in front ah' you that you were rollin' on the 28. The pulpit floor used to get so hot that you couldn't touch it with your hand. Even though you were cool in there because they had big air-conditioners, so one time I said, "I believe you could fry an egg on the floor here." And I brought an egg in and cracked it on the floor, and it did fry it, right on the floor.

Now that, those are the kinda stories I'm lookin' for in this book.
NF: Yeah. I didn't wanna eat it though.

Because nobody, well no you don't wanna, because the floors weren't really that clean at Bethlehem Steel. I mean Lord have mercy, I can remember them bringing special equipment in during the shut down periods just to clean the floors. You probably seen it yourself.

NF: Sometimes we hadda wear wooden shoes depending what we were doin'.

Yeah. OK. So yunno, now the Combination Mill comes along at the Saucon Mills and, and how did that change your job, how did that affect what you were doing?
NF: Initially it didn't because they started rolling, rolling shapes on the Combination Mill, an' they were having trouble initially; it didn't wanna' work right, and I really didn't get over there a lot till the end of my career but, they kept all the mills goin' initially. Then finally after, after a few years, they shut the 28-inch mill down. And then they used to shut the 42-inch mill down but then they'd start it up an' shut it down, start it up, an' this went on for years, because they could roll the same sections on the old mill as you could some of the sections on the Combination Mill. But a lot ah' guys who had worked on the 42-inch mill, the rollers and stuff, they moved them over to the Combination Mill. And then, when they would run the 42- inch mill and they were trouble gettin' section. In the beginning a lot of the rollers that were trained to run that mill didn't know how to eliminate the problems because they didn't have the experience. Yunno, there was no school you go to to learn how to roll steel. You have to learn from the older guy, and he wasn't there; he was over on the other mill.

OK now, you just made the statement, they couldn't make section. Could you explain to people what exactly you mean by making section.
NF: Well, a bar, a bar ah, takes uh, the web has to be so thick, the flange has to be so thick, it has to weigh so much a pound. And every bar that was rolled at Bethlehem Steel was a piece was cut off; it was might be flanged, webbed, and weighed for how much it would weigh a foot. And then every piece of every bar was tested in the test stand. And we were the only company that custom cut a bar for the customer. Every other steel company had a policy, if you bought a bar off 'em, you took the whole bar, whereas Bethlehem Steel, uh, cut the bar to the customer's specification.

I understand that the, the tolerance were as little as a quarter of an inch. Is that what you're familiar with? If you ordered 35 an' a quarter you would get within a quarter inch one way or the other. And you would never get it short; you would always get it a little longer.
NF: No. You got it right on the button.

Yah. It was that close. And nobody else was doin' that. 'Course nobody else had the grey mill initially too when that first came in.
NF: Well that's right. That rolled the biggest sections in the world, the grey mill.

OK. Now, as, as time goes on there I'm sure you must've seen a lot in the shop, because you know, just coming to work and doing the same old thing, I mean, the guys fooled around a little bit didn't they? There musta been some horseplay goin' on in some, Steelworkers were famous for playing tricks on each other.

NF: You hadda or you'd ah' went nuts in that place. You hadda laugh.

That's right. Can you have any examples for me? Some of the things the guys used to do on a regular basis. Just to ...

NF: We used to put a Styrofoam cup above the door with a tack in it, fill the cup with water and we had a string, and when a guy would come in and sit down, we'd pull the string and the tack would come out and the water would start drippin' on the guy. Uh, we used to hook a coil up an' give guys shocks. Uh, one time, Derby invented a thing where this, we had this short little guy; he couldn't reach on top of the locker, but he always threw his helmet up there. So Derby put it outa reach, and he made this board up and he had a packing spring on one end and a rope on the other, but you couldn't see the rope. So it was time to go out after our lunch break; when Claire went to get his hat he looked; he would have to look first because he, he couldn't look up there and reach at the same time. So he'd look to see where the hat is, and when he'd go to reach it Derby would pull the rope. Well then he'd back up again and he'd look and he'd see it's a foot further than what he thought, and he didn't have good eyes at that time so I guess he thought, well, yunno, and Derby keep doin' this; then when it get all the way down to one end, Derby'd let go ah' the rope and the packing spring would pull it all the way back. Well pretty soon he was chasing it with the broom handle tryin' to get it. And he got it. We, we played so many tricks.

Let's face it. Most of us had a good time there. How would you, how would you describe your years there? Uh, what's the best way to say I, I really enjoyed it, I enjoyed the guys, I enjoyed everything; there were jobs I didn't like, what's the best way to wrap it up?

NF: I liked the guys, I miss 'em, I don't get to see many of 'em. Uh, some jobs I liked. Technical jobs I liked. I didn't like the big jobs where all you needed was brute force and strength. I liked the job that was, you hadda' do it right or, it wasn't gonna' work. Some things I didn't like were things like, we hadda' go to the machine shop, and we'd take parts over there to machine 'em. Well, one Saturday we went over there, and uh, we saw these blueprints there, and it said SSQ, and we didn't know what SSQ meant in the Bethlehem Steel. You know how they used to have those numbers. And so we asked the machine shop foreman. He says, "That stands for Stodard Slate Quarry." So we said; "Whadda you mean?" And Elworth Slateworth was our superintendent of maintenance. Well, here he scheduled out machinists on a Saturday for overtime and used Bethlehem Steel machinists and Bethlehem Steel materials to make parts for his slate quarry in Bangor.

Wow. I'll tell you what.

NF: Now, that I didn't like when I saw that. Because that, that, you can't stop the tape now, it has to keep going.

Yunno, that's, that's one of many stories I've heard, and I'm sure I'm gonna hear more. But yunno, when you talk about working there at Bethlehem Steel, there was pluses and there were minuses. Was there a particular job that you really liked to do? That, yunno, maybe it didn't come up very often or anything.

NF: I liked running the 46 bloomer and 48 One, rollin' steel. That was a challenge runnin' that, an' runnin' it right.

Yeah. That actually wasn't part of your job but that was something that you did get to do?

NF: Oh no, I hadda do that if somebody got sick or there wasn't a, a, somebody reported off, or maybe they didn't have a, near the end there I did that a lot because there wasn't enough engineers.

OK, I wasn't aware of that. Yah. You were up there with big Jack Wenner then, huh? Jack I hope to interview later on, yunno, for the book. Now did you, were you involved with the union at all while you were there?

NF: No. Just that I was a member.

Well OK then. Speaking about the union, would you ever have wanted to work at Bethlehem Steel without the union?

NF: Well maybe, maybe after the union was formed and we got where we were, maybe then, but not when they first started the steel. They, I heard stories, I knew guys that said they had water boys come around with water, they didn't even shower. Yunno, they didn't, they didn't have anything like we had near the end there.

They had no safety program to speak of.

NF: No, no safety program at all.

I remember talking to one individual who told me that the drop forge was the first place in the plant where they wore hard hats and hearing protection.

NF: Well, St. Luke's Hospital was built here in Fountain Hill because of the injuries at the Bethlehem Steel plant. That's why it was built.

The captains of industry, I understand, all went to the same church. Right over there at the end of the Hill to Hill Bridge, and maybe that was a good thing for the employees, because, yunno, even though it was a dangerous place it's still a lot more comforting to know that there is a place they could take care of you. God bless the 800 an' something guys though that went to their early deaths workin' down at the plant. Yunno, from the time I started, which was right before you, a couple weeks before you, there were 31 guys died in that plant by the time I left, which was April 30th of '97.

NF: Well how 'bout the day the pit walls fell in on the 3 guys; they just started. Now you know, I blame that on, as time went on, they went after the, the foremen with education, and they were intelligent people, but they didn't know the job. The old foremen, yeah they couldn't read or write good, but they knew all the hazards, they knew how everything went together, because they started at the bottom of the ladder and worked their way up.

Everybody had a line of progression.

NF: Where they started hirin' people in the middle of the ladder. Well, if their job was to go to the college every day and take an exam, they'd all be and they'd all shine like a bright star. But when it came to the job they, they couldn't help you. They didn't, they just couldn't help with that old equipment that.

So you feel that, a lot of the management people at the company were hired more by "relative ability" than anything else? They knew somebody is what I mean.

NF: Well, in the old days. I don't say in the new days they didn't do that. They, that was a, that was a problem and they weren't allowed to do that. But in the old days, yeah, but those older people knew what they were doin'.

Yeah. Well, I wanted to ask yah, based on everything we talked about here, do you think the plant could have been saved?

NF: Yeah, because in the beginning when they first built that, they had no competition. The plant just rolled on. They got supervisors in there an' upper management who, who more or less could just coast. They didn't have to make any changes. I went to that Elworth Stodard one time and proposed that we modernize the plant a little. Get rid ah' these engines, put motors in. And his statement to me was that, ah, "We're making money hand over fist; we don't even have any competition; we're not gonna change anything." And I said, "Well, yunno, if we're making money hand over fist, somebody's gonna' wanna' get in on that. And they're gonna' build a new modern building, and they'll force us to compete with them rather than them compete with us." And that's exactly what happened. In time, of course, he was retired then, Donny Granado where he lives, and when that happened he wasn't there to see it, but that's actually what occurred.

Now had they made changes way back, you can't. They tried too little too late with computers and everything, and it was just too late. We had too much competition. But when we shut the doors on the 48-inch mill, my friend Dick Roberts who ah, used to handle the orders for customers, he had people beggin' him for four years after he wasn't even there no more an' he worked at another steel plant process, for our big sections. So the need was there for our big sections. Apparently they couldn't get 'em at that time yet except off us, and we weren't makin' 'em anymore. Now we had rolled a whole lot ah' those big sections, even when they weren't ordered, no orders, to stock pile 'em. They were hauling it out least knee high an' settin' it there, because they knew when they shut down that they were gonna need those sections. And the, those sections were all eventually sold. The way I understand today yet, they still bring steel down there to cut it from other companies. A customer will buy it, and when he gets it to, no one can cut it, so they bring it down to our plant and they still cut the steel there, even though our plant shut down.

Well. What year would you say you finally come to the realization that we were on our way out?
NF: Umm. I'm gonna say the '80s. I'm gonna say 1980, already, I saw that comin'.

1980. It was long before they had Partners for Progress and restructuring then?
NF: Well, they would hire, every time they would build somethin' new, they would hire a German engineering company, and when you'd ask them, well why? And they'd say; "Well they're the sharpest engineers in the world." And they are. But then when they'd get a bill, like A battery down at the Coke Works, then they don't listen to the German. The German said, "You can't run this half way, you have to start it up an' run it full bore." Same thing with the 59-inch mill, the engineer told 'em what to do and they wouldn't listen to him. I said; "You hire these guys, 'cuz they're the best in the world but then you don't listen to 'em." So A battery the walls started to fall in. So he asked the German; "What do you do when you have, when you're making coke and you don't need it; how do you slow your ovens down?" They said, "We don't. We run 'em wide open, and we stock pile the coke and then we put it in road beds when we build highways, instead of usin' stones, we use coke." Us, we used to throw it out on the ground, then when things got better we'd re-screen it, we'd send it to the Blast Furnace, but because it was laying on the ground out in the sunlight, it wasn't as good, and those people down at Blast Furnace knew right away when you sent 'em re-screened Coke. They knew right away it wasn't fresh, and they'd start raising cain.

That's because ah' the moisture content. They knew it, they knew it immediately when it'd hit the furnace, somethin' wasn't right.

NF: And the fact that it was out in the sun, you can't lay coal or coke out in the sun and let the sun hit it; it does somethin' to it. Regular coal, if you set it on the ground for ten years and then you go to burn it, it'll burn but it won't have the BTUs or heat of somethin' just mined.

Now I heard you make the statement about the German engineers and the 59-inch mill, but no one yet has said to me; "Frank, this is what the German engineer said to me about running the 59-inch mill." What did you hear, what would they have done?"

NF: He said, "You don't even need that mill down at 48 Two." He says, "That man down there is countering everything I do up here. You don't even need that down there. All you need is this 59-inch mill." He said, "If you had a continuous caster, you could start the bar right here and finish the bar right here." And that 59-inch mill, that worked, that work good.

Well that's, that's good. So uh, I'm looking here on your sheet and it's telling me that you spent some time outside of the area, down at, what was it here?

NF: The Coke Works. it hadda be '78 because I bought a brand new Jeep Wagoneer then, a 1978 truck. They pushed me down there on a layoff. And then, when it was time to go back to the mills, the guys down there talked me into staying, so I stayed. But then I wasn't happy with how they handled things down there; for instance on gas jobs, they used go give you a hard time, and I explained to 'em, I'd put the, if I was the back-up man I would put the gas mask on and fire the cartridge off, so in case my buddy went down I was ready to run in. They didn't want you to do that; they wanted you to keep the gas mask off, and then if somebody went down, put it on, pull the cord, set your timer and test the mask. Well, I was in a hazardous area already so I got the mask, we really had a going around about this, so they brought the people from up, up above that, and they said, "Why that man's exactly right. He should have the mask on and ready to run in there. If someone falls, you want 'em outa there as quick as possible."

That's right. A couple breaths and you're finished yourself.

NF: And has, and me being a fireman for years, volunteer an' a policeman, I was off, and I rescued people, I asked him, "How many people did you ever rescue?" "Well none." "Well, I did and I'll tell you what, you're all thumbs. Yunno, unless you do that every day, you're all thumbs." So then their answer down there was, "Well, we won't make you go in gas jobs anymore." And so then I didn't have to go on gas jobs anymore. And uh, so

I didn't, uh, they weren't as, uh, strict on safety as, uh, they were up above. So then, they posted for jobs up above and I bid and by this time I had a lot of seniority and I got right back up there. And I went back to my old department some time in the '80s.

Like '85?
NF: Coulda been. I was down at Coke Works about five years, I'd say, five or six years.

OK. Now, all this time, yunno, you were married right? You had children?
NF: Yep, yep.

And how did they cope with your time at Bethlehem Steel? I know it wasn't easy, the vacations; it took a long time until you could go where you wanted to go. How'd that work out?
NF: Well, when they were little they really didn't care much but there were a lot ah' activities, like at school, like plays, and band concerts and stuff I couldn't come to, and they were in that.

You were a middle shift.
NF: Because I was middle shift. Well, then by the time I could get my vacation in the summer, the youngest boy, he was playing little league baseball and they'd always have this all-star game or somethin'. So then I couldn't go away on vacation anyway because he, he was playing the all-star game; so, they just grew up really basically without me. They just seen me come and go.

So, cuz your wife was actually, like, really in charge of the family.
NF: Yeah, you could say that.

Well, most steel workers would come right out and they'd tell you that. If I wouldn't have had the woman I had, I woulda been in trouble.
NF: I think that's true; though with anybody that works shifts where you, where you go around the clock with shifts…

Yeah, but then again, when you think about it, yunno, the people that were working at PP&L, MAC Truck, Rollersmith, big operations around here, a lot of 'em didn't work middle shift. They didn't know what middle shift was.
NF: And yunno what other problem with working middle shift where you get dirty like that, you'd get, you'd work till' quarter of 11 at night, now you go take a shower. Well, that wakes, if you take a shower at 11 o'clock at night an' then you walk a mile in the cold air to get to your car, then you can't sleep when you get home. So you wind up goin' to a bar or somethin' and havin' a pizza and a couple, you don't get to bed till two, three in the

morning. Then the next day you can't get up. Well, finally when it's time to get up, it's time to go back to work. So they don't get to see yah'. And nobody understands that except the guy who hadda do that, somebody who had to work middle shift.

Well, I'll tell you what, who ever picks up this book and reads about Ned Fink is gonna understand that. Now Ned, were you lucky enough in your time there to, to have a, relative low number of injuries?

NF: I didn't get many injuries, just minor cuts an' stuff.

You never get, you ever have injuries that you had to miss work?

NF: Not because of in there. I used to get gout and I couldn't walk an' stuff. I never got injured that I couldn't work in there.

OK, and when someone says to you, uh, "Ned, if you guys wouldn't ah' been makin' what you were makin', and having the benefits you have, the people in the Lehigh Valley woulda been better off, the health care woulda been cheaper, the dental care woulda been cheaper." What do you say to these people? I run into this all the time when I used to work.

NF: I don't see health care got expensive because of us. I mean yeah, we got the health care for free, but now the company doesn't even exist anymore and health care, they tellin' me health care in the next ten years is gonna' double, I don't think that had anything to do with the company. Uh, a lot ah people though thought when you went in there you didn't do anything. And you'd see all this smoke and hear all this banging and boomin' and trucks comin' out with steel; well somebody hadda be doin' something.

That's right. I mean, why were we in there workin' every holiday is what I wanna know.

NF: Yeah. Why would they pay you 20 hours wages?

And why is the Golden Gate Bridge and all those big buildings in New York City, where did they come from?

NF: And they're not fallin' down either.

No, they're not fallin' down; isn't that ironic?

NF: Yah. They still standin'.

Now, in your time there, did you have any cooks in your shop?

NF: Oh, we all cooked. Yeah. Always cooked.

I, everyone's telling me that yunno' and the people in the outside they'll say, "Hey Frank, you'd still be workin' today if you wouldn't ah been cookin' on middle shift and sleepin' on night shift." But they don't understand how we worked.

NF: Well, when we cooked it was like a pot ah' hot dogs you'd put on, and then you'd go out in the job and by the time you came back and you had 'em on low they were done, hot dogs an sauerkraut and stuff like that.

And, and guys could come in anytime they want it an grab 'em.

NF: And they don't understand, some jobs in there, let's say you had a job, maybe you worked in combustion or somethin'. Your job, now I never worked in there but I saw the guys, they hadda watch meters, and there were emergency things that would occur and then they'd have to act upon it. Sorta like a man who works in a nuclear plant today and he's gotta watch. OK, that guy might sit there and doze off every now an' then; well, you would too when night shift sittin' there watching these meters. But I think guys used to exaggerate. They'd make it sound like they go to work every day and they go to bed or something.

Now Ned, did they have a nickname for you down there?

NF: They used to call me Fountain Hill Fats.

Fountain Hill Fats. Now that is an original.

NF: Well, that's because I used to shoot pool, and one time we went to the Ag hall and there was supposed to be some kinda expert there and I kept beatin' him. So they called me Fountain Hill Fats. {Laughing}

Well how 'bout that. Now, you had a pretty tight group ah' guys because you worked in a lot ah' dirt, you worked around a lot ah' noise. I mean did you have pension parties and things like that, or …?

NF: We, we had pension parties; uh, you, everybody would donate so much to have a pension party when we had a lot ah' men. But near the end we didn't have enough men, we were down to fifteen men. Now, how you gonna have a pension party, so we sold these tickets in the, in the plant. These strip tickets. And that would generate about 22 hundred dollars a year. Because you couldn't sell 'em, uh, when there was a shut down cuz the guys were off and you couldn't sell, so you, we would have a pension uh, for free. Nobody had to pay anything. And we'd invite all the pensioners and we'd invite all the guys who were gonna retire and everybody who worked. We went to the Fountain Hill Hosey when we did that. We had lobster, clams, shrimp.

No kiddin'. You're livin' high on the hog, huh.

NF: Yeah. Well, it cost, that party cost about 15 hundred dollars when we had it.

Yeah. That's great. I'm glad to hear, yunno, that you did something like that. Now, so many things went on in there, but if I had to say to you, Ned, we've talked a little about, about everything that you did. I wanna give you this opportunity right now, to just say what you want about Bethlehem Steel, and we'll basically like wrap this thing up. We heard a little bit about everything: we heard about safety, we heard about scheduling, we heard about vacations, we heard about how important the wife was, raising the kids; we heard everything but, yunno, this time is yours, I'm not gonna cut in; I'm not gonna say a word. You just pretend you're sittin' back here and you're talkin' to a classroom of kids a hundred years from now, and they're gonna say to you, Ned, tell us why Bethlehem Steel isn't there anymore. Let's hear what you have to say.

NF: Well, first of all I was lucky to get a job there; that's the first thing. And I don't regret workin' there because I owe a lot ah' what I have today that I did work there. Uh, but, I would break it down into quarters. I would say that the Bethlehem Steel isn't there today, I'd blame uh, a quarter of it on the government with environmental controls, even though we hadda do that, we couldn't keep pollutin' the Lehigh River and pollutin' the air and things like that. I would blame about a quarter of it on the market; sometimes the market fluctuated, and I would blame about a quarter of it on management. And I would even blame a quarter of it on us, the union, the union, because uh, when we would ask for things, uh, for instance, I wasn't there when they went for the 13 weeks vacation but ah, I can imagine whoever negotiated for the company at that time, instead of saying, well that's ridiculous, they said, "Hey, if they get it, we get it." And maybe they shouldn't have done that, maybe they shoulda said no, but a lot of things they received because we received it, so, so I don't even think management negotiated as fair as they should've for the company. But you add everything together and the, and the, and then you take modernization of all these mills, where you didn't need people watching gauges, and you didn't need this army of men to do certain jobs because machinery did it. Well, then you can't compete. You got, I mean when, when we went out there on a day when they were rolling steel, we couldn't fix anything, we could fix little auxiliary equipment. We were there in case there was a break down. Well, today in modern steel mills, they probably just have a small group ah' men who handle everything instead ah' specialty groups like we were. But in the end there we were startin' to integrate an' help. One of our guys became, he wasn't only an A millwright, he was a B welder, and he was a B motor inspector. He kept goin' to school, and he started to diversify. And, but that was, a little, too little too late I think. We shoulda been modernized, instead of sittin' on it there with your feet up on the desk and sayin', "Keep doin' what you're doin'," We shoulda always been on top of everything and modernized and everything and, re-engineering things so we didn't have the same problems. And that's what I think caused the demise of, not just the steel industry but any old industry. Take the cement mills. They went outa business and the French came over, now the same cement mills, well they're OK now. They're, they're, they're back in the business. And you take uh, when this Wilbur Ross; he bought all of Bethlehem's plant and LTV and all, he made money with those mills. Of course, they were non union, but he made money with it and eventually sold it all to Mittal Steel, and now those are still some of the same mills workin' today, although they're more modern.

Well okay Ned. You said it all. Thanks a lot.
OK.

WILLIAM MOLITORISZ
43 years of service

Mill Roller

Bill was a bloomer roller in the Saucon Mills, one of the most important jobs at BSCO. Other than a half hour break, he operated his mill 7 ½ hours a shift.

* * * * * * * * * *

Today is October 29, 2008. We're here with William Molitorisz. William, did you have a nickname in the plant, or they just called you Bill?
WM: Yeah, Bill.

Okay. I'm looking here, and I see you started in the plant in October of 1952. How did you find out about the job, and how did you get hired?
WM: Uh, my dad worked at the Bethlehem Steel.

Okay, how about your grandfather?
WM: He worked there at the Bethlehem Steel. I had aunts and uncles that worked there too.

Yeah, now, an interesting point. Did they offer you your choice of jobs when you were hired? Or what did they say, "We're sending you down to the merchant mill to be a mailman"?
WM: Yeah.

And you did that for how long?
WM: Uh, from October until January when I enlisted in the Marine Corps.

Okay, all right, so you were in the Marines for awhile. Now, when you first got down into the plant, what was your, what's the first thing you thought of when you got in there? It must have been completely different for a kid right out of high school. Well, a lot of people couldn't believe the size of it. Couldn't believe how loud it was.
WM: The size. Yeah, how big everything was.

Yeah, and you walked back and forth through the merchant mill area delivering mail, between shop offices and things like that?
WM: Right

Yeah, I remember a couple of guys down there, that when I started in '65, you know Al Standing, and some guys like that, and, but I didn't know a lot of them.
WM: Well, I was mostly in HDM.

Yeah, and what did HDM stand for? It had something to do with tool steel.
WM: Tool steel yeah. But uh, they used to make, I know they used to make some kind of cylinders for aircraft and for the Army and Navy.
Drill collars.
WM: Yeah.

For the oil industry, things like that. I know when I started up there in the merchant mill, we were making all the crankshafts for Ford Motor Company, nine by nines, that were coming off the thirty-five inch mill. And things were real good when I started. It was like days of wine and roses.
WM: Oh yeah.

So you go into the service, you come back, and I see that you ended up in the electrical department. You weren't there long, how long?
WM: That's right. Uh, maybe a year, maybe a year.

Yeah. And what were you doing there? You were like a helper?
WM: I was, uh, yeah, I was a floor helper.

And you worked all over the plant?
WM: Just in the electrical shop.

That must have been a good thing. How was the scheduling?
WM: Uh, well I was steady day shift.

Wow, there weren't many people in the plant at that time that could say that. Were you married at the time?
WM: No.

I'm looking down here, and I see you were with the bricklayers a while also.
WM: Yeah, that was for maybe three/four months.

And the same thing, a helper?
WM: Yeah, yeah, well, no, '57 or '58 there when Eisenhower came into office. That's when everybody got laid off. And then between '58 and '60, '61 we were in and out in this department for three months and then out, and then maybe in the department for one month and out.

Plus you were going through a strike in '59. What was that strike like?
WM: '59, that was 118 days.

What can you tell us about that?
WM: Uh, all I can tell you is I was caddying out at Saucon Valley Country Club for seven dollars a day, maybe one or two days a week.

And you were glad you had that?
WM: Yup. I remember the wife and I we would, I was married then, and we would use one tea bag for about four cups of tea.

You were doing what you had to do. Do you remember much about the strike? You were on the picket line or?
WM: No, I wasn't doing anything. I don't remember much.

Yeah, okay, so. I see down here Billet Yard also. When did you end up in the Billet Yard?
WM: That was during that time too, down at New Street there. Well it wasn't New Street, it was up from New Street there. There was a building that had the billets in.

Now you have down here you ended up at the forty-eight inch mill. About what year was that Bill?
WM: That was '60 or '61.

And there's where you found a home?
WM: Yeah.

You stayed there until 1994? And you started out there as a laborer? And you just moved up?
WM: Scaleman, well a scaleman they called you.

Yeah, you moved up through the ranks. Describe some of the jobs you did.
WM: Well, according to my record, I did 17 different jobs to get to roller, the highest job up there.

So like, take us, walk us through some of them jobs. What exactly did they do?
WM: Well, the first job you get is greaser, they called it greaser. First sample you carry, you went down to the mill for samples and carried them back for the roller to measure. Then there was the greaser on the mill where you greased the bearings. And then guidesetter, second guidesetter, first guidesetter, and then...

The guidesetters, what exactly was a guidesetter doing?
WM: He took care of the guides that went into the mill.

The guides actually guided the steel into the…
WM: Guided the bar through the mill, yeah.

And they were adjustable, or what?
WM: Yes, yes, they were adjustable.

Okay. So that was all part of the Steel rolling process.
WM: Yes

Everything had to be set before the first bar came through
WM: Or it didn't come out the other side.

And that's what you called them, ingots, or did you call them blooms, or what did you call them?
WM: Ingots. At the bloomer they were ingots.

Yeah, all right. And uh, this was a big mill, the forty-eight inch mill. Steam powered, right?
WM: Yes

Do you remember what year that mill went in? I know it was prior to 1910, that's for sure. It was there a long time.
WM: I heard so many different stories.

Part of it was legend, part of it was truth, and part of it was in between. So, now you get in, you do the guidesetter job, and where do you go from there?
WM: Then from guidesetter, I went to cable operator, and the pulpit.

Now you're enclosed, you're not actually outdoors anymore?
WM: No.

I mean exposed to the elements.
WM: Yeah, I'm operating leverage to send the bar in and out of the mill.

Okay. All right. And then where do you go from there?
WM: The screw down operator is the guy that ran the mill up and down and in and out.

And how did you, did you have a voice communication on where to set that, or was that just something you knew from experience from operating?
WM: Yeah, we had books from, guys set up books and then, uh, on the drums that went around, drums that you put, that's what the greaser would get a sample for the roller, the roller would measure the sample, and then he would make adjustments. Cuz, uh, you just had a basic standard way of rolling or running the screw down, in and out, and then depending on

the hardness or temperature of the steel, the roller would have to make adjustments.

Yeah, and when you talk about the screw down, you're talking about a device that actually lowers the rolls and raises them? It's actually big screws on both sides of the mill, like…

WM: Yeah, and there's sides that go in and out.

Okay. So now we're into the screw down job, where do we go from there?

WM: Then from there I went to the, they would call a manipulator at the bloomer. He ran, he operated the side guards in and out, side guards and flipped the, the ingot over.

And about how many passes would you, would you make on a let's say an eighteen inch section? How many passes would you make from an ingot from beginning to end, roughly? When we're talking passes, we're talking about through the mill, back again, back through again. Describe that process to us.

WM: Well, you start out with maybe an ingot, uh three foot by five foot, by maybe five foot high in length, and then you reduce it down into a shape, to send it down to the number one mill, that was the roughing mill, and then he'd send it down to number two, the finishing mill.

Yeah, and that was a process, and each bloom would take how much time? Just an average. I know everyone's different.

WM: In time? Maybe three to five minutes.

And naturally, if everything was going right, the name of the game was to produce it in three minutes if you could. Because that's how you made your money, that's how you made your incentive gain.

WM: And again, depending on the heat of the steel, you could do it. Say, say the normal is thirty passes, maybe you could knock it down to twenty-four passes.

Yeah, if it was the right temperature.

WM: Yeah, and then instead of rolling say 10 an hour, you could roll 12/14 an hour.

Yeah, that was the difference between a good shift and a bad shift.

WM: Right, the more you rolled the better your bonus was.

Yeah, and that, and that's why people are at Bethlehem Steel. They didn't go in to see their buddies, they went into make money and to feed their families. Okay, so you went up to manipulator. And then the next move up was?

WM: The bloomer mill.

Okay, now how long were you a manipulator?
WM: Uh, maybe three, four, five years.

Yeah, and then you became a roller about what year, did you remember?
WM: Uh, probably in 1988, '87, '88.

Okay, and you stayed there until you retired or the mill shut down?
WM: Right, the mill shut down in '94.

Yeah, now the roller, was that the top job in that department?
WM: Yes.

Okay, so financially you were doing pretty well at Bethlehem Steel when you became roller?
WM: Uh, in '87 I was doing good, yup. But then our great American hero Ronald Reagan was in office.

And then what happened?
WM: Probably when I started at roller I was making $23 an hour. And when I left I was making $17.50 an hour. So then we were working four days a week too.

That's strange. But that's reality. Yeah, now let me ask you this. When did you come to the realization that that plant was in trouble, about what year?
WM: Uh, I would guess we all realized it in the early '80s when Trautlein came there and started cleaning house.

Yeah, you knew something wasn't quite right? And it was reflected in how much steel was actually being rolled.
WM: And then they came out with that golden parachute. And then...

Was that the one for the working guys, when it trickled down it turned yellow in the snow?
WM: Yeah.

That's the one we got. I remember that one. But overall, your time in Bethlehem Steel, would you say it was a good time?
WM: Oh yeah, yes.

I mean everything can't go perfectly, we all know that.
WM: No, no. The only bad time was in '57/'58 when we went on, laid off, and then the strike came.

Yeah, we were all over the place.
WM: Yeah, those were the worst times, that was the worst time. From then on, the first, my first 15 years in the plant, I probably worked seven,

seven years out of them 15.

Yeah, then you were pretty steady after that down at the forty-eight inch mill.
WM: Yeah.

Well, that's good. Now you probably were involved with some of the attempts by the management and the union to start communicating the Partners for Progress and stuff like that? What did you think of that? I mean, that was an attempt, you know, for, to get ideas from the guys on how to run the place better, but in return the company promised some benefits to the men in the way of earnings.
WM: I don't know if you want to hear this.

Well, no, I want to hear anything you have to say.
WM: Partners in Progress was the beginning of the end to shut the place down.

Oh, okay. I mean everybody looks at it different.
WM: Cuz I remember we used to have bosses come in and sit down, have coffee with us, and guys weren't doing their job, you know, they were sitting there talking shooting the breeze with the boss, boy, he's the nicest guy in the world, the next thing you know we got thirty guys laid off. Because we didn't need those guys if they could sit there and talk to that boss for an hour or two, they didn't need those jobs. In the '80s, the early '80s we had like 163 guys in the department. In 1994 when we shut down we had 75.

Yeah, and actually you have a feeling that the company considered that progress?
WM: Sure for them. Because every time we got guys laid off, they got a bonus.

I'll tell you what. You're not alone in the way you're thinking. I don't want you to think that you're standing out in the crowd, because you're not. I've heard people praise Partners for Progress and say, I wish we would have had it 15 years sooner, because it was always better to get our ideas across in order to have something run better, than it was to do things the old-fashioned way and not make any progress. They liked it along them terms. But they also did what you just said. To a lot of people it represented the beginning of the end, because it was an efficiency move.
WM: Yeah, it was just like when they brought the computers in, they said, uh, this was for better you know, and the first thing we all said was, hey, this is big brother, he's going to know who makes the mistakes.

Now you know Bill, one of the reasons I'm writing the book is, you know, I'm tired of hearing people say all we did was cook on middle shift and sleep on night shift. What do you have to say about that? Because you know the general public in this area has that consensus of steelworkers.

WM: Well, they should've come down to my job. Where I sat in a chair and operated levers for eight hours.

And you ate in between.

WM: Yeah, you sat there and ate in between, but then, well I forget what year it was, they gave us a half hour spell. We had a spell man, and he used to come around, and we'd get a half hour spell.

That was like a big event after all those years of doing...

WM: Oh yeah, just sitting in the chair.

But by the same token, the spell guy was also getting some time on the equipment, and that was good.

WM: Yes. Yes, he had to be a guy that could operate all that.

Were you ever injured in the plant?

WM: Yes.

Yeah, how long were you out of work? Do you remember what happened?

WM: Oh, many months, I don't remember how many months. I broke my fibula.

Whoa. Slipped somewhere?

WM: No, a roll, we were changing rolls, and a roll spun around and hit me against the platform.

Yeah. You're lucky.

WM: I still have a mark where I can stick my fingers in. How that never came off, I don't know.

Yeah. Well, there's been a lot of accidents over time down at the Bethlehem Steel that hardly anybody knows about. You know, like my buddy said one time that worked in the bank, "Jeez all you had to do is a little bit of working, and probably still have a job." I said, "Hey, how many of your buddies did you carry to the ambulance? How many funerals did you go to?" You know, that shuts them right up on the spot, because they just have no clue that we weren't paid so much for what we do, but for the hours we worked and the conditions we worked under. How many holidays do you figure you worked in 43 years?

WM: Almost every one of them.

That's right, because you're on a steady schedule. The mill was rolling, you were working.

WM: Yeah, that was 24/7, for 30 years.

Did you hunt? Were you ever a hunter?
WM: No.

No, do you fish?
WM: I did in the beginning with the kids.

Yeah, now let me ask you something. As far as summer vacations, how many years did you work there before you could get a vacation to take your family away in the summer?

WM: Oh, I worked about 30 years before I got a summer vacation.

Whoa boy. See, this is what the majority of the people know nothing about. This is one of the main reasons I'm interviewing this, because it means more coming right from you, a guy that was right there doing it, than it means for me telling the story. That's why I'm doing this on interview basis.
WM: The only summer, the only time we took vacation in the summer was when I had the long weekend, Friday, Saturday or Sunday off, and then I'd take Thursday and Tuesday off, so we'd be out, so we'd have a five day vacation.

You did what you thought you had to do?
WM: Yeah.

You couldn't do it any other way?
WM: No.

Yes sir, I'll tell you what. What do you miss most about the plant?
WM: The guys.

You had a good time down there?
WM: Yeah.

Everybody had nicknames, everybody knew everybody else's family.
WM: I always used to say, I'd laugh like hell how you could fight on the job, but when something happened, how everybody stuck together.

Yeah, and at the end of the shift everybody went up to Vinny's and had a beer.
WM: Yeah, yeah. You could fight all day and walk out friends.

Yeah, you could forget about it at the end of the shift. And you know the one thing that has become obvious through these interviews is even though guys came in and had the same job every day, every day the job was different. It was different absolutely different every day. You could never get bored going to work at Bethlehem Steel.
WM: No.

I don't ever regret having to go into work.
WM: Yeah.

There were days I didn't want to go into work, but you know once you were there it was like, well, here I am, so I'm going to do what I have to do.
WM: Did you ever see a roll change down on the forty-eight inch mill?

I saw one on the forty number one when I worked there but not on the forty-eight.
WM: It's amazing nobody ever got killed. We should have had at least one killed every day.

Yeah, in other words, it was that dangerous?
WM: Well, the fact of the matter was you couldn't do it safely. There was only one way you could do it, and uh,

And you had to get used to it. Just make sure you made no mistakes.
WM: Yeah

Well, is there anything that you want to say in this interview, you want to get off your chest or, make a statement on Bethlehem Steel? How did the union treat you?
WM: Oh, the union was good, yeah sure.

You were active a little bit with the union?
WM: Yeah. It upsets me today when I hear people say that the unions were the cause of the Steel going down the tubes.

Do you think you could've worked there without the union?
WM: No. Definitely not. Because you would have been fired. You would have been fired every day by a different boss. You couldn't last an hour in there, somebody would be firing you.

Well, I never heard that one, but I'll tell you what, that's why you do these interviews, because you're trying to get these unsolicited answers. So, let's just say it was 20 years ago and they picked up the phone and called you and said, "Bill, we want you to come back to work." What would you do?
WM: Hell no.

No, you wouldn't. Okay Bill I want to thank you for that, and I wish the best to you and your family.
WM: Yeah.

VINCENT J. ZOPPI
34 years of service

Saucon Roll Shop

Vince has a brilliant mind coupled with a sincere desire to "get the job done." He was a misunderstood individual as Chairman of the Plant Grievance Committee. I would be honored to have him in my foxhole in a time of war. I know what he did on behalf of steelworkers in the Bethlehem plant. A true hero of the working man.

* * * * * * * * * *

Today we're talkin' to Vincent J. Zoppi on this March 25th, 2008. How ya doin' today Vince?

VZ: Fine.

Vince, you know everybody down at Bethlehem Steel had some sort of a nickname; did you have one? Or were you just Vince the whole time you were there?

VZ: Yeah.

So that's what we're gonna use, we're gonna use Vince. Vince, I see you started here in May of 1956. How did you come to become a steelworker, how did you get the job?

VZ: I just went in there and applied for, an application, and they gave me a job. They were lookin' for help.

Wow. Okay, so they were hiring at that time?

VZ: Probably, not too many.

Not too many, but you were there at the right time?

VZ: Right.

Okay, and I'm lookin' here, and I see your base unit was the Saucon roll shop, and it was the only place you worked the whole time you were there.

VZ: That's correct.

Would you say that was a little bit unusual, or do you think, do you look at it as normal?

VZ: No, that's unusual. When we went to the pools, people could move around throughout the whole plant, and they did that.

Yeah, okay. Now I'm lookin' here, uh, I see you ran machinery in there. What exactly did they do in the roll shop?
VZ: Okay, what we did, we dressed the rolls that all the mills in the Saucon division rolled steel; we made the rolls that formed beams.

Okay, those rolls used to come back in periodically and actually be resized and brought back to the original condition, correct?
VZ: Uh, well no, not really, only the 28s and the 18-inch mill were doin' that. 48s and the 42s and uh, were rolls that were resized and put down into different sections. In other words for the 48s they started at 36-inches wide and went down to 8 inches. The 42s started about 24-inches wide and went to 6 inches. The 18s and the 28s they stayed the same, and all we did was take the wear out of them and redress them.

So the bottom line was without these rolls there wasn't too much steel getting made down at the Bethlehem Steel, at least in the beams anyway.
VZ: Well, there was no steel at all made if we didn't turn the rolls.

Okay, so you guys were sitting right up at the top of the food chain, and without those rolls, I mean nothing was gonna happen.
VZ: Correct.

Now, when you started there, how were you treated by the older guys?
VZ: No problems. It was in the '50s, and uh, the older guys took you under their wing and made sure that you didn't get hurt or made sure you were doing everything right. There wasn't no major problems, because these guys were in their 50s and I was in my 20s.

Well you know, the only reason I brought that up is some of the shops, some of the people I talked to, Blast Furnace people, hourly division people, they always used to say, "Well, the old guys didn't say much to us until they got to know us, and they never told us how to do anything until they knew for sure that we were there, you know, we were one of them." You didn't experience any of that?
VZ: No, because when you started on the floor and you start hooking up rolls, so they depended on you to change the roll so they could make money, so they didn't really take us on. They made sure because there was a lot of hazards there when you were hooking up rolls that you had to do it right. So they made sure that we didn't get hurt.

Okay, so you know they needed you as much as you needed the job?
VZ: Correct.

Beautiful. And I see here looking down here at some of the things you did. I'm lookin' here and it says you ran a tracer lathe. Was that a job that was at the top of the seniority order, or where did that fit in there? I mean, did you start there?

VZ: That was the highest paying job in the shop, so when you got seniority you went to become a tracer lathe operator for money. Roll turner was a craft job, but it didn't pay as much as a tracer lathe operator so you jumped from roll turner to tracer lathe operator.

So when you first started out you were a roll turner then?

VZ: No, when I first started out I was a crane man.

Okay, and how did you progress?

VZ: And then I was a machine hand, which turns the 42- and 48-inch mill rolls. Then you progressed to the next level, which was a roll turner, and you went into where the bloomers were, where the first initial rolls, where the beam went through the roll first, it was called a bloomer, and then you stood there, and that was a roll turner C. As you progressed in hours you went to B and A, and then when you were in A then you did everything.

You did everything?

VZ: Yup, from as far as redressing the rolls and making 'em new, we also turned the rolls to make 'em new.

Okay. Uh, I'm lookin' here and I see along the line you got involved with the union pretty heavily. I see that you were a guide. You were also on the grievance committee, and you were chairman of the grievance committee. How did you get started with the union?

VZ: Uh, Nick Kiak, roll shop boys, the bosses ran the shop; in other words, they were king. So Nick got me in and said you wanna become a shop steward and that's how I started.

So you were always active, basically from when you started?

VZ: Uh, about eight years. That was '56 to '84.

Yeah. So that was, uh, that was quite an experience, I guess? And uh, you were very active, I know, with incentives. How did ya get going with that? And tell us what incentives were in the plant.

VZ: Okay. What they did, they set a rate for you, say they gave you 500 minutes to do a roll, so you had to accomplish that roll in less than 500 minutes.

In order to make additional money.

VZ: Yeah, and it was, I guess it started at 3 cents a minute, I'm not sure.

Yeah, everything was based on a negotiated rate between the union and the company.

VZ: Well, yeah, they gave you brochures. And at the 42- and the 48-inch mill the guys didn't make too much money, so we started working on incentives, and we had to go through negotiations because the incentive plans were established that long, and the eight percent wasn't very much at that time.

Yeah, so actually as the smarter you got at your job, the more you realized that there was a lot more money to be made here than the company was willing to pay. And that's what it was really all about, it was negotiating. Because of that, I see here you moved onto the grievance committee. And what year did you become a grievance committeeman?

VZ: 1976, Tony Buffo became staff, and I ran for his position to fill the rest of his term, and I started in '76 and I wound up in '85.

And you saw it all during that period because that was a period of tremendous change in the plant. You worked on the final pool agreement. Wasn't that one of the first projects you were doing on the grievance committee, changing the pools into one pool?

VZ: One of the major ones, yes. We made some agreements in different departments. Because I was a chairman. I had to go into the department whenever the grievance committeeman that was handling the department…but the first major agreement was the pool.

And we had something that no other plant, and we had where a 20-year guy with 20 years experience, if he was on layoff could stay on layoff, and a younger guy would work in his place.

VZ: Yeah, and he could do that. And I don't recall, but I think it was 90 days and he had to come back.

And, you know the amazing thing about that was, uh, as some of our people when the plant was winding down went to other plants, nobody else had that in the Bethlehem corporation. We were the only ones, and boy I'll tell ya the senior guys at the other plants they were saying, "Hey, when are we gonna get with the program here? How did Bethlehem get this?" Well, we always, our guys would come back when they'd be at these other plants and we'd see 'em, and they'd say, "You know what, I hate to tell ya this, but you know we were way ahead of those guys," and I liked to think it was because of guys like you that had the insight, you know, to do these things, and you had such a rapport with management that you were able to convince them that this wasn't just for us, but it was gonna be a benefit for them, and uh. Tell me a little bit about your some of the highs and lows of your time with the grievance committee. You were involved in a lot of negotiating. What jumps out? What sticks out in your mind?

VZ: Well the 48-inch number 1 mill, uh we negotiated 500 jobs to get the mill with the promise that they would do some upgrades, and they never lived up to their promise, and finally they closed the plant, but we saved the plant for about 16 to17 years and got a lot of people on pension so that was a highlight, even though it was a down for me because we had to cut jobs, and the union was never for cutting jobs, but we had to do something to save the plant.

And uh, so you're saying basically from your time when you started on the grievance committee, you knew at that time that the days were actually numbered for the plant?

VZ: Oh yeah, we knew.

At least you strongly suspected it.

VZ: Well, no, no, 1980 I was chairman and I was also, what the heck you call it, I can't think of it. But I went out to negotiation with McHale, and Williams was the President of the international, and he told us flat out that if we don't do something in the plants, Bethlehem and I think it was National and US Steel were all in trouble because of the imports. Imports were there since the '60s. Now, they really took, they exported their unemployment to us; in other words they were subsidized and we couldn't do nothing about it, so we had to do something to compete.

And naturally because you had to do something like that, that anybody that was involved in doing anything of that nature, because the people didn't fully understand the ramifications, that always put these people in a bad position didn't it?

VZ: Oh yeah, I lost the election over it.

I mean there wasn't a lot of people that were in love with you, so to speak.

VZ: No, no, no, they voted me out in '85.

Well, you know, I believe, you know, when you were, actually after you were voted out, uh, in the early '90s I remember people saying, "Boy, it's a good thing we did what we did, where we probably already would be shut down." So you know, just if you've never heard that, you heard it from me, and you know that came from people unsolicited.

VZ: No, I never heard that.

One of the things I want to bring up is the '59 strike. You went through the '59 strike. What was that like?

VZ: Well, you gotta remember there was nothing out there to subsidize us, you know. After 20 years I think the union started subsidizing these people that were on strike. We went out there, we got nothing.

So anything that was forthcoming came from the goodness of the local union more or less.

VZ: We didn't even get anything from the local union; you had to be, these local unions didn't have that much money to give out, so you had to be dedicated, you know; you had to have a family of five and you were going hungry, then the union would help you, but uh, they couldn't help everybody.

In other words, they did what they could.

VZ: Yeah, it was, at that time there was somewhere in the neighborhood of 12,000 and 13,000 in the plant, so you know, it was kind of tough.

And the union at that time, what was the big issue of the '59 strike?

VZ: Seniority.

Seniority. The company wanted to make changes?

VZ: Oh, sure they did. They didn't want seniority, They wanted to pick their own people. That's why we had to stay out 120 days. And after that there was no strikes because neither side could afford it.

Okay, now did you ever hear anyone say that the '59 strike opened up the eyes of the world that there were other places to buy steel?

VZ: I don't think so.

No?

VZ: I think the imports were gonna come no matter what we did.

Okay, all right. You know I heard that from people already.

VZ: That's a falsity. Imports were coming, because like Britain, France, and all those people, they didn't want to lay their people off, so what they did; they exported it out and they subsidized the steel industries over there and shipped it over here. So the steel industry could sell their steel cheaper by even shipping across the ocean by boat.

But they, I guess their idea was it was cheaper to do that than to pay people to do nothing, which is what it would have been. And that's right what we ran into. So now, you're unsuccessful in your bid with the grievance committee, you go back into the plant. What was that like?

VZ: No, I didn't. When I was unsuccessful I was…

That's right you went on and you did what?

VZ: Partners for Progress. I was a coordinator for the union and it was Partners for Progress. Now, that never worked out because I think the union never bought it, and the company never sat down, and what it was designed to do was to help the company get productive, and the company had to turn over part of their management skills to us to let us put our input in there, and that never happened.

Do you think if we would have had Partners for Progress ten years earlier, it would have had a bigger impact?
VZ: I don't think the union was ready for Partners for Progress. Only the people on the top. The people on the bottom…

Was that a trust thing? Did that go right back to trust again that the employees didn't trust…
VZ: I think the company wasn't honest. I think they only did it cuz they were told to do it from the higher ups.

Ah, in other words, they wanted to project an image that they were doing everything they could, you know to make things right.
VZ: And they were supposed to tell us how much salary they made and all that, that never happened.

Yeah, it never happened.
VZ: Nope, we knew because we organized. I think it was payroll department. We had a couple people that were organizing there; that's how we knew all the salaries, but they never told us what they were making.

Now, what was the number one thing during your union time that you're really glad you were involved in, or was it just overall being involved with the union period?
VZ: I think the grievance committee. When I first went on, the learning experience, how to go to arbitration, how to arbitrate, uh, how to negotiate, um, until I think '81 it was really enjoyable to do it because you helped people out. In '81 even though we were helping people out, there was a lot of animosity toward us; in other words, we went in department where we got a job, people hated us. Marvin and I went in there, you know, as soon as we showed up we were the enemy.

In other words, they didn't see it as a temporary inconvenience leading to a permanent improvement. It wasn't perceived that way by anyone?
VZ: Nope, nope.

And it had to be a hard thing to do too, going completely against the grain of the way the union was taught to operate.
VZ: Well, it goes against your own way. Let's face it, you were brought

up that, you know, sometimes we over-extended and got more jobs than we really needed, but you're going in there and you're taking a guy's food out of his mouth and out of his children's mouth, so what do you think he's gonna do? How is he gonna react? How would I react? You know. It was something that never bothered me because we knew we had to do it, or else the plant was gonna be shut down way before they wanted.

And a lot of people would have never got a pension out of that?
VZ: Oh no. How 'bout they got TRA, these guys got health benefits out of it until they were '65, you know. There was a lot of stuff that came out the good of it. Unfortunately, some people had to suffer for other people to gain, so, that's the way that life is.

What would you say was your low point, or would you say your high point and your low point were basically the same thing?
VZ: If I stayed there another four or five years I'd be a dead man today. I would, I couldn't handle it.

Just too much stress involved with what you were doing?
VZ: Well, yeah, because then they took another, then they went and they cut another 500 jobs. So I don't think I could go through that twice.

Now, you did the Partners for Progress part, etc. etc.; eventually that ended up, you ended up back in the shop. It must have been by the time you got back to the shop it was like, you were like, reborn, you know, all you had to do was go to work and do your job.
VZ: Unfortunately, the job that I got as a tracer lathe operator, I never worked that much, I just learned that job and that's when my seniority put me, so it was kind of tough to last five years because it was starting all over again and learning something.

But as far as stress-wise, it wasn't nowhere near like being on the grievance committee.
VZ: No, there was no stress.

Now, here's a question and you might have to think about this a little bit. Let's say you had been in 1980 in a position, okay where you could do things in that Bethlehem plant that would make it more productive, okay, and would give it a better chance of survival. What would you have done? This is all in hindsight, but it's really important that people hear this from employees that were actually on the inside.
VZ: What would I have done? I don't know what I would have done. They wouldn't stick no money into, there was nothing we could do unless they wanted to stick some money in it and modernize it and go to like

instant coffee, and they wouldn't do that. They had to put a caster there. That was the first thing we would have negotiated if we had any smarts, and we were after them to put a caster in there, and the British Steel fell through for whatever reason; uh, the British wouldn't honor the union I think it was, and uh, they were gonna put a caster in the plant, but Bethlehem Steel wouldn't put a caster there. They put one in Burns Harbor and Sparrow's Point, those two survived, Bethlehem Steel went down. They could've kicked their rears too, because they could have made money with structured steel.

Yeah, I would imagine.

VZ: And if they would have modernized, they should have took the BOF out of there; see, our hours per man hour per ton of steel was too high. I think it was 5 or 6. When we cut jobs we got it down to about 4. Uh, Nucor came in and really killed us. So we had to get down to about three or two, and we couldn't do it with the facilities we had. We had to have some modernization because it was just too many man-hours to make a ton of steel.

Now, if you, most of the guys I've talked to have already told me they'd never trade the years in the steel for anything because of the relationships they had with the men. They spent more time in there in that plant usually than they did with their own families. How did that affect your family when you were there?

VZ: My wife was good about it.

She was used to it.

VZ: Yeah, if I go away, she never moaned. Yeah, she was very supportive, so I never had that problem.

Good for you, good for you. Cuz you know I've run into guys, I have interviewed some people in the past couple weeks that had 20 or 30 different areas they worked in the plant. It just so happens they were '73, 1973 hires, and these guys were all over the place. And boy, could they, they could tell ya some stories. They could tell ya some stories. Well, Vince I'll tell you what, this is a real pleasure getting to talk to what I call one of the icons of the union movement here in Bethlehem, and I hope all the best for you and your family. Thank a lot.

EARL KURTZ
36 years of service

Electronics Department

One of only 8 men hired in 1963. Many came from the Penn State associate degree program in Allentown. Electronic's repairman supreme. Active union representative.

* * * * * * * * * *

Today is May 22, 2008. We're here with Earl Kurtz from the electronics department. Earl, does everybody call you Earl? I know a lot of guys had nicknames. Just Earl?

EK: Earl is my name. It was my grandfather's name, and I continued to use it.

Okay, now, I see here that you were one of the few who were hired in 1963. Tell me how you became a steelworker.

EK: I had just graduated from Penn State as an associate electronic and electrical technician, and my dad had worked at the Steel for many, many years, and he let me know that there was an opening for an electronics apprentice course. And I applied for it and I was able to get it, because of my college training, without too much trouble. I had to take a battery of tests but I did rather well, as my friend, Bernie, did and another gentleman, Frank Waha. All three of us came from Penn State so all three of us got in.

Well isn't that some story. Now correct me if I'm wrong, but most of you guys were hired right around the same time, weren't you?

EK: There were ten of us hired on that day.

Where did you set in there seniority wise?

EK: Well, because we were hired all in the same day, it went by date of birth, so I was number four.

Okay then, when you first came into the plant, first impressions I know are really strong. What did you think when you first got out there where all the noise, the dirt, the dust, the movement; what did you think about that? Tell me what your first month was like.

EK: Okay, well, first of all, my grandfather and my father were mechanics, and I wasn't afraid to get dirty. And I pretty much knew what my dad was doing as a mechanic at the Steel. However, on my first day or two, I had to go—and all ten apprentices—to a meeting that supervision was having. And they explained that we shouldn't come with our best suit, okay; we should come with our second best suit. And my first day on the field, I actually had a white shirt on without no tie, and I went out in the field, and I think my first job was to travel down to the auxiliary yard, okay, and work in the carrier garage, and work on a communications system there. So, you know what that was like going in there with my second best suit on.

Absolutely. You know I had a guy that got hired—this is funny—because you know when you come down there, and your family and your relatives and your neighbors work at Bethlehem Steel and all of a sudden, you get hired. And they say to you, "You're going to be an inspector." This guy showed up with a suit and a tie, and they took him down to the Beam Yard to be an inspector, and he says it took the guys like three days. Their sides hurt for three days from laughing. Who's this bozo who just came in? He says, "Now picture this, Frank. I have hair halfway down my back, right out of the service. I'm not one of these, how would you put it, take-charge-type guys, very unassuming." He says, "It took me less than 24 hours to realize, you don't come to work like that."

EK: Yep. Well, I didn't come with a suit, but the very next day I put something on that I didn't mind so much if it got dirty. But it wasn't a big surprise, but I was told by the "powers to be" this is the way you should dress; and I, of course, listened to them.

Yeah, well, naturally. Anybody's going to do that. But, you know, your first job was down at the auxiliary yard at the Beam Yard. All over the Beam Yard, believe it or not, it was actually one of the cleaner areas of the plant. But you could find some really filthy holes there. I mean nasty work. I mean, "Look out!"

EK: Beth Forge, on the Number One Press Forge, there's a really greasy mess. And going down into the Combo, in the basement, the sluiceways, and it goes on and on and on.

And because you were electronics guys, the company was always trying to make things better in the sense that, if they could have electronic control that could do things and was more dependable, they wanted to use it. So you must have worked all over the plant.

EK: There wasn't one part of the plant that I didn't set foot in. Okay, when they talk about technology, at the blast furnaces we had nuclear gauges to check the moisture in the coke. I worked that job. You go all the way down to the opposite end of the plant, the Coke Works. We put in the remote control locomotives. We even had radar detectors to try and catch the cars as they were coming out of the dumper, which failed miserably, and they ended up having another remote control locomotive to actually catch the cars. But that's sort of from one end to the other, and I worked everything in between. The machine shops, the mills, there wasn't anything in my 36 years of experience that I didn't work on. It seemed like, because of my engineering background, I was on almost every new startup. I was on the Basic Oxygen Furnace startup in '67. I was on that startup team. The funniest thing, I was offered a foreman's job, because the foreman was afraid of the first day, and he took vacation to go hunting. And I was a new man there, and I had to be the electronics foreman for startup of the BOF. Never forget that day.

Amazing, amazing. So you did have occasion where you did perform as a temporary foreman over the entire time you were there. And that had to do with what? Vacations, illnesses, and things like that?

EK: Right, uh-huh.

Now your shop was known probably more than any other area to use a lot of working leaders. Tell me about that. What is a working leader?

EK: A working leader was very similar to a temporary foreman. The name was sort of coined because of the rotation at the Combination Mill. It was imperative to have electronics repairmen out 24/7. And they needed somebody to direct, for lack of a better word, that was totally familiar with the mill, because you would have people on vacation from the mill, and somebody from another area would fill in, and they wouldn't know anything about it. By having a working leader that was knowledgeable, the two people could go out. As you know a working leader wasn't really allowed to work, but in electronics capacity, they certainly could make voltage tests and read prints and stuff like that, and they could do almost the entire job, and they would come down to a part they could tell the new fellow who was filling in to merely change this part. And I forget what the cost, I don't know if I'm right on this, if it was five thousand dollars an hour that the mill was down. You wanted to get the mill up as quick as possible. So obviously, the working leader, in my opinion, in electronics, that's where it got its start.

Yeah. Now, the electronics department everywhere all over the plant, was there a particular area that you liked more than others? Was it machine shops? What was it?

EK: I would say, I found out that I was assigned certain areas and I grew to like them, only because I was there, I got to know the people. I would say my longest tour of duty, so to speak, was working in machine shops. I worked in Number 2 Shop, in Number 8 Shop, and while I was at two shops and just took care of two shops for a while, moved on to some other areas, and then was recalled, and I was assigned at 8 Machine Shop. At 8 Machine Shop I was responsible for 8 Shop, the press forges, the treatments there, and also Saucon Machine Shop. I would say I probably enjoyed that the most. I worked almost totally by myself. Had my own little shop, and my office and desk, and I worked on all the equipment, repaired everything there. I had all the test equipment I needed. It was an interesting, the 8 Shop is kind of unique because it was so large. It had a very large lathe, a 10-inch horizontal lathe, a 100-inch face plate, and let's say, a 150-feet long bed.

So when you talk about a face plate, that's actually like a chuck for a drill, right?
EK: That's exactly right.

So when you talk a hundred inches, you're talking some big stuff here?
EK: Yeah, contrast that with a vertical lathe, which you could walk and stand on, 25 foot across. All the bells for the blast furnace were turned on that lathe.

Yeah. Amazing. Now Number 8 Shop was big and had real big machinery in it and lathes, but Number 2 Machine Shop was monstrous. Describe how big that was.
EK: Yeah, Number 2 Shop was extremely long. I'm thinking getting close to a quarter mile from one end to the other. And on the end of it was some sort of treatment or something that might have been shut down or something like that. But it was very large, and the upper ends had all the vertical lathes. I think their biggest lathe was like a 12 foot, or 14 foot I think the biggest. And then you go all the way down to the other end of it, they had honing machines, where they would bring in the larger guns, and they would do some honing there. So in between there was some horizontal lathes, some milling machines. They had the tool crib where they would grind all the tooling for the lathes and so forth. Covered a lot of ground. And a very interesting thing at Number 2 Shop, they had a big sound system so that they could announce things. And they found it very inconvenient to always run it through the microphone. So one of my projects was to design something that you could call a number on any telephone, and that would get you right into the sound system, and you could announce whatever you had to. Made it very convenient. So that was like a first for the Steel, and I'm very proud to design that.

You were the guy that put that together, or instrumental in getting that off the ground. Now, you worked in the machine shop when they were actually still working on guns for the Navy and the Army.

EK: That's correct.

How big of guns are we talking about here? They're actually rifles I guess.

EK: I have to qualify that. What sticks out in my mind more than the guns is the new technology for the rolling mills, the rolls that they used. They would bore a hole through the roll, and when you forged it, all the bad steel went to the center. And then they would bore that out, and then they would hone it to a real fine mirror finish, and then they could run electronic equipment called ultrasounds and they use a reflectoscope. And they could ping outward from the inside and look for flaws, and then on the outside they would ping from the outside in, and they wouldn't miss anything that way. So, I'd have to say I had more experience seeing jobs like that rather than the guns. The only thing I know I was involved with, the 16-inch shells for the Battleship New Jersey that they used over at Nam.

Where were they made?

EK: That was down at the forge next to Forge Specialty. And they actually put a press in, that they would take the steel and punch a hole in it, and then machine the shape of a shell.

I know those babies, I mean we actually, when I was in the Navy, we had the New Jersey fire over top of us. And we knew what the gun target line was, and when you looked up there first you would see a flash, then you would see smoke, it's way out on the horizon, and then you would hear the sound maybe three, four seconds later, and then you would look up to what you knew was the gun target line. That was the line that was from the gun to the target. If you knew what that was, if you looked up there, you could actually see these rounds pass overhead. They look like big, black cigars. And I'll tell you what, when we were on the firing range, and they were landing like only five thousand yards beyond our ship, when they would start coming down, they would tumble. They wouldn't come in straight. And you would get this woo-woo-woo-woo-woo-woo, and when these babies hit. Boy, I'll tell you what, they really moved some dirt. It was an impressive thing to see, and you know it was all done at Bethlehem Steel.

EK: Right. I'm not saying during my tenure there that they didn't make guns, I just might not have been in the shop at that time.

Now, you did basically the same thing the entire time you were there—electronics. Was there like a time when they got into actually new types of technology, new types of equipment that you started installing? Do you know what I mean by that? Tape lathes or things of that nature, you know, were retrofitted onto the lathes.

EK: Okay, let me just say this. People said that the Bethlehem Steel didn't modernize enough and that's why it failed. It did not fail because of that, because I'm here to tell you that I worked on every new piece of gear that came into the plant. And I can tell you, they were always modernizing. Maybe they didn't have enough money to make everything with a brand-new piece on it, but they would retrofit. Many of the lathes were retrofitted and added. You had mentioned tape control lathe. There were many, many lathes that were tape controls. Some of them were actually bought brand-new and put in place. However, they would take older lathes, totally rebuild them, and put all the controls on them. So, we had tracer lathes, where you actually could, they could, toolmakers would make a design, and they put it on the lathe, and the tracer would come and follow the shape of whatever they made. They had numerical control lathes where a designer would design what a generating roll would look like, and that was called a CNC lathe or an NC lathe. Then they went one step further and they bought CNC lathes. It actually was a full-blown computer. It did basically the same thing as a CNC, or an NC, I'm sorry. The difference between NC was it read every step off a punch tape, where a CNC lathe you could go in there with a floppy with the whole design of the roll. And then you could put maybe 5 or 6 and then keep them in memory. But the bottom line was, it had very accurate positioning because the computer and the position feedback always knew where it was. There was a smaller lathe at Central Tool; it could hold 7 ten-thousandths.

Wow. And these CNC lathes, was there any particular area that they more of them than others?

EK: Well, Number 2 Shop had a number of them, Number 8 Shop had a number of them, Forge Specialty had a number of them, Saucon Roll Shop had some also. Saucon Roll Shop, you talk about sophistication, I don't know if you ever heard of a SPARC workstation, but it was basically a high-end computer, where they would graphically design the shape that they wanted the roll to be, and they would download that whole finished program right to this, they called it a DNC. You didn't have to go in there with a floppy. It just passed the software right to it, and the operator would come in there, start the machine up, and just put the right tooling in, it would tell him what tooling to use, and start the job off, and do the whole job. And that was trackable to the customer when it was designed; all that information went in there, as part of the whole program.

So that was part of a quality control program on top of it. So you know that the quality of the stuff that came out was as good as you were going to get.

EK: Right. And they could always tell where, if the customer asked, "Well where's this load of steel?" or whatever, especially if it was something unique. They'd say, "Well, the designer is designing the rolls for it right now." We could go in and see what date he started it, what date he completed it, where it was on the line as far as machining the actual rolls, and then track it further to when it got installed in the Combo.

Now Earl, schedules, I know they worked round the clock, how did you work in there?

EK: I worked 24/7 at times, and I would work Tuesday to Sunday day shift, and then I would work Wednesday would be 6-7-7, whatever that works out. I would end up on a night shift, going home on a night shift on a Friday morning.

So you end up working all three shifts. And you did that for how many years?

EK: Yes. That's when I was assigned to the Combination Mill. That wasn't one of my favorite schedules, so I did everything I could to get out of it, and that sort of dropped me over to union. I was elected shop steward, and I elected to get out of working that rotation.

Okay. So how did all these schedules and stuff, how did it affect your family life? Vacations and things like that?

EK: Well, working 24/7 was really tough. It took me a day or so until I was able to get back to myself, and to be quite honest with you, there was some people that liked working night shift. I ended up giving most of my night shifts away. I normally would probably only work two night shifts and then the next five days would fall in another week, and then I usually always found somebody that would take that. So I was more of a day shift and a middle shift person, for the most part.

Now somewhere along the line there, you actually became active with the union. When was that about?

EK: That would be 1974.

1974. Was there any particular person that took you under their wing?

EK: Yes, the former shop steward was really looking for somebody, a go-getter so to speak, and he's the one that talked me into running for shop steward. Russell Buckneller was his name.

How about that. And what exactly did you do with the union, other than being a shop steward?

EK: Well, I first straightened out some scheduling issues. We used to use seniority to pick holidays, and we had four- and five-day schedules, so I worked up agreements on how the general foreman could schedule four- and five-day schedules and share the overtime agreement. After I got through that, I started looking into our incentive plan. We had a time-measured incentive plan. It was based upon how many man hours we worked versus how many hours a plant person worked, and that was multiplied by the average performance of all these groups in our plant. And it was counterproductive to us, because we would put in new technology to eliminate people, which would cut our incentive. Our incentive always kept going down. And then I would ask for a change or a revision to our incentive. And I'll never forget the day I went over to the union hall to ask about the incentive. Owen McFadden, he was the number one incentive person over there, and we went through our plan, and he explained the whole thing. And I says, "Owen, I understand. It's simple math." And he looked at me and he says, "You're the only one that I explained this to that understood what I was talking about."

Well you know, you probably know, and I know for sure, Owen McFadden was a legend when it came to incentives. When we would go away with the union to other plants and sit down with other grievance committees, the first thing out of their mouth would be, "When can we talk to McFadden?" They wanted to have an hour or two just to sit down and talk incentives or grievances with McFadden, because McFadden was, how would you put it, an old-line shop steward that had a tremendous mind that could think on his feet like nobody I ever ran into. I mean he came up with stuff that was out of this world. I got two days off one time for having my hard hat and glasses off on a holiday. The division superintendent caught me. Then McFadden came over when my case was being heard, and after they presented everything, the superintendent says, "Well, this is pretty well an open and shut case." And he looked at McFadden and he says, "Don't you agree?" He says, "Now wait a minute. Hold it. This man has a chance to confront his accuser. Where is he?" "Well, he's over in France on company business." He says, "I rest my case." He says, "This man is telling me he never did any of these things. Now what are you going to do?" Well, I won that case. McFadden came out; he says, "They'll be talking about that for some time." And he says, "He wasn't happy about that." But you know what, when you think about it, I was sitting a hundred feet from the building, after getting done a job in 100 degree temperature, and what happened was I was just wiping the sweat off of me is all I was doing. And he was just amazing the way he came in and he says, "Wait a minute, this guy has a chance to confront his accuser. Where is he?" I never even thought of that!

EK: Nope. Many people didn't care for Owen, because he told you right up front whether you had a case or not. And a lot of people didn't want to hear that. But I must say I have to thank Owen, because I'm sure he's the one who recommended that I be part of the incentive committee.

Well, you know an interesting thing about that is one of the guys who used to hang on his every word was Lester Clore. And Lester always used to say, "Hey, the truth is the ultimate defense." He says, "If you can't handle the truth, you have no defense." And I always used to listen to that and I used to tell that to people and they'd look at me like, "What are you talking about?" I'd say, "Think about what I just said. The truth is the ultimate defense." "Yeah?" I says, "As long as we stick to the facts when we go in there to hear these cases, we're not going to really have a lot of problems." I says, "Because there's right and there's wrong and then there's contract and then there's non-contract. We got to strike a happy medium here to get something done." And, you know, it would work. So Earl, when did you actually reach the point where you knew the company was in trouble? About what year would you say it was?

EK: Let me qualify what you're asking. Because of my seniority, I knew the plant was in trouble. I don't know if I could pick a day, but I'm sort of qualifying it that I sort of felt, because I had so much seniority, if they had one small part running, I would still have the seniority to keep a job. So it wasn't until that they actually decided to close the Coke Works, that's when I decided that it was all over. But as far as answering your question goes, I would say I knew Bethlehem plant was in a lot of trouble was, didn't we have a contract around '90ish or something like that, where they promised to put in a continuous caster and we voted for the contract and we approved it and, what was it, six months later they backed ....

Yeah. In fact they went so far as that they actually started sinking the foundations out by the BOF.

EK: That's right, because I was involved in the, what do you call it department at that time, the electrical engineering department, where I worked as an electronic technician. And there were many, many plans started. And when they cancelled that, that's when I knew we were going downhill for sure.

That's really something. Now if all that time you were there, what's your best memory of the plant?

EK: I have many, memories and it's hard to…oh boy. I remember one thing, this is sort of comical. I remember I used to also teach apprentices for a short time, and the superintendent of the electrical department, who electronics reported to, he said electronics was gonna be a passing fad. And here I am just a young guy starting out, and he was my superintendent, and he was a Mason, he was like up top there, and this is the kind of mentality I was dealing with, and that's when I decided not to go with the company and stay hourly. So I could keep my sanity. He said that all the remote control locomotives, once they do a post audit, they're gonna throw them out. Well, guess what? They bought two, and I think they went up to six alone at the Coke Works, they bought two or three in Ingot Mould. They converted all the narrow gauge over all with remote control; well, I rest my case.

Yeah. Do you think that that was just a fear of technology more than anything else?

EK: Well, yes. Because he was a very good engineer, electrical engineer, and I don't think he knew enough about electronics and, to be perfectly honest. My general foreman at the time didn't get along with him, so I think that sort of comes from that. But still as a young person, hearing those words coming out of his mouth, they rested pretty heavy on me.

I talked to a shop steward who I had also interviewed who had dealings with this gentleman that you're describing, and he found out that the way to this guy's heart was to say to him, "Look, if we do it this way, there's gonna be peace and harmony in the shop, everything's gonna work smooth, and you're gonna see me less than you're seeing me right now, because everybody's gonna be happy." And he says he would then throw him a bone. "Okay, we're gonna forget about this one. Okay, but I don't want to see this guy in here anymore." A lot of these guys, they were old-line superintendents, old-line general foremen, but they, most of them treated the guys pretty good. Overall the foremen you dealt with in the plant, do you think most of them were, you know, on the right page?

EK: Most of the foremen, yeah. I had some issues with some foremen in my department, namely my general foremen, but the only way to solve the issue was to tie his hands. And I did that by creating the four- and five-day share-the-work agreement and the overtime agreement, and then he learned to live within the rules. We have very few grievances; he actually got "atta boys," because there were so few grievances, and everything worked out in the long run.

I know you were never the type of guy to brag, but I can see in this case here, you realized real early that, if you made fewer problems for him, the better it was for everybody.

EK: Absolutely.

There's no doubt about that. Now, we already know all the things you did in the plant, we know how you dealt with foremen, we heard about your union activity, I want to know now, Earl, and think about this one time. What if you had been in the position, let's say like 1985, to call the shots in the Bethlehem

Plant, sort of like general manager? I know this is kind of weird to even ask you this. What would you have done to try to save that plant?

EK: Well, first of all, I would not have listened to all my immediate supervisors that reported to me. I think I would have been smart enough that they weren't telling me the truth. I would have gone down to another level and find out where the real truth was. And, in hindsight on my part, in my opinion the Coke Works was the biggest money-losing place there was. We put very few technology into the Coke Works, and nobody really wanted to work there. Had the Coke Works been taken out of the picture, and we could have gotten cheaper coke to the Blast Furnace, I think we could have saved the Blast Furnace. If we could have saved the Blast Furnace, that would have saved the plant.

That's interesting, because I haven't had a report like that from anybody. I haven't done a lot of work with the Coke Works people so far. I'm going to be talking to them in the next 30 days. But I was always under the impression from the Blast Furnace people that every time they used coke other than coke from our plant, they had problems.

EK: Well, you're absolutely right. Our coke plant made very good coke. But at some point you have to look at how much you're paying for it. And believe me, the technology was there to modify the way they made the iron with a lesser quality of coke. They were taking the easy way out. And here again I make my point, if you can't be listening to your direct supervisor, you have to get down to a lower level. Now, because I worked in the entire plant, I got to see the whole picture. Most people would go to their one little shop and they would work there every day. But I worked through the whole plant, and I think I have a much bigger picture of everything that was happening. And what you say is absolutely true. Ford Motor Company bought our coke because it was such great quality coke.

And they used it in their actual steel mills.

EK: Absolutely, I have nothing negative about the quality of the coke, it just cost too much to make it.

Yeah. Well, I'm sure when the bean counters came in, the Donald Trautleins of the world who, I'm gonna be honest with you, I always felt that we should have seen Donald Trautlein 15 years before he ever showed up. And I think if that would have been the case, we would have done a lot better. Well, Earl, I want to thank you for participating in this, and I wish you and your family all the best.

EK: Well thanks so much.

LARRY SHEA
20 years of service

Hydraulic Engineers

A gift handed to Bethlehem Steel from the U.S. Navy, Larry came to BSCO after twenty years of serving our country. He started training classes in hydraulics in the plant and was an advocate of in house repair, saving the company untold expense.

****

Today is May the 12ᵗʰ, 2008; we're interviewing Larry Shea. Larry how ya doing today?

LS: Okay pretty good.

Okay, Larry, you told me earlier you didn't have a nickname, so I guess for the purposes of this interview, we'll just call you Larry. Ttell us how you became associated with Bethlehem Steel.

LS: I started in World War II. I worked in the Bethlehem Steel as a minor employee in 1943, 1944, only for, like, the summer.

Okay. Was that right here in the Bethlehem plant?

LS: Right in the Bethlehem plant, I worked down in the electrical department, and I worked down in Forge Specialty.

How did that work as a minor? You had only worked so many hours?

LS: I worked like a regular shift and all, and there were restrictions where I could go and work, and I worked with the repairmen down there, and it was Forge Specialty at the time; it was called Forge Specialty.

And we're talking …

LS: Over at the Saucon plant.

Yeah, we're talkin' at a time when the plant is in full production. They're lookin' for people everywhere, anybody they could get their hands on, they hired.

LS: Yup.

What was your first impression when you walked into the plant?

LS: I was amazed as a 16-year-old guy coming in, a boy coming in the plant. I was just amazed how, how large the plant was and the operations of the plant. I just still could remember the first couple days I was in there. It was just really something.

I had a lot of guys tell me right out … I didn't know if I was gonna last out the week. How did you feel about that? Did that ever cross your mind?

LS: I felt all right, because my dad had worked in the Bethlehem Steel, and he told me all about it, so I was more or less, you know, I heard words about it, so I wasn't actually scared. I just was very cautious going in and looking around; that's the only thing that kind of startled me a little bit, but after a while I got used to it, and was okay. So I worked there until I went in the Navy.

And what time was that?

LS: I went in the Navy the end of '44, at the end of '43, '44 I went in the Navy, and stayed in the Navy till after World War Two. I put about two and a half years in the Navy and come out, and went back to school, and after that I played ball and went back into the Navy again for a while until I got married and more or less got out after that, and then finally went back in again and stayed in for a little over twenty years. I got out in 1969, I got out of the Navy.

And you somehow drifted back towards the plant?

LS: Yeah. I went back. I put a resumé in, and being that I had moved around quite a bit in the Navy, I was always in naval air in the Navy. And what happened, I sent a resumé in to Bethlehem Steel, and I was working in hydraulics. I worked in hydraulics in the service and I taught hydraulics in the service on aircraft. I was always involved with aviation in the Navy. And I worked on aircraft and I taught hydraulics in the Navy. I went to school in the Navy, for instructor's training school, and so I had a resumé in and sent that into Bethlehem Steel and that particular time that they were a little short, engineer, the hydraulic engineer that they had in the plant was a very knowledgeable gentleman named Francis Braun. He was out sick at the time, and I guess you want to call it luckily I picked up my resumé at that particular time and called me in for quite a few interviews, which at that time I was still in the Navy. I was stationed at Lakehurst, New Jersey then.

How about that. So eventually I guess they finally hired ya?

LS: Yeah, they hired me, and I started about a week after I retired from the Navy, so I worked there at different positions, and worked myself up to hydraulic technician. I took a test in Washington, through Washington as a hydraulic engineering technician. So I ended up working as a hydraulic technician, and after that when I filled in for the hydraulic engineer.

Did Bethlehem Steel actually have a pre-requisite for that position that they would want you to have that license?

LS: No, they just come in, and just hired me. Actually, there was nobody in the plant doing hydraulics at all, except Francis Braun; he was a hydraulic engineer. I filled in for him for a while, and then he came back to work, and I worked a few years, and then he retired. So, then I worked for another engineer, Jim Anders. I worked for him for a while, and then I ended up setting up the hydraulic shop for hydraulic repairs for Bethlehem Steel.

I see. Were you training people at the same time?

LS: I was teaching up at millwright training for a while up there. I taught up there off and on for about two and a half years.

Well, that's, that's really interesting to hear, but you know, uh, when you talk about hydraulics, very few people know anything about that, and they have no comprehension about the size of the equipment. Tell us some stories about some of the projects that you worked on like the breakdowns and things like that. What comes right to your mind?

LS: Well, I think the longest place I was at, two places in the plant, was when we put A battery in, down at Coke Works. I was down there for about a year and a half, uh, close to two years, because we put the screen station in first, and from the screen station they worked on A battery, and uh, worked on all the pushers and larry cars, and what they called a blue goose where they used to, it was like a quenching car, and we walked on all the hydraulics in there, and that was quite a project down there. It was a lot of hydraulics in there, and eventually taught millwrights down there hydraulics, which that ended up a little longer than say two and half years maybe that I was actually down in Coke Works.

And give us some sort of an idea about like the size of the blue goose and exactly what did it do?

LS: Okay, what it was it was like a mobile quenching car.

And a quenching car does what?

LS: It quenches the hot coal, coke coming out.

The coke comes out, it's red hot, it's pushed out.

LS: And it goes through this process, and then they could move the car on the railroad track. It was a car similar to like a big long, similar to like a locomotive on the front of it, which you could move. They used to name it the blue goose account of the color and so forth. But the biggest project, I think, down there in the Coke Works was the screen station for a while. What happened, they would, it was set up near automatically that as the cars would come in, railroad cars would come in and get ready for the coke. What happened, they had large hydraulic cylinders implanted in the ground, so what would happen as they would move forward, they had different sizes of coke, and what would happen after we got it set up, the cars would be pulled up, put under the, which was a large building where the coke would be processed and come through, and what would happen as this coke would come in three different tracks, cars would come in three different tracks; we had different sizes of the coke, and what would happen there, they would fill the, this is automatically, would fill these up, and they had like program that as soon as it was approved, when it would get up, the coal would get in the car, would come up so far, and it stopped, and then we'd fill it up and there would be a probe telling it okay, that was, and this was all run by hydraulics. The track would move up, and the gates would open, electronic, electric control.

So to make it short, you had an automated system that was selecting various sizes of coal to go into the coking process?
LS: Yeah, which would go into the cars.

And then it would end up eventually in the blue goose and, you know, be distributed, taken up, probably almost all the coke at one time went up, to our blast furnaces.
LS: Yeah, but uh, blue goose was like a separate part of that system. That was, I would say between that and the battery itself, there was a lot of hydraulics on the battery, so that, the whole Coke Works, there's a lot of hydraulics involved with the whole Coke Works.

How big, Larry, were we talking about as far as these hydraulic cylinders, physical size, and like a capacity?
LS: I'll tell ya a good explanation of that there; when they put it in, people from the system that contracted, built it, engineered it and come in, they would say figure like a cannon. Look at the size of a cannon, a large cannon, and that's how, they called the cylinders were quite big and were cables that ran on cables. After the cylinder come out, it hydraulically wrapped around with a cable. So that would move the car forward. , and uh. My recollection, I think they had three large cylinders.

And the reason for the hydraulic, it was the most dependable method of moving the stuff around.

LS: Yeah, like for the cylinders, yes, the easiest way.

And you did that for a while.

LS: That was about two and a half years I was down there.

Yeah, did you ever do much work in the BOF?

LS: In the BOF, I worked in the BOF, and it used to dump scrap into the furnace, and it had like a cart up there, and that was hydraulic. It would push the steel, the beams into the furnace. It was probably every place in the plant I can remember there was hydraulics, and that was one of the hardest things, too, which was hard in there. There was no hydraulic repairman in the whole plant, and there was a training program to try to train people to get people trained in hydraulics.

So in reality, if you went into the BOF and there was a problem, you would more or less be like the, like, an overseer. You'd make sure everyone was doin' it the way it had to be done. But they were actually under the direction of their own foremen, you were an advisor.

LS: Well, it ended up that way. It looked good on paper, but uh, to be honest with you I had a lot of grievances filed against me, because, Well, what happened, the men, a lot of the men, weren't trained in hydraulics, and you'd go in there and have to be working with the guy, so number one in safety that nobody got hurt, and then they knew what to do and how to do it, and how to set up. All of these systems have to be set up by pressure and tweaked and, that would happen to make sure that the pressure's okay, that something didn't, you know, happen through over-pressure. So this is one of the problems that I think that we lacked in the training of hydraulic people. Now what they have throughout the United States in the hydraulic industry is hydraulic men, hydraulic positions where you would go to school and get trained in hydraulics, so you'd come out as a hydraulic technician or hydraulic repairman.

So you were actually involved in like cutting edge as far as that job went? You were, like, you were doing what you could based on the knowledge you had from the military?

LS: Yeah, and the years that I put in there, yeah.

But by the same token, the company really couldn't go out on a job search and pull in a lot guys like you, could they?

LS: No, no. There was hardly anybody. I think I, and oh, I would say I was about the only hydraulic technician at one time, and I think it was four of us in the State of Pennsylvania at the beginning when we started this, and what happened you would have to take a test, and you could become an engineering assistant, and you would have to get three professional engineers to sign for you, engineers, to sign for you that you worked on a system and you could set up a system, but you would have to have a regular professional engineer to sign for ya. So it, that's the only thing lacking, that I was really against the Bethlehem Steel for not training your men on, into hydraulics. And it was very hard to, you know, to explain things to people, because everything was more or less into a production phase in there, and I could see the company's problem, and I could see the problem of men working in the hydraulic, you know, shop and all that, you know, because they didn't have anybody in hydraulics per se in the plants. There's a real good friend of Mike Stullo down in Sparrow's Point who was a hydraulic engineer down there, and more or less they didn't have a training program set up either. They had, different shops had different people working in hydraulics to make sure some people repaired their own cylinders and some people repaired their own pumps to a certain degree, which they did a lot of shops in the plant here.

Do you get the impression that the guys that you worked with in the various shops were eager for training and it just really wasn't available to 'em? How did that work? I mean, I talked to guys when I worked in the Beam Yard that they always used to say, "Boy, we wish we could get up to Larry's school" and things like, but it didn't always work out for them.

LS: Well, yeah, the thing that I think that was really lacking at the time, the hydraulics come in and the advancement of hydraulics all over in the plant and steel industry it wasn't cut out. What happened, they would call your service people in, whether it was Vickers or Racine or Rexroth, and uh, therefore they were contracting more or less into them to set up the systems for 'em, and then they would leave, and the plant had no back-up people to stay there and get the system, keep the system going, and it was hard that way, and that's the thing; I thought it was very lacking, I would say in the plant, Bethlehem Steel, oh I would say Sparrow's Point, Bethlehem, uh, and I got to go to a few schools while I was in, that they were service schools from the companies, and the company would always say, "Well, you know, who do we have back in Bethlehem that's gonna be doing this?" And it's very hard, you know, it was like having a fire truck with one hose and ten fires, so you'd be running around and trying to get things squared away, and each department there was a lot of good men in each department that I went to, the Coke Works, the Beam Yard, and the BOF, up in Alloy.

There was a lot of good men, and you know, it's a shame that, you know, they didn't have the training that could help them. You know, down the

Beam Yard we put the punches in down the Beam Yard, the saws, worked on all the saws in the Beam Yard. I don't think there was a … and in MERF I get called down on MERF. I'm working mobile hydraulics, so it was a field that was very lax on training anybody in the plant, and I would say it was darn near that way all over. But it was a shame, that's what I think, it was lacking in the plant. And it was a shame because there was a lot of good repairmen I ran through, like down at Coke Works, the Beam Yard, and the plant had enough good people to keep the systems running.

I could picture, I can picture what you're saying in the sense, you mentioned earlier that there were grievances involved with this, and I could picture that because once the people like Rexroth and that would put in the equipment and leave on the shifts and week to week 24/7, the guys were there taking care of it until they ran up, ran into the wall, and then you had to come in. Now we're talking about you got a superintendent, a general foreman, are all saying, Larry we gotta get this going, it's gotta get going, and you're trying to get this thing going, coordinate all this; at the same time these guys are actually bitter because you're there, but you're actually there to help 'em. And the only way, the only way that they can get any attention, okay, is to file a grievance. Hey, how come no one's teaching us how to do this? How come Larry's gotta come down and do it? Well, Larry came down because there weren't enough people trained. Yeah, that makes perfect sense to me; I mean, it's like human nature.

LS: Yeah, it was just something that was left behind, and, well, what happened, somebody could foresee this, and they have a lot of good technicians, electronic people in the plant that I would get involved with, because later on everything was electronic hydraulic, and you need a good electronic person to go out with you troubleshooting, and that was another part of the plant that was ours.

So those were the controls, yeah.
LS: Yup, so this is what you had.

Well, you know in the time you were down there, I mean, overall did you enjoy working for the company?
LS: Yeah, I enjoyed it. It was very educational for me, and I met a lot of good people, and it was a good company to work for, I thought.

Well you know, everybody's telling me right now that if the company called 'em back, they'd go. Which, you know, is, I find that a little ironic, but, you know, from listening to their stories I can understand why they'd be saying that. They spent more time there with their buddies from Bethlehem Steel than some of them spent with their own families because of the amount of hours they worked. And I think the general public doesn't understand that. I mean, we really, especially the last ten years, I mean it was like a war zone down there. There were guys that sometimes they'd be home once or twice a week, the rest of the time be working double shifts, and uh … When did you first come to the realization that the plant was in trouble?

LS: I would say I was there a few years till I, took me awhile to understand, and when I first started out, they never had a hydraulic technician, and I ended up in the electrical department with engineering, electrical engineers. And uh, they would take me down to the combo mill and show me the combo mill and seeing how that worked, and then they took me other places in the plant, so I stayed with them because somebody had set up a program to set up a hydraulic shop, so I went down and set up a hydraulic shop for them in the lubrication department utilizing the lubrication repairmen, and they did some repair work on all the pumps and valves, certain types, in the plant. So I set up a relatively small hydraulic repair unit for Bethlehem Steel, and we had testing valves and pumps and so forth, and we did that, and it was pretty, I would say a pretty nice set up that they had there toward the end where they were doing, we went into doing all the filters in the plant. We went up to research and got an ultrasonic cleaner, that we could ultrasonically clean the filters in the plant, which was a saving for the plant; we would go to different departments, would set them up and did the filters there, and we set that hydraulic system up and we moved up the line from lubrication, we had to set up a hydraulic shop over in the Saucon engineering building over there, so things worked out pretty well that way.

But yeah, you could see the need, you know each year that was happening, and it was happening all over in the industry, not only for Bethlehem, but the National Floor Power Society, I don't know if I was lucky or it was handed down; I was the educational chairman for the Lehigh Valley Floor Power Society for two years, and it wasn't only in the steel industry, but it was all over, but, getting people involved in hydraulics, it was hard. There was no training for them, there was no actual hydraulic school, although community college had a set up, and I was teaching basic hydraulics toward the end over there. At one time I taught over at Lehigh Valley, Northampton Community College, over at NCACC for a couple courses of hydraulics, and it was something. You know the whole industry was very lacking of training. And what happened, you know yourself, and everybody knows, that electronics went hog wild on training and so forth, their electronic people were an industry; the hydraulics, they weren't training the hydraulic people to be hydraulic repairmen.

Yeah, well you know, we were fortunate in the 414 department; we had a guy named Dean that did all our hydraulic work. He just had his own little area; nobody bothered him; he ordered all his own parts and stuff, and I guess from time to time if he got stuck he probably gave you a call, but we were really lucky because the department, you know, our general foreman, John Chunko, he said, "Wow," he says, "We're just lucky we got a guy like that or we'd be paying through the nose getting all this stuff done." And I guess they had another guy when he came down to the Beam Yard to work over at the 1- inch mill area, they had another guy up there that had worked with him that took over up there at the Saucon mills and was doin' the same thing. But I don't think there were too many areas in the plant where, you know, they were actually doing that.

LS: Well, it seemed like everybody had their own little place that, Coke Works had a place, the guys that were doing their work, and Beam Yard had a place, the mills up in the rolling mills and up in the Saucon division, they had Reinhard, a fellow named Reinhard. Will Reinhard did the repairs up in Saucon, and uh, we worked together with him, and there was, each department more or less had their own hydraulic, they would repair like simple things: cylinders and valves and so forth, but that's what kept everything going, and I think that way was all over in the industry that way. And we ended up ... I think I taught about 900 guys in the plant through the what, five-, six-year period, where everybody would set up. I think you were in one of the classes, if I wasn't mistaken.

I might have been, but I don't think I was in the hydraulic part of it. I think I was up there at the millwright school, okay, when you had the hydraulic school going on, yeah.

LS: It was a good thing for the guys, but that was a whole bit of the hydraulics that I could see in the plant that was very lacking and it was, and it was, I think it was that way all over, and I got involved a lot of times down at MERF, which was our mobile hydraulics.

Mobile Equipment Repair Facility. All the moving equipment in the plant, bulldozers, regular dump trucks, you name it. I mean, the MERF garage was a big place. I remember, I think at one time they had close to 250 people working in there. That was a, down East Lehigh, they called it the cabbage patch.

LS: Yup, yup, and I worked in East Lehigh when the mill was running, so I went out, I seemed to be all over in the plant hydraulically, so...

So here's something. There had to be a point. I would say it was probably around 1985 where most of the people in the plant had a pretty good idea that our days are numbered. Now a lot of people didn't want to believe it. Would you say that that's pretty close to about when people were coming to the realization that if something doesn't happen around here, we're not gonna be here long?

LS: Well, I talked to a lot of people that had been in the plant way longer than I was and different departments you could go to, and they were seeing that, well, you know, the talk of the people that I ran into. I worked more with the guys that were working there in the engineering department in the plant, that asked why we didn't put a continuous caster here. And why, we should be doing this, and, you know. I was like the young kid on the block; I didn't know, you know, I thought what the heck are they talking about? And you could see, you know, guy's minds were changing that we should be doing this or doing that. It was, you know, it was startling to the guys that were there I think that, you know, why aren't we doing this, and we should be doing this or doing that, but...

Well, let's say it was 1985, you were in the plant about 15 or 16 years. If someone would have came to you and said, "Larry, as far as the hydraulic end of it goes, you're in charge; here's your budget; here's what we're gonna give ya." How would you have handled that? Now I know this is in hindsight, but I'm saying to you, what steps would you have done to insure that the plant had a good future, other than the school, which was limited.

LS: Well, I think I would have sent people out for training.

Outside of the plant?

LS: Outside of the plant for training. That they could cope with the people that are bringing the equipment in, and new engineering that's coming in, that they could get involved before the product would come into the plant. Uh, a good example of that was when we put the, which they have up in the Press Forge, which is still operating now under a different company up there is the largest open die press in the United States, which is a hydraulic press; years ago they had steam. So, what happened, Rexroth come in with the hydraulic press, and then all the presses up there were your regular steam presses, or, you know, we're coming in with a hydraulic press or, somebody could have went out and went to the school with the people, engineering, over at Rexroth, and worked, you know, hand by hand until they come in, which would have saved company money, and also, and the down time of the equipment. That would be one thing I would have did I think at the time, and plus the training. You know, and my biggest pet peeve in there was the training, that they should have had more training, and probably I would say it would have lasted a little longer that way hydraulical.

Okay. So overall you enjoyed your time at the plant, you could never get bored in the job you had, cuz things were changing every week, sometimes everyday. And I imagine there were probably a couple days where they changed every hour. So what about the safety end of it? How did that tie in with the hydraulics? I mean that had to be a, like a critical thing in a lot of different areas.

LS: Uh, what we tried to do, they had your JSA's.

Yeah, Job Safety Analysis. Those were, like, how-to books.

LS: Yeah, and what I would do is review a lot of these in different departments, because as a new piece of equipment would come in, you would have to write a JSA on it. And I got involved with a few departments on writing JSA's and the hydraulic part of it. Uh, they had nothing in there pneumatically for, you know, that I was involved with, but that's one thing that I would say was critical in there that they had to have and, which each department more or less would write up their own JSA's for the hydraulic equipment you have. So that was the one big feature safety-wise, and thank God we never lost anybody hydraulically to my knowledge. Maybe before I got there or anything, but it was critical that, you know, you have to watch. Especially, I used to get a little scared down the Beam Yard, because you know the saws would be running and I had to go out troubleshooting somewhere down there, and I always used to try to get a foreman to go with me, either Frank Dowling when he was down there, or Chunko or somebody that, give me somebody to take me out to the different place of the plant where they had a problem or in the yard where they had a problem. That more or less, any place in the plant, even up at the BOF I wasn't too … I used to get scared down the Beam Yard. I don't know if it was mental or what.

I think it was probably a combination of the movement and the noise.

LS: Yeah.

I mean, I remember when I was down the Beam Yard. We'd see these guys come in from other departments because, you know, they were pool jobs; they were laid off, and they'd get down there to the Beam Yard, and I mean these guys were like a nervous wreck for; it'd, take 'em, you know, like ten days to thirty days before they felt comfortable just walking around down there because of the movement. And then it didn't help any that the guys would be telling 'em war stories about, you know, before they had the aprons on the roller lines; how many guys that met an untimely end down there, and it was, it was a circus; it was a real circus. But you know, we came to be used to that, and it became a way of life. Did you ever, were you ever injured at the plant?

LS: No. Luckily, I got hit with oil a few times, but other than that, no I lucked out. Never got, I think I was a little more tentative, a little more careful about where I was going and what was happening at the operation of it. You know, I was in a lot of hairy spots in the plant, uh, and the hydraulic pressures went up. Right now the hydraulic pressures in the plant before it closed and everything it was 5000 PSI, so you're going from years ago where 500, 1000, 1500 PSI. Now you're working with 5000 PSI. You have to be very careful then, that, you know, and that's where the training came in of safety got involved in the plant, about teaching the fellas what to do, how to work on a system, make sure it's shut down, make sure you bled the accumulators and you could work on it. It can, uh, you had to be very careful; the men had to be very careful. And like I say, thankful, you know, thank God that everything worked out and didn't have any hydraulic casualties to my knowledge. Maybe before, but not when I could remember, getting killed hydraulically.

Actually, Larry, you're one of the few guys that I've interviewed so far that can speak on the technical aspects of the job. You know when you talk to a Blast Furnace guy, he talks about doing repetitious dangerous work. You talk to an ore handling guy, he talks about handling ore. You know, you talk to a Coke Works guy, he talks to you about, you know, the hazards involved at the Coke Works; you know the heat, the gas, everything like that, but this was very interesting in the fact that you know, you were actually in a more technical aspect than anybody I've had so far, and I really like to thank you for this interview, and I wish the best for you and your family.

LS: Thank you very much.

Okay.

CARL RIEKER
44 years of service

Carpenters

Carl lived up to his nickname, "Tiger." To know him was to love him. Always a go-getter, Carl still runs reunions for the men he worked with.

* * * * * * * * * *

Okay, it's August 29th, 2008, and we're here with Carl Rieker. Carl, how you doing today?

CR: I'm doing very well, thank you.

Carl, did you have a nickname in the plant?

CR: Yeah, they used to call me Tiger, T-I-G-E-R.

Tiger, so what should we call you for this interview?

CR: Well, you can call me Carl, please.

Okay. Okay, okay Tiger, ooh, that's right, it's Carl. Carl, I see here you started in the plant back in November of 1952. How did you even find out the company was hiring?

CR: Well, I went down. I used to carry newspapers in Catty when I was a kid in high school, and there was a fellow that I used to carry out in East Catty. His name was Ray Wert, and he asked me, and I used to play ball with his kids and everything in high school, and he asked me, "Why don't you come down to the Bethlehem Steel when you graduate from high school?" Well, I went down to the Horseshoe in Catty because I didn't have a car, and I worked down there at the Horseshoe at Front and Race, at Front Street in Catasauqua, I could walk there, and then I decided after I had appendicitis that I'm gonna try to get a job at the Bethlehem Steel. I hitchhiked to Bethlehem Steel, and I found a job as a laborer. November 19th, 1952.

What were you in the Lehigh or the Saucon plant?

CR: I was at the Saucon plant, and my boss' name was Nick Glosen, and we were with six guys. We worked together with six guys every day cleaning the furnaces out, cleaning the soaking pits out. And one day I saw Ray Wert, who was a carpenter foreman. He said to me, why don't you try to get in to carpenter apprenticeship, so I thought, "Well, what prayer do I have, all I did was graduate from high school." He said, Try it," and I did, and I made it, and I started in the carpenter shop in March of 1953 as a carpenter apprentice. I worked my way through carpenter apprentice school, it was a four-year course. I did it in four years, I got my A rate after six years, and I was in the carpenter gang until 1977.

Okay. Now, that first day in the plant, you must have been like, what am I doing here? What was it like?

CR: The first day I started in the plant, I thought what did I do? They gave me a pair of wooden shoes to wear over my shoes, they sent me into a hot furnace to throw bricks out that were knocked down from the roof in an open hearth. I had to, after that was done the next day I had to go down into what they called the flues which was in the cellar of the open hearth. I couldn't stand up. It was too small. We had to shovel dirt into buckets that were on conveyor lines and shove 'em over into openings in the floor so that the guys up on the top could lift them up and dump 'em and send 'em back down empty, and this was for eight hours, and I thought, "My God, what did I do?" I had a nice job in the Ford shop at the Horseshoe down in Catasauqua, but I thought well, this is the only way I can get into apprenticeship. So I slugged it out in the labor gang with guys that were tough guys, and I finally was able to get in as a carpenter apprentice. And some of the jobs that I did in the labor gang were unbelievably tough, and people don't realize how tough.

Hot.

CR: Hot. We wore handkerchiefs over our faces so that our mouths wouldn't burn. Now they have respirators and everything. In those days we just wore handkerchiefs, and our ears were burning and everything else, and we wore gloves and long sleeves and sweaters so that we wouldn't burn up when we worked on the pan, where the hot metal was. As soon as they would tap a furnace at the open hearth, when they were done, they would let it cool off a little bit until it turned black. Then we went in there and we had to clean everything out so that the carpenters could put the pan scaffold in. The pan scaffold was just a scaffold for the bricklayers to stand on and work. It was made out of bars and plank, which usually burned up, but the firemen were there to put water on to quench it in case it caught fire. And it was a tough job, let me tell ya.

I'll tell ya. That's the best description I've heard so far from a laborer about what it was like working in them open hearths, and I talked to some guys that did it for years. And the one guy came right out, he told me, he says, "Look," he says, "passing out in them furnaces was a way of life." I says, "Well, were you taking salt pills?" "They always used to push salt pills," he says, "but I never took 'em," he says, "because I ran into an old guy, he says don't take the salt pills, they're worse for you, and they don't do you good." He says, "Just make sure every time you go in there you drink water." He says, "You're gonna sweat," he says. "Y gonna get tired, but" he says, " if you take the salt pills there's no telling what'll happen to ya." And you know the company finally discontinued their use. Nobody could prove they did any good for ya.

CR: No, they didn't do any good for ya. And everybody tried, some people took salt pills. They said that it put some of the salt back into your system that you're sweating out, but I never took any, because when you're 18, 19, 20 years old you figure I can handle anything, so you didn't do it, you know. Today maybe it's a different story. But when I was in the labor gang, they hooked me up with people that live in Northampton that I could get a ride to work every day, and on the way home from signing my papers at the Bethlehem Steel that I go the job, which I never saw Bethlehem in my life. In those days you didn't travel too far like kids today. I come out of the employment office and I saw an old Dutch Brewery truck, and I know Old Dutch beer was made in Catasauqua, and I asked the guy if he is going to Catasauqua after he's done with his deliveries, and he said yes, and I said could I have a lift home, and he said absolutely, and I got in his truck, and about an hour and a half later I got back to Catasauqua, and my mom said where were you, and I told her that I quit the, that I'm working at the Bethlehem Steel starting tomorrow, and I got a ride to work the next day, and I got with a gang that took me to work every day, and in March I got a job in the carpenter gang, and in the carpenter gang they had people from Catasauqua that lived, that I knew since I was a little boy. They got me back and forth to work, and that's how I communicated from Catasauqua to the Bethlehem Steel until I got my own car.

Yeah, now that apprenticeship was it on the job training?
CR: Apprenticeship was on the job.

In addition to classroom, right? Tell me how that worked.
CR: Oh yeah. The apprenticeship was on the job training. We worked every day; we worked Monday, Tuesday, Wednesday, and Thursday. Friday morning we went to apprentice school, which was on the third floor of Number 2 machine shop, and the boss there his name was John Shook, and his secretary was a guy named Mr. Zink. I can't think of his first name.

But they treated us with dignity, and there was all different trades in there, and it was the ICS course, International Correspondence School, and it was a four-year course, and I did it in three years because we did a lot of overtime in the carpenters in those days, so I got my 6,000 hours in before the four years were up, so I graduated as a C carpenter, and after six months I became a B carpenter, and after six months I became an A carpenter, and I had my own gang after that. So I had my own gang, and a carpenter gang, which was another dangerous high job, and I did that job for 27 years, and we were secondary indirect, which I never could understand what secondary indirect means, our incentive pay was secondary indirect, which I never could understand what that was, and so I transferred from the carpenters in 1977 to the riggers, which was indirect, and there I made more money than I could make in the carpenter shop, and everything went better for me there, plus it was a little more dangerous, a little higher jobs and they knew that I could climb and everything like that. I went into the riggers as a rigger helper and worked my way to a B rigger after I passed my tests. And I was happy with being a B rigger for 17 years, and I wound up with 44 years in the plant.

As a carpenter, describe some of the jobs that you would do?

CR: In the carpenters I used to have to go up on the roof with a gang of guys, and most of those guys were good climbers like I thought I was. We had to tear off old sheet iron on buildings that were 90, 110, 125 feet high. We had to put new sheet iron on. We tried to do a bay, a bay and a half a day, it all depend on how big it was. We had bosses that were very good to us, and they understood that we had to rip it off, we had to chop the old rivets off, we had a ground man. We had four guys. We had a guy running a drill, a guy with a nut runner to put the bolts back in. We had a couple of guys that worked ahead of us tearing the sheets off. It was a tough dangerous job because you always had to worry whether or not you were stepping on deteriorated old sheet iron that you could fall through, which I saw somebody do it one time. His name was John, I can't think of his last name, he lived in Northampton. He fell through the roof, and he landed on a crane, thank God. He landed on a crane which was like 20 feet under him, and uh, he lived through it, thank God for that. And they wanted us to wear safety belts on jobs that were really high, but like I said when you're young and you don't care, you don't feel like you should wear safety belts, it is the thing to do. And in fact later on I'll tell you that when I was in the riggers I did fall, and after I fell then I decided that I think it is time now to wear a safety belt.

Yeah, I can imagine. That educated you real quick.

CR: Real quick.

It doesn't take long to figure out, you know, when your life's at stake here, you gotta do the right thing.

CR: When you have time in the hospital, you think, "What did I do wrong?"

So you were on a roofing crew there. What else did you do at the riggers? Did you almost stay with that exclusively?

CR: I was mostly on the roof gang and the carpenter gang, because they used to put certain guys on the roofs all the time, and in the wintertime when things were tough they put us like in the machine shops putting new hardwood floors in, things like that, you know. But most of the time, even when it was cold out, we worked on the roofs, and top of the blast furnaces, we worked putting scaffolds in for different trades, the electricians, the riggers.

Scaffolds were a big thing weren't they?

CR: Scaffolds was the number one job for most trades. We went into all the pipes at the blast furnace, which were bustle pipes, bleeder pipes, you name it. We went in there, and we did all of the work for the laborers. We put the main scaffold in the blast furnaces without lookers. We did all that work so that the laborers could go in there with jackhammers and they could knock the brick down that the furnace was lined with. We put scaffolds in every pipe in the blast furnace so that the laborers could go in there and tear the brick out, and brick layers could use our scaffolding, and after we rebuilt it back up again to put the new brick back in.

Now, when you were with the carpenter gang, how many guys were in that shop? Did you know?

CR: When I started in the Bethlehem Steel company in the carpenter gang in 1952, '53, March of '53, there were 365 carpenters in the shop. In those days everybody carried a carpenter box full of tools, and as things progressed, people didn't have to carry tools anymore, because they had power equipment then. They had, when I started there we had two man saws to do car blocking and machine shop, when we blocked big forgings in that with big timbers, we used two man saws back in the early '50s. Then we had power drills. We had chain saws. We had electric drills. Everything was electric then, and things progressed. Today they have battery powered drills and battery powered saws, where in those days we used everything by hand, and uh, so when I started as a young fella in the carpenter gang, you had to have a complement of tools, and they made sure, the carpenter foremen made sure that you had a full complement of tools, because that was very important in those days that you have yourself a hammer, a saw, and a hatchet. Today nobody uses hatchets because they have electric stuff. Everything is taken care of.

What would you use a hatchet for?

CR: Well, when we were on a big form job, like when we worked down East Lehigh on a big form job when I was in the carpenter gang, the job was a mile long and it was several forms, and we were on that job for one year, and we had to use the hatchets to make stakes to hold the braces that were holding the forms. There were so many things that we had to use hand tools for. Today they have tools that are battery powered, where they can just drive a nail in with a battery powered gun. In those days, we used hammer and nails, and uh, everything is different today than it was then. But that job down at East Lehigh, we put a new rolling mill in for them people down there. It took one year, and we did several, several, several form jobs, and in those days.

Out of the 12- and 14-inch mill.

CR: That's right, in those days the labor gang made more money pouring concrete into our forms than we did as carpenters building the forms. As a carpenter I used to holler about that, and I was told it is none of my business, and that is a fact, and we could never do anything about it. Our job was to build the forms.

Well, from listening to over 80 people already talk about the incentive in the plant, it's obvious that the incentive in the plant was a tool used by management to hold down wages.

CR: That's right.

And what it was, it was a mind controlling thing. They would tell you it was just like Joseph Goebbels, they would tell you so many lies about why you couldn't make more money. You actually began to believe 'em yourself. And consequently, when you started doing that, they did nothing, and nothing got done.

CR: Nothing got done. When we finally got an incentive program in the carpenter shop, we were called secondary indirect, and we had to go, and I could never understand why a secondary indirect person, there is nothing that is secondary indirect. There, you can't explain what secondary indirect is.

Well, it's just a rate of pay that's derived by man hours.

CR: That's right.

That's production.

CR: When I used to ask people in other departments, like a machine shop guy, I have all the admiration in the world for a machinist, but he got direct incentive because he was producing a product. But without the carpenters fixing his machine up with platforms and you name it, he could not function at his job. So I always thought that we were involved in his job in some way or another. We went on top of the blast furnace in the middle of the winter to put a scaffold up, and we were paid secondary indirect so that somebody down below could get direct incentive. And as a shop steward I yelled and hollered about it, and that's one of the reasons why I guess maybe today we're on secondary indirect as carpenters and direct and indirect as riggers, I guess we never advance from there.

So you did everything as far as carpenters went from making doors to framing?
CR: Oh yeah, everything. When we had a job, we had a job where we had...

A lot of concrete forms?
CR: Oh everything. We did everything that you could think of. In fact, I thank God every day for the knowledge that I gained as a carpenter because it helped me build my own home, and every time I got laid off, which was eleven times in thirteen years I was laid off from the Bethlehem Steel carpenter department, I was laid off eleven times, I found work with contractors, and I got jobs building homes, and I knew what I was doing, knock on wood, thank God.

Okay. Okay. Now we're gonna talk, because you told me that you put this house we're in right now, you put it up yourself. What year was that Carl?
CR: That was 1955 I built this house.

Well, you were just a young puppy then.
CR: I was only 21/22 years old when I built this house, and it was all farmland, and I had to borrow the lumber, I got the lumber from Whitehall Supply Company, who I had worked for when I was laid off. They gave me the lumber to have it built, to build the house until I had it on the roof then I could get a mortgage. I went to the Catasauqua Bank, they said I was too young for a mortgage, I had to go to the Palmerton Bank who didn't even know me, and they gave me a mortgage for $75 a month, $75 a month. And I keep thinking $75 a month, and I had to beg.

Do you remember what your initial cost was to build this?
CR: I built this whole house, $8,900. and it's all brick, even the brick ends, and I built the two homes down on the next street there with a contractor, so I know what ours is worth, and as years went by, then I put the garage on, and I often wondered why you pay $1,000 to put a garage

on and put a $50 car in it, and that's all the car was worth in those days you know.

Yeah. So now you're into the riggers. What do the riggers do?

CR: Well, the riggers had more dangerous high jobs than anything, and uh, we had to go on top of the blast furnace. We had to make sure we put the rigging up so that the people could get brick up to the top of the blast furnace. We had to go and we had to do all the welding and all the sanding and everything, grinding that took care of, so that we had to grind all of the bad spots out so that the welders and the riggers could weld it. We had to go and we had to put new girders in. We had to reinforce the blast furnace so that it wouldn't fall down, and to this day I still don't understand how A furnace is still standing when the girders must be like razor blades. That hasn't been maintained in how many years? It wasn't maintained when I was still working, and I don't understand how it's still working that they have it there, but we had five blast furnaces in those days. We had A, B, C, D, and E, and we used to go on E blast furnace, and we would, I'll never forget we had to rebuild every year, because the Great Lakes was frozen, and they couldn't get ore down the Great Lakes, so they used to always schedule a blast furnace rebuild in the middle of the winter, and I never could understand it until they told me that is why. The riggers used to be a climbing outfit, and that's the way it was. I was at the blast furnace in 1980. I fell 27 foot there, and I had a fellow that was with me, his name was Bobby Mertz, one of the best, he lives in Palmerton today, and he told me that I fell. They took four discs out of my back, and they said that I would never walk again, but with a lot of prayers I walked, and I'm back in the riggers. When I came back in the riggers about eight months later I got back to work again, and they told me they made me a ground man, and I worked my way back up to the top, but then I wore a belt, because I didn't want to fall again. I guess you have to get hurt in order to have a little brains.

What year was that that you had your accident?

CR: That was 1980. 1980 I fell. I was in the hospital for the longest time. They had me in the hospital and they had for me a lift, I used to go, they had some kind of a rig set up on top of my bed where I could go and lift myself up to try to build my arms up and my body up a little bit, but I couldn't move my legs. They were gone. But everything is back to shape now, thank God in heaven, you know. I'm back as a normal person, and after I was about another 13 years before I quit the Bethlehem Steel, I was 62 then. Well, the Bethlehem Steel was ready to shut down in another month or two before I got out of there, so I had my time in and everything was good.

Carl, with the riggers, what would you say was the most challenging job you were ever on?

CR:　The most challenging job I was ever on was going up on the top of the roof where the bricklayers have the, the bricklayers do the submarines, they brick the submarines. We had to go up on the roof.

The submarines were what?

CR:　The submarines were the subs that are full of hot metal for the blast furnace. They bring that in on the railroad car, and they were called subs, submarines. And we had to go into the submarine shop and that was between Saucon and Lehigh, between Lehigh and Saucon, that's where this mill was. We had to go up on the top of that roof. They had, and they had, on top of the roof they had a monitor, also a monitor, and we had to go up on there, and in order to get out there to put new steel beams in, we had to get the dirt off the walkway which was rounded off.

That was pretty bad, and that was pretty dangerous, and you think of all the dangerous jobs, which I'll think of tomorrow probably, but one that really pops into my mind now, when I was in the carpenters, I'll never forget we went to the high house, which is, you can see the high house from the Minsi Trail Bridge, you can see the high house. They used to use the high house to make any aircraft guns during the war, and they used to take these 35, 40, 50, 60, 100 foot beams, big guns and shove 'em down into something to get 'em strong. So we had to go up on the roof, and I'll never forget, I'm walking down the roof, a guy was holding my safety belt, and I was standing on the lap screws to make sure that we would start to take the sheet iron off. Now this was a highly pitched roof, and didn't the rope break, and thank God in heaven I caught myself on a lap screw, or I would've went down about 200 foot and got killed, and that has to be one of the scariest jobs that I think I was ever on as both a carpenter and a rigger. I think I can remember that, and every time I drive across the Minsi Trail Bridge just to see how things are changing down there, which they have, I look at that building and I think, look at that roof, it's still there.

Another one was when I was in the carpenters we were on a swing scaffold. We were putting sheet iron up on Number 2 machine shop, we had to put a new elevator in Number 2 machine shop, and through the roof we went with a big shanty for the elevator mechanism, and since we were on secondary indirect the first thing you think of is "I gotta make money on this job," so we had a ground man, and we had lugs welded on these big channels for our swing scaffold, which had to be about 125 feet in the air. So when we got done putting the sheet iron on this section, we had to jack the scaffold all the way to the ground, which would have taken maybe three quarters of an hour, but myself said what I want everybody to do go back up on the roof and we're gonna tie the swing scaffolds up to those lugs with ropes, we're gonna disconnect the cables, we're gonna put them over on the other ones, and when they are connected, we're gonna cut the ropes and let the swings swing over, and then we're ready for the next section. We saved ourselves maybe two hours of work, and I think that we had to go to the main office to find out how we made so much money on that job knowing that it was a dangerous job and we didn't get much pay for it. So we got more money for it.

I filed a grievance one time, and I said one of the guys that used to be in my gang was now a rate setter, and I said in front of all the big shots and all the union people, and in front of all the people from the industrial relations that set our incentive up, how come that if this fellow, and I pointed to the old fellow that was in the carpenter gang with me, and me worked on a job for many many years, and it always took us eight hours, why are you only giving me six hours to do the job now? And when they walked out of the carpenter shop office to have a little pow wow, my boss, who happened to be Phil Sabatino, a carpenter boss, he said to me, "You got 'em now." When they came back in, they said to me, "We're gonna eliminate our book work. However we calculate a job and the way we're gonna make the job is exactly how we have it, you and this fellow, pointing to the guy that used to be in the gang with me, must have goofed off all those years, because this is a six-hour job, not an eight-hour job, and I said to my boss, "Now that's it. Now I'm going to the riggers because you people are unbelievable" and that's why I went to the riggers.

Wow.
CR: One of the reasons I went to the riggers was you just could not get through to the incentive program that we as carpenters, hard working people, could get through to these people, so.

So, uh, what do you have to say now to the people that you meet on the outside that will make comments like, if you wouldn't have been cooking on middle shift and sleeping on night shift you'd still have a job. What do you say to those people?
CR: I say you're full of baloney. Because if everybody that you think of says, "Aw youse walked through the main gate with a six-foot plank to sleep on," that's wrong. And I admit there were days when I had good days, but there was more days that I had rough days, and I would say if I had

one day a month that I had it good where I was a ground man or I was a watchman, or I was just watching, that's great, but I would honest to God say that it hurts, it hurts, it hurts. I talked to a guy one time, he was a school teacher, which is a great job, and I won't even say what school district he was at, but he crossed the picket line to go to work when the janitors were on strike, and this is wrong because in unity there is strength. You never, ever, ever cross a picket line. When I was building this house Two Guys from Harrison who I did a lot of business with buying paint and stuff like that, they went on strike, I did not cross their picket line, and I told all the fellows at work not to go through their picket line, if they did I don't know, but…

Do you think you could have worked in that plant without the union?
CR: No, absolutely not. Because if I would've worked in that plant without the union I probably would've been fired in about six months, because first of all in the summer time when a boss' kid comes home from college, the kid needs a job, so right away they're gonna get rid of me and give the boss' kid a job, and that's, and the union would stop that,. They would stop that immediately, thank God for the union. And all the arguments I got into, and most of the guys that were, I would say everybody felt the same way. If it wasn't for the union, we wouldn't have a job, and that's the honest to God's truth, and I'm still a die-hard union man. You know, like when I drive somebody and I see somebody doing something, I say, I hope it's a union job, and they laugh like crazy, and it is.

Now, when you finally had some time there in the plant, you know like over 30 years, you moved onto Ingot Mould foundry, what did you do there?
CR: Yeah, I went to Ingot Mould, I had 38 years in the plant, and I went, the guy that was a carpenter at Ingot Mould, we were down in Ingot Mould oh maybe six months before that, we had to put new girders in the sand-slinger shop, and it was a tough job, and he said to me, and I knew him because he used to be in the carpenter gang when I was in the carpenters, and then I went to the riggers for 20 years, but he said to me, you know I'm going pension next month, why don't you put your name in for this job? Now that job is strictly seniority, but you had to have some knowledge of the trade. So I put my name in for it, and by God I got the job, and when I got the job at Ingot Mould nobody was allowed to go into that carpenter shop, and I said this is wrong, this is wrong. And I'm not bragging about it, but I made benches. I made chairs for people to come in and sit down instead of standing out there in the middle of the winter warming their hands over cold buckets of coke, come into the carpenter shop where it's warm and let's do things for you, whatever you want me to do. Whatever

I had to do, I had to do a lot of things for the department, and I got along good with them. I organized things like picnics and caterings, and we had a nice time, and we all get along, in fact we have a picnic once a summer all the guys in Ingot Mould foundry, and there's some people that I don't even know because I got there they had already been on pension, but then I had guys that came from the riggers, and the carpenters used to come down and say hello to me and see how things are going, you know, and I had no problems at all. I got out of the Bethlehem Steel in 1995, and I honest to God, I can say I made a great living there. I had four kids.

And what do you miss the most about it?

CR: The most I miss about it is to go in there and see the guys again. You know what really hurts the most? I went to a viewing down in Coopersburg. I drove down past the plant to go to this man's viewing who worked in the carpenter gang in the riggers with me, and I look in and I thought my God what happened to this place? All of a sudden Bethlehem Steel is now a casino. Now right away they blame the union for that, but the union didn't bring people over from China and Japan and show 'em how to make steel, the company did. And that's what makes me mad, and I'm not blaming the company for everything. Maybe the union could've stopped it, but I just think that every time I look at the Bethlehem Steel now, and when I was working there and people would come in that took their pension 10/15 years ago and we blah blah blah we'd have a good time talking to them all, then I think now I don't have that. I can't go back into the Bethlehem Steel and say hi to people that I knew all those years, you know, it's a chance meeting at the mall or something like that, or a picnic like we have or something like that, and I think that something should have been done.

What year, what year did you come to the realization that plant was in trouble?

CR: I came to the realization that the plant was in trouble about 1985. When I saw Comfort Inn on the other side of the Hill to Hill bridge, building that Comfort Inn with foreign steel while the Beam Yard was a mile and a half down the road, now something stinks. Now that wasn't the union's fault, that was the company's fault, that was the people that built the Comfort Inn with foreign steel and foreign labor, and I don't want to be a racist or anything like that, but I still say if the Bethlehem Steel is right here on the corner, you do not use anybody else's steel but the Bethlehem Steel's, and when I saw that big coliseum being built at Beijing for the Olympics, I thought to myself, wow, what a wonderful thing for us if we would have had that building to build. It's all built with foreign steel, it's foreign to us but it's not foreign to them. They didn't use American steel to build that building, they used their own steel to build that building.

Carl, if you had an opportunity during your time at Bethlehem Steel to change something that was being done over and over again, what would it have been?

CR: It would have been to keep all foreigners out of the plant as salesmen. They would not be allowed into our plant. I want to know what they're doing in there? If a guy was building a house across the street from me and he came into my house and said how did you build this, I want to build one just like yours, and I want to undersell it, I would kick him out of my house. Now you mean to tell me that the Bethlehem Steel left foreigners, and I don't say what kind of foreigners they were, left them into our plant. What were they coming in for, for the hell of it? They came in to find out how we made steel, and they undercut us. When I was a kid.

They came in and ate our lunch.

CR: Absolutely. When I was a kid I could walk through the alleys in Catty and North Catty, and I would see women in there with sewing machines making clothes for different, like Town & Country, Polera Brothers, Phoenix Clothes. Today you're lucky if you can buy an American flag made in America, and that is the honest to God's truth. It's a shame. And you know what worries me more than anything else, I wonder what our grandchildren's, our great-grandchildren's lives are going to be like in this country.

Well, Carl, I want to thank you for this interview, one of the best ones I've come across so far because I could tell from the way you were, how would you put it, continuing on with your speech that this wasn't something that was rehearsed or anything. It came from the heart.

CR: Aw no, absolutely.

Alright, I wish the best to you and your family. Thank you.

CR: Thank you Buddy, God bless ya.

LESTER CLORE
32 years

Riggers

Served 20 years on plant grievance committee. Chairman of the plant contracting out committee. His favorite saying was "the truth is the ultimate defense for slander."

* * * * * * * * *

This is the interview with Lester Clore from the rigging department. It's February the 15th, 2008. Lester, how you doing today? Let me ask you something, when did you start at Bethlehem Steel?

LC: I started at Bethlehem Steel on July the 6th, 1964.

Was there anything remarkable about, you know, how you came to be hired? I mean, how did you get there? Why did you show up that day?

LC: Well, my father worked for Bethlehem Steel, and at that time Bethlehem Steel was hiring. I went down for my employment interview, and when I was interviewed, they gave me an option of working at the Blast Furnace, Ingot Mould foundry, the yards. Well, my wife and I had five children, so I asked them, where can I make the most money? And they said probably the place you'd make the most money is Ingot Mould foundry, but you might want to go down to look at it before you decide to work there.

Well, you know, that's ironic that you would say that, because so many guys said to me, "The only way, the only reason I ended up in Ingot Mould foundry was that nobody, nobody, knew any better, and I didn't know any better either." Well, how was it down at Ingot Mould foundry?

LC: Well, uh, Ingot Mould in 1964, the dust was so heavy in that shop, the sand from the slingers, and making sand molds, that's what we did, we made sand molds, and then poured iron into 'em, molt lining, and we made ingots. And if there was another worker twenty feet away from me, he looked like a shadow Frank. I mean, that's how bad the dust was in that department, and in that dirt, that sand was of course bedinite, pitch, which is a coal derivative, and it was pretty nasty.

And did you know at the time it was loaded with silica? Was that sort of like a best-kept secret when you started?

LC: Well, I'll tell you a little story. I was working, and here come a guy, we called him the organ grinder. He had just like an organ that they used to have the monkeys on, he cranked the handle and sucked air, and he took air samples, and I asked him, I said, "Hey, buddy, will this dirt hurt me?" He said, "Don't worry about it, sonny; it's too big to get in your lungs."

That's, you know, that's really amazing, because over the many, many years, you know, that both of us worked at the plant, we always used to hear, it was like a joke to us. If it had to do with safety and it cost money, they didn't want to know about it.

LC: That was in the beginning, that's how it was.

And there really, really was no industrial hygiene, I mean, to speak of. Okay, well you know the first couple of years you were there, like the first ten years, how would you say the company, like looked on their employees? Just as another number, or thank God we got somebody that works here? How was it?

LC: I think Frank at Ingot Mould it was kind of unusual, because of the conditions, they were so bad, that the guys really stuck together. At that time in '64 we had 700 people working in the Ingot Mould foundry.

And I'll give you another example, I was a laborer, and worked out of line up, and the foreman's name was Steven Swedis, and Stevie says, "Uh, Clore, pitch cars." Now the pitch cars were railroad cars, and in the railroad cars they had bags of pitch, and I forget exactly what the weight of the bags was, around sixty pounds, but if you got assigned to the pitch car, it was your job to take those pitch bags, throw 'em on top of a big metal box, and they gave you a knife, and you sliced open a bag, and you dumped this pitch in this metal box. From there that metal box was taken, it was mixed in with the sand and the mullers. Well, on a windy day, that pitch just blew all back over you. When you sweat, that pitch, your skin was like raw. I mean it just burned you. And they gave you a little bottle of green soap that was supposed to cure all. It was a little bottle of lanolin soap, and you were supposed to go in the shower at the end of the shift and use that, but the next day, you were still all wet. So I came out the following day, Swedis says, "Clore, pitch cars." I said, "Wait a minute, wait a minute, look at me, my skin's all red, I'm all raw for Christ's sake; it's somebody else's turn in the box. He said, "You don't want to do it? You either get in there or go home." So I made my way to the phone, called up the union hall; the union hall within a couple of hours had a representative down there. The outcome was, and they said you either change this or we're gonna shut this shop down. And I'll never forget the guy that came down, his name was Owen McFadden.

A legend at the Bethlehem plant.

LC: What a great guy. And anyway, the result was the union got involved. The company agreed to build silos, where a car would come in with a hopper on the bottom, it would open up, and the pitch would go in the hopper and then be taken into the silo, the pitch silo, so that we didn't have to empty that car by hand anymore. So, in return for doing that, we agreed to continue the work until they could get it built, and within six months they had it built.

So would you say that that was your first sort of like official dealing with the union?

LC: That was my first experience with the union.

Well, I can see right now it made a big impression on ya, and for the people who are going to be looking at this interview that we're having, they're gonna understand further down the road when they read what we're talking about. Now, you know when you're down there, tell us about the good times you had at Ingot Mould? There's gotta be something sticks out in your mind.

LC: Well, like I said, we had 700 people. Uh, we were scheduled off Wednesday and Sunday; we never got a weekend off, and that was because of the way the hot metal was sent to Ingot Mould. We were the, on the bottom of the list. And every Friday, I'm sorry every Saturday, those of us that were working said, that's it, we're going home early. So we would get our pieces all made, and the foremen would kind of turn their back, and we would go home a couple hours early. And of course we punched out, there was nothing illegal about it, and they kind of worked with us in that respect. But the biggest thing were the guys Frank. It was like a big family. They were always joking around, always kidding, as hard as the conditions were.

That's amazing. How long were you there?

LC: I was, uh, from 1964 to 1971 I worked in Ingot Mould foundry.

And then in '71 what happened?

LC: 1971 there was a posting that went up for a rigger apprenticeship, so I put in for the rigger apprenticeship, and by then the company had, they agreed to go ahead and let me take the apprenticeship. I was a successful bidder. But at that time, in order to get released, your department had to agree to release you. If Ingot Mould would've said no, we're gonna keep him here, then I would have been stuck in Ingot Mould.

That was prior to the consent decree.

LC: That was prior to the consent decree. But Rudy Ashman, who, and Slim Kardis, Slim was the general foreman, and Rudy of course was the superintendent; when I talked to them about it, they said if that's what you want, we won't stand in your way.

I understand Rudy Ashman at one time was one of the highest paid superintendents in the plant. Do you know anything about that?

LC: Just rumors, Frankie. We were the highest producing foundry in the world, tonnage-wise.

Right here in Bethlehem, PA.

LC: Right here in Bethlehem, PA.

All right, that's really something. I can remember stories about guys that couldn't get released. Did you have like some inside information on the riggers, or was it just something you wanted to get out of the dirt?

LC: Well, I just wanted to get out of those conditions. It didn't take a genius to know that it was no good to suck that dirt in all the time.

And it wasn't easy work either, was it? Actually going to the riggers was almost like a break for ya?

LC: Yeah, I figured it out, and when we made bottoms, and we did all the shoveling of sand by hand at that time to make bottoms, I figured I shoveled about sixty tons a day.

Wow. That is really something. Now, what can you tell us about the riggers?

LC: Well, I went to the riggers in 1971 in the apprenticeship. I put 8,000 hours in the rigger apprenticeship. I graduated from the apprenticeship as a rigger C. That was in 1975. So, by that time I had become involved with the union, and I decided to just take a rigger B test. I took the rigger B test, and uh, I was given the rating of a rigger B. Then again in about 1987 I took the rigger A test and became an A rigger.

Now during this time, though, you ran for elective office at the union hall.

LC: I ran for the grievance committee in about 1973.

Okay, did you win the first time?

LC: Yes I did.

How long were you on the grievance committee?

LC: Total of about 23 years.

Wow, that's really saying something. That's like fighting a war in itself. You were a veteran, too, weren't you Les?

LC: Yeah, I was a veteran during the Vietnam era. I was fortunate enough that I didn't have to go to Vietnam, but I was in special forces, the 101st Airborne, and the last outfit I was with was the, was called the 11th Air Assault, and I went to the 11th when they were just forming to help them form the 11th, and uh, right after I got out, they disbanded the 11th Air Assault, renamed it the First Air Calvary, and shipped the whole division over to Vietnam.

Wow. Now, now there's some talk going around, Les, that I heard at your pension party about your group with the Fifth Army being the first to ever wear the Green Beret?

LC: Yes, special forces. We were the first to wear the Green Beret. We always called ourselves Kennedy's elite.

Yeah, I understand President Kennedy was so impressed on the review of the troops one time that I guess one of your colonels said to him, "You know, the guys are really looking for their own place in the sun," and he more or less put that idea in his head about the Green Beret, and it stuck. I mean there's a story I bet hardly anyone has ever heard. I'll tell you what, that was really something. Now look, you know, when you talk about your wages at Bethlehem Steel, how did you feel about your wages? Did you always think you made a good buck for what you did?

LC: No. When I started Ingot Mould in 1964 I made about $28 a day, and that was a high paid incentive job.

Okay, that was one of the highest in the plant. In fact that was back in the days before the people in the Beam Yard were making the money.

LC: Yes it was. But the only reason we were paid that much, Frank, was because of our incentive program. You got paid for what you produced.

Yeah, in other words you could go in there and work, and if you didn't produce anything, you were like any other employee of the Bethlehem Steel. That's really something. Now, how did this rate of pay you had there when you worked at Ingot Moulding when you started at the rigger department, how did you feel about that compared to the rest of the Lehigh Valley? Did you feel as though you were sort of up to par, like in the working world, like a first class citizen?

LC: Frank, at that time a laborer in construction made more than a steelworker. So if you were an outside laborer, you actually earned more than you did at Bethlehem Steel. Mack Trucks at that time earned more than the Bethlehem Steel employees.

Would you consider that like one of the best kept secrets in the Lehigh Valley?

LC: I believe it was.

Well, we have to laugh about it, because we both, went through it. We know exactly. Okay, when you talk about schedules, schedules and families, what was that like? Getting days off, how you were scheduled, what kind of vacations you got.

LC: Frank, that's another reason I left Ingot Mould. I mentioned that we got every Sunday and Wednesday off, and if I wanted to work the job, I was a finisher at that time, which was a fairly high paying job, and if I wanted to continue to work that job, I had to take steady middle shift. So now I never got a weekend off to be with our kids, and when I came home from work at 11:30, the kids were in bed. When I got up in the morning and went to work, the kids were going to school. When the kids were coming from school, I was going to work. So my wife had to raise those children practically by herself for most of the years. Now of course during the summer months, I got to see them during the summer months, but there's nothing that'll ever make up for that time I lost with my family.

Yeah, that's true, that's true. But uh, the thing about it is from my knowledge, you know, your wife did a good job in your absence; thank God for that, huh?

LC: Yup. Now, Frank, you ask about the money. The money was so good that to make ends meet, and I lived in a half a double block on Center Street for 28 years, and to make ends meet I worked three jobs. With five kids.

Okay. That like says it all.

LC: And then eventually we had another one. We had a sixth child. So we had four girls and two boys, and we raised four girls and two boys in a house that had one bathroom.

Wow. Now, I guess planning vacations and stuff like that was pretty tough?

LC: Yeah, vacations were, we always found a way during the summer. I would take at least two weeks, and my wife's from San Antonio, Texas, and we would load all the kids in that old station wagon, and because we didn't have enough money to afford to stay in hotels on the way down, my wife and I would switch off, and we'd drive straight through from Bethlehem, Pennsylvania, to San Antonio, Texas, which is 1,800 miles. We'd drive straight through; we'd make it in 36 hours.

Wow. Well I can see right now the way you worked at Bethlehem Steel had a big impact on your private life. And you know, these are some of the things that the people in the Lehigh Valley have no clue, because the only thing they ever really see is what's been in the newspaper, what Bethlehem Steel basically told 'em to say. Now, be honest with ya, I want you to tell me here: Do you think the company treated you pretty good, or they could have done a better job, overall?

LC: I think they treated me pretty good overall, Frank. I think they could have shared the wealth a hell of a lot more than they did, but at that time, and especially in the early '60s and '70s...

Were you ever laid off?

LC: I was laid off one time, uh, and that was 1969. I was laid off for three weeks. I found out that there was somebody who was junior to me still working, went over lodged a complaint, and I was back at work the next day, and the company of course back paid me. Not because they wanted to Frank, because the union...

Now here's a real broadside question: Did you feel in the time you worked there that the company was somebody you could trust?

LC: No, I felt that there were individuals within the company that I could trust, but the company as a whole, no. I think actions speak louder than words, Frank.

Okay. Were you ever injured in the plant?

LC: Oh yeah.

What happened?

LC: I was chipping at Ingot Mould foundry and I had three pieces of scrap in one eye and six pieces in the other. And I went to the dispensary; the doctors tried to dig it out and they couldn't get it out, and the nurse said, "It's in too deep; you won't get it out." Finally they stopped, and they sent me over to Dr. Ogers who was an eye specialist, and he was able to remove the scrap. But, and that's another story of just how they were. I had to stay at home with bandages on my eyes. I couldn't take them off, because the light was, it was just so painful. And after a couple days at home, I got a telephone call, and they said, "We're going to pick you up in the morning to come to work. We don't want you sitting at home watching television," and I told them, "Well, in the first place I've gotta keep my eyes bandaged, because I can't expose 'em to light." They said, "Well, we're going to pick you up and bring you to work," and they did. They had a guy that used to come around, Jimmy, and I don't recall his last name, but he drove a station wagon for the company, and that was his job to go pick up all these people who were out hurt, bring 'em in to work. They brought me into work, and they sat me down on the bench in the welfare room, and...

The welfare room wasn't actually the cleanest place in the shop was it?

LC: Oh no, no, no, especially at Ingot Mould foundry. I mean, it was terrible. Eventually they built a new welfare room, and that's the one I had to sit in, where at one side you put your dirty clothes and the other side you put your clean clothes so that you didn't have to mix them and expose your family to that, but you still exposed them of course when you took your clothing home to be washed. But I sat there a couple of days, and then, uh, a foreman come in and he says, "Look, instead of just sitting here, do you think you could sweep up a little bit?" Now here I am, you have to picture this, sitting on a wooden bench with my eyes bandaged, and big bandage around my head so I couldn't get any light in my eyes, and this jerk is asking me if I could sweep up.

Did you understand at that time that Bethlehem Steel was self-insured under the worker's compensation law?
LC: No.

Well, that's probably the reason why they were getting away with that stuff.
LC: I understand that they didn't want a lost time.

This was prior. I guess this was prior to you becoming a union official?
LC: Yes it was.

Okay. Now, when we talk about safety in the plant, when I mention the word safety to you, I'm going to make a statement, One hundred just dropped dead, go get 101." What does that mean to you?
LC: Just get somebody in there to replace him. You're a number, you're a number, get the other guy in there.

I've heard that statement from so many different people. One hundred just dropped dead, go get 101. And I guess it means the same thing to all of us who worked in there: "fill that position," because that's the only thing that matters is getting the steel out the door.
LC: Yup, don't hold up too much production.

Do you think the company looked at you as an asset or a liability?
LC: I think they looked at me as an asset.

That's good, I'm glad to hear that. I'm glad to hear that. Do you think you could have worked at Bethlehem Steel without a union?
LC: I don't think I would have lasted very long, Frank.

Overall, the guys that you worked with in the plant, how do you think that they perceived that?
LC: I think they were thankful, uh, that they had somebody that would help them stand up to things that were wrong and that knew how to use the union, and uh, I became a union representative in Ingot Mould, a shop steward, and in the riggers a shop steward, and then eventually a grievance committee man full-time, but uh, most of the people that worked for Bethlehem Steel, Frank, just wanted to come into work, do their job and

go home. I mean, they weren't there to raise hell. In fact I saw too many that took too many risks because they didn't want to slow production; they were interested in the company, and most of them were proud to work for Bethlehem Steel.

Yes, I've heard that myself. Now, if I said to you, I had people tell me, "Frank, you'd still have a job at Bethlehem Steel if you wouldn't have been cooking on middle shift and sleeping on night shift." How would you answer something like that?

LC: It infuriates me. Because I know we didn't sleep on middle shift or night shift. And I know most of the people didn't. I'm not gonna say that there weren't a few jobs, meter readers and people like that, who uh, it was their job just to sit in one place, stay in the shanty and watch those meters. But it was an important job. Now they didn't have to get out in the weather and work like we did, physically work like we did. But I'm sure their job was just as hard.

Well, you know, I ask this question to maintenance people; you know what they said? "When we're not working, the company's making money."

LC: Oh yeah.

He says and if by chance somebody did fall asleep, he says no one worried about it. The only thing they worried about is if something broke down, were they on the job, and how fast did they get there, and I think that was more or less the name of the game. When did you first, Lester, when did you first realize the company was in trouble?

LC: Well Frank, one of my part-time jobs other than the Steel was working for ABE Airport, and I was a fueler out there, I was a fuel chief, five in a crew that we fueled all the airliners. So I was familiar with Bethlehem Steel and their hangar and the number of planes they had, and at that time they had two Conairs, and then they got two G1 Gulfstreams, G1s and two G2 Gulfstreams, and uh, I used to call it the Bethlehem Steel airforce, and I always said that when I see them get rid of their airforce, then I know they're in trouble, and that did happen, Frank.

Well, you know it's ironic that you would say that, Lester, because I was with some of our union brothers, and we were in Washington, D.C., the lobby in front of the steel caucus, and when we were done lobbying, we were at the Washington National Airport; it's Ronald Reagan Airport now, and Don Trautlein walked up to me and he said, "Frank," he says, "I'm gonna tell you something because I've known you a few years"; he says, "This is the last scheduled flight of a Bethlehem Steel plane going back to Bethlehem. Tomorrow at 9 o'clock in the morning we are going to announce the end of the Aviation Division." Well, I'll tell you what,

I knew right then and there we were in trouble. Lo and behold I come to the union hall the next day, and you already knew basically what was going on, and I came into the grievance room and I reported that, and they looked at me like I was from another planet. I says, "Turn the radio on," and like clock work they had "and breaking news from Bethlehem, PA"; whoa, that was really something. Lester, when...

LC: Let me just tell you one story about their planes. Bethlehem Steel had two beautiful Conairs, which were two-turbo prop. And they had doplar radar. I assume they had everything in them, so they were their pride and joy really, and one day there was a breakdown at the Bethlehem plant, and I happened to be working at the airport on night shift, and uh, they came out and they wanted to use the plane. Well, there was no Conair available. One was off on business, and the other one Mrs. Cort had taken with her friends on a golfing expedition some place. So they weren't happy about that.

Lester, do you think the company did all they could to save itself?

LC: No. Absolutely not. I think if they would've gone through with their plans, uh, to put in the continuous caster and lived up to their agreement with the union at that time, I think Bethlehem plant would still be there.

Yeah, I can remember having talks with Jack Roberts when he was the plant general manager, and he had some great ideas, but he started getting a lot of resistance from the Board of Directors. He just pulled everything up and moved on. He said, This is something that I really can't do." He says, "If I don't have any support, nobody to back me up, I'm wasting my time here." Okay, now...

LC: A lot of people don't know that Bethlehem Steel, Bethlehem plant, actually built the first continuous caster in the eastern hemisphere.

Oh, absolutely, back in the early '60s up there at the old Number 3 Open Hearth. In fact the guys from my shop 413 department were deeply involved with that.

LC: Yeah, we sent people down. They picked certain people from throughout the plant to go down to work with that caster.

Did you ever hear the company make or anyone from the company make the statement, "Don't worry about a thing, you'll get it in the end"? What does that mean to you?

LC: Well, I never heard anyone put it exactly those words, but I always felt like I was gonna get it in the end.

And lo and behold. Now do you, Lester, do you think the union fought a good fight, or do you think they were just involved in a no-win situation?

LC: Uh, I think they fought a good fight. I think they did everything that any union could possibly do. Frank, it's hard to convince people doing the kind of heavy labor and dangerous work that we did that the company they were working for was in fact in financial trouble and that there had to be changes, especially when the auto workers, the Mack Truck of the worlds, are, you know, they're all getting raises, but uh, I think they could have done a lot more.

Tell us a little bit about your union time? What were some of the highlights that you would consider; something that really made you happy working for the union?

LC: Well, Frank, what made me proud, especially to say that I was a United Steelworkers, because I got to go to negotiation in Pittsburgh, and I got to work with guys like you, Frank, I mean guys that cared about the people in the plant, you know, and uh, I got to meet people that most people forgot their names by now, and I'm sure you have, but the Owen McFadden and the Julius Baylus, Dominic Tuscano, Nick Kiak, and you know all those old guys who...

"Hey, this here, hey," remember that? "This here, hey." I said, "Nick, what do you mean 'this here hey'"? "You know 'this here hey.'" We never did find out what "This here, hey" was, but Nick said it all the time. And how about Tony Buffo?

LC: Oh, and Tony Buffo, yes, and those were the guys that worked there in the plant when it was really tough. It was tough when we worked there, but when those...

They were the founding fathers. And how about the guys from the other plants, Art Sambuci? The guy could get up and preach; he should have been the pope is what he should have been. He could talk people into anything.

LC: Art Sambuci. Yes he could. But you know the United Steelworkers did more things, and when I stop and think about them ... They were directly responsible for having the ERISA law passed. Had they not pushed to get the ERISA law passed, Frankie, you and I would have gotten nothing for pension.

You're right about that.

LC: That was the United Steelworkers directly.

That was really big. That was really big.

LC: OSHA Frank. We talked about the conditions in the plant and how bad they were when we first started, but when OSHA came into being, which again was another birth child of the United Steelworkers along with industrial unions, but the United Steelworkers were the head, and when they got the OSHA law passed and afforded some real protection for the workers, you know, other than just what the union can do, but in conjunction with the government, it just made me so proud.

Well, I remember when OSHA first came in. I remember talking to other union people through the labor council, and they would come right out and say, "You know you steelworkers had more protection in your union contract prior to OSHA than most places combined." Especially, you know, Article 14. Tell me a little bit about Article 14.

LC: We were the only union, Frank. Article 14, Section 3, and that section of the contract said in that article that if I was working and what I was doing posed an imminent threat to my well being or health, I could refuse to do that job.

And ask for a review.

LC: And ask for a review and union representation, and until that was resolved and that job was made safe, no one was allowed to work on that job.

Do you think that directly saved a lot of people at this plant?

LC: Absolutely.

I feel the same way about it.

LC: Frank, I worked with a guy at Ingot Mould who happened to be related to my father, a distant relative; his name was Mike Skrimkoski, and he kind of took me under his wing when I started there, and I'll never forget Mike. He was an expeditor, and when he went through the grab hooks onto the molds, because we were working incentive that crane man was going up, he wasn't waiting for a signal. I mean you were standing on the edge of the mold hanging there to begin with, and he'd climb down there, he'd look up at that crane man, and our crane man's name was Stengal, and he hold his fingers up. Well, three of his fingers were just stubs, and he'd holler at Stengal, "I put my kids through college." Because at that time you remember you get paid so much for every joint that you lost. And it never slowed him down. I mean he just kept going. He was never bitter about it, and that's the kind of people I worked with.

And how many years did you actually put in?

LC: I retired in 1996.

1996, what'd you do then?

LC: Then I went to work for Brandenburg Industrial Services, who were contracted to actually dismantle the Bethlehem plant.

Did you work with other steelworkers there?

LC: Yes I did. We had a provision, and we reached an agreement between the company and Brandenburg and the union that any steelworker, when Brandenburg came in to do the work, any United Steelworker had preference for the hiring, so before Brandenburg could go outside and hire anyone from outside of the United Steelworkers or from the Bethlehem plant, they had to exhaust the list of all the people who wanted to work for Brandenburg in dismantling the plant in Bethlehem Steel.

You know a funny thing about that Brandenburg, uh, I remember when you first started working there, you were there about a year, and every now and then I would get sort of like a word from a little bird, and it would say, you have to go down and see these guys at this area; they got a problem. Well, I knew none of those guys were ever gonna call. I always suspected it might have been Lester, might have called the union hall from a discreet phone location, but we're not going to ask you if that's true or not, because Brandenburg is still there. I see they just removed the electric furnace. It almost broke my heart. But you know that was one of the shops I worked in. So Lester, we had a real good interview here, we got an idea about what you did there, what you liked, what you didn't like, how it affected your family. I'm just gonna ask you at this time, you know, if there's anything you want to say about your time at Bethlehem Steel. Let's hear it right now.

LC: Well Frank, all I can say is I wouldn't have traded it for anything. The people I got to meet and the people I worked with, I made friends for life. In fact, we still get together, we have breakfasts, we have a reunion coming up in March for the riggers and pipe fitters, and it was like family, and I'm just thankful. And Bethlehem Steel allowed me to raise my family, to provide for them. I got one son that's an engineer, and they're all doing well, so, but more than anything I'm just glad I got an opportunity to meet all those people and to work with guys in the union and get to learn about the union and the union movement. Now don't get me wrong, Frank; there were people that I don't care if I ever see 'em again, but that's not 99 and 9/10th percent of the people. And it seems all the steelworkers, most of them managed to do well even after the Steel shut. There was life after Bethlehem Steel, and that was because the guys, because of their work ethics, and it was good, the people were good.

Well, I want to thank you Lester for your time here, and uh, continued good luck and health for you and your family. And that concludes the interview with Lester Clore. Thank you Lester.

LC: Thank you.

RICHARD CHECK
43 years of service

Riggers

"Mr. Rigger" Richie knew every job the riggers performed. He never turned down a job. He was a legend in the plant. With his brothers and sisters they gave 441 years of service to BSCO.

* * * * * * * * * *

Today is June 12, 2008, and we're here to interview Richard A. Check. Richard, what did they call you in the plant?

RC: Either Checky or Richie.

Okay, so what should call you for the purpose of this interview, Richie or Checky?

RC: Richie.

Richie, ok Richie. I see here you were a regulator, graduated from high school, went to college for a while, and you started in the plant on, of all times, Valentine's Day, 1951. Tell me what that first day was like. What did you think of it?

RC: Horrible. I was scared from top to bottom. That general foreman, when he talked to me, he was about a six foot, he looked like a linebacker. He was a six-foot-five, about two hundred seventy-five, German. He was my general foreman. And he talked to me and he said, "School boy, you got yourself into something that you don't know what you're gonna get." And I was scared. Why did I ever pick to be a rigger? Because I was an apprentice that they sent me to school for four years.

No kidding. You went through the rigger apprenticeship?

RC: Yes I did, for four years. It was either eight thousand hours or four years, whatever comes first.

All right. And you figured you'd learn more going through the apprenticeship.

RC: Well you went to school one day of the week and the other four days working on the job.

So when you were going to school, during that period of time, did you work mostly day shift or how did they do that?

RC: No, when it was required for my services to be on the middle shift or night shift, I worked it.

In other words, although you probably worked it you did more day shift than anything. Now, I was told that the new guys that came into the rigger department, you were like kept in the shade most of the time. They didn't really let you see what was going on until they knew what kind of a person you were, is that true?

RC: To a small extent it was. And actually, to tell you the truth, I saw; and I didn't like that, that they were excluding me. I wanted to get myself more involved, so by going into the office and telling them, the problem stopped. I got involved with what was going on.

In other words, you let them know from day one that you were there to learn the job and to do the job.

RC: Yes, that's right.

Of course, now you came from a long history, a long family tradition. How many brothers or sisters did you have working in the plant?

RC: Well, I have to tell it to you this way, when Mom and Pop came to our America in 1910, they were 19 and 20 years old. Mom was older than Pop. And Pop got himself a job, 1910, with Bethlehem Steel.

Year of strike, in 1910, yet on top of it.

RC: All right, so Pop gets himself a job in the blast furnace as a common laborer. Okay, as life went on and with our family that grew to be nine sons and five girls. I am the eighth son of nine, and the thirteenth child of fourteen. So, when the boys became eligible to go to work for Bethlehem Steel, six of them went to work with their father. One went to the iron foundry, Bartholomew. Emil, the younger than me, went to be a general carpenter; and I became an apprentice rigger.

So at one time, the nine of you were in the plant along with your dad?

RC: Yes. Now, also add on one sister that she worked for 26 years in the billing division over on Eighth Avenue, used to be on Third Street first. Then they built it over on Eighth Avenue. And my oldest son, we gave them a total in our family, 441 years.

Of service at Bethlehem Steel.

RC: Of service, Bethlehem Steel, just in my family.

In your recollection, did you ever hear of anyone with the company putting in that much family time? That's a real interesting question; I'd love to know the answer to that.

RC: To tell you the truth, Frank, no, nobody. And I can even tell you the story how the company recognized our family. There was an article at one time; Bethlehem Steel had a magazine that went out every month. It was called The Steel Review. They reviewed articles in there for all the eight plants that they had all over our country, and this one man from Steelton came from a family of seven. He said there's seven of us working for Bethlehem Steel Corporation in Steelton Plant; can anyone top this? So my brother, Steve, says, "Heck, that's no problem with us. We have ten of us with our father. So Bethlehem Steel put that in the magazine.

I remember my grandfather was a general foreman at Central Tool Treatment, and he used to get that every month. That was really a nice magazine.

RC: It was up to date. So with that, the company honoring us, they took us, all of us - the wives, children, no matter who wanted to go in the family - to Saucon Valley Country Club, and treated us to a dinner.

No kidding. Not many people are able to say that. Now, as you are going through your apprenticeship, you're done with your apprenticeship, what happened then?

RC: I became a C-rigger.

A C-rigger. Was that like automatic upon completion? And then you had to put hours in to actually move up rate?

RC: Yes. Six months and automatically I got the B rate. And six months later, I became the A leader automatically.

All right. Now you guys, riggers, what exactly do riggers do, Richie?

RC: My definition of a rigger is this: he never goes around, over, or on top of anything; he goes through it. He wants to find out. That's my definition of a rigger.

Okay. In other words, the jobs that other departments didn't want to tackle, didn't know how to do, were all performed by the riggers.

RC: Definitely. That's very good.

Well, I would say that one thing that came out of that that was good is that the riggers probably in the plant had the best reputation in the entire working force.

RC: And the fewer accidents.

Well, that goes without saying. You guys were always together. Everybody knew everyone else. And that was important. When I talk to Blast Furnace people that worked on the cast floor, they said, "Hey, everybody out there knew the job." Everybody did the job. If somebody slipped or missed something, we were right

there to handle it. And we had to, because you had a limited amount of time. So,
give me a typical job that the riggers did that nobody else did.

RC: Over in the drop forge, the first day in the washroom and the welfare room, I looked at the slip on the bulletin board where your name was and your number. Most of the time, your number, because once you started with Bethlehem Steel, you lost your name. You became a number. My number became 40964. So every day, for every day you came out to work, the description of the job on top, it said typically: "drop forge R and R anvil." That means "remove and replace anvil." And I looked at this and I thought, "Well what the heck kind of job is that?" So I go over by my A person. I says to him, "Joe." He was one of the most, of the three men that I would do anything for, them three men that I worked for, especially this guy Joe. I said, "Joe, what's this all about?" "Ah," he said, "Richie, it's too much for me to tell you. When we get there, you're going to understand when we start talking and working." So we get over there to this drop forge, and I noticed as soon as I come in, this part where we're gonna be working removing this anvil. Now this anvil weighs 90 tons of solid steel. Ninety tons. And this roof is pitched; there's no crane over your head. Now how are you gonna get this 90-ton anvil out of the ground that's in the ground 14 feet? How are we gonna get this 90 tons of solid steel out? So I said to Joe, "How are we gonna do this?" He says, "Rich, it's gonna get easier. We'll be here for at least ten days." And he says, "Every day's gonna get easier. You just watch yourself, and what I tell you and the rest of the guys." There's about eight of us in the gang. Now this big hole that this solid mass of steel was in this hole, there's dirt all around it. And on the bottom of this 90-ton was cork. Now this cork is now pulverized from this hammer, this 90-ton anvil being hammered upon. That's the idea. Remove the anvil, replace the new cork, put it back, and you're back in business. Now I never saw anybody any place in the plant do something like that. And the job went so smooth. It's the idea of putting a steel frame up around this anvil, and on four corners, each corner has a 100-ton jack. And four men are constantly jacking and pinning. You jack, you pin. You jack, you pin. So you don't lose 90 tons.

Hardened steel pins, what about how much in diameter, an inch?
RC: Oh yeah, an inch in diameter and about eight inches long. And you just jack and pin.

So you take it up a little bit at a time.
RC: That's it. You watch at the other guy.

And how long did it take you to get it to the height you needed?

RC: To get it above floor level, two feet above floor level, that takes three shifts.

I guess you get tired of jacking after a while, huh?

RC: No you don't. Honest to God you don't. You don't, because the guys are just talking. You're batting the baloney and you're talking. And if you get tired of jacking, you stop. The four guys stop; two, three other guys take your place. And you get a break, go have a smoke.

It was teamwork.

RC: That's right. Has to be.

In fact they have a terminology for it. I think it's called "labor of love." Some guys would say a love of labor, but I like a labor of love. So, you got this in there and these people that you're doing this for the drop forge, I mean they're probably down on their hands and knees kissing your butts, because they were so happy this was being completed, and there was no problems with it. Minimum down time.

RC: And nobody getting hurt.

Yeah, yeah. Now I bet you had a lot of people came around just to see that operate.

RC: There's always visitors. Visitors always from that department. Coming and, "How the hell do you get this thing out of the ground?"

Do you remember who the superintendent was? Was it Bill Redder?

RC: At the time, gee, oh that was pretty long ago to remember who that was.

So, you did a lot of work in the blast furnaces. What was like the standard big job in the blast furnace? Changing the bell?

RC: Well, the biggest thing and time working there was when the furnace was going to be rebuilt. That's a six-month guaranteed job, working seven days a week as many hours as you want. Honest.

In other words, every minute that you could put in towards getting this furnace back on campaign was money in everyone's pocket, and it was job security on top of it.

RC: Oh, definitely, and it was at times it was a hard job, but it was a good job. It was. It might have been dirty at times but it was still good.

And you worked with all the other different crafts in the plant.

RC: Electricians, carpenters, pipefitters, plumbers, everybody.

Everybody worked together.

RC: All the time, all the time.

Now, Richie, one of the reasons I'm writing this book is because I got tired of people in supermarkets saying to me, "Just think, Frank, you'd still have a job if you wouldn't have been cooking on middle shift and sleeping on night shift." But you know what, how did the work get done? I mean did little leprechauns come out of the Lehigh River and do the job?

RC: They better not let me hear that.

Yeah well, I'll tell you what, you know, I want people to know 100 years from now that Richie Check worked on the blast furnace for six months straight, had a good time doing it, everyone worked hard, everyone put in a lot of hours; and everybody, you know, they made the job what it was. These were tough guys.

RC: Yeah, every one of them.

Tough guys. They spent more time there then they did with their own families most of the time.

RC: Yes you did. Yes you did.

I'll tell you what, I never got around to riggers much to see other than down at the sintering plant. We used to see them every Thursday; they'd be down there on the pressures.

RC: Shut down, shut down.

Yeah, on shut down. They'd be down there welding up a storm. That was a dandy job. I mean that was a regular job, and you know we used to do that at one time. But the guys would whine and carry on, "Oh what are we doing in here. You know this is a job for the riggers." Well, guess what George Yasso said. "You're right." And he gave it to the riggers.

RC: Oh yeah, yeah, but, uh, I heard lots of times, you know, that people would say, about your work, you know, this and that and this and that about it. And you wonder, "Are they waiting for me to complain them?" Well, I'll tell you the truth, very little did I complain. And people would ask me, "What was a good day like? What was a bad day like?" I would say to them, "There's no such thing as a bad day. You know why?" They'd say, "Well, why?" I'd say, "You make it good. You make that day good."

That's right. And by the same token you can make a bad day, too.

RC: Yes, you could, but there's more plentiful of bad days in a sense, but with cooperation of the men working in the gang, they're good.

Well, you know I had a maintenance foreman would tell me one time. He said, "Listen what I'm gonna tell you. In, out, and on to the next job." He said, "That's all you got to know in the maintenance department. Get in there and fix it. Get out, and get ready for the next job." He said, "Now it goes without saying, we don't want you to get injured while you're in there." He says, "You know what I mean. You can't do dumb things." He says, "And that's why we have people in there with you, you know, there's somebody got your back all the time."

RC: What I liked about working with all kinds of men, in all parts of life, no matter what kind of guy he was…

Yeah, it was like working for the United Nations, how about it?

RC: As I was going through my apprenticeship, and then when I did get my rates – C-rate, B-rate - now these men that I was working for and under them, now I was gonna be their leader. And what I liked about it, when I was working with them, I gave them all the respect, no matter who the guy was. If he was somebody - and I don't like to say it that way - that I did not like, there's nobody that I did not like. I just did not associate with them. I did it in my life outside. Nobody that I did not like. You can't say that.

Yeah. Now when you talk about the outside, I would imagine because you were in a group that was together all the time, you guys spent a lot of time actually outside of the plant together, too. Is there a particular place like in South Bethlehem like the riggers hung out? A certain barroom or something? I often heard stories about this, but I want to hear right from you.

RC: Every day on the day shift, on the corner of Fourth and Pierce streets, it was called the Linden Tavern. That's where the riggers used to go on the day shift after work. Now, as a young apprentice, young snot-nosed kid, I couldn't afford it. But this guy by the name of Stevie Gombosi, Joe Zaun, and I'm trying to think of another guy, anyway I thought that Joe Stran or a guy like him would be there, but no. But anyway, they would stop there, and there was usually like about a dozen, a dozen to fourteen of them. Shot and a beer, shot and a beer, shot and a beer. Now me being that snot-nosed kid, I don't have the money for that. I don't have the money for that. So everybody would get their turn. Now it come to me, they'd jump over me. Stevie Gombosi would say, "Checky, keep your money. You need it for the kids." Because we had two kids at the time, two boys. So, I couldn't buy. I just couldn't buy. They wouldn't let me.

Wow.

RC: My turn would come around again; they wouldn't let me. And the bartender knew it. But Stevie already told him, "When it comes to his turn, you don't take nothing off him. Give him his drink, whatever he's drinking, and then that's it." I couldn't pay for nothing. Honest to God.

You know one of the first jobs I had was scarfing up in the billet yard. What a miserable job that was, but it paid good money. And I remember the first week that I spent scarfing on Friday. Everyone was scheduled Monday to Friday that week. We got up to the washroom, and there was a guy up there, Hunky Joe.

Hunky Joe said, "We go to Gert's after the shift." He said, "You make sure you're there." He said, "We drink lots of beer." And I went over there, you know, and I wasn't 21. But it didn't really matter at Gert's, because if you were a steelworker and your money was in front of you, it was good enough for her. And we'd go over there and we'd drink up a storm. And I'll tell what, these guys could dump 'em down. But, when they were really in a good mood, they used to go to the Tokay Hotel because they said they had the best shots in town. Thirty cents for a shot. This is back in the '60s. And boy, I'll tell you what, and you know they always used to say, "What we like best is those shots are always filled right to the brim. Right to the brim." They liked that. You know they figured they were really getting their money's worth up there. But that's the thing; the camaraderie among the guys in the plant was tremendous.

RC: It was.

And when they'd leave the plant for whatever reason, it seems to be the number one thing they talk about. "We really miss the guys." I said, "What about the job? Do you miss the job?" "No, we don't miss the job. We like the idea of coming in, and everything, everyday, something was different." You couldn't get bored.

RC: Right; that's what I liked about the riggers.

Well, in the riggers it was really true. Now, you worked in the Coke Works, too, didn't you? What were some of the technical jobs down there?

RC: Working on the battery.

Rebuilding them?

RC: Yes, with the bricklayers.

How big of a job was that?

RC: Oh that was, well, if steel was worn out inside the battery, why you'd have to replace it. Channels, angles, you know, things like that. Or another good job, believe it or not, was in the cold tank. Honest to God, it was a dangerous job, because you had to go in there with a safety belt, see, and every now and then a scab would accumulate inside the cold tank and they didn't like that. See, so our job as a rigger, when they got at that level, then we had to go down in there with your safety belt on, and you're down maybe 20-30 feet and trying to break that scab off itself so it falls down, see. And you didn't know about your footing. If you hit a pocket or something, and if you wouldn't have had your belt on, you'd get buried instantly. And you'd be coming up and you'd suffocate. And it was a good job, but it was dangerous. Or going out there on the top of the dome of the cold tank, we had to install stainless steel, trying to think of the proper word, snow guard. See, because if the snow would come without that guard off the top of the cold tank, and it would go down to the ground and anybody's walking around, you'd get killed.

Yeah, it was that big, huh?

RC: Yeah, a good chunk of it. So you'd have to go out with your safety belt and go down about 10-12 feet, hanging; and in the back, somebody got you tied off and you'd go down there with the welder and installed these snow guards. He had clips built on also that you got to weld onto the roof. And when do you think they wanted you to do that? Not in the summer; in January. To go out, well, you're nuts!

At least you thought they were nuts, right? Until you found out they were serious.

RC: They were (laughing). The same thing like working in the open hearth. They rebuilt them open hearths in July and August. And you're working down the cellar. Why they're nuts again!

Well, I guess they figure if they're not working, we got to get them working. That's what we're here to make steel. That's it.

RC: I used to pity them laborers though, when they rebuilt the checker chamber in the open hearth.

Yeah. I was talking to one of those guys that used to go in there. They said, "Hey, we'd be in there about eighteen minutes every hour." He said, "We'd go in there six minutes at a time, come out, another crew would go in." He says, "When you added it all up, we were in there about 20 minutes every hour." He says, "And you know what, sometimes that was too much, depending on how hot it was." I said, "Did you ever get carried out?" He said, "More than once." But you know what, that was more like a regular part of the job. I think they took a lot of chances with heat exhaustion and heat stroke back in those days.

RC: Because I watched one of them laborers who was there working. Before they go down the ladder into the checker chamber, he put his soft cap on, and then with his burlap bag, he dipped it in a bucket of cold water and put it back over his shoulders. Then he went down the ladder into the checker chamber and took the whole brick with ice tongs and threw them in the charge pile. And when the box was full, the craneman would take it away. They used to get half of a penny to remove three thousand brick. And then they would get a whole penny to install new fire brick, the laborers. They had to share that with a hundred or so men, the three thousand brick. Honest to God.

Amazing. A lot of things went on down there that people had no clue. And it was at one time that I really believe Bethlehem Steel considered most of their employees as liability. They didn't really look at them as assets until maybe the last ten years the plant was open. And you were getting out, in 1994, and it was only open four more years after that. So you were actually there when the furnaces and everything were still running.

RC: You can't believe what you saw. The only way to say it, Frank, you had to be there. You had to be there to see it, what was going on. In all them years, when I started in the '60s, in the '70s, in the '80s, you couldn't believe it.

How did you do it holidays, Richie, when you had all those kids? You had three children. I mean how that work? You worked them no matter what?

RC: Well, I'll tell you, holidays never bothered me, because that was an excellent time to make yourself good money. And she didn't mind and the kids didn't mind, even as they grew up.

In other words, you had them trained real well. They said Pop's working Christmas, but we're gonna eat real good when he gets home.

RC: And we did, we did. That's the way it went. The job come first. Actually family came first, so by having the family, you go to work. And many, many, and many a Sunday, Frank, we're going down from our house by getting ready after church, 10 o'clock, 10:30 Sunday morning, right?

Which church did you go to?

RC: Saint Cyril and Methodius. So we're all packed up, ready to go, out the door, and the phone rings. She didn't say nothing. I walk over to the phone, "Hello." "Richie, would you come out to work?" "When?" "Now." "Yes, I will. Good-bye." I hung up. That ended the picnic. But, they said they were going to picnic in the backyard.

Okay, because they didn't want to have a good time while you were working. Well, that was nice of them.

RC: Oh yeah. When it happened, Frank, it happened. It happened. They didn't want to go. "We're going to stay at home."

Most of the people that went down there to St. Cyril's were all steelworkers.

RC: Every one of them. Very few people in the whole neighborhood there that worked there like Mack Motor. Now some individuals they had a gas station. Back alley mechanic, they were good mechanics. They were good mechanics. But I would say nine out of ten, even places ten out of ten, they went to work. Steelworkers.

Do you think the company did all they could to save themselves? Or do you think it was too little, too late?

RC: No, the men that were in there in that administration running the company, they got too old. Honestly, that's my opinion. All them guys like including Mr. Grace; then go to A.B. Homer; Martin; Foy; Cort; Barnette, the attorney; Bransco; all them guys they were too old. They were up in their 70s going into 80s. And they were all stockholders. And they bring accountants in like they did and lawyers. You got to have steel people.

Yeah, well you know what; you're not alone in what you're saying. A lot of people told me the same thing.

RC: Why sure. You can't blame, and I don't blame the company that they took away all my medical. I can't blame them for that.

You can blame the federal judge on that, because he had the authority to grant it. He gave it to the stockholders instead. The only thing he had to do was take care of the people on Worker's Comp, and he established a trust fund for them. But that was a sad day when that happened, because we had a contract, a labor agreement. Their obligation was to pay us first, and they really dropped the ball on that one. But then again, you look at who's sitting there in Washington right now, and you don't have to be a real brain surgeon to figure out what was going on. And you know it was a shame, it was really a shame, because over the years both Democrats and Republicans had a chance to stop the steel imports and stuff like that. It didn't happen. It didn't happen, and what those foreign companies were doing, they were importing their unemployment to this country, until finally the burden became so heavy, you know, we couldn't carry it any more.

RC: No. I was hoping while what was happening in late '80s and early '90s that the company would have stayed and went small. That's what I was hoping for. For the next 10, 20 years for young guys that want to work, that this company's still here.

Yeah, I'm sure they could have kept the Combination Mill open. Made standard lengths. They had the best sheet piling in the world. They could have kept doing that. The Beam Yard was already there. You know we had it set up and, you know, you take a look at the machine shops and the press forge, those guys are making more money the Treasury has a hard time printing enough just to pay them. They're really making money hand over fist there. And, well you know what was happening with us? We were taking care of shops that were losing money big time. And it was all in one big pot and it always looked like there was a loss. But the moneymakers, like you said, they could have kept them going.

RC: Yes, that's what I was hoping.

But you know: "would've, could've, should've." You know what the queen said, "Balls: if I had them, I could be King." And you know it was that simple. Really it wasn't that simple, you know what I'm saying now. Even if the company would have come back and says, "Hey," to the union, "hey look now. It's costing us; we're going deeper and deeper with payments for medical. How about we get together and let the worker pay half and we'll pay half?" Well they tried all

468

that stuff. They tried it too late. Now Richie, if you, let's say you had been in a position, let's say around 1985. You knew what you knew, you had already been in the plant over 30 years, and someone came to you and said, "Richie, we're gonna give you the authority to change the things you know aren't right." What would you have done?

RC: Well, somebody in that administration, just when that happened, they should have did what they did when I started to work in 1951.

And that was?

RC: Combining all the crafts. They should have did that day one when I started. Because I would go on a job, and I'm not ashamed to say it; if there was pipe in the way, if there was wood, if there was electrical wires, you stop, got a hold of an electrician or a carpenter, call the department, which I did, "This is in the way. That's in the way. We can't work." And like say it was one o'clock in the afternoon and you approached that position, something was in your way, you didn't do nothing the rest of the shift.

Yeah, that was considered jurisdictional lines.

RC: Yeah, and everybody upheld it.

Well, you know that was part of the thing that you're probably right they should have been talking about long before they talked about it. They started talking about it around 1985, '86.

RC: Thirty years too late.

But yeah probably should have been talking about it at least 15 years earlier for sure, like 1970. And everyone's job actually would have been more secure.

RC: It would have been. Yes.

A lot of people, when you say that to them, you know what they say? "Well, you know, what if that was the case, they probably wouldn't have hired anybody."

RC: Oh no, they would have hired more.

In 1973. Well, no, I don't know if they would have hired more. They probably wouldn't have hired as many, but they would have hired them steadily.

RC: Oh yeah, they would have. They would have.

But life's a bitch and then you die, how 'bout it?

RC: There was too many, too many had jobs that I was on, Frank, with the gang, leading the gang. And I'd get on the job and, Jesus Christ, the pipe's in the way. And then the pipefitters agree maybe up to eight inches you could take, remove it. But if it's anything bigger, see then you run into trouble. But I thought it was an eight, but it was a ten. See? Now they file a grievance. See?

Well, I guess that would work on you after a while, but then believe it or not, this is true: there were certain groups of guys that work with each other pretty regular. If you went and did some of those things, they didn't say anything. They were happy. You know why they were happy? Because they got done sooner on their job and they made more money. So you know who said steelworkers didn't know what they were doing?

RC: No, no they did.

Damn right. Now, Richie, what's the number one thing you missed about being out of that plant?

RC: To tell you the truth, the work and the men. I'd say the work first, because the work as my years went by any kind of, Frank, if it was a big job, a little job, it didn't faze me.

You reached the point within your career that there was nothing you couldn't handle, that's what you're saying? So everything became like easy for you?

RC: Yes it did. Honest to God.

Well, not many people who worked in the plant in the capacity that you did are able to say something like that. Richie, who built the U.S. Navy?

RC: Bethlehem Steel.

Who built the Golden Gate Bridge?

RC: Bethlehem Steel.

Who built the Empire State Building?

RC: Bethlehem Steel.

Who built almost the entire skyline in New York City?

RC: Seventy-five percent.

There you go.

RC: Yah, yah. And Mackinac Bridge in Michigan.

There you go. Well look, I'm going to tell you this: you know it's a real pleasure talking to you. I wish the best for you and your family. I really appreciate you taking this time, you know, to come here and sit with me.

RC: Oh, you're more than welcome.

And the best for you.

RC: My pleasure.

Thank you, sir.

GEORGE PINKEY
35 years of service

Pipe Shop

"Pink" as he was known in the plant, truly enjoyed and appreciated his job at BSCO. An accomplished storyteller, he took a keen interest in history and tells a compelling story of himself in his interview. Currently Vice President of the Pennsylvania Labor History Society.

* * * * * * * * * *

Today is June 10, 2008. We're here with George A. Pinkey. George, did you have a nickname in the plant?

GP: We were born with a nickname, Frank. You know, Pinkey. So all my brothers were Pink or Pinkey and that's the way it went. When people got to know you they referred to you as Pink or Pinkey. Some of the guys called me George but I'd say less than ten percent. I was either Pink or Pinkey and that's what we went by.

So what should we call you for purposes of this interview?

GP: Well, George is all right. If you flash back to Pinkey, that's fine, too.

George is good, because that's all I have always referred to you. Ok George I'm looking here and I see August 4, 1964. Do you want to tell me how you became a Bethlehem Steel employee?

GP: Yeah, that's kind of a long drawn-out story, too. See I was going to college. I was studying forestry at the University of Maine, and in the fall of 1963, I made the decision that I was going to drop out. I was really hammering an organic chemistry and a physics course, and I knew I wasn't going to pass the physics course, and normally the foresters took two semesters, four credits of physics. I tried to combine it into one seven-credit engineering physics course, and I just didn't have the math for it. So I knew in the fall of '63 I was going to drop out. I took the finals in

January of '64. I packed up my car and I came home. I went to work clear and right away for Blue Ridge Real Estate at Lake Hauto, and in June, my buddy got out of the Navy, and he got a job as an electrical helper in 4 Open Hearth, and he's showing me his paychecks where he was working sometimes three and four days a week, as he was drinking and carrying on the other time. He wasn't making a full 40 hours. He was making more money in that three or four days than I was making ten hours a day, six days a week, time and a half over 40 and over 8. So in June, I went for an interview down at Bethlehem, and at that time they were doing their own hiring, the old ship construction building was till across the street from the plant office. I took my tests and all and I went over to Route 28 for an interview, and the gentleman interviewing me said that we don't have anything in research right now, and when something opens up we'll give you a call. Now that was June of '64. I'm still waiting for the call. Nothing opened up in research. I think I had a little too much college. My sport coat with the tie and my briefcase with the resume, that just didn't make it for a job at Bethlehem Steel.

Now, do you think you just wowed them to death, more or less?
GP: Well, I think that they were worried, I mean, hey. I still have serious reservations whether that was the mechanical aptitude test or whether that was an I.Q. test, and I think that was an I.Q. test. The lowest guys went to the labor gang. The second lowest went to the bricklayers and the carpenters and pipe fitters and up the line. I don't know and I'll never know but that's my opinion in the thing.

Well, eventually they did hire you.
GP: Eventually they started hiring through the state, and I went to Tamaqua to the state employment office, and there was a fellow there, Joe Ambrose, that was an old friend of my family's from Coaldale days. His family was involved with a drugstore operation in Coaldale. But Joe saw me and he said, "You did very good in the test." He said, "But when you go for your interview," he said, "wear a flannel shirt, put the sleeves rolled up to your arms, leave the briefcase and the sport coat and tie at home." He said, "Don't worry about your resume. All the paperwork that they need will be down there." And he said, "Just make sure that he sees your forearms and you'll do all right." Well, I went to the same room 28; son of a bitch, I'm looking. There's three people doing interviews, a woman and two guys, and you're moving up a chair, and I thought, "That same guy's going to interview me now. They're going to interview me in June." I guess I started to sweat or something. I was getting nervous. I sat down, yeah, yeah, and he didn't even ask me any questions. He says, "We have

openings in the labor department or a bricklayer helper." Well, bricklayer helper sounded a little more, a little less servile, should I say, so I said, "Well I'll take the bricklayer helper." He said, "When do you want to start?" I said, "When could I start?" And he looked over his shoulder. And I can remember it was ten minutes after 11 in the morning, on August 4, 1964. He said, "You could start at four o'clock this afternoon if you want to." I said, "I'll be there." And he got a paper. He gave me a map of how to get to the Saucon bricklayers, and he told me I would have to buy a pair of shoes, and he would give me the other required safety equipment, but when I go there, they'll take care of things. Well, I came home and I had to notify my employer. I told them I was only taking the day off. You know, come to think of it, but I think that was a Thursday, because I told them I was going to be off and I would be back tomorrow. Well, when I came home I called Kirk Kemmerer, the boss of Blue Ridge, and told him that I took a job with Bethlehem Steel. Well, he said, "Good luck. Just make sure you get back and finish your college." And that's how my career with Bethlehem Steel started. I went down there, and my good buddy Eddie McHugh, who was driving a truck on that operation for Fazio, who was the earth moving contractor for Blue Ridge, he's sitting in the shape-up room in the bricklayer's shanty at Saucon, and he says, "What the hell are you doing here?" I said, "What are you doing here?" He said, "I got a job here yesterday." So for the rest of the time we were there, Eddie was one day ahead of me on the seniority list.

Wow. So what was it like when you started with the bricklayers? You must have been in awe of the noise, everything going on, the activities.

GP: The whole steel mill affair was completely different than what I ever expected it to be. I thought that I would take a job there, earn a couple bucks, maybe work through the winter, and in the following fall I would be back at Maine, finish my schooling. But in that washroom, with that old timer there helping me find the basket and the smells and the noises and everything, till I got over to the bricklayers shanty, I thought, "Boy, this is quite a place." And I went to work in 2 Open Hearth. And anyone who was never in an open hearth can't appreciate what went on in an open hearth, but anybody that was there knows that that was one hell of a beehive of activity, the noise, the fire. After I thought about it for a little while, the noise, the dirt, the sight, the fire all over the place, guys capering around with silvers on, it was just amazing.

Silver suits you're in reference to? Those were like what? Aluminum coated?

GP: Well, aluminum-coat asbestos. Most of the guys wore the leggings. Some of them wore the bib overalls and trousers, and some of them wore big ankle-length coats.

And all of this was designed to protect you from sparks.

GP: Because every time they opened those doors on those open-hearth furnaces, they were throwing alloys or dolomite or something in there, flux. Fire, sparks, would be flying out and things like that and they had to be careful.

So you must have thought originally you are in some sort of an annex of hell.

GP: You know I thought about Dante's "Inferno." But to me, I don't know, I was always since a kid I liked fire, like building fires in the Boys Scouts. I mean the place was like poetry and music. I said it was like a big symphony being driven by the devil. That first week or so was orientation. Within a couple minutes after the safety meeting and the shapeup, I walked out and I'm going out to the floor to Open Hearth, and Rocco grabs me by the neck and pulls me back as a big bucket of hot metal goes flying by on a car with a guy ringing a bell being pushed by a little locomotive. "Boy, kid, you got to be awake around here," he said. "You almost walked right in front of that hot metal car." And that was it; you were on the knife's edge. And, you know, as you worked, you got used to this stuff and you started recognizing the hazards.

So how did the old timers treat you? They sort of like take you under their wing?

GP: The story was there, Johnson was running for election, you know, after Kennedy got shot and everything and you guys will be here until after election. The old conspiracy theory the government was pumping life into industry, particularly Bethlehem Steel, and they were hiring all of us so we would get the feeling of prosperity, and after the election we were going to get laid off. It didn't matter much to me, but I would say within the first week about half of the people that I talked to reminded me that I would only be there until after the election. There was a caste system in that bricklayers: there were old timers that didn't want anything to do with you; there were old timers that tried to take you under their wing more or less as a grandfatherly type to protect you and make you aware of the hazards; and then there was a group of guys that would say, mostly like the Korean War veterans that were seriously interested in seeing that you made the adjustment, you made the takeover, and eventually you'd become a long-term employee of the Bethlehem Steel, because you were going to be the guy behind them as they grew older. And I didn't know anything about that system at that time, but as I worked there over the years, you know there were the old guys, there were middle guys, and there were the young guys. Every team, every group that you worked with, the older guys were the brains of the outfit, more or less directed the job; the middle guys did the work; and the younger guys were the gophers, they did the hard climbing and the heavy lifting and pulling and pushing and stuff.

I guess you found out real early how important seniority was. And there was no doubt about it, the more you had the better off you were.

GP: Oh yeah. And in the bricklayer, the incentive system was such that the hotter the job, the more the incentive. And if you were assigned to a hot job so-called, and you had one day less than some guy that was working down at the soaking pits or up on the Blue Mountain doing a car-bottom furnace or something and he found out, well pretty soon you were headed where he was and he was headed for the place you were. They called that getting bumped off a job, so when a roof would fall in or an end wall or a side wall would fall in on an open hearth furnace, there would be a shuffle, and the older guys would migrate to this job that was being set up, and the younger guys would be moved to the other positions, and stuff like that. But seniority was all important, and there was actually in some of those older helpers especially, not so much the bricklayers, because they had their job to do. As a helper you didn't compete with them but you competed with those old helpers, and they would get angry if the working leader or someone would assign a younger guy to a job. They'd get pissed off and start hollering and screaming and carrying on. You were pretty soon on your way. Once in a while you'd slip by, and you know, you'd get some ridiculous seven or eight dollars an hour incentive on a job where you're only getting a dollar seventy cents, the base rate. But depending on how that crew performed and got that thing patched up and all, anywhere around the hot metal where your incentive was based on hot metal, you did pretty good, and then you learned that all the way through the incentive program down there. But seniority was all important in the bricklayer.

How long were you with the bricklayers before you moved on?

GP: Well, I started August 4th and October 7th I got my draft notice, and the last day I worked was October 26th. I went to the draft board there in Wilkes-Barre. I got on a bus and went to Philadelphia. October 27th I was marching in the United States Army. So from August until October, two years later I came back, I got an early discharge. Instead of waiting until October 27th, there was a plant opening on October 6th, so I got a plane from Rhein-Main Air Force Base to McGuire Air Force Base. October 7th, I landed in New Jersey at McGuire Air Force Base and on October 8th I came back to work in the bricklayer helper.

How about that? So I hear Rhein-Main, so I'm guessing you were in Germany.

That must have been an experience in itself.

GP: Well, hey, you know what? I hated every day that I was in the Army, but the 11 months that I spent in Germany, other than the working hours, it was like a paid vacation to the old country. And if it wasn't for being drafted in the Army, I probably would have never got to Europe. And I was in a pretty good outfit. My commanding officer was my brother's roommate at West Point in his plebe year. Colonel Moran was his name. And, he took care of me. I mean I worked hard for him. I did a job there getting his S4 straightened out, his supply section. I was trained as an artillery surveyor, but he put me in the supply. And, when work was done, I had a pass. I could leave and I didn't have to make the nightly bed checks at midnight. So I did good.

So after you came back, how long did you stay with the bricklayers?

GP: Well, the first thing, I was really disappointed because some of those middle guys, particularly there was Lessy Wargo from up in Haddock, up near McAdoo. He was a bricklayer and he told us, he said, "You got to get out of this department, because if you don't, in 20 years you're going to end up with a weak back and a weak mind." So he said, "You want to get out of the bricklayer helpers, because this is not the bottom but almost at the bottom level." He said, "You got to get into some other department." And you know, in 1964, you could already bid departments and things, and those old timers didn't realize that when they went department to department, the vacation schedule and things like that were interfered with. That was before the consent? But with us guys just starting out, we had nothing to lose. The big disappointment coming back from the service was that Eddie McHugh was still in the bricklayer gang. He had improved to the spraying gang, where there were long hours of wait between jobs, if you're spraying asbestos around and stuff. I said to Eddie, "We got to get the hell out of this department." And when we were working night shift on Open Hearth and the bricklayer helper gang, we would see these pipe fitters come in, and they'd set a cooler up and the guys packed up the wells and they'd disappear, then they'd come back and weld. In about 8 hours, they might have worked about 3 or 4, and I said, "That's the gang that we want to get into. They don't look like they're wearing out a pair of gloves both sides of the shift handling bricks." So then in May of '67, an opening came, and Eddie and I and three other guys from the labor gang went as pipe fitter helpers into the pipe shop. One of the things about the pipe shop, basically you only work one weekend a month and it was day shift and you had a steady schedule. You didn't have to work that murderous swing shift where you were working three shifts, sometimes three shifts in one week.

Well that can really impact your family life, too.

GP: And, hey, a young guy that's making that kind of money, he doesn't want to be working night shift and middle shift in a steel mill on a Friday or a Saturday night when he can be at the Legion dancing and drinking.

Sure, sure. And you know you were driving about roughly 50 miles right on the nose?

GP: It was 50 miles; from where I live now to the main gate is 50 miles. On a good day you could do it in maybe 50 – 55 minutes. And there were days when in the winter time or because of tie ups on 22 it took me three hours coming home. Bad weather, instead of leaving like at 6 o'clock for an 8 o'clock start, you left at 5 o'clock automatically.

How did the company treat you when you came in late? They had an understanding about that?

GP: Well, working in the maintenance department wasn't as bad as the production department. If we were going to be late, we would stop somewhere, get to a phone, and call the clerk and tell him, "Hey, we got tied up in traffic. There was a wreck on 100. We're going to be a half an hour late." And until you call all these guys, you know, you give them the numbers of the shops. Like some guys working at the Coke Works, call their shops and tell them they're going to be late. The production people were pretty rough on that lateness or absence. They didn't go for that stuff.

So now you … because what? Were you an apprentice or a helper?

GP: No, I was a helper. I started there in May as a helper in 1967. And then I worked until 1972, where an opening as crane man in the shop opened up. That was instead of job class 4, that was job class 6. And the crane man in the shop was a good job. You didn't have to climb a ladder to get in the crane, you could either climb the steps or ride an elevator to the second floor, and then there were five steps, a little steel stairway built to get in the crane. And sometimes when you were working, if they were working on big pipe, like 36- or 48-inch pipe, you'd set the guy up; you might have to make two or three lifts in the shift, and it worked out pretty good. What happened on there, I had been out 1973 with a hip operation, and when I came back, I went back on my crane job. I had gotten married, my wife was a teacher, so it was good to have the middle shift job, because we wanted to have children, and I was 29 when I got married so I had to get going. And we figured I would watch the children during the day; maybe an hour a day, we would need a babysitter at home. So I kept that craning job, but then the old fly came in the ointment. In August of 1974, when I went back to work, they posted for a pipe fitter. Now, because of that year off being sick, they had an apprentice program that started, and I would have qualified. I would have been able to use my G.I. Bill, but to take the apprentice program you have to be physically qualified to do the job, and because I had the hip operation and was on crutches, even though I was going to be back work by the time the apprentice program started at the time that it was offered, I wasn't physically qualified. And I got pissed off about that. I tried to fight that through the union. Hey, the union says, "This is the way it's written up. There's nothing we can do, you know." He said, "Try to get better and get back, and when you get back in January, maybe we could do something at that time." Well, in August they posted for pipe fitter. Now, what am I going to do? I have an opportunity to become a pipe fitter or do I go into the program with apprentice where it might take me three or four years to get a pipe fitter? I have to go to school for a year before I could even test. I took the test. In 1974, I was the first guy that ever tested for pipe fitter that made a pipe fitter right off the bat. And they didn't like me.

How did you pick this up?
GP: Well, the thing was, with the college and the math that I had, figuring those angles and offsets, I'm not a wiz at trigonometry or anything like that, but I understood the trigonometry involved where other guys knew that you multiplied something by 1.414 but they didn't understand what was going on. Plus, I think I had a good work ethic, and the thing was I thought that helpers were greatly taken advantage of. That crap of having to carry the pipe fitter's bag and shit like that, I never went for that. Hell, I was hired to be a helper, not to be a slave. He's getting the big money, you know.

So you're saying a lot of the pipe fitter helpers were probably as good as the pipe fitters?
GP: Yeah, absolutely, especially the older guys.

It's just a matter of who took the test?
GP: But that business about education, people have fears of failure. And I went into the thing, I didn't care; like I said, I was a ball breaker. I filed grievance after grievance about safety issues. I never lost a grievance, because they were good solid things. In fact, one time after I got to be the fabricator, the assistant general foreman told me, he said, "You know when you were a helper, you were the biggest pain in the ass in the shop." He said, "Now that you're a fitter, you're one of the best men that I have." And

I went into that test like there was no tomorrow. I didn't care what they threw at me, I figured it out, I worked through lunch, I was lucky to get, like, good helpers and good welders that worked with me. John Harkins from Summit Hill, we nearly burned the iron foundry down one day when we were going to bat. But, after six months of testing, they didn't want to do it, but they had to give me the A rate, so I came out way ahead of the rest of them. Some of those guys that went into the apprentice program didn't get that A rate for three or four years down the road.

So now you're a pipe fitter, you've got roughly ten years in the plant. Now this is a question; maybe you got to think about it. What do you think the company's attitude was toward the employees, back those first ten years? How did look on their employees?

GP: Well, I think that their attitude in the pipe shop was they recognized good workers and they recognized talent. The other hitch in this thing, you know, I talked earlier about that middle shift job, now I have a little girl, I'm an A pipe fitter. Well, I'm headed for day shift. Well the guy on the bending table, they call them the B team, where the fabricators three shifts and then there were the B team three shifts, the guys on the bending table. Old Charlie Hallum, they call "Broom Bear," because every day he ate a baked potato for his evening meal. He announces that he's going on a pension, so they put me with him for two months to understudy him. Then I could get a middle shift job. And Bobby Enright came to me and said, "Hey there's a position opening up on middle shift. Do you still want it? I'll put you down there with Broom Bear to learn how to bend pipe." So I jumped on it. And I'm down there on the B team. You know I worked 13 years on the 4 to 12 shift so that I could raise my kids and someone else didn't have to, and my wife watched them on night shift, and I watched them on day shift. So I'm one of the few fathers of that era that got to see them take their first steps, say their first words, and all of that stuff.

Well, that's a good thing that it worked out for you like that.

GP: And that bended job, again, because of the little bit of knowledge that I had in math, old Broom Bear had a whole composition book where he had all the sequence written down. You didn't only bend pipe, things were slow you made U bolts, you made I bolts; if they needed anchor bolts for a construction job, you bent the anchor bolts. He had everything written down for what size pipe, what size stock you had to use, how long the thread had to be, how long the bar had to be before you bent it. That son of a bitch wouldn't show me nothing. If we were bending a piece of eight-inch pipe to a certain radius, he would wait until I went to the toilet or I went for lunch, and I came back, and everything was marked out. Then we started heating the pipe up.

I heard the same story from some of the riggers.

GP: I didn't give a shit. A month after Charlie left, I was better than he was with bending pipe. But I'm not bragging; it's just a fact of the matter.

Well, he must have showed you something then. Or did you pick it up from just watching him?

GP: You watch him. And you know at that time, you bend a lot of pipe. I mean there were times when we went for seven or eight months where all we were doing for six and a half or seven hours out of eight was bending the pipe. And we went pipe anywhere from the smallest one-eighth tubing all the way up to, well, the biggest pipe I think that I ever bent was a piece of twelve-inch extra heavy pipe.

Well, you know, you're down there now and you get onto this job, you're on middle shift, you were there for quite some time, how was it as far as getting your vacations, getting a day off when you need it, or otherwise planning things that happen in the family. Did you get cooperation?

GP: You know seniority ruled and in those early days, '67, the '70s. I didn't have the seniority, so I got vacation whenever there was vacation left. The other thing was, in the maintenance outfit like the pipe shop. The production outfit shut down every holiday: Thanksgiving, Christmas, Easter, Fourth of July. Every Thanksgiving for the first 15 years, every Christmas, every Easter I was in the Bethlehem plant, I knew that I was going to be there. And I couldn't get vacation at that time, so Christmas dinners were held when I got home.

Well, here's a good one. Do you think that the company treated you right or do you think they could have done a better job? Do you think they worked within the system and that was it?

GP: Given the nature of the work that had to be done for the production office would shut down on the holidays, give their men vacation, given off, I don't know how else they could have worked it. Hey, our bosses were right in there with us. I'm talking about the general foreman and assistant foreman. They were in there on those holidays right with us. And Christ's sake, some of those guys had 35 years already, you know, they were going. But they more or less took it in stride. Hey, sometimes, you know this, if you're working on Thanksgiving, somewhere in the welding rod oven or somewhere there's a turkey cooking and you sit down with your other family, namely the guys that you work with, from 12 or until quarter to 1 or 1 o'clock you're eating a turkey dinner with all the trimmings, because some guy was a good cook. A lot of times that fell on me, because from the

Boy Scouts and stuff, I could cook on open fires and stuff. It wasn't hard in the steel mill to find a hot place that you could roast a turkey or a ham or something like that.

Yep, and did what you had to do.

GP: And you know what, on those occasions our bosses would sit down with us and eat at those holiday dinners.

Were you ever injured at work? Lose any time?

GP: Burned. I never lost any time. One time when I was a pipe fitter helper, I was on workman's comp. I was reduced in my responsibilities. I slipped on a wad of grease and dislocated my right shoulder. So I think for six weeks I had a thing on here where my right arm was immobilized. And they took me off helper and put me on job class 2 labor. I was filling out time reports and safety reports, even though it was hard because I'm right handed, and I was working over at the blast, moved me from the Saucon Mill gang up to the Blast Furnace and the system general foreman, Bob Keller, I was his clerk for those six weeks.

Now, you're living up here in what the people down in the Bethlehem area would call "north of the Blue." So they called you guys the "up homers." Now, it was always my opinion, that the up homers could be trusted on the job to do more work than anybody. Do you think that's that just an ingrained something that comes from the coal regions?

GP: I think this. I think that we come from an ethnic background. Our grandparents were immigrants, and they came to this country for the opportunity, and they brought with them a very, very good work ethic. I learned that work ethic from a little boy from my father and my brothers and my uncles and things like that. Up homers, I think, were maybe more dependable than some of the local. Now, keep in mind, those people came from the same immigrant background, but they weren't driving 50 miles to get to work.

Yeah, that's right. And they hadn't gone through what had happened in the coal regions.

GP: And the other thing that used to amaze me, and it used to amaze the bosses: bad weather, snow. And you know in the '60s and '70s we got some pretty bad snowstorms. I had a '73 Dodge Power Wagon, and I used to have to plow the roads to get to Bethlehem. Guys that lived a mile away would call in; they can't make it, the roads are closed, and guys that lived 50 miles away would be there an hour early. The bosses said, "What? I can't figure this out. Guys can't make it a mile and you came 50 miles. What the hell time did you start? It ain't four o'clock this morning." So you might have been on the road two and a half or three hours before the shift. And then, of course, when it was like that, they couldn't get in, so there was a little opportunity to grab a little overtime, because they had to have you there to do whatever had to be done. But up homers and coal crackers, the guys from down there they called it coal crackers in a demeaning way, but we took that as a compliment.

I never felt that way about it, but I knew that other people did. I think what it was, there were people who were down in town, when they spoke about coal crackers, they just didn't understand the life these people led. They didn't know that. They had a hard time relating to that, so they thought, "Well, these guys, because they're different, they're strange." And I didn't find that to be true at all. Some of my best friends were the so-called coal crackers and up homers, because they were fiercely loyal people. And they were workers.

GP: I would just use the word dependable. To me the guys that drove 50 miles for a job, I think they might have appreciated that good wage and the fact that you had good union protection and stuff like that. They might have appreciated it a little bit more than some of the local characters down there. But it wasn't universal. Hey, I could say sometimes very seldom on a hanger that someone referred to you as up homer or coal cracker. Most of the time it was in jest or something like that, and sometimes, like, if you did something dumb.

Were you ever laid off?
GP: Never laid off.

Never laid off? You were one of the lucky guys, huh?
GP: Thirty-four years, Frankie, never laid off, never had to walk on the picket line. Got a paycheck even when I was sick with the operation and the heart attack and everything, I got my SIP, I got my money. Hey, them SIP checks aren't enough to go out and buy a new car or make a down payment on a house, but they paid the bills.

George, do you think you could have worked in that plant without a union?
GP: I wouldn't want to work there without one.

Why's that?
GP: Well, everything. You know, just the day to day operations. Safety. The company claims safety, the company claims safety, but there were people that would try to pull shit with you. They try to get you to take shortcuts to do stuff. You know, in 34 years of working, in 35 years of service, I never ever had to do anything that was unsafe, unless I made that decision to do it myself where I was gambling for an early quit or a little

extra time on the bench. If there was something that wasn't right, and I told the boss, he made it right. And if he didn't, you filed a grievance, and when you got into that superintendent's office, I think that superintendent sometimes made fools out of foremen that tried to make us do things that were unsafe.

Yeah. When did you first come to the realization that the company was in trouble, George? About what year?

GP: Well, the facts of the matter I think speak for themselves. '79 was the record profits for Bethlehem Steel. They made more money in '79 then they ever did before that; and by 1982, they were laying off salaried people. I would say 1980, '81, and '82 there was a noticeable difference in how that plant was run. As a maintenance person I noticed one thing, there were no more big projects of renewal and rebuild. It was patch, fix, and get it going. If a pipe was rotten, instead of replacing two or three lengths of pipe, you cut out a foot-long piece and welded a piece in. And that's the first thing. You know, in hindsight, they started talking about harvest mode. I would say that somewhere in the early '80s in some meeting either in the plant office or in the company office, someone made the decision that that plant went on harvest mode. There was a noticeable difference in how we operated beginning in the early 1980s.

Yep, you're echoing what a lot of other people interviewed said.

GP: In hindsight, again, I always want to give credit to the union, because while it was going on I didn't always agree. You probably heard me screaming and hollering just like a lot of other people. But our union did a masterful job in stretching out the shut down of that plant. That is to say, I think the company made a decision in 1981 or '82 to close that plant down, and our union struggled in the best way that they could to bring as many of us into the 30 and 35 year for those pensions.

So guys could get a pension, yeah.

GP: They could have made the decision like they did in other places, like United States Steel did in Homestead. Shut 'er down. That's it. We're done. But our union, well I guess there were some good people that they were able to get on the industrial relations, and the guys in our union, they did a masterful job. Hector Nemes, some of those giants that struggled to keep that thing going. Hey, I hope that everybody's as grateful as I am that the union did the job that they did in stretching out the shutdown.

So you feel that they fought the good fight but they were actually in a no-win situation?

GP: I think the cards were stacked against them from the beginning.

It was only because of good faith it was built up between union people and company people that they were able to prolong that shutdown. I don't think all of the managers received their pension.

Do you think the company looked at most of their employees as assets or liabilities?
GP: I think the company looked at most of the employees just like they looked at a pile of taconite pellets or a pile of limestone. It was a commodity. How little do I have to give these guys to get as much as I can out of them? And I think that that's a flaw in almost all labor/management relations in that period.

Now, the Partners for Progress, the Juran training programs that came in the early '80s, is that something that probably would have helped us a lot more if we would have had it in the early '70s? Do you think it would have helped?
GP: I think that if the company were participating in an enlightened management style, there wouldn't have been a big announcement. There wouldn't have been a program. That stuff would have been ongoing, day-to-day. Frank, how many times did you try to tell one of your immediate supervisors a better way to do something, and they'd completely ignore you or told you that you were full of shit? And when it came to some of the stuff like, I was a believer in Partners for Progress. I really thought that if that took hold, that that was going to make a difference and we could turn that place around, because the waste and the mismanagement and the way we did things was so obvious. I don't think you had to be a Harvard MBA or I don't think you even had to be a high school graduate to see that the place was being terribly run. And I think if you were an intelligent person regardless of what your degree of education, you could talk to another intelligent person, and the two of you could come up with a better way to do things. I don't think our management was acceptable or amenable to that. I think they had their mind set that they were somehow better than us, and their deal was to get as much as they could out of us and pay us as little as possible. Some of the stupid shit that they did, just unbelievable.

Yeah, George, now I'm only going to ask you one more question. If you had an opportunity to do one or two things that would have dramatically helped the company out towards the end, what would you have done? Some guys tell me, "I would have gotten rid of all the foremen and put on working leaders." Some guys say, "We were in a no-win situation, because people didn't know what was going on in this plant."

GP: Frank, the crew chief position was in the contract book for a long, long time. I don't know exactly when it came in, but it was never used until the mid '80s. And the fact of the matter comes that the crew chief in the pipe shop, Lehigh pipe shop in the Lehigh plant...

You did that for a while yourself, didn't you?

GP: I did that job down there where, you know, I could count as high as thirteen or as little as seven salaried people that did the work that I was doing with one material person from material control department in one plant. The three of us were doing what from seven to thirteen people did from time to time that were salaried people. You know there was a guy in our department, the only thing I could figure out what his job was to keep track of the welder gloves. When you went for a pair of welder gloves, you had to sign your name and he'd put your name in a book, and if you came back there too soon he'd give you shit.

And you know I filed a grievance one time, they wanted us to wear them big asbestos mittens on a job down the Coke Works where you couldn't even hold a three-quarter-inch nipple. And I said we should be using welding gloves, and when we got to the superintendent, he said, "How much do these gloves cost?" The asbestos gloves were 75 dollars a pair; the welding gloves were 15 dollars a pair. And the superintendent said, "Mark, I see no reason why they can't and shouldn't use the welding gloves. They're more efficient, they're cheaper, what's the problem?" But that's the kind of shit that they were to me. They had a job. It's safety inspection on tools. Every air winch, every electric drill, everything was supposed to be inspected on a monthly basis. And you know what that was? That was a bookkeeping exercise. That guy never pulled that cable on that air winch out and inspected it for spikes or kinks or anything like that. He simply took the number off that winch and marked a checkmark. The books were beautiful. They looked like something in an engineering graphics class, but they had no basis in reality, and that guy was pulling down a big salary for that, because he was related to some guy in the main office. I mean, it was bad. The other thing I often say, and I think there's room for a book, I call it "Out the Gate." There was an awful lot of stealing and an awful lot of leakage. And this started with the salaried employees. When I first worked there as a bricklayer helper, I used to see stuff going on. Basically, the salaried people were filling their trunks up with you name it, they had it. And in the end, everybody was carrying stuff out in lunch buckets and everything else like that. I don't know what the dollar value of the stuff was, but it could have contributed to the profitability of the plant. Fact of the matter is the plant patrol, the trucking department, and everybody at every level was stealing, and it just seems that, again, when things got tough when it should have gotten better, it got worse starting in the mid '80s. A lot of stuff carried out that gate that could have contributed to the profitability. Hey, a lot of good work was done. I did government jobs, for churches, for community groups, for fire companies or stuff like that. I almost think that that was a company policy, because I know that we did stuff for churches that people in the Bethlehem Steel office requested, and I don't think that there's anything really wrong with that stuff. But the personal stealing, the stories about hunting cabins and things like that, that made a hell of a big difference there. And just what it contributed to the attitude, that, hey, if they can do that and approve that kind of stuff, what the hell I do isn't important to the salvation of this company.

Yeah. Well, George, I'll tell you what. You described it pretty good. I see you were there until June 28th of 1998, you put in 35 years of service, and what's probably the biggest thing that you miss about Bethlehem Steel?

GP: I just miss the whole place. You know there was an old salaried foreman who said that there's no place on earth to work like Bethlehem Steel, and I mentioned earlier about my opinion about the plant before I started to work there and once I got in. That was a fascinating place. You know until the last day, I could never walk by when they were rolling hot steel, without stopping for a few seconds to pause and look. I couldn't pass where they were pouring iron or steel. There was just something fascinating about the whole thing. And when you think and learn about the history of that plant, all the way back to Civil War times, making rails, and what that contributed to this country, as far as skyscrapers and bridges and everything else like that. You were a part of the history of the building of a nation, and that was part of your everyday life. You know Frank, I'm sure you worked with people that used to curse that place and hated to come in there.

Yeah but I often wondered, "Did they really mean it or are they just mad at the moment."

GP: If I hated a place as much as you claimed to hate it, I'd quit and I'd go somewhere. Go to Mack Trucks, or go to Western Electric, or something. I loved the place. You know, I never, ever, and you could ask my wife, you could ask my brothers, anybody. I never hated to go to work. Every day was a challenge.

That's exactly the way I felt about it.

GP: There was something there. And I actually had a good time when I was there. Hey, did I drop some blood and sweat? You bet your ass I did. Them cold nights down there on the 84-inch water line along the river, fixing a leak and joint, or replacing pipe when it's seven degrees above zero and the wind's blowing, yeah you suffer. Some of those hot days in the summertime inside a boiler replacing tubes or in an asbestos enclosure sweating your ass off. You know, you left some blood and sweat. There's a reason why, hey, we noticed guys that worked until they were 62, they lasted three or four years. Guys that worked until they were 65, a year, a year and a half you were going to their viewings. There's a reason for that. It was hard work; but it was satisfying work. Because of the union, you were well compensated. Did you have to take risk and chances? Did you work in a dangerous place? Yes you did, but you were paid and you knew that you were doing it. And, the union made all of that stuff bearable. I can't imagine what that was like before 1941. Now my father-in-law was there before 1941. Forty-four years he put as a crane man in the Steel. And some of the stories that he told me. They had a big fright of the bosses, there were "kiss asses" that were bringing anything from the local, the produce from their gardens, strawberries, peas, beans, chickens, pheasants in hunting season. You know what I'm saying? And they were afraid of their jobs. I never had to be afraid of my job. I was assigned a job; if I did my job, the boss never came after me. If he thought that I wasn't doing my job, and I was doing the best I can, when he barked at me, I barked at him. And if I had to file a grievance to get a job made safe, sometimes it was enough to tell him you're going to file a grievance, and the job was made safe.

Yeah. Well, George, you did a very commendable job of telling us about your time at Bethlehem Steel, and I want to thank you and wish the best for you and your family. Thank you.

JOHN W. PODHANY
32 years of service

Pipe Shop Safety Shop

"Pot" was a very well-known pipe fitter in the plant. He never lost a union election.

* * * * * * * * * *

Today's date is October the 16ᵗʰ, 2008; we're here with John W. Podhany. John, how you doing today?

JP: Quite well Frank, how are you?

Now John in the plant, there's a long history in the Bethlehem plant with people having nicknames, did you have one?

JP: Yes I did. Pot.

Okay, John, I see you're a high school graduate. Where did you go to school?

JP: Liberty High School. Graduated in 1965.

It was a good year. I see here you started very soon thereafter in July of '65 down at the plant.

JP: Correct, three days after my birthday.

Wow, that must have been something. Now, was this something that you knew about? Was there something in the paper? Did a relative tip you off? How did you come to be a steelworker?

JP: Well, I actually started working at EFM in Emmaus.

Oh, okay, the foundry.

JP: During school. And uh, when I turned 18, then I went right over to the Bethlehem Steel, and I think it was just word of mouth because my father worked there and my grandfather worked there, and I went down, took the test, and I got hired three days after my birthday, 18. I started in Safety Shop.

And what did they do in the Safety Shop?

JP: Oh, we made all kind of guards for machines, ladders, handrails, anything that pertained to safety out in the plant.

Okay, and in other words that was sort of like a caretaker for all the shops, because they didn't want to be spending time doing … that was done at a central location?

JP: Correct, and then we'd go out and install.

Yeah. I understand you had quite a few characters in that job. Do you remember working with some of those guys? Who was the foreman they had there? He was like a legend down at the plant.

JP: Joe McCoskey. That was our foreman.

How long were you down at the Safety Shop?

JP: I think I worked there for 12 years, then I got laid off.

Wow. What was it like the first day you walked into the plant? You must have thought you were like on the surface of the moon or something?

JP: That is correct. Actually, the first day in the plant my father, who had worked there at the same time, told me where the Safety Shop was, so I walked in the Minsi Trail Street gate and ended up at number 2 Machine Shop, wrong shop.

No, you weren't that far off, thank God for that. So you got in there, and what's the first thing that stuck out in your mind?

JP: Oh, what a huge place and how dangerous it could have been, the places that I saw, just working in there, all the big mills and everything I looked at. It was unbelievable from the inside compared to what the outside looked like.

Yeah, in other words, for years and years, you drove across that bridge and never gave a thought to what was going on down there. Well, I share your feelings, because I always used to tell my wife, you know, one place I never wanna work is down there in that sintering plant, and I ended up there. And I'm gonna tell you right now, it was the best place I ever worked. And I'll tell you why. It was so dirty in there. We always used to joke if the plant got an enema, that's where the hose would go. And nobody wanted to be in the dirt, especially the foreman, so they'd give you a job, you'd go out and you'd do it, you'd go over to a shanty and sit down; the only thing the foreman wanted to know was what shanty were you in. If another job comes up or anything breaks down, we'll come get ya. And that's why it was a good place to work. You know everybody just did what they had to do. So in the Safety Shop, what exactly did you start off with?

JP: I started off actually as a helper, which was a class 5 that job. We used to help the sheet metal workers. And we would help load trucks. I mean we were like high class laborers, I guess, you know.

It was just like a utility position more or less.

JP: Correct, I mean if they told me to paint in lines or whatever they did or help a sheet metal man hold his job to put together while he tacked it up, that's what we did.

I'll be interviewing a guy later this month that's gonna talk about, you know, his stint at the carpenter shop. Now, 12 years you were there, were you there 12 years steady or were you, like, in and out?

JP: Yup, 12 years steady. I got laid off, the first time was 1970, was it '75, '76, somewhere around there. It was '76 I got laid off.

That's a pretty good run compared to most of the places in the plant. I was lucky also like you in that I started out in the Alloy Division, went in the service, came back, was laid off, got kicked around a few places, and then started in '72 in the maintenance, the 413 Maintenance Department, you know, for Alloy and Tool Steel maintenance, and I hung around there a couple of years, then went down to the sintering plant. But, uh, in my time at Bethlehem Steel I think I was only laid off like seven weeks in 30 years. I've run into a few people I've interviewed were never laid off, and that's astounding for working down there. So the Safety Shop, how was it working in the Safety Shop? Was it, it's something that you do a lot of day shifts? Did you work swing shifts?

JP: I was steady days, Monday through Friday, 8-4.

Boy, it's almost enough to break your heart as a steelworker, huh?

JP: That's correct, and the reason that I got that job, I think, because of Dick D'Augustino. He placed me there basically. Because I was a machinist out of high school and I went for my interview, and I used to know Dick from the outside, and he said he had a job at Central Tool for me. He says, you know what, and I told him I really didn't want to be a machinist, but you know, and he said, how about going in there? And that's where I started. That's where I learned my welding trade, that's where I learned my burning trade. And of course I took a sheet metal test there also in that shop.

All in the Safety Shop, amazing. And is there anything about that, working there, that, like, jumps out at you, like jobs you like, jobs that you didn't like?

JP: No, it was actually an excellent shop to work with. I mean, I had one of the best shop stewards in the world, George Capauano, if you know that name? Cappy was, well he's passed away now I think since then.

Yeah he did, yeah. Moved over to Central Tool later on. He was uh, I dealt with him when I was on the grievance committee, and he was one of the more, how would ya put it, intelligent guys contract-wise that I dealt with. He was a guy that wouldn't ask me any questions, okay, unless he absolutely didn't know. You could talk to him about the contract, and he knew everything about it. I mean, we had a lot of guys like that, you know, and unfortunately because they were that good, people took 'em for granted, and you know, didn't realize what they had. And you know what I'm finding out from the guys that went to the other plants, this is what they're telling me. The worst grievance man or worse union official they thought they ever had at the Bethlehem plant was a genius compared to the other plants. And I'm sorry to put that into the record, but this is what people are telling. I can't say that I experienced it first-hand, but it's amazing the stories that come back to me. So after 12 years there now you're moving on, where ya headed?

JP: I get laid off. I finally got laid off in 1976 I think it was, and I was laid off for ten months.

Wow, that was a good lay off. Where'd you end up at?

JP: Then I came back, then I went down to the lumber yard, you know, two three months here, and then keep bidding on jobs, but with the Consent Decree I was not getting my welding job, because they had to hire so many you know females or minorities prior to me.

Yeah, there had to be two postings before you were actually in the running.

JP: Correct. So that's when I got my bid in the Pipe Shop. And that's where I ended up.

That's where you ended up. Now by nature of being in the Pipe Shop, that really put you, like, all over the plant? So everyone got to know the famous, the one and only John Podhany?

JP: Uh, some of 'em did.

Yes they did. Course now this did serve you well down the road when you became active with the union. There's no doubt about it. In fact, I think you may hold a record over there that is very enviable; you never lost a union election. Is that true?

JP: Uh, that is correct also.

Unfortunately, it's a record that can't be broken. But don't you wish somebody could break it. Now, what would you say is the number one thing you miss about the plant overall?

JP: Oh, definitely the people I was working with. You know they were…

Yeah, you worked with a lot of good people.

JP: Oh, my God, I mean, I can't actually say there was, I mean there was a couple of people that you didn't care for, but that's any place you work. I miss the, I even see, I see a couple of guys, like Johnny Wise, and they would say, "If they would call you up tonight to go back there, would you go" and I said, "Definitely, right now I'd leave. If they wanted to start something up or do something, I would go back."

I often call guys for these interviews, and I'll call, and they don't know who I am, because I haven't talked to them in years, and I'll start off by saying, "Hey listen, we need a chain man in the 16 run hole down the Beam Yard tonight, can you come out?" "I'll be there." he says, "Where do you want me?" This is Frankie Behum. Get out, what are you calling me for, and then I tell 'em, you know about the book and stuff like, and I end up interviewing 'em. So you go into the Safety Shop, you get laid off, you come back, you working a few places, you get down there and now you're in the Pipe Shop, and it's what around 1977, when was the first that you actually gave some thought that the plant might be in trouble?

JP: I'm trying to think when we gave our money back.

It was in the '80s, early '80s.

JP: Early '80s we had to, remember we gave that dollar…

Concessionary contract.

JP: Yup, we gave money back, and they promised to put the caster here and everything else, and that's when I thought the company had lied to me, or us. And that's when I knew they were in trouble. Later on in life, I can say when I became a union official, I would talk to the salaried, the people in the unemployment office, and I think they had plans of shutting this place down back in the middle or late '70s.

Yeah they did.

JP: We didn't, I mean I didn't see it, or maybe I just didn't believe it. But they had plans back then to shut it down.

Well, you know John the name of the book that I'm writing here is Thirty Years Under the Beam, and the reason I picked that name is that I believe that the men in the plant, including members of management, did everything they could the last thirty years to keep this place going, and I feel secure in that I haven't run into a person yet that's disputed that, and you worked with good foremen, I know you did. But it was like any other place, every now and then you'd find a guy that, he was actually in over his head a little bit, thought he had to be in the office all the time, you know rattin' on somebody. But you know, when you found out who these guys were, you worked around 'em, and it was like one big happy family. I mean that didn't prevent you from going up to Tammany Hall to have a beer after middle shift. Because that's the way that it was. Do you think you spent more time there in the plant with the guys than you did with your own family?

JP: Oh my God yes. Even at the end, you know, when we were working doubles and triples, you actually spend more time with the guys you worked with than you did with your own family.

You know a lot of people have more or less taken me to task because I haven't interviewed very many of the wives about this; in fact I haven't interviewed any of them, and they were actually in it as much as we were in it, because you know they were the ones that stayed at home and say, I wonder what he's doing. You know one of the biggest problems we had over in that union hall was right after we had the tours in the mid '80s. We actually would have women that would call us at the hall and say, is there any way that he can get out of that job? They were like appalled to see the conditions that some of the guys worked under. I saw some women come into the electric furnace and leave in tears. Does he work here? He sure does. Is this the place where the guy got killed? I says, "Well, there were several of 'em killed here." Oh my God, and you know everything changed after that, and you know, I'm in over at the supermarket one day and a guy says to me, "Just think Bamie," he says "if you would have done a little bit of work, wouldn't have been cooking on middle shift and sleeping on night shift, you'd still have a job." And I said to him, I said, "Hey Bill, over here at the bank, how many of your buddies have you carried to an ambulance? How many funerals do you go to? How many guys did you counsel because they were busted up at work on how to get their worker's comp because the company was giving 'em a hard time about it?" And you know, they just don't understand that, but I'm hoping that this book puts a lot of that to rest. The funniest part is that when I brought that up to the guys at the Beam Yard on the piling crew, they said, "You know on night shift we used to lay down, and little guys used to come out of the river and do our work, and then wake us up in the morning and we would go up and take our showers, and we would get paid for that." And you know, they thought it was a big joke.

JP: Well, I know for a fact that there were more people killed in the Bethlehem plant in the years, from 1980 I think it was, than there was in all of the state police in Pennsylvania.

Yeah, in fact I believe from the time you started, cuz I started also, in '65 I believe there was 31 people killed in that plant. And uh, it wasn't a real safe place to work, but you know, you could say that the company had complete control of the press in the area, so when I say to people about this book, I tell 'em it's the real story, because it's the story told by the employees, not by the newspapers or Bethlehem Steel. And there will be some people from Bethlehem Steel that'll say, "Well, you really made us look bad." I said, "No, all I did was transcribe what people told me in these interviews. I'm not out to make anybody look bad." You know, you have to decide yourself what's truth and what's fiction. I'm not gonna say to you, "John Podhany, you're full of shit." Whatever you tell me is good enough for me. Now, John when we got into the middle '80s and we finally started having, how would you put it? Maybe getting in bed with the company with the Partners for Progress, where we were actually communicating, they were asking for our help to save the plant. What did you think about that program?

JP: Well, in the beginning I was skeptical, because when I first started there I could not even associate with my bosses outside the plant. It was tabooed you know when we first started there, but after that a lot of these guys were my friends; in fact two of them were very good friends of mine and ended up being bosses, and when I was a union officer, and I told both of 'em, I says "Hey between 7 and 3 you're my boss, I'm the union rep. After 3 o'clock we're friends again." But I did, and maybe I was gullible, but I thought that, and I hate the wording "Getting in bed with the company."

Well, that's just a figure of speech.

JP: But people, you now, uh, I thought we could work together. You know, mergers, the inter-departments, you know, cutting down men, unfortunately people got laid off, thought maybe save the plant and there would be a future for some younger kids coming up, but guess what?

Didn't happen.

JP: Wasn't gonna happen, no.

Wasn't gonna happen. A lot of people when I mention this, about this time, they said, "You know, it would have been nice had that started fifteen years earlier than it did, who knows what could have happened." Then there's some people that'll go, they'll bring up, you know, names of people from the corporation and stuff that they took offense to, and I said, "Hey look, some of those guys maybe if they had come around fifteen years earlier we wouldn't have been in this fix." Were you aware that in 1994 there was a conglomeration of gentlemen that wanted to buy this plant? Tthey were gonna retain 1,250 jobs; it's a deal that fell through because the company wouldn't buy into it, and a lot of people think to this day it was because they thought the higher ups, you know, would lose their golden parachutes and their pensions, etc. etc. There was a lot of reasons that people, you know, that knew about this, and the union never really mentioned it, because it never. Can you imagine what would have happened if that would have, people would have known there was an ongoing negotiation? Well, life would have been unbearable, but uh, it happened. One of those gentlemen I interviewed, ya know what he said at the end of the interview? "I want you to know one thing, when they decided where are we going to go into the steel business, and they wanted to turn this plant into a mini mall." Dick Adams was his name, I'll tell you right out, he came out and said, "I was in several plants, and the work ethic in the Bethlehem plant was bar none the best there was," he says" because we had as many as five generations of steelworkers working in this plant," and uh, it made me feel good to hear that. Can you think of anything off hand that you would have done yourself, okay, to maybe turn things around in that plant? What jumped right out at ya?

JP: Well, as a young kid, I didn't realize, you know, what you have to do to become a team player in the plant, and as a young kid I was, just give me the money and I'm going home. Now the older you get you figure, you know what, I'm not here, and as I became a union officer, you know I guess a light bulb went out and say, "Hey, you just don't have to come in the door to get your money, you gotta do something for it." And there was many guys that had that attitude, they thought they had to come in the door, you know.

Come in one end walk out the other.

JP: Stay here for eight hours and come out with a check. Hey the boss tells you to do something, you do it. If it was unsafe, you didn't do it. But this is the way I felt. What I could've done, uh, I can't think of anything that I, you know, personally would have. You know, like I say, I remember an old timer telling me one time, he says, "Kid, whatever you want to be in life, be the best you can." He said, "Even if you're gonna be a bum, be the best bum you can," and that stuck with me after years. I guess, I've been driving bus and whatever I've been doing in my life, I try to be the best I can.

And what have you done, John, since you left the plant? I know you drove bus for a while, right here locally in the Bethlehem area.

JP: Yup, ten years with Carl Bieber for five and Transbridge for five. I delivered meats for B&M Meats, I sold cars, I...

Did a little bit of everything.

JP: Yeah, then I went to North Carolina of course.

Yeah?

JP: And came back into the welding field, and uh, retubing factory, factory company called Jomor and Company, and my wife and I thought that, you know, down there would be a place for me to retire, and it was cheaper living, but we missed the area, so that's why we're back. We were down there for over a year.

Well, I'll tell you what, John, it was a real pleasure talking to ya, and I'm hoping you know a hundred years from now someone will pick up this book, they'll go and they'll see John Podhany and they'll find out here's what John thought about working at Bethlehem Steel, here's what he did, here's what he liked, here's what he didn't like, and he got out of there in one piece.

JP: That's correct.

And that was important.

JP: Yup, all your fingers, all my toes, I mean we had some accidents and this and that, but we got out of there, most of us did.

There you go. I remember when old Tom Petro used to tell the story about the merry go round of life; he'd be going around in a circle, and he said every now and then you could reach out for the brass ring. He says, but you know what, he says when you're missing a couple of fingers, you could never grab it. And boy that summed it up in a nutshell. Okay, John, thank you.

JP: All right Frank.

Best good luck to you and your family.

JP: You too, thank you.